Mollie Katzen's Sunlight Café

MOLLIE KATZEN'S
SUNLIGHT CAFÉ

MOLLIE KATZEN

WITH ILLUSTRATIONS BY MOLLIE KATZEN

"Breakfast served all day"

NEW YORK

FOR PATTY

Printed in the United States of America

For information address:
Hyperion
77 West 66th Street
New York, New York 10023-6298

Library of Congress Cataloging-in-Publication Data

ISBN: 0-7868-6269-6

Written and illustrated by Mollie Katzen
Book design and typesetting by
Deborah Bowman, Berkeley, California

Hyperion books are available for special promotions and premiums.
For details contact:
Hyperion Special Markets
77 West 66th Street, 11th floor
New York, New York 10023,
or call 212-456-0100.

FIRST EDITION

10 9 8 7 6 5 4 3 2 1

CONTENTS

I am one
Who eats his breakfast
Gazing at the morning glories.

—Bashō

ACKNOWLEDGMENTS

As my work on this book unfolded over a period of four years, I was blessed with constant support and enthusiasm from my esteemed editor, Will Schwalbe. I've also had the tremendous privilege and good fortune to work with two truly gifted and dedicated women: Deborah Bowman, who designed every page of this book with great thoughtfulness, talent, and loving attention, and Rebecca Pepper, whose copy editing has made the final prose as effective and useful as I think and hope it is.

I want to thank Bob Miller for placing his faith and trust in me for the last number of years. I also owe a debt of gratitude to Jennifer Lang, whose cheerful, calm, can-do attitude kept the inner sunlight shining on this project. Many thanks to the rest of the team at Hyperion: Adrian James, Navorn Johnson, Linda Prather, Lisa Stokes, Ellen Archer, Michael Burkin, Jane Comins, and Mark Chait—as well as to the proofreader, Victoria Mathews, and the indexer, Lisa Kleinholz.

I am grateful to Eric Sartenauer of The Phoenix Pastificio in Berkeley—and to Nancy Flynn—for generously sharing the amazing tart recipe that became the basis for Divine Apple-Pear Crostada. I also want to acknowledge Suzanne Dunaway, whose recipe for homemade ricotta inspired mine. Many thanks to Christine Swett, Jennifer Carden, Randy Milden, and Lorraine Battle for helping me with some of the recipe tests. Jackie Wan was there for me at the beginning of this project, and Torri Randall, Aaron Wehner, Nancy Austin, and Hal Hershey all provided support, advice, and various recommendations that were enormously helpful. Mona Meisami, Photoshop artist par excellence, helped prepare some of the art for reproduction. The people at Cantoo, in Berkeley, did all of the art photography with such meticulous care and concern that I actually began to worry about them.

At various times I needed to get away from my home office/kitchen/art studio and just plain write. I am so grateful to Esta Brand for giving me a key to her house so I could camp out there with my laptop from time to time while she was at work. I also want to express my gratitude to the folks who run the Maui Writers Conference—and to Joe and Gayle Ortiz in particular, who personally invited me there. It was an incredible work retreat for me, as well as an opportunity to get "sparked" in the presence of so many colleagues and peers.

And speaking of colleagues, I want to thank my fellow travelers, Frances Moore Lappé, Anna Lappé, Jesse Cool, Michele Anna Jordan, Dana Jacobi, Linda Williams, Elizabeth Fishel, Janet Peoples, Adrienne McDonnell, Marissa Moss, and Shirley Corriher for sharing their invaluable experience, encouragement, knowledge, wisdom, and humor. I would also like to acknowledge the groundbreaking, visionary work of Anna Thomas, whose classic, *The Vegetarian Epicure*, blazed the trail for me and many others. I will always be in her debt.

It's been my great honor in the past few years to have gotten to know and confer with Walter C. Willett, M.D., Dr. P.H., chair of the nutrition department at the Harvard School of Public Health. His work has taught me so much! I am grateful to Dr. Willett for inviting me to be a member of the Harvard School of Public Health Nutrition Roundtable, which has provided a unique opportunity for studying—and coming to understand—the most current nutritional research.

Love and thanks to Ken Swezey, and to my dream team: Deke Jamieson, Debra Joester, Joanne Loria, Jane Kraemer, and Maury Rogoff, who have helped propel my work further into the big, wide world. And most of all, thanks to my husband Carl for his unwavering support—philosophical, personal, and practical; to my extraordinary parents, Betty and Leon Katzen; and to Sam and Eve, my daily breakfast customers, as well as my most honest critics and greatest inspiration. You are so much fun to feed!

INTRODUCTION

Breakfast is everyone's favorite meal—yet ironically, relatively few of us seem to make the time to actually prepare or enjoy it. Instead, we rely on something from a box or from the pastry case where we stop for coffee—or, worse, we eat nothing at all. What is it that we love about this often-illusory meal? What does it symbolize? And how can we bring the whole notion of breakfast back down to earth and make it real, so that a good morning meal becomes an integral part of our every day and not just a special event reserved for weekends? | Addressing the first two questions, I have a hunch that, for many of us, breakfast symbolizes the encouraging notion of a fresh start, even if only on a very modest scale. Literally and repeatedly, breakfast is the first meal of the rest of our lives, associated with positivity and optimism—a small, bright keynote that revives us from sleepiness and fuels us for action. The forecast for an entire day can somehow be encoded within a piece of toast or a bowl of fresh fruit, promising a sense of renewal as we shift out of our dream state and crank ourselves up to face the business of daily life. | The answer to the third question is more complicated. Our morning schedules are often hectic, and many of us are as pressed for appetite and inspiration as we are for time. Throughout this book, I show you many ways you can approach breakfast—strategically, spiritually, and sensually—so that you can not only make space for this cheerful, important meal but embrace it and look forward to enjoying it each morning. If the ideas presented in these pages help you to rise and shine—and not just rise—and if your daily breakfast becomes a wellspring of peace and pleasure—and not just another a source of stress—I will feel I've done my job.

—Mollie Katzen

MAKE ROOM IN YOUR LIFE FOR BREAKFAST

I know that on rushed weekday mornings it's hard to have to choose between a few extra minutes in bed (or on the tread-mill or in the shower) and a quality meal. That's why it is very important to have strategies in place and to plan ahead. Otherwise, many of us will look at these recipes and feel hopeless or even think they're a joke. "I'm really going to cook and eat *that* at 7 a.m. on a weekday?" Actually, if you adopt some of these strategies, you *can* eat "that" (whatever it is) on a weekday morning, but you will possibly have cooked it ahead and reheated it—or you may eat it at 10 a.m. at your desk or during your break.

If you would like to rework your routines so that a good, balanced breakfast becomes part of your every day, here are some pointers that might be helpful. Remember, if we are mindful about breakfast during other times of the day, we can allow ourselves to be blissfully mind*less* about it in the early morning, which is the state many of us are in at that hour any-way. We might as well enjoy it!

- First, make a commitment—a decision to elevate breakfast to a top priority. Then allow yourself the luxury of time spent pondering and planning. This planning time can be really enjoyable, but for some reason we fight it. It might help to think of it this way: Planning is like dreaming, except that it's real.
- Read through the book, and list the recipes you'd like to prepare, as well as the ingredients required. That way, when you shop, you can get everything you need in an efficient way.
- Set aside time to bake, make granola, cook whole grains, and so forth on weekends and in the evening. Most of the dishes in this book are designed to store and reheat very well. (In fact, many of them are even better reheated because, if done properly, reheating can cause the flavors to deepen and the texture to actually improve.) Detailed instructions for storing and reheating appear in individual recipes throughout the book.
- Set up your kitchen in such a way that breakfast becomes a regular—and joyful—reality. Focus on small, aesthetic touches that might make your eating area a haven where you can take a breath—in addition to taking a few bites—early in the morning.
- Read through the Equipment Notes on page xvi to get a sense of how you can streamline preparations.
- Cleanup is a big issue for people who need to get themselves out the door in a hurry. You can address this in part by preparing a large tub of hot, soapy water (perhaps while you're waiting for your tea water to boil). Just plunge your dirty dishes into the tub before you leave, and rinse them off when you get home. It's not a perfect solution, but this one extra effort can make a big difference to you later in the day.

FAMILY STRATEGIES

Families with children tend to experience weekday mornings as the first and worst of the daily rush hours. Even without breakfast, getting everyone up, washed, combed, dressed, packed up, and out the door can be difficult enough. (I know what I'm talking about. Until recently, my own morning schedule factored in a good eight or nine extra minutes just to help my daughter find her shoes, which always seemed, mysteriously, to vanish during the night.) Clearly, we need to get some version of breakfast into our kids on weekday mornings before we send them on their way. If our children barely have time to sit down amid all the hubbub, how on earth do we feed them wisely and efficiently, without resorting to sugary toaster pastries—or worse?

We can embrace a middle ground between junk food on the one hand and a home-cooked three-course sit-down meal on the other. It *is* possible to feed our children quickly and well, even if they end up eating whatever it is we give them on the bus. In this imperfect world, that's better than letting them run on empty.

Here are some suggestions that you can both follow and also use as a springboard for your own (or your kids') ideas. Note that most of these items can be prepared—fully or partially—in the evening, to take pressure off the morning crunch.

- Fresh fruit—whole, or cut into thick slices
- Yogurt sweetened with a little pure maple syrup
- Smoothies (see pages 10 through 12)
- Breakfast sandwiches (peanut butter and honey on toast, scrambled eggs in a pita)
- Protein bars and other healthy cookie-type foods (see chapter 12)
- A toasted, buttered homemade muffin (see chapter 4)
- A Nibble Bag (great commute item): Combine nuts, pretzels, dried fruit, and a few chocolate chips (for energy, of course) in a zip-style plastic bag. Hand this to your child with a banana and a thermos or carton of milk for the road.
- Cereal from a box with fortified milk (see page 17) and a subtle sprinkling of wheat germ

 BREAKFAST AROUND THE WORLD

We are familiar with the traditional English breakfast of eggs, toast and marmalade, bacon or sausage, tomato, and so on—as that concept was readily imported to the New World (as well as to all the areas colonized by Great Britain) and is now seen as the norm. We are also familiar with the "continental breakfast," consisting of just a hot beverage with some form of bread and butter. Less familiar are the foods people eat for breakfast in other parts of the world, many of which seem odd until you realize that they are often derived from last night's dinner. Some examples:

EASTERN EUROPE Fruit juice; cold cuts; onion-laced cheese spreads; hot peppers; sausages; pastries

MALAYSIA Meat curry with coconut rice

PHILIPPINES Fried rice with eggs and seasonings; dried fish

VIETNAM Rice with fish and vegetables; sweet potatoes; pickled vegetables; salted eggs; *pho* (noodle soup)

MIDDLE EAST Yogurt; cheeses; olives; bread dipped in olive oil and spices; bean dishes; hummus; falafel; eggs

NORTH AFRICA Skillet mixes of vegetables, eggs, and meats; various specialty breads

ISRAEL Vegetable salads; olives; pickled and smoked fish; cheeses; yogurt; bread; eggs

ITALY Pizza bianca (plain, unadorned pizza), sometimes topped with cheese (midmorning street food)

SPAIN Potato omelets ("tortillas") and lots of coffee

ETHIOPIA *Injera* (spongy bread made from a grain called teff) and stew

CARIBBEAN Tropical fruit; eggs with hot sauces; fried plantains; vegetables; fish soup; pastries

JAPAN Miso soup; rice; fish; pickles

SINGAPORE Noodles in broth; rice porridge with eggs and vegetables; rotis (flatbreads) with soup

CHINA Rice porridge with pepper sauce and organ meat; warm soy milk; sesame cakes; dim sum

HOLLAND, GERMANY, AND NORTHERN EUROPE Bread; cheese; meat; eggs; chocolate

SCANDINAVIA Fish and sandwiches

VENEZUELA *Arepas* (griddle breads made from flour ground from a very starchy cooked corn)

MEXICO *Huevos rancheros; chilaquiles* (leftover tortillas baked in a casserole with other leftovers)

BREAKFAST FOR METABOLIC HEALTH

Eat breakfast as a king, lunch as a citizen, and dinner as the beggar on the corner.
—Hungarian proverb

They say that breakfast is the most important meal of the day. And once upon a time, not that long ago, the role of breakfast in people's lives was very clear. Most people worked long and hard in the fields—or labored at physically demanding jobs— and they walked or rode horses as their primary means of transportation. A large breakfast made sense for this deeply active way of life, and good nutrition was generally thought of quantitatively, with the aim being to get enough calories to accomplish the day's work. But as industrialization set in and a new professional class arose, metabolic needs shifted. People who worked in factories or at desks simply could not burn off the calories they might once have ingested from a larger, more traditional farm breakfast. As daily life became mechanized and thus supposedly more "convenience oriented"—and as we evolved into a basically sedentary population—we somehow became *hurried,* and thus less willing to make time for full, good meals. At some point, on a cultural level, we seem to have decided that there would always be something more urgent to attend to than the careful and loving preparation and consumption of food.

As the world has modernized, and as opportunities for obtaining fast food have sprung up everywhere, the very definition of breakfast has become more elusive and unclear. Rushing out the door on weekdays, many of us tend to shortchange or sidestep this meal, a pattern that leads to feelings of deprivation and outright hunger later in the day—sometimes as soon as late morning. The result? We compensate by snacking indiscriminately, escalating over the hours in a pattern that, for many, culminates in bouts of overeating in the evening—and of just plain eating poorly in general.

When we eat inadequately at the start of the day, we fail to take into account that our bodies need *real fuel.* The car analogy is a good eye-opener. We never question the wisdom of filling our car with gas at the start of a journey, and we'd find it downright absurd to begin a long trip with the gauge near empty. Furthermore, when "feeding" our car, we never question the wisdom of choosing a fuel of the proper composition and richness to do the job efficiently. Somehow, though— perhaps because we don't like to think of our bodies as machines—we tend not to treat ourselves with the same consideration as we treat our vehicles. How modern human beings became so counterintuitive about feeding themselves is a subject for a book in itself. My main point here is that a good breakfast, whatever that means to each of us, is the fueling stop that launches the journey of our day, helping to bring our systems into balance. If we think of it this way, perhaps our start-of-the-day eating will improve—and, ideally, the quality of our lives will follow suit.

WHAT CAUSES AN ENERGY CRASH?

We wake up with what is known as a "fasting blood sugar level." When we ingest food this level rises, at a rate that depends on what food we eat and in what combination. The ingestion of simple carbohydrates all by themselves on an empty stomach can cause blood sugar levels to spike quite suddenly. Our pancreas then responds by producing a large rush of insulin to "go after" that blood glucose and bring it down to a more normal level. When this happens, we tend to experience a precipitous drop in energy and concentration and an attack of hunger. We might even feel shaky or lightheaded. So we reach for another quick fix in the form of additional simple carbohydrates (commonly an empty-calorie snack), and the process repeats itself. This pattern has an adverse effect on our health in many ways—not just in the short term, as an energy roller-coaster, but in the long term as well, with implications for our general health.

WHAT IS THE SOLUTION?

The trick is to eat in such a way that our blood sugar level escalates at a moderate rate and doesn't shoot through the roof in a short period of time. This means eating well in reasonable amounts and at appropriate intervals. It also requires that we be aware of the form and quantity of carbohydrates we ingest, and that we skew our choices toward certain foods—and food combinations—that will be absorbed gently and slowly. The most rapidly absorbed foods are the simple, highly refined carbohydrates (including most ready-to-eat breakfast cereals, bagels, breads, and so on) that contain very little fiber. However, when such foods are accompanied by other, more slowly absorbed elements—such as high-quality fat, fiber, or a good hit of protein—the loading of sugar into our system is slowed down. Look at it this way: The absorption rate of simple carbohydrates is affected by the company they keep.

It's also important to note that not all carbohydrates are the same. Those that are less refined (whole or coarsely milled grains with larger particle size) contain more fiber and have more of a "time-release" effect on our blood sugar level, so there is no dramatic rise and fall. Instead, a slower, more gradual rise occurs, lasting longer and leading to a gentler landing later on. This eases the demand for insulin, so our pancreas will not be working as hard and we will be less exposed to midmorning cravings, hunger spells, or fatigue. And if our blood glucose remains at a fairly even level throughout the day, our energy and focus will be steady too.

What does this look like in terms of actual food?

We are all very attached to our morning habits and are understandably resistant to making significant changes. And that's fine. This book is about small changes, not a dramatic dietary makeover! If you love your morning meal of coffee and a pastry, you needn't overhaul your routine. You might find that you can achieve the desired effect simply by changing the pastry ever so slightly.

- You don't need to give up your beloved piece of toast; just add a little cheese or nut butter instead of eating it plain. Have a piece of whole fruit (or purée whole fruit into a smoothie) instead of drinking sugary fruit juice.
- If your daily bowl of cereal is a highly personal, defining moment in your life, keep it, but maybe sprinkle it with nutritious touches, like cooked whole grains, wheat germ, seeds, or nuts.
- If you genuinely have little or no appetite first thing in the morning and are repelled by the idea of an early full meal (especially one with savory flavors), it might be helpful to think of the breakfast time frame as relative, not absolute. So if you can't eat early, just eat as early as you can. "Breakfast" can become a quality grazing experience that you enjoy while sitting at your computer, and you can cultivate some new, expanded snack habits (such as the bars, gems, and nuggets in chapter 12).
- Discover the fun of sneaking delicious yet unexpected ingredients—and touches of protein and extra fiber—into your baked goods (chapters 4 and 12).
- Stretch your concept of morning food to include beans and soy foods, vegetables, and puddings.

Within these pages I hope you'll find many ways to begin looking at breakfast with fresh eyes—and with renewed interest and curiosity. My wish for you is that your energy be steady and strong and that you look forward to breakfast every morning—and then look forward to facing and enjoying your day from that delicious and satisfying vantage point.

A Few General Pantry Notes

I like to cook with ordinary, wholesome ingredients that can be found in basic grocery stores and natural food stores around the country—not just in upscale metropolitan areas. Throughout this book, whenever a slightly unusual or unfamiliar ingredient appears in a recipe, I have offered an explanation on the same page. In this section, I discuss a few general categories of frequently used ingredients.

MILK

In general, when a recipe calls for milk, you can use regular cow's milk (whole or lowfat) or plain, unflavored soy milk. For a richer taste, you can also use evaporated milk (whole or lowfat).

BUTTERMILK

Many of these recipes use buttermilk, so I suggest you keep a quart or two on hand. Buttermilk has a longer shelf life than regular milk, although the solids tend to settle as it sits, so be sure to shake it well before using. Leftover buttermilk can be used for making refreshing cold drinks (see page 16). If you prefer, you can buy a package of powdered buttermilk and just mix up as much as you need for a recipe.

RICOTTA CHEESE

Soft, mild ricotta is a lovely eating and spreading cheese. It is also a terrific baking ingredient, and I use it frequently—especially in muffin batters. There are big taste and texture differences between whole-milk and lowfat ricotta, and unless I indicate otherwise, I generally recommend using the whole-milk variety in baking. You'll get superior results.

BUTTER

When butter is part of the body of a recipe, I specify unsalted butter (which is virtually the same thing as "sweet" butter). I prefer unsalted butter because it enables you to control the amount of salt in the dish. However, when butter appears in a recipe just for the purpose of sautéing or for greasing a pan, I don't indicate salted or unsalted because it doesn't really matter—you can use either kind.

EGGS

Unless otherwise specified, all the recipes in this book were tested with grade A large eggs. For many more details about eggs, see pages 115-16.

FLOUR

- All-purpose flour comes by its name honestly, working very well for breads, cakes, and pastries alike. Unbleached all-purpose flour is my basic flour.
- If you prefer a touch of whole wheat, you can substitute whole wheat pastry flour for all-purpose flour in any recipe except those for yeasted bread doughs. Whole wheat pastry flour is very finely milled and low in gluten, and will give you a tender, light result. (Please note that this is not the same as regular whole wheat flour, which is much more coarsely ground.)
- A few recipes in the book use other types of flour, all of which can be found at natural food stores—either in bulk or packaged. Buy these in small amounts, and store them in the freezer to keep them fresh.

CORNMEAL AND POLENTA

Cornmeal is finely ground; polenta is coarser in texture. These two grades of ground corn are only rarely interchangeable, so I have specified which to use in any given corn-based recipe. Because ground corn has a tendency to become rancid, store cornmeal and polenta in the freezer.

PROTEIN POWDER

- For baking: There are many different types of protein powder, most of which are made from soy or whey. In baked goods I like to use the fluffy, beige soy-based protein powder that can be found in the bulk bins at natural food stores. Many of the baking recipes in this book indicate that this powder can replace a certain amount of the flour.
- For blending into drinks: I find that the more highly processed protein powders—the ones that come in cans and have additional esoteric ingredients—tend to dissolve much more readily in liquid than the variety sold in bulk bins. Provided you like the flavor of these "designer" powders, they are the ones to use in smoothies and other drinks.

YEAST

I like to purchase active dry yeast in bulk from the natural food store and store it in a zip-style plastic bag in the freezer, which will extend its shelf life. Bulk yeast is much more economical than those familiar little square packets sold in grocery stores. But you can also use the packets—the yeast inside is the same. Each packet contains about 2½ teaspoons of yeast.

HONEY

A rule of thumb about honey: The lighter the color, the milder the flavor. That's why I call for "light-colored" honey in these recipes. I like honey's gentle sweetness, but I don't want its flavor to dominate.

MAPLE SYRUP

Like honey, maple syrup is milder in flavor when it is lighter in color. But unlike honey, maple syrup tends to be more expensive the lighter it is. The highest grade of syrup, AA, is downright subtle and ethereal. But sometimes I buy grade B because I like its dark, thick maple flavor in certain contexts. Store maple syrup in the refrigerator to maximize its shelf life.

NONSTICK SPRAY

Nonstick spray is a very helpful item that can greatly streamline kitchen operations. Beyond the obvious applications, such as spraying baking pans, I use nonstick spray in many contexts where food might stick. For example, I often spray a measuring utensil before measuring something sticky, like honey. I also spray my hands—and the work surface—before kneading yeasted dough. It really helps! My favorite brand is Spectrum Naturals Super Canola Skillet Spray.

OILS

There is a lot of confusion about which oil to use for what. I like to keep it simple, and this is my general plan: I use olive oil (virgin or extra virgin) for sautéing over medium heat. In some recipes, I add a little butter to the olive oil to give a more complex taste. And occasionally, if the flavor of olive oil just isn't right for the dish, I'll sauté with canola oil instead. For serious frying—when I want to get the oil to a very high temperature in pursuit of an ultra-crisp result—I'll use high-oleic safflower oil (see page 155), which works beautifully over strong heat and leaves no greasy residue.

WHOLE GRAINS, DRIED FRUIT, NUTS, AND SEEDS

A monthly field trip to the natural food store can be a lot of fun, like an old-fashioned foraging expedition in a modern urban setting. Once you have incorporated the whole-grain recipes and concepts described throughout this book into your repertoire, the vital act of keeping your kitchen stocked with all these good things will become an enjoyable and creative routine. Instead of making a list, I just wander through the bulk-bin aisle and fill my cart with bags and containers of a great variety of grains, fruit, nuts, and seeds. When I get home, I pack most of them up for freezer storage but keep out a small amount to become Nibble Bags for my kids' portable breakfasts (see page xi). The granola supplies usually go straight into my big granola-making bowl, and I get to work.

CANNED GOODS

These canned goods are always on hand in my house: beans, pumpkin, tomatoes, green chiles, applesauce, fruit (packed in juice), and artichoke hearts.

Equipment Notes

I assume that your kitchen is already set up the way you like it, with your pet gadgets and trusty utensils and appliances at the ready. Keeping that in mind, I've composed this list of specific, possibly supplementary equipment that can greatly streamline breakfast preparations and also help you effectively store and reheat many of the recipes in this book, so you can have better breakfasts more easily and more often.

MICROWAVE

In our household, the microwave is used exclusively for defrosting foods and reheating leftovers. As many of the recipes in this book are "do-aheads," the microwave will be an indispensable tool for making a daily good breakfast a reality. A microwave will come in especially handy when you want to reheat a nice big bowl of whole-grain cooked cereal made the night before. Note: use a microwave for defrosting breads, but not for reheating them. (Microwave reheating will make bread and muffins rubbery.)

TOASTER OVEN

Plain old toasters are great for toasting sliced bread of a given dimension. But many of the baked goods in this book assume larger and odder shapes than most toasters can accommodate. (Use a toaster oven, and not a microwave, for reheating and toasting bread.)

TEN-INCH (OR LARGER) SAUTÉ PAN

Many of the potato dishes and hashes in this book need to be fried or sautéed in a thin or single layer in order to get the optimal texture. A large pan is a must, because you can't get crisp results if the pan is crowded.

METAL SPATULA

A metal spatula is the most effective tool for really scraping the bottom of the griddle or pan so you don't lose any of the bottom texture of whatever it is you're cooking.

NONSTICK EIGHT-INCH OMELET OR CRÊPE PAN

One good pan can be used for eggs and crêpes alike.

GRIDDLE SITUATION

If you are fortunate enough to have a cooktop with a built-in griddle, by all means use it! You can also purchase a large cast-iron griddle (they're not expensive) and place it over two burners of the stove to cook pancakes or French toast. You can also use the 10-inch skillet mentioned earlier, but it will not be as roomy.

HEAT ABSORBER

This thick metal disk sits on your burner under your pot and helps keep the heat evenly distributed when you cook whole grains. This allows them to cook all the way through without scorching on the bottom.

ELECTRIC SPICE GRINDER

Buy an electric coffee grinder, and use it exclusively for grinding seeds and spices—and for milling small amounts of whole grain (like quinoa or oats) into flour. (If you already use one of these inexpensive machines for grinding coffee, buy a second one to use for food, to keep the lingering flavors separate.)

BLENDER

A blender is indispensable for making smooth purées. A food processor doesn't do this job nearly as well.

FOOD PROCESSOR

I use my food processor constantly—for making many kinds of dough, for grinding nuts, and for grating cheese and vegetables.

LIQUID MEASURING CUPS

Keep both 2-cup and 4-cup liquid measuring cups on hand. They are very convenient for both measuring and mixing the liquid component of many muffin and cake batters, thus simplifying the cleanup process ever so slightly. (Every little bit of simplification helps.)

SHAKERS

I like to keep shakers of powdered sugar (page 247) and spice mixtures (page 260) on my kitchen table for sprinkling over all sorts of sweet and savory dishes. These inexpensive utensils are really fun, and they make your kitchen feel like a bona fide café! The best shakers to use for powdered sugar are the lightweight, round metal variety with a cap that you can pry off with your thumbs. For savory spice mixtures, I like to use glass shakers with screw-on metal lids—the kind you see in pizza parlors, filled with red pepper flakes or grated cheese.

PLANE ZESTER

I use a lot of grated citrus zest in my baking recipes, and I know that zesting can be daunting. The easiest tool for quickly grating a quantity of zest is a plane grater, which is a long, rectangular metal utensil with tiny sharp holes. You should be able to find one at any kitchen equipment store, and you will be amazed by the effectiveness of this tool!

OVEN THERMOMETER

Even if you have a very good stove, the oven calibration might be inaccurate, which can greatly affect the results of your baking efforts. I strongly recommend using an oven thermometer to help you monitor the temperature and to guide you in adjusting the controls, if necessary. Think of it as a baking insurance policy.

JUICER

This is a good tool to own if you are inclined to drink fresh, homemade fruit juice or vegetable juice (page 165) for breakfast. Unlike blenders or food processors, which purée food, leaving every element in the mix, a juicer extracts only the juice of fruits and vegetables, separating out and discarding the fiber and other solids and giving you a pure liquid that is highly digestible. In the case of vegetables, which have a rougher, less absorbable type of fiber than fruit, this can be especially desirable, allowing you to dramatically increase your vegetable intake with ease.

For Storage

FREEZER

Create a special breakfast section or compartment in your freezer (I use a large, plastic rectangular tub), and store all kinds of things in it—baking ingredients (for optimal freshness) and baked goods, as well as fruit and many other things that are noted as "freezable" in individual recipes.

ZIP-STYLE FREEZER BAGS OF VARIOUS SIZES
STORAGE CONTAINERS WITH TIGHT-FITTING LIDS

I recommend using storage bags and containers, not only for freezing and refrigerating food but also for transporting it when you have to eat on the run or when you bring breakfast with you to eat at your desk while you work.

GOOD LABELING PEN

Although it may seem obvious, I promise that you will forget (or possibly not recognize) what you put into those bags or containers in that special section of your freezer unless you tell yourself with a nice, clear label. Use a permanent marker.

① BEVERAGES

CONTENTS

BEVERAGES

We bring a certain orthodoxy to our morning beverage. Even those of us who are strictly secular about everything else approach that first sip with sacramental devotion. Why is it that even the most easygoing among us tend to have precise needs and notions not only about *what* we drink first thing in the morning but also when, where, and how? The cup, spoon, teapot or coffee paraphernalia, temperature, brewing method, and social context (newspaper or radio? conversation or silence?) are all critical factors that can set the tone for the new day ahead. We don't just drink our beverage of choice in the morning, we *have a relationship* with it. Often this includes physical interactions with the end product—and its chosen delivery vehicle—that go beyond just taking a sip. For example, I find myself really *holding* the hot mug on a cold morning—or the cold drink on a hot morning—as a way of absorbing temperature and energy through my hands. And the heady aroma of hot water hitting freshly ground coffee summons a clarity of mind that seems not to have existed just moments before. Our morning beverage is more than something to drink—it's a transitional ceremony, easing us from our cozy dream world into the sometimes unpleasant state of having to be alert and ready for action.

Chances are you already have an established routine for preparing whatever it is you drink in the morning, and you don't need a recipe as such. There really is no right or wrong way to prepare coffee or tea, especially when you're making it for yourself, nor are there principles of correctness about juice. Habits and preferences develop over a lifetime, based on a personal sense of ritual as well as individual taste, kitchen space, personal style, budget, and time. So rather than provide recipes for the standard breakfast beverages—orange juice, coffee, and tea—I've included a *discussion* of them, along with pointers for making these basic drinks taste excellent and not merely good. (I did include a recipe for hot chocolate, however. It's my family's favorite cocoa, so you *must* try it!)

You'll also find a few unusual ideas here: Hot Spiced Cider, Miso Soup, Breakfast Gazpacho, and Cucumber-Mint Lassi, all of which are surprisingly delectable first thing in the morning. Another category of breakfast drink is the healthy shake, which can be very useful when you're crunched for time and short on appetite, but you still need to get some good (and good-tasting) nutrition into your system. Somehow, we can often manage to drink what we can't quite eat, even if it adds up to the same volume. To that effect, I've included a section on fruit smoothies, enabling you to create bright, healthful blended drinks on a regular basis—and with great enjoyment.

About Orange Juice

I thoroughly enjoy squeezing a glass of fresh orange juice for breakfast, and I recommend doing it once in a while. It doesn't take all that long, and it adds a touch of what I like to call "soulful intention" to my early morning routine. But if you can't spare the few minutes required for squeezing oranges—and soulful intention is not on your list of priorities—you can still have fresh-tasting "not from concentrate" orange juice, thanks to the high-quality brands available at the market these days. These products are *almost* as good as hand-squeezed. (The main challenge in buying fresh juice is navigating the maze of choices, which includes "with pulp," "no pulp," "some pulp," "lots of pulp," and "calcium-enriched"—or various combinations of calcium and pulp—all of which can be *really* confusing! But I digress.)

Frozen orange juice concentrate was invented in the United States in the mid-20th century, and within a short time the changeover from fresh fruit to frozen concentrate approached 100 percent. By the early 1970s, however, consumers began moving toward chilled fresh juice and away from concentrate. By 1986, chilled juice sales had surpassed juice from concentrate, and the gap continues to widen. According to the Florida Department of Citrus, chilled juice now accounts for over 60 percent of all the orange juice sold in this country.

WHICH ORANGES SHOULD YOU BUY?

You can't tell the quality of an orange by its appearance. And color is not an indicator of ripeness, juiciness, or sweetness either—rather, the color reflects the temperature at which the orange was harvested. A green orange can be fully ripe, and a bright orange one can be far from ready. (Cold weather brings out the orange color, and warm weather turns the fruit green again.) So when purchasing juice oranges, don't be seduced by a vibrant orange color. *Feel*—rather than look—for firmness and heaviness. Also scratch the skin a little, and sniff for fragrance.

California oranges develop a thicker skin than those grown in Florida, as California has a drier climate and the thick skin is an adaptive mechanism to protect the fruit from drought. Florida oranges are juicier because Florida is a wetter place (logical, isn't it?). This means you will get more volume for your money with Florida oranges.

The best juice oranges are Valencias. Yet this variety, with its thin skin and a tendency to bruise, is not the best looking. Navel oranges are considered the best for eating because they are seedless and attractive—and they peel easily. But don't overlook Valencias as good eating oranges too, even if they aren't as pretty or as peelable as navels—and even though they have seeds. They're just *so* sweet and delicious!

A $3 BILLION INDUSTRY

According to the Florida Department of Citrus, that state produces 48 billion oranges a year, the vast majority of which are squeezed into juice that is sold commercially. In a given year, as many as 230 million boxes of oranges—weighing 90 pounds each—will be used for commercial orange juice, while only 9 million boxes (or fewer) will be sold as fresh fruit.

The northeastern United States is the biggest market, consuming 40 percent of all the orange juice produced in the country. (The New York City area alone consumes 17 percent of the national output.) Each week Tropicana sends 5 full trainloads (52 million gallons per train) of orange juice to its packaging plant in New Jersey. It must smell really good in there!

STRANGELY, ORANGES ARE NOT NAMED FOR THEIR COLOR

The name "orange" is believed to derive from the Sanskrit *naranagah,* which became the Tamil *naru,* meaning "fragrance." The letter "n" still appears in the Spanish *naranja* but was dropped in both the Italian *arancia* and in French, where the original version, *une narange,* became *une orange*. This, in turn, led to the modern English name for the fruit, which—in relation to the color—is pure coincidence.

About Coffee

Coffee is consumed daily by roughly 49 percent of the U.S. population, and most of us coffee drinkers have our brewing and drinking patterns firmly embedded in our morning routine. Some prefer the concentrated intensity of a shot of espresso, while others are propelled through the day by the bottomless cup. Many of us embrace this beverage not only for the ritual and the caffeine buzz, but also for the dark, sensual enjoyment, experiencing coffee's powerful essence primarily through our sense of smell. And to many, coffee's aftertaste (referred to as the "finishing" by aficionados) is as important as the first sip. According to true enthusiasts, the best coffee is still pleasing for a good while after the last drop is swallowed.

Coffee grows on trees, and the beans come from inside the fruit, which looks like a cherry. All coffee is grown between the Tropics of Cancer and Capricorn—in the Pacific, the Americas, and Africa and the Middle East—and each region brings its own unique approach and techniques to the cultivation and harvesting of the beans. Coffee beans are hand-picked, and there are about 4,000 of them in a single pound of specialty coffee! Add to that the fact that there are more steps in processing coffee from tree to cup than there are in making fine wine, and you'll understand why premium beans sell for a premium price. By knowing what you like about coffee, you can search out coffee origins and roasters and then experiment with various brewing methods until you find a complete scenario that delivers what you are looking for.

A FEW WORDS ABOUT CAFFEINE

Caffeine is an odorless, bitter alkaloid found in cacao beans, coffee beans, cola nuts, and tea leaves. It is a stimulant to the central nervous system and a diuretic. The amount of caffeine in coffee depends on a number of factors, including the variety, where it is grown, the particle size used (the "grind"), and the method and length of brewing. Decaffeination is the process of dissolving the caffeine out of coffee beans—through any one of several processes—before they are roasted. Usually these processes remove about 98 percent of the caffeine.

The challenge of a good decaf is to retain the coffee's flavor and character, and some decaffeinated coffees are available that taste just as good as the regular brew. If you think about it, decaf *has* to taste good, because when people are not drinking coffee for the stimulus, flavor becomes the sole purpose. So you might conclude that people who drink decaf like the taste of coffee even more than do those who drink the caffeinated variety.

 WHAT DO NOBEL PRIZE WINNERS EAT FOR BREAKFAST?

The Nobel laureates at MIT report beginning the day with the following:

- David Baltimore (Physiology/Medicine, 1975): Half a bagel with a couple of slices of Swedish farmer cheese, black coffee, and fresh-squeezed orange juice

- Philip Shart (Physiology/Medicine, 1993): A glass of orange juice, a grapefruit half or half of a melon, a muffin with jelly, and two cups of black coffee

- Clifford Shull (Physics, 1994): Corn flakes with milk, a mélange of peaches, bananas, blueberries, and/or strawberries, black coffee, and an occasional English muffin or roll with butter

What common thread do we see in all the above? They all drink black coffee. Hmmm . . . could this be the true brain food?

Coffee-Brewing Pointers

If you would like your cup of java to taste not only better but *great,* here are a few details that will make a difference.

HOW SHOULD I BUY COFFEE—AND FROM WHOM?

Buy your coffee from a company that knows its beans and has perfected the fine art of roasting. Carefully chosen "top of the crop" beans, uniform in size and free from defects, are half the story. The other half is the roasting process, which helps determine the color, aroma, acidity, and body of the final product. A skilled roastmaster makes many subtle judgment calls throughout the process, resulting in a variety of roasts (light to dark) from which to choose. Experiment with various types of coffee beans—including blends—until you find one or two that you love.

HOW SHOULD COFFEE BE STORED?

Once it has been roasted, coffee must be packaged and stored correctly to preserve its freshness. Quality roasters produce small batches and ship them right away, packed in specially crafted airtight bags that have one-way valves designed to release carbon dioxide while preventing oxygen from entering. (Oxygen, light, heat, and moisture are the major culprits in flavor degradation.) For best results, store coffee right in the roaster's bag, tightly closed—with as much of the air pressed out of it as possible—and keep it in the freezer.

WHAT'S THE BEST WAY TO BREW COFFEE?

- If possible, buy whole beans and grind them just before brewing. (Ground coffee goes stale 100 times faster than intact beans.)

- Use the appropriate grind for your chosen brewing method. For press pots, use a medium to coarse grind (about 10 seconds in an electric blade grinder). For the drip method—paper or gold filters—use a medium to fine grind (15 to 20 seconds in the grinder). Espresso requires a very fine grind (up to 30 seconds in the grinder).

- Good water makes good coffee. If the water tastes funny, so will the coffee. If your tap water is unpleasant tasting or heavily chlorinated, use bottled or filtered water. Begin with cold water and bring it to a boil, then let your kettle rest for a minute or two after boiling to reach the best brewing temperature (195°F to 205°F). Preheat the cup, pot, carafe, or thermos by pouring in hot water and then dumping it out right before you begin brewing.

- Measure 2 tablespoons of ground coffee for every 6 ounces of water. Keep this ratio consistent, no matter how much coffee you're brewing. (Add hot water afterward, if it's too strong.)

- If you use a press pot, brew coffee for 2 to 3 minutes to produce full flavor without the bitterness of overextraction.

- If you're using a drip method, remove the grounds before the last few drops of water have drained through, as these late drips tend to be bitter. Coffee made with the drip method will be stronger initially and grow weaker as the infusion continues, so stir your cup or carafe before serving.

- Brew only as much as you need. Serve the coffee as soon after brewing as possible.

- Coffee can be kept warm on a burner or a hot plate for only about 20 minutes—at *most*—before the flavor starts to become bitter. Reheating coffee—even a little bit—will ruin its flavor. An airtight thermos preserves the flavor for several hours while keeping the coffee hot, but if it is left there too long the coffee will eventually develop a thermos taste.

Specialty Coffees at Home

You don't have to head out to a chic café to enjoy a cup of specialty coffee. All you need to create your own coffee bar at home is a bag of great beans, a grinder, an espresso machine, and a description of what to do.

- ESPRESSO is not a kind of bean, nor is it a "roast." It's a way of preparing a small dose of strong coffee with sublimely concentrated aroma and flavor, meant to be drunk quickly while still hot—not slowly sipped. Espresso is made by forcing hot water through finely ground and tightly packed dark-roasted coffee under high pressure. The resulting beverage is thick, strong, rich, and smooth—and topped with a naturally occurring light brown foam. A single shot of espresso is made from the same amount of coffee you would normally use to make a 6-ounce cup. The true appreciation of espresso lies in both the aroma and the aftertaste, which should last—pleasantly—for as long as 30 minutes. Thus the memory of espresso is almost more important than the immediate experience.

- CAPPUCCINO is one or more shots of espresso topped with an equal amount of steamed milk, followed by an equal amount of milk foam.

- CAFFÈ LATTE consists of one or more shots of espresso (one third or less of the total volume) topped with steamed milk (two thirds or more of the total volume) and layered with ¼ inch of milk foam.

- CAFFÈ MOCHA begins with an ounce of chocolate syrup and one or more shots of espresso (one third of the total volume). The cup then is filled with steamed milk (two thirds or more of the total volume) and topped with whipped cream.

- CAFFÈ AMERICANO is 2 shots of espresso diluted with enough steaming hot water to produce a 6-ounce cup.

- SWISS-STYLE CAFFÈ MOCHA is something you won't find in coffee bars but can have fun serving at home. With no espresso machine necessary, it's a shortcut "faux" specialty coffee or, put less politely, a "cheat." Serve a regular cup of your favorite brew with a plate of milk chocolate candies on the side. Let the candies melt (wholly or partially) in your mouth as you drink the coffee. What a treat! This lovely ritual is a true Swiss tradition.

 FLAVORED COFFEE IS NOT A MODERN IDEA

In the 1980s, flavored coffee was very much in style in the United States. But it wasn't a new phenomenon. Since coffee was first brewed in the Middle East—its place of origin—centuries ago, people have been adding spices to it, not so much out of preference but out of necessity. Here are some examples:

- Bedouins add cardamom to their coffee. This tradition probably arose because the Bedouins were always on the run and never had time to roast their coffee beans correctly. So cardamom was needed to mask the bad flavors that were not adequately "roasted out."

- Yemen was once the world's only source of coffee. The Yemenites have a traditional coffee spice mixture containing ginger, cloves, and bishop's weed (which tastes like a blend of thyme and cumin). Like the Bedouins, they added this mixture as a remedial element to make inferior beans more palatable.

- In Europe, coffee beans often were not only inadequately roasted, but also rancid from the long shipping voyage. Thus, spiced coffee became common in Europe, especially in England, where there is a record of people actually adding *mustard* to coffee. That might explain why British culture became known for its tea.

About Tea

Tea is nearly five thousand years old. According to legend, it was discovered by a Chinese emperor when some tea leaves accidentally blew into a pot of boiling water, creating an irresistible brew.

True teas are made from the dried leaves of the tea plant, *Camellia sinensis,* which was first cultivated in China and was also found growing wild in India. Chinese monks and European traders introduced tea to Japan, Sri Lanka, and other countries. From there, it was brought to Europe and eventually to North America. Today there are more than three thousand varieties of tea, each with its own distinct character and named for the district in which it is grown.

In many cultures, tea has been the focal point around which spiritual and hospitality rituals have evolved. Tea has inspired the creation of exquisite cups, ceremonial bowls, earthenware pots, silver service sets, samovars, furniture (the tea table predates the coffee table)—and even entire buildings. For many people, a cup of hot tea, fixed "just so," is the centerpiece of the early morning routine—a defining moment in the often challenging quest to wake up and get going. And recent studies in leading medical journals have provided even more reasons to drink tea, showing it to contain powerful antioxidants, with implications for heart health, cancer prevention, immune system strength, and general detoxification.

Tea breaks down into three basic types: black, oolong, and green.

- BLACK TEA has been fully oxidized or fermented, producing a hearty-flavored, dark amber brew. Some of the popular black teas include English Breakfast (a good breakfast choice, as its flavor mixes well with milk), Darjeeling (a blend of Himalayan teas with flowery overtones), and Orange Pekoe (a blend of Ceylon teas—the most widely used of the tea blends).

- OOLONG TEA, popular in China, is a cross between black and green tea. It is only partially fermented to achieve a delicious fruity taste and a lovely pale color. Elegant and mildly fragrant, oolong is sometimes called the "champagne of teas." Originally grown in the Fukien province of China, the highest-grade oolongs (Formosa oolongs) are grown now in Taiwan.

- GREEN TEA is produced by steaming fresh-picked leaves before they are dried, skipping the oxidizing or fermenting step that distinguishes black teas and oolongs. Green tea thus has a more delicate taste than other teas and is a light golden-green color. A staple in Asia for centuries, green tea is gaining popularity in the United States due in large part to recent scientific studies linking it with reduced risk of stroke, heart disease, and cancer—and showing it to have a high content of vitamins and minerals. These include vitamin C and several B vitamins, which are water-soluble and quickly released into a cup of tea, making them readily available. Green tea also contains magnesium, potassium, manganese, and fluoride.

  Some of the most popular green tea varieties are Jasmine, Gunpowder, Dragonwell, Genmai-Cha, and Bancha. Each one has a distinct flavor that should be savored on its own. I don't recommend mixing them.

- TISANES, OR HERBAL INFUSIONS, are created from the flowers, berries, peels, seeds, leaves, and roots of many different plants. These botanical ingredients are often combined into interesting blends to create complex, evocative flavors. Tisanes are good for refreshment, relaxation, and rejuvenation—and are sometimes also used for medicinal purposes. Mint and fruity varieties mix well with black teas, and many of them are delicious chilled—plain, or combined with fruit juices. Herbal infusions, although commonly called "tea," contain no true tea leaves.

How to Brew a Perfect Cup of Tea

• Start with fresh, cold water. In areas with poor tap water, use bottled or filtered water. Never use hot water directly from the tap—rather, let the water run for a few seconds until it is quite cold. This ensures that the water is aerated (full of oxygen) which helps release the full flavor of the tea leaves.

• Bring the water to a rolling boil. Don't let it boil too long, as it will boil away the flavor-releasing oxygen and result in a flat-tasting cup of tea.

• Preheat the teapot or cup by pouring in some of the hot water, letting it stand for a moment, and then dumping it out.

• For each 8-ounce cup of tea, use 1 rounded teaspoon of loose tea leaves (2 teaspoons for oolong).

• Pour the boiling water directly onto the tea leaves or tea bag in the pot or cup. (With green tea, let the water cool down for a few minutes before brewing.)

• Brew black tea or oolong for 3 to 5 minutes. Steep green tea for 2 to 3 minutes. Tisanes can steep for up to 8 minutes or even longer. In all cases, longer steeping yields a stronger brew.

DOES TEA REALLY HAVE MORE CAFFEINE THAN COFFEE?

The question of tea's caffeine content is a point of confusion for many people. While coffee and tea are both sources of caffeine, the amount of caffeine in any single serving of these beverages varies significantly. However, an average serving of coffee contains up to twice as much caffeine as an average cup of tea. Here's where the confusion comes in: Ounce for ounce, tea contains more caffeine than coffee *when measured in its dry form*. But of course, we never consume it that way, so for all intents and purposes, coffee prevails in the true caffeine delivery contest.

TEA INVENTIONS IN AMERICA: ICED TEA AND TEA BAGS

• In 1904, the United States hosted the first World's Fair in St. Louis, at which merchants from all over the world gathered to show off their products. One exhibitor, a tea plantation owner, planned to give away free samples of hot tea to fair visitors as a promotional device. When a heat wave hit, to save his investment of time and travel, he dumped a load of ice into the brewed tea and thus served the first iced tea. Along with the Egyptian fan dancer, it was the talk of the fair.

• Four years later, a tea merchant in New York inadvertently developed the tea bag. He carefully wrapped each sample that he delivered to restaurants for their consideration, then recognized a terrific marketing opportunity when he noticed that, to avoid dealing with messy, wet tea leaves when it came time to clean up, the restaurants were brewing the samples in the bags he had wrapped them in.

SMOOTHIES

My basic smoothie method is very low-tech: I just throw all the ingredients into a blender and push the button. This is a perfect morning project, because you can make it before you're fully awake, and it will still come out fine.

I like to make smoothies with seasonal fruit whenever possible. The recipes on these two pages are designed to be made in the summer, and the three that follow (page 12) feature winter fruit. Of course, if you use frozen fruit (opposite page), you can make any of them any time of year.

- Use a high-quality yogurt that has live cultures and, if flavored, is not too sweet.
- Soy milk (plain or vanilla) can be substituted for the yogurt in any of these recipes.
- You can replace the orange juice with other kinds of fruit juice. (Guava and passionfruit juice are especially good.) You can also vary the fruit and experiment with other flavors of yogurt (lemon or strawberry, for example) besides vanilla. In other words, these recipes are entirely flexible.
- Smoothies keep for several days if stored in a tightly covered container in the refrigerator. They will thicken slightly during this time.

YIELD: 1 to 2 servings per recipe
PREPARATION TIME: 5 to 10 minutes per recipe

Strawberry-Banana Smoothie

½ cup orange juice

1 medium-sized ripe banana

8 to 10 large strawberries

½ cup vanilla yogurt

1 to 2 tablespoons fresh
    lemon juice

1. Combine the orange juice, banana, strawberries, and yogurt in a blender and purée to the desired consistency.
2. Add lemon juice to taste, and serve cold.

A SMOOTHIE DOESN'T HAVE TO BE SMOOTH

If you prefer a more textured smoothie, stop the blender a few seconds sooner than you normally would, leaving small pieces of fruit laced throughout the drink. If you use chunks of frozen fruit, they will turn into tiny, flavored ice chips that will keep the drink cold—especially delightful on hot summer mornings!

FRUIT SECONDS

Don't toss a piece of fruit because it's unattractive. In fact, purposely buy fruit "seconds" for your smoothies. (Remember, it doesn't matter what the fruit looks like, because it will be blended into a drink.) It's especially nice to do this if you purchase fruit directly from the growers at a farmers' market. It will be a mutual service!

Honeydew Smoothie

½ cup orange juice

2 to 3 cups honeydew chunks

¼ cup fresh lemon juice

½ cup vanilla yogurt

A handful of fresh mint leaves
 (optional)

1. Combine all the ingredients in a blender and purée to the desired consistency.
2. Serve cold.

Cantaloupe-Peach Smoothie

¾ cup orange juice

1 cup cantaloupe chunks

1 cup sliced peaches

½ cup vanilla yogurt

1 to 2 tablespoons fresh
 lemon juice

2 to 3 tablespoons pure maple syrup

1. Combine the orange juice, cantaloupe, peaches, and yogurt in a blender and purée to the desired consistency.
2. Add lemon juice and maple syrup to taste, and serve cold.

 USE YOUR FREEZER!

If you freeze some of your smoothie ingredients, you can get a thicker, frothier shake. Freezing also enables you to preserve summer fruit at its peak, so you can enjoy it a few months down the road. Here are some tips for using your freezer to maximize your smoothies:

• You can freeze just about any kind of fruit for smoothies: cranberries, strawberries, blueberries, chunks of banana, sliced plums or peaches, melon cubes. With the exception of cranberries, which you can freeze directly in the bag they came in, fruit needs to be frozen in individual pieces first—spread out on a tray—before being packed into bags for longer-term storage. This keeps the chunks separate, so you can just take out and use the amount you need at any given time.

• Freeze soy milk or coconut milk (used in the Piña Colada Smoothie, page 12) in ice cube trays, then pack the cubes into zip-style bags and use as desired. (It's easiest to keep track of the volume if you consistently measure 1½ tablespoons per cube.)

Cranberry-Pomegranate Smoothie

• Pomegranate molasses is available in specialty markets and Middle Eastern groceries.

1 cup fresh cranberries

¼ cup pomegranate molasses

1 cup apple juice or pear nectar

½ cup plain or vanilla yogurt
(optional)

1. Combine everything in a blender and purée to the desired consistency.

2. Taste to adjust the molasses, and serve cold.

Piña Colada Smoothie

1 can (20 ounces) crushed
pineapple packed in juice

8 coconut milk ice cubes
(see preceding page), or ¾ cup
cold coconut milk

¾ cup vanilla yogurt

1. Combine all the ingredients in a blender and purée to the desired consistency.

2. Serve cold.

Vanilla-Pear Smoothie

2 medium-sized, very ripe pears,
peeled and sliced (or 2 cups
sliced canned pears)

1 to 2 tablespoons fresh lemon juice

¼ teaspoon vanilla extract

1 cup vanilla yogurt

Pear nectar or apple juice

Pure maple syrup

1. Combine the pears, lemon juice, vanilla, and yogurt in a blender and purée until smooth.

2. Thin to the desired consistency with pear nectar or apple juice, and sweeten to taste with maple syrup.

3. Serve cold.

FRUITED SWIZZLE STICKS

Add a festive touch to birthday mornings or holiday brunches—or plain old rainy Tuesdays—with a fruited swizzle stick garnish for your smoothie. Just thread chunks of fresh, seasonal fruit (such as whole strawberries, pitted cherries, melon cubes, banana chunks, peach or plum slices, citrus wedges, thick slices of orange peel, or grapes) on a bamboo skewer, and slide it into the drink or place it across the top of the glass. Children, especially, will love this!

MAKE YOUR SMOOTHIE INTO A SUPERFOOD

While the smoothie recipes on the preceding pages are delicious on their own, they also offer a great opportunity to incorporate some "nutriceuticals" (functional foods) into your diet. This approach works splendidly with kids, and it's a real lifesaver if your children are fussy eaters. Within the safe, luxurious—and deceptive—format of an innocent shake, you can mask healthy supplements that might otherwise cause youngsters to run for cover. (And if your kids don't finish the smoothies you give them for breakfast, pack the leftovers into a thermos to include with their lunch.)

To boost the nutritional profile of any juice or smoothie, try one or more of these options:

CHILLED GREEN TEA OR FRUITY TISANES
Chilled green tea or fruity tisanes (page 8) can replace some or all of the fruit juice in a smoothie. Balance the flavor with some maple syrup to taste, if desired.

POWDERED MILK
For extra calcium, add up to 2 tablespoons powdered milk per cup.

OAT BRAN
Add up to 2 tablespoons oat bran per cup to get more fiber.

PROTEIN POWDER
Give the smoothie a protein boost with 2 tablespoons protein powder (any kind) per cup.

VITAMIN C
Vitamin C is widely available in powdered form, and it readily blends into any juice or smoothie.

VITAMIN AND MINERAL CAPSULES
If you take vitamin and mineral supplements in capsule form, but you dislike swallowing them whole, open the capsules and empty the contents into any juice or smoothie, mix it in, and just drink it down. (You can also get liquid vitamins and minerals, which you can just stir in.)

"GREEN STUFF"
"Green stuff" (fresh wheat grass juice or powdered barley grass) contains chlorophyll, potassium, calcium, and magnesium, and can be quite nutritious in small doses. Wheat grass juice, especially, is very intense and quite sweet. Usually, with wheat grass juice, we're advised to take a maximum of 2 ounces per serving. With powdered barley grass, follow the recommended serving size on the package.

FLAX-SEED OIL
Slip some supernutritious essential fatty acids into your smoothie by adding 1 to 2 tablespoons flax-seed oil (or a fresh-pressed blend of omega-6 and omega-3 oils, available in the refrigerated section of many natural food stores) to each serving.

Miso Soup

In Japan, miso soup is a traditional breakfast food—sipped hot, directly from the bowl. As complex in flavor as it is simple to prepare, a single portion of miso soup can be put together in roughly the same amount of time it takes to brew a cup of tea. Try transferring the soup to a wide-neck thermos and taking it to work with you. I can't think of a more soothing and fortifying way to start the day, especially in winter.

If you are too hurried to make even this simple recipe—or you don't have the ingredients on hand—there are some very good brands of instant miso soup powder available. They come in single-serving packets, and all you need to do is add hot water and stir. Consider keeping a stash at work, for midmorning nourishment.

- The best type of miso to use for breakfast soup is "shiro" or "mellow white."
- Although miso soup stores and reheats well, some of the beneficial enzymes in the miso will be destroyed if the soup is boiled. So if you reheat it, do so gently.

YIELD: **1 serving (easily multiplied)**
PREPARATION TIME: **5 minutes**

1 cup water or vegetable broth

1 tablespoon light-colored miso

1 to 2 tablespoons diced silken tofu (tiny pieces)

1 small scallion, very finely minced

1. Heat the water or broth until it reaches a boil. Place the miso in a generously sized single-serving bowl, and pour in about one third of the hot water or broth. Mash and stir until the mixture becomes smooth.

2. Add the remaining liquid, along with the tofu and scallion. Serve right away.

(VARIATIONS) **A HEARTIER MISO SOUP**

Miso soup is delicious plain, sipped as a hot beverage. You can also make it into a heartier meal by adding any or all of the following:

- A few spoonfuls of cooked grains (wild rice or barley are especially nice)
- A poached egg
- A handful of daikon sprouts or radish sprouts
- Wakame (a sea vegetable that is sold dried), soaked in water for 15 minutes, or until tender
- A few small spinach leaves

 MISO, THE VENERABLE SOYBEAN PASTE

Rich in enzymes that aid digestion—and a good source of protein—miso is a salty, deeply flavored paste made from aged fermented soybeans and grains. There are many different varieties of miso (determined by variations in the soybeans, the type of grain used, the length of fermentation, and so on), and they are often referred to by their color (such as red, yellow, brown, or white). Because it is already fermented and aged, miso keeps indefinitely on your pantry shelf.

Breakfast Gazpacho

The famous cold vegetable soup—with its slightly spicy, eye-opening edge—can double as a deeply refreshing, brightly flavored cold breakfast drink. Thickened with vegetables rather than with the traditional bread used by Spanish cooks, this light gazpacho is thin enough to drink but still has enough heft to make you feel as though you've had a meal. I especially recommend this to those of you who like a glass of cold tomato juice upon awakening—just a short ride through the blender with a few additional ingredients will turn that plain drink into a full-fledged liquid breakfast.

- You will get a smoother purée in a blender than in a food processor.
- If you don't have fresh tomatoes on hand, substitute 3 cups puréed canned tomatoes—it will still taste great.
- Breakfast Gazpacho keeps for a week or longer if refrigerated in a tightly covered container.

YIELD: **About 4 servings**
PREPARATION TIME: **10 minutes**

1 pound very ripe tomatoes

1½ cups cucumber chunks, peeled and seeded

½ cup chopped bell pepper

A handful of parsley

1 medium clove garlic

¼ teaspoon cumin (rounded measure)

½ teaspoon salt (rounded measure)

1 teaspoon red wine vinegar or cider vinegar

1 teaspoon light honey

2 teaspoons fresh lemon juice

1 tablespoon extra virgin olive oil

Cayenne

1. Core the tomatoes, and cut them into large chunks. (Peeling and seeding are unnecessary.)
2. Place the tomatoes in a blender or food processor with all the remaining ingredients except the cayenne. Purée until it is as smooth as you like it.
3. Transfer to a container, and add cayenne to taste. Cover and chill. Serve cold.

A "VIRGIN MARY" FOR BREAKFAST

If you are a tomato juice-for-breakfast person, and you'd like to give your morning beverage some zing—but you don't have the time or ingredients to make Breakfast Gazpacho—you can very quickly throw together what is sometimes called a "virgin Mary" (a bloody Mary without the vodka).

For each serving, combine in a glass:

- 1 cup cold tomato juice
- A drop or two of Tabasco sauce or Worcestershire sauce
- ½ teaspoon prepared horseradish
- Lemon juice to taste
- Black pepper to taste

Whisk or stir until thoroughly blended, and garnish with:

- 1 large stalk celery

Cucumber-Mint Lassi

Lassi is a cold buttermilk drink—lightly seasoned and sometimes sweetened—that is often served in Indian restaurants as a mouth-cooling accompaniment to hot curries. It also makes a delicious, light breakfast beverage. This ultra-refreshing variation has become my new favorite guzzling habit. It's the cleanest-tasting drink imaginable.

- Plain yogurt—thinned to your desired consistency with a little water—can be substituted for the buttermilk.
- Cucumber-Mint Lassi keeps for up to a week if stored in a tightly covered container in the refrigerator. It will separate into layers. Shake or stir or before serving.

YIELD: 1 to 2 servings
PREPARATION TIME: 5 minutes

1½ cups cucumber chunks, peeled and seeded

1 cup buttermilk

⅛ teaspoon salt

OPTIONAL ADDITIONS

1 teaspoon sugar

1 to 2 scallions, chopped

6 to 8 fresh mint leaves

1. Combine everything in a blender and purée until smooth.
2. Serve cold—plain or over ice.

VARIATIONS

SAVORY SPICED LASSI

Add pinches of the following ground spices to plain, cold buttermilk:

- Cumin
- Fenugreek
- Fennel
- Coriander
- Salt

Taste to adjust the seasonings, and serve cold.

MANGO LASSI

For each serving, combine in a blender:

- ¾ cup buttermilk
- 1½ cups ripe mango pulp

Purée until smooth, and serve cold.

Chai-Spiced Milk

Chai is the word for "tea" in both Swahili and Russian. In Hindi, it's chaay; in Mandarin and Portuguese—and in British slang—it's chà. In current American coffee bar vernacular, "chai" has come to mean a sweet, spiced, milky tea drink that satisfies many cravings. Here's a tea-less milk drink spiked with chai spices, followed by a variation that also includes the tea.

- For a more pronounced flavor, you can increase the spices and/or let the drink steep for up to an hour, then strain and reheat.
- This recipe can be made with any kind of milk, including soy milk or rice milk.

YIELD: **1 serving (easily multiplied)**
PREPARATION TIME: **10 minutes**

1 cup milk

1 cinnamon stick

1 teaspoon fennel seed

8 cardamom pods

4 whole cloves

¼ teaspoon ground coriander

Honey

Ground cinnamon

1. Pour the milk into a nonstick saucepan and add everything except the honey and ground cinnamon. Place over medium heat.
2. Just before the milk reaches the boiling point, turn the heat down and simmer, uncovered, for 5 minutes. (If a skin forms on top of the milk, just stir it back in.)
3. Strain the mixture into a mug and stir in honey to taste. Lightly sprinkle with cinnamon, and serve hot.

VARIATION BACKWARD CHAI

Normally, chai is spiced tea with plain milk added. This backward version is spiced milk with plain tea added, allowing you to vary the amount of tea without sacrificing any of the flavor. It makes 2 to 3 servings.

Make the main recipe, doubling the spices. Add:

- 1½ cups hot black tea, brewed very strong

FROTHING MILK

Create a lovely foam on top of your milk by whipping air into it with a frother—a gadget (available in specialty coffee shops and upscale "cuisine" stores) that looks like a small immersion blender. You can froth cold milk and then heat it in a microwave. Or if the milk is already heated, as in these chai recipes, transfer it to a deep vessel—such as a 1-quart-capacity jar or pitcher—and froth it there, to prevent splashing. In addition to foaming the top surface, a frother adds volume and transforms the texture of the milk. You can also use this handy gadget to whip small amounts of cream in seconds.

FORTIFYING MILK

Increase the protein or calcium content of milk by stirring in some protein powder or powdered milk. For best results, use the kind of easily dissolved protein powder made especially for use in drinks. (See page xv for more information about protein powder.)

My Family's Favorite Hot Chocolate

There are some days—and some moods—when hot chocolate is just simply the *answer. And there might not even have been a question! This recipe hits that indescribable spot.*

• Soy milk—or a combination of milk and cream—can be substituted for the milk.

YIELD: **2 servings (easily multiplied)**
PREPARATION TIME: **10 minutes**

¼ cup semisweet chocolate chips

1 teaspoon sugar

3 cups milk

A pinch of salt

¼ teaspoon vanilla extract

OPTIONAL TOPPINGS

Whipped cream

Cinnamon

1. Combine the chocolate chips and sugar in a medium-sized saucepan. Pour in the milk, then add the salt and vanilla.
2. Place the saucepan over medium heat, stirring slowly as the mixture heats up and the chocolate melts. Don't let it boil.
3. Serve hot, topped with whipped cream and a light sprinkling of cinnamon, if desired.

 ## A BIT OF HOT CHOCOLATE HISTORY

Introduced to Europe by the Spanish conquistadores—who had been served this mysterious elixir by the Aztecs in the New World—hot chocolate became *the* drink of the European elite. This fad lasted until the Industrial Revolution, when Europe's leisure class dwindled and a business class arose, requiring a stronger dose of caffeine to begin the day. Coffee and tea then replaced chocolate as the prevailing morning beverage, and hot cocoa was relegated mostly to children. Several centuries later, this rule has been greatly relaxed, and chocolate is now a universally acceptable breakfast option for people of all ages.

WHY DOES A SKIN FORM ON HEATED MILK?

That skin on your hot milk is actually a protein called casein, which evaporates and dries out on the hot surface of the milk. As you may have noticed, removing the skin while the milk is still heating doesn't do much good, since another layer will soon appear in its place. That's a good reason not to bother. Here's an even better reason to leave it alone: The casein is very nutritious, and every time you skim off a layer, you are removing some of the protein from the milk. Food scientist Shirley Corriher, in her very entertaining and informative book *Cookwise,* suggests an inspired solution to this dilemma: "With hot chocolate, the simplest solution is to add marshmallows, which melt on the surface. They contain an egg white foam and gelatin, which coat the surface and prevent the casein from drying." On behalf of all of us who harbor a secret passion for marshmallows on our cocoa, I want to thank Shirley for this permission!

Hot Spiced Cider

You might normally think of hot spiced cider as something to brighten up a dreary, cold Sunday afternoon, but it can also be a wonderful breakfast beverage as well. Consider bringing a full thermos to work with you on a crisp autumn or winter day, so you can sip it throughout the morning. This recipe, gently laced with ginger and black pepper, will provide heat in every sense of the word.

You can play with the amount of spice according to your taste, so consider the recipe below a formula, open to interpretation. You can simmer the mixture in the evening, let it sit out overnight, and reheat it in the morning. Note that the flavors get stronger as the cider sits around with the spices in it.

YIELD: 3 to 4 servings (easily multiplied)
PREPARATION TIME: 5 minutes, plus at least 25 minutes to heat, simmer, and steep

6 cardamom pods

½ teaspoon whole cloves

2 teaspoons whole peppercorns

1 quart apple cider

2 sticks cinnamon

2 thin slices fresh ginger

1. Place the cardamom, cloves, and peppercorns in a tea ball.
2. Combine everything in a saucepan and bring to a boil. Cover the pan, lower the heat, and let the mixture simmer for 10 minutes. Remove from the heat, and let it sit for at least another 10 minutes or longer.
3. Fish out the spices, and reheat the cider just before serving. Serve hot.

 WHAT'S THE DIFFERENCE BETWEEN APPLE JUICE AND CIDER?

Both apple juice and cider are made from pressing the juice from apples. Apple juice is usually pasteurized and filtered and is often chemically treated to prevent fermentation. It is then bottled and stored on the shelf, needing no refrigeration until after the bottle is opened. Cider, on the other hand, is a fresh product—unpasteurized, unfiltered, and unprocessed. Therefore, it has a much deeper apple flavor—and retains more vitamins—than apple juice. Cider also requires refrigeration, as it is highly perishable.

Hard cider is simply fresh cider that has been allowed to ferment. Hard ciders, like wines, vary greatly in taste, from sharp and dry to fruity and sweet. Lately, they have become a very fashionable drink in upscale bars and pubs throughout the United States (as they have been for years in France and England). Taking it one step further, when you distill fermented cider, you get apple brandy, also known as applejack (or Calvados, if you're in Normandy, France).

② FRUIT

CONTENTS

FRUIT

Fresh, ripe fruit in season just screams to be eaten—no instructions necessary. All we need is to get it in the house and in front of us. The rest falls deliciously into place.

And even though it's the world's juiciest pleasure to just pick up a ripe peach and bite into it, a platter of sliced fruit, cut just minutes before, will always be welcomed as a special event. A big part of this is the loving care that goes into preparing and arranging the fruit. I sometimes get up a little early and make individualized plates of sliced fruit for my kids, organizing it into clusters or designs. It takes maybe 10 minutes—if that—yet I feel as though I've created an edible, juicy little picture-poem to greet them as they drag themselves into the kitchen on a school morning. It's actually a pleasure for me, since I like a little quiet time alone in the kitchen first thing in the morning anyway. It's a meditation—an opportunity to soak up the early light and a sweet way to begin the day.

If plain, ripe fruit is so good and compelling on its own, why bother with a whole chapter of fruit recipes? Because good fresh fruit isn't always available, and when it is, it's often not as good as it looks. This is especially true when it has been grown in distant places and then packed and shipped for miles before arriving in your kitchen. Covering all these possibilities (or as many of them as I could think of), I've presented you with some recipes for a range of fruit, including ideas to help you salvage specimens that are not inspiring on their own.

I also want to encourage you to use some of the better canned and frozen fruit products, with or without fresh, in-season additions. These items are often perfectly good and can come in handy during the off-season or when you just can't get to the produce market.

IMPERFECT FRUIT 911

Who is not familiar with the frustration of opening a beautiful melon or pineapple only to discover that what you purchased was actually only a melon- or pineapple-shaped object? You want to quickly close the fruit back up and tape it together again—hoping no one will notice that it was ever opened—and leave it to ripen on the windowsill. But alas, that won't happen. So you feel obligated to eat the imperfect fruit even though important qualities, like texture and flavor, are missing. It is so sad!

But here's the silver lining: Fruit can be imperfect and still have great potential. The next time you find yourself with a disappointing melon or pineapple, consider the following.

(Note that some of these solutions can work with overripe *or* underripe fruit.)

OVERRIPE FRUIT CAN BE USED IN:

- Smoothies (page 10)
- Instant fruit jam (page 247)
- Berry Sauces (page 248)
- Mixed Fruit Compote (page 32)
- Fruit Crisp or Cobbler (page 38)
- Bread Pudding (page 236)
- Tropical fruit salsas (pages 250 to 252)
- Blintz filling (page 196)

UNDERRIPE FRUIT CAN BE USED IN:

- Caramelized Fruit (page 27)
- Mixed Fruit Compote (page 32)
- Roasted Fruit (page 36)
- Fruit Crisp or Cobbler (page 38)
- Bread Pudding (pages 236 and 237)
- Tropical fruit salsas (pages 250 to 252)

For two ultra-simple recipes for rescuing underripe fruit, please turn the page.

LETTING FRUIT RIPEN

PEACHES, PLUMS, APRICOTS, AND PEARS will ripen in your kitchen—quickly but not always beautifully. If you miss their best moment, consider turning them into a smoothie or a compote. You can tell when any of these are ripe simply by smelling them or by squeezing them gently.

PINEAPPLES, FIGS, AND MELONS will not ripen once harvested, although they will get softer, which is a nice way of saying they will rot. Keep your eye on them, and keep them cold. (In the case of figs and melons, eat them as soon as possible.)

How can you tell when they're ripe? Figs should be slightly soft. The rest is luck. Pineapples and melons should be fragrant and have warm, golden tones in the skin, with no green. Honeydews should be a creamy color. Pineapples will "give" a little when gently squeezed.

MANGOES AND PAPAYAS ripen well on your windowsill, away from direct sunlight. (You can hurry this along if you put them in a paper bag.) They're ripe when they emit a good fragrance and become slightly soft to the touch.

BERRY POINTERS

- Ripe berries will have a deep and even color. Overripe berries will appear dull, soft, watery, or moldy.

- Don't buy berries if their container is stained or leaking, as this usually indicates crushed or moldy berries within.

- To help berries stay fresh longer, store them in a single layer on a paper towel–lined tray or jelly roll pan. Cover with another layer of paper towels, and keep in the refrigerator.

- Don't wash berries until just before using them.

- Once chilled, strawberries will stay fresh for 3 or 4 days, and blueberries will stay good for 10 days to 2 weeks. But blackberries and raspberries are so fragile, they should be eaten as soon as possible.

FROZEN BERRIES can be a really good solution to the painful brevity of the fresh berry season. I have found that I use frozen berries much more often than I do fresh ones, especially now that high-quality organic berries—unsweetened and packed in sealed bags—are readily available in the frozen food department of many grocery stores. And if, when fresh berries are in season, you are blessed with an overabundance, it is very easy to freeze your own fruit (see page 11). This is a wonderful way to cheer up your household in the dead of winter!

Fruit Rescue Glaze

You can greatly improve the flavor of underripe fruit by "cooking" it in a marinade of acid and sugar, such as this lightly sweetened reduction of fruit juice and vinegar.

It's fun to mix and match different flavors in this recipe, and the finished glaze will always be an exquisite color. At various times I've made this with orange juice, pear nectar, apricot nectar, and guava juice—and with raspberry, cider, and balsamic vinegar—all in different combinations, and all of them delicious. Each mixture is so pretty, I actually went out and bought a set of small see-through glass bottles just for storing the assortment of fruit glazes I now have in the refrigerator at all times.

- This recipe can be multiplied. Just be sure you use a large enough pan so the mixture can remain shallow (1 inch deep or less) throughout the cooking process.
- Fruit Rescue Glaze keeps for months if stored in a tightly capped bottle or jar in the refrigerator. I recommend having some on hand for spontaneous use. (You never know when you might cut open a piece of fruit that isn't ripe—it's not as though we plan these things!)

YIELD: About ¾ cup (enough to resuscitate 1 large cut-up melon or its equivalent)
PREPARATION TIME: 40 minutes, plus time to cool. Once poured onto the fruit, allow 2 hours for the fruit to marinate.

---

1 cup fruit juice

1 cup vinegar

⅓ cup sugar or honey (possibly more)

1. Combine everything in a wide, shallow saucepan, and stir to dissolve the sugar or honey.
2. Place the pan over medium heat, and bring the mixture to the boiling point. (Open your windows—this will produce major fumes!) Turn the heat way down and simmer, uncovered, for 20 to 30 minutes, or until reduced by about two thirds.
3. Taste for sweetness, and add more sugar or honey, if desired. When the glaze has cooled to room temperature, it can be stored in a tightly covered container in the refrigerator until you need it.
4. To use the glaze, simply drizzle it over disappointing fruit. Cover, and let it marinate in the refrigerator for at least 2 hours, longer if possible. You will be amazed by the result!

THE BALSAMIC VINEGAR TREATMENT

Here's another good way to make dull fruit sparkle.

Slice the fruit, place it in a shallow pan, and sprinkle it with enough sugar to lightly coat every surface. Let it stand—at room temperature or in the refrigerator—for 30 minutes to 1 hour. Splash in a little high-quality balsamic vinegar (approximately 2 teaspoons per cup of sliced fruit), and it's ready to serve.

Caramelized Fruit

To dramatically transform fruit that is underripe or boring—or to bring aged dried fruit back to life—just cook it in a little butter and then add a touch of sugar, which will caramelize into a sweet crust. The whole thing can be done on the stovetop, or you can use a combination of the stovetop and the broiler. The fruit gets quite soft from the cooking, so be sure it is fairly firm to begin with.

This recipe calls for ½ to ¾ pound fruit. With fresh fruit, this translates more or less into any of the following: 2 medium-sized apples, peaches, or pears; 6 average fresh apricots or figs; 3 to 4 plums; or half a medium pineapple. (With dried fruit, just weigh it.)

• If you intend to broil the fruit, make sure the pan has an ovenproof handle.

YIELD: 2 to 3 servings
PREPARATION TIME: About 20 minutes

½ to ¾ pound fruit, fresh or dried

1 to 2 teaspoons unsalted butter

1 tablespoon vinegar (raspberry, cider, or balsamic)

¾ to 1 teaspoon sugar

Orange juice (up to ¼ cup)

Squeezable lemon or lime wedges

1. Prepare the fresh fruit: Halve apricots and plums. Quarter or thickly slice peaches, apples, and pears. Cut figs in half. Peel and trim pineapple, and cut it into ¾-inch slices. (Leave dried fruit whole.)
2. Place a medium-sized skillet over medium heat for about a minute. Add the butter, and when it melts, swirl to coat the pan. (Optional: Preheat the broiler.)
3. Reduce the heat to medium-low. Place the fruit skin side down in the melted butter, and cook for about 5 minutes, or until it softens slightly.
4. Turn the fruit over, and press it down gently. (Press dried fruit flat.) Drizzle with the vinegar, and cook on the second side for about 3 minutes, or until tender. Sprinkle the sugar over the top, and continue to cook just until the sugar melts.
5. If desired, place the pan under the preheated broiler for 3 to 5 minutes, or until the sugar turns golden. (Check every minute after 3 minutes, to be sure it doesn't burn.) In the case of dried fruit, broil until the sugar forms an exquisite chewy crust.
6. Remove the pan from the heat, and transfer the fruit to a plate with a rim. Any sauce that comes out of the pan easily can be spooned over the fruit.
7. Pour the orange juice into the pan, mixing to dissolve the remaining sauce. Spoon this over the fruit and serve hot or warm with squeezable citrus wedges.

VARIATION **CARAMELIZED BANANAS**

Follow the main recipe with these adjustments.

For the fruit, use:

• 2 medium-sized bananas (not too ripe!), split lengthwise down the middle, then cut in half

Replace the vinegar with:

• 1 tablespoon fresh lime juice

Add with the sugar:

• A pinch each of cinnamon and nutmeg

THREE SIMPLE FRUIT SALADS

A bowlful of cut fruit, complete with all the juices, is a timeless delight. At the peak of the summer season, this is the world's most sensuous no-brainer—an embarrassment of riches, especially if you shop at your local farmers' market. At other times of the year, though, or in other circumstances, when fresh fruit is not nearly as compelling or abundant, you may need a few suggestions to get inspired. Here are the three approaches I use most often. Please note that these are road maps, not specific recipes. Proceed intuitively.

MINT-INFUSED FRUIT SALAD

Certain types of fruit absorb the flavor of fresh mint incredibly well, and the result is stunningly refreshing.

- Grapefruit sections (fresh or canned in juice)
- Honeydew melon
- Cantaloupe and other muskmelons
- Pineapple (fresh, or chunks canned in juice)
- Citrus juice or Fruit Rescue Glaze (page 26; optional)
- Several handfuls of fresh peppermint or spearmint leaves

A combination of all the above works really well, but these fruit are not necessarily in season at the same time, so play it by ear. Simply cut the fruit into bite-sized chunks. Grapefruit and pineapple will produce enough of their own juice. With cut melon, you'll need to add some citrus juice (lemon, lime, and/or orange) or, if the melon tastes "pale," add a splash or two of Fruit Rescue Glaze to perk it up.

   I like to add about 5 fresh mint leaves for every cup or so of cut fruit. You don't need to chop the leaves—leave them whole, or just tear them in half if they're large. Mix well, cover, and refrigerate for at least 3 hours, or ideally overnight. Remove the mint leaves before serving, as they will have wilted dramatically from steeping in the acidic fruit juice. Replace them with a few small, fresh leaves, for garnish.

PANTRY FRUIT SALAD

Keep all of these items on hand, so when you haven't time to go to the market, you can still have a lovely fruit salad any season of the year. Sometimes we need permission to use convenience items. Here it is.

- Frozen unsweetened berries (any kind)
- Canned mandarin oranges, drained
- Canned pineapple (crushed or in chunks) packed in juice
- Canned grapefruit sections
- Canned sour cherries packed in water, drained

Empty the berries into the bowl while they're still frozen, so you can catch and keep all the lovely juices they give off as they defrost. When the berries are thoroughly defrosted, add any or all of the canned items, including the juices, if they're not too syrupy. If you have fresh fruit on hand and you'd like to include it, slice and add it just before serving.

WINTER FRUIT SALAD WITH POMEGRANATE

If you don't normally think of making a fresh fruit salad in winter, think again. You can usually find fresh pineapples, oranges, grapefruit, apples, bananas, and pears in the produce department.

Pomegranates have a very limited season (mid-fall through January), which makes them all the more special. So celebrate the winter solstice with this beautiful, tart fruit salad, adorned with glistening, scarlet pomegranate seeds.

Note: These days you can often find fresh summer fruit in the market in winter. It's generally been imported from the Southern Hemisphere, which has opposite seasons. If you don't mind paying the price and using this nonlocal (and usually nonorganic) fruit, go ahead. This is up to you.

- Pomegranates
- Fresh pineapple (or canned pineapple, packed in juice)
- Fresh orange sections
- Fresh grapefruit sections
- Apples
- Pears
- Bananas

Juice some of the pomegranates and seed the others, placing seeds and juice in a bowl. Stir in the pineapple and citrus sections, including all the juices. Slice and add apples, pears, and bananas just before serving, so they won't discolor or wilt.

EXCAVATING A POMEGRANATE

MINING THE SEEDS Pomegranate seeds are juicy little jewels—bright red, tart, and crunchy. The problem is, they're encased in a hard, tight skin, which, although lovely to look at, is difficult to break into. When you finally get the skin open, another challenge lies inside: The precious seeds are buried within a copious amount of pith, and you have to coax them out. Don't despair! Here's a method that I hope will change your relationship to pomegranates forever.

Have ready a large bowl of cold water. Slice the pomegranate into quarters, right through the skin, with a good, sharp knife. Place the pieces in the water, then pull the pith out and pull the seeds from the pith. Everything will yield quite readily. To make things even easier, the seeds will sink to the bottom of the water and the pith will float to the top—like magic.

EXTRACTING THE JUICE Juice a pomegranate exactly as you would an orange: Cut it in half through the middle (crosswise) and use a citrus juicer (manual or electric). Hold the fruit firmly in place and move it around to get maximum yield.

FREEZING POMEGRANATES Another nice thing to know about pomegranates is that they freeze very well. Just pack whole fruit in a heavy, zip-style plastic bag and store in the freezer. They will keep for a good, long time. Defrost before cutting open and juicing or extracting the seeds. Buy and freeze pomegranates during their very short season (late fall to early winter), and you can enjoy them anytime.

Berries in Buttermilk

We normally expect a fruit dish to be sweet, but this one is a refreshing surprise! A delightful tart and tangy flavor takes center stage, and the sweet touches are merely accents. I like this best made with frozen raspberries, black-berries, or blueberries, because they produce wonderful, deeply colored, flavorful juices as they defrost.

If you're making this with strawberries, use only fresh ones that are perfectly ripe and in season. (They don't work as well as the other berries if they've been frozen first.) Slice them thinly ahead of time, and let them sit for about 15 minutes before adding the buttermilk.

• If you're using frozen berries, defrost them right in the bowls, so all their juices will be included.

YIELD: 2 servings (easily multiplied)
PREPARATION TIME: 5 minutes (once frozen berries have defrosted)

½ cup berries (fresh or frozen, defrosted if frozen)

¾ cup cold buttermilk

Sugar (1½ to 2 teaspoons per serving)

1. Divide the berries between 2 servings bowls, then do the same with the buttermilk.
2. Stir gently, sweeten to taste, and either serve right away or cover tightly and refrigerate for up to a day, then serve cold.

Faux Fool

In culinary language, a fool is a light dessert consisting of fruit folded into whipped cream. This "faux" version replaces the cream with yogurt and makes a lovely light breakfast or midmorning snack.

YIELD: 2 servings (easily multiplied)
PREPARATION TIME: 5 minutes

¾ cup peeled, mashed mango, peach, or papaya

¾ cup plain yogurt

1. Mash, stir, or purée the fruit and yogurt together until uniformly blended.
2. Serve cold.

Green Apples and Red Grapes with maple yogurt

I can't think of a more perfect autumn fruit dish! This arrangement is very pretty, with contrasting colors. It also juxtaposes wonderful textures—and tart and sweet flavors. I like this best made with whole-milk yogurt, but you can make it with lowfat yogurt if you prefer.

YIELD: 2 to 3 servings
PREPARATION TIME: 5 minutes

1 cup plain yogurt

2 to 3 tablespoons pure maple syrup

2 medium-sized green apples

1 cup or more seedless red grapes

½ cup slivered almonds, lightly toasted (optional)

1. Place the yogurt in a small bowl, and sweeten to taste with maple syrup, stirring until the yogurt is thin enough to drizzle.
2. Cut the unpeeled apples into thin slices, and arrange them on a serving platter or on individual plates.
3. Spoon the yogurt over the apples in a zig zag pattern that doesn't cover them completely, so their lovely green peel still shows.
4. Scatter the grapes, whole or halved, over the top. If you like, you can also toss on some lightly toasted slivered almonds. Serve right away.

THIS JUST IN: GRAPES ARE SERIOUS STUFF!

"To a long life" may be more than just a wine drinker's toast. It's actually a *statement*—a key to the puzzle known as "the French paradox." Americans have always wondered with envy how French people can eat all that rich food and still be healthy. This is partially explained by the French tradition of serving smaller portions. However, new findings show that this phenomenon is also related to the consumption of wine—more specifically, the grapes from which the wine is made.

Although grapes have been cultivated and appreciated for millennia, their outstanding nutritional profile has just recently been discovered. Grapes, particularly red and purple varieties, are now known to contain powerful phenolic compounds, which are antioxidants that may help prevent heart disease and cancer. This doesn't mean that eternal health automatically springs forth from a wine bottle, nice though that would be. But it does confirm that reaching for a big bunch of red or purple grapes at snack time is a very good idea.

Mixed Fruit Compote

If you need a use for overripe or underripe fruit, this tremendously flexible recipe covers all the bases. And there's no rule saying that you can't use perfectly ripe fruit as well.

My favorite way to make this is to cook fresh apples and pears and then to add dried apricots. Adding dried fruit about halfway through cooking infuses the juices with layers of flavor. It's fun to vary how you make it from one batch to the next—and to vary the fruit itself, too. That's the beauty of this dish: It never comes out exactly the same as the time before.

If you're using apples or pears (any kind other than Bosc), you don't need to add any cooking liquid. If you're using Bosc pears, or very ripe peaches or other stone fruit, keep the heat low, and add small amounts of water to prevent sticking. Also note that softer, riper fruit will cook faster.

Serve Mixed Fruit Compote in a bowl, accompanied by a thick slice of whole-grain toast spread with nut butter, and perhaps a wedge of aged cheddar. This also goes well with Potato Pancakes (page 193).

- If you'll be adding the optional dried fruit, slice larger fruit (apricots, figs, or plums). Leave smaller fruit (cranberries, cherries, raisins) whole.
- "Sweet spices" is vague on purpose, in the hope of stimulating your creative spirit. (Broad hint: Try touches of cinnamon, cloves, allspice, cardamom, and coriander.)

YIELD: **6 servings (about 5 cups)**
PREPARATION TIME: **10 minutes, plus 40 minutes to cook**

---

2 pounds fresh fruit, cut into 1½-inch chunks (peeling is optional)

1 to 2 tablespoons fresh lemon juice

A dash or two of salt (optional, for underripe fruit)

OPTIONAL ADDITIONS

Dried fruit (up to 1 cup)

Honey or pure maple syrup

Sweet spices

OPTIONAL TOPPINGS

Plain yogurt

Toasted walnuts

1. Place the fruit in a heavy saucepan over medium heat. Cover and cook slowly, checking in every 5 minutes or so to give it a stir. (If you're cooking stone fruit or Bosc pears, add small amounts of water as needed.)
2. After about 30 minutes, add the lemon juice, salt, and dried fruit. Cover and cook for another 10 minutes or so, then taste. At this point you can sweeten it or add a touch of spice—or just leave it plain. You can also cook it until it is soft enough to mash or let it keep some texture.
3. Serve at any temperature, plain or topped with yogurt and toasted walnuts.

Raspberry-Drenched Rhubarb

What to do with rhubarb? It is so sour that it requires frightening amounts of sugar just to become tart, *let alone sweet. Here's my favorite treatment for rendering rhubarb just right. The syrup from the raspberries is the main sweetener, and a touch of fruit juice completes the job.*

- For a variation, you can use frozen sweetened strawberries instead of raspberries.

YIELD: About 4 servings
PREPARATION TIME: 5 minutes, plus 15 minutes to cook

¾ pound rhubarb, cut into 1-inch pieces

10 ounces frozen sweetened raspberries

⅓ cup apple juice or grape juice

A pinch of salt

Plain yogurt (optional)

1. Place the rhubarb, raspberries, juice, and salt in a heavy saucepan. Cover and bring to a boil.
2. When the mixture reaches a boil, reduce the heat and remove the cover. Simmer uncovered for 15 minutes. Remove from the heat, and cool to room temperature. Transfer to a container with a tight-fitting lid, and refrigerate.
3. Serve cold, plain or with yogurt.

 ABOUT RHUBARB

Rhubarb is peculiar in that it is botanically a vegetable but is considered a fruit and is treated as such culinarily. (The opposite is much more common—that is, botanical fruits being regarded and used as vegetables. Examples include tomatoes, winter squash, zucchini, and cucumbers.)

Even though it resembles pink celery, rhubarb is actually a member of the buckwheat family and a close relative of sorrel. Rhubarb is very sour and quite fibrous. The stems are the edible part of the plant; the leaves are actually toxic. Look for moderately thin pink or red stalks. The greener, thicker stalks are stringier and more sour. Rhubarb must be cooked, as it is inedible raw. It must also be sweetened, as its sourness is so extreme that it is unpalatable unsweetened, even when cooked.

Rhubarb keeps for a week or even longer if stored in the refrigerator in a zip-style plastic bag. It also freezes perfectly, and since its season is so short (spring), I often freeze a few batches for use throughout the year. You can freeze rhubarb in whole stalks or cut into any size. Seal it in a heavy, zip-style plastic bag, and freeze it as is, without further fuss. You can cook or bake it directly from the freezer, without defrosting it first.

Dried Fruit Compote

You can make any combination of dried fruit into a delicious compote simply by soaking it in hot water. The deep flavor from the fruit infuses the water, making a rich sauce. In turn the water softens the fruit, which becomes plump and tender. Choose dried fruit that is "natural" and untreated (not the stiff, processed, sugar-coated pieces that are sold as snacks). I like to serve this compote with pancakes or on cooked cereal. Top it with nuts, or just eat it plain.

- It's okay to leave the pieces large and, if you're using dried plums (prunes), you can leave in the pits.
- This is a great way to perk up leathery old dried apricots or figs that may have been sitting in your cupboard for years.
- Store this compote in a tightly lidded jar in the refrigerator, and it will keep for several days. It can last more than a week if you add enough extra citrus juice to cover the fruit.

YIELD: 2 cups plump fruit
PREPARATION TIME: A few minutes, plus 1 to 2 hours to steep

2 cups mixed dried fruit

1 cinnamon stick

A few strips of citrus zest (orange or lemon; optional)

Boiling water to cover (1 to 2 cups)

3 tablespoons fresh orange juice (possibly more)

1 tablespoon fresh lemon or lime juice (possibly more)

Squeezable wedges of orange, lemon, or lime

1. Place the fruit, cinnamon stick, and optional strips of citrus zest in a medium-sized bowl. Pour in enough boiling water to generously cover the fruit, then cover the bowl with a plate or a piece of foil. Let it sit for a minimum of 1 to 2 hours or even longer—until the fruit absorbs the water and plumps up. (How long this takes will depend on how dry the fruit was to begin with.)

2. Add the orange and lemon juice and mix well. Fish out and discard the cinnamon stick and citrus strips, then transfer the mixture, including all the liquid, to a jar with a tight-fitting lid and store in the refrigerator. If you want the compote to keep for more than a week, add enough additional citrus juice (any kind) to cover the top surface of the compote. It will act as a preservative.

3. Serve cold or at room temperature, with squeezable wedges of orange, lemon, or lime.

 YEAR-ROUND FARMERS' MARKETS

We often think of farmers' markets as a hallmark of summer. But in many places around the country these markets are open year-round, selling specialty items in addition to whatever produce is in season. I have found the *best* dried fruit—including many varieties of plums and nectarines, hand-picked and dried with love by the growers—in the farmers' market in the middle of winter! Check out your local scene to see what you can find.

DRIED FRUIT JEWELS

It's wonderful to have these lovely little morsels on hand to grab for a commute or to snack on while at work. You can make a bunch of them ahead of time and keep them in the refrigerator, then just pull them out as desired. Spend some time making these on a weekend afternoon, while visiting with a friend. Children can help prepare them, too. Rather than give you a detailed recipe for these, I'm just going to provide a general description.

• Dried fruit (pitted plums/prunes, whole apricots, figs, pitted dates)
• Softened cream cheese
• Pecan halves (or walnuts or almonds), lightly toasted

Slit open the fruit and place a dab of cream cheese inside. Place a nut on the cheese. Gently squeeze the fruit around the filling, to close it slightly. That's it! Make a million of them and have fun! They will keep in the refrigerator for up to a week.

DRIED FRUIT IS CONCENTRATED GOODNESS

Fruit doesn't have to be juicy to be nutritious. In fact, dried fruit is very good for you! Whether the fruit is dried in the sun or through a hot-air treatment indoors, it retains iron, potassium and other minerals, antioxidants, and fiber. (It loses only vitamin C and water through the drying process.)

Other good things about dried fruit:

• It is lightweight—a good portable snack.
• There are many types to choose from, so you can buy a variety to keep it interesting.
• It stores well, with little or no spoilage.
• It's neat—no sticky, juicy mess.
• Dried fruit can deeply satisfy cravings for junk sweets and highly processed carbohydrates.

If you are worried about the intensity of the sugar in dried fruit, here is some good news. Studies have shown that, for many people, blood sugar levels stay low when they snack on dried fruit, partially because the high fiber content slows down the glycemic load. However, my dentist wants me to remind you that dried fruit does promote tooth decay, so be sure to brush your teeth and rinse with fresh water after a dried fruit snack.

THE FRUIT FORMERLY KNOWN AS PRUNES

The humble prune—a delicious and quiet hero rich in fiber, vitamin A, and potassium—has unfairly been the object of ridicule and disrespect since time immemorial. But a new dignity is on its way! The Food and Drug Administration recently granted an official name change, and this fruit shall henceforth and forever be known as the "dried plum." According to the California Dried Plum (formerly Prune) Board, this name change immediately increased sales. Prune juice is still called "prune juice," though. (I guess "dried plum juice" just didn't cut it.) And the dried plums that are shipped abroad (where there was never any stigma to begin with) will still be called prunes.

Roasted Fruit

Roasting is a dry cooking process that surrounds the food with intense heat, causing it to cook from the inside out, literally steaming from its inner juices. Because no additional liquid is added, the juices evaporate ("reduce" in culinary-speak), and the proportion of natural sugars and fiber increases. What you get is a chewy, intensely flavored, sweet result—like a fruit that has been partially dried. And all of this takes practically no work on your part; your oven does most of it!

You can eat roasted fruit as a snack or add some flavorful liquid and make it into a delicious compote. It's also a great substitute for homemade jam—just spoon it onto a thick piece of toast.

Roasting fruit is a process that, once understood, is intuitive and inexact. Keeping this in mind, I have presented this concept more as a description than as a recipe per se, hoping to teach a technique and take the pressure off the need to do it "exactly right." In fact, the end product is greatly determined by your own powers of observation and taste. Allow about ½ pound of fruit per serving. Make as many servings as you desire (or as can fit in the baking dish).

- For a lovely light, portable breakfast, pack a container of Roasted Fruit plus some sliced cheddar cheese and a handful or two of nuts. Take it to work with you and munch at your desk.

YIELD: flexible (see headnotes)
PREPARATION TIME: 40 to 50 minutes

FRUIT YOU CAN ROAST:

Apples

Pears

Underripe bananas

Papayas

Pineapples

Stone fruits (peaches, plums, apricots, cherries)

Grapes

YOU WILL ALSO NEED:

Nonstick spray

1. Preheat the oven to 425°F. Spray a ceramic baking dish, large enough to hold the fruit in a single layer, with nonstick spray.
2. Cut the fruit into fairly large chunks. Peel bananas, papaya, and pineapple. Leave other fruit unpeeled.
3. Place the chunks of fruit either peel side down or on their sides in the baking dish. Spacing is not important, since the fruit shrinks as it roasts. Just make sure the pieces are in a single layer. Put the dish into the preheated oven, and let the fruit roast for about 30 minutes. (Softer fruit, like peaches and plums, will cook more quickly than harder fruit like apples or pears.) For grapes, which tend to leak sugary juices and stick, check on them around 15 minutes into the process, and gently loosen them with a spatula and shake the pan to keep them from sticking. I like to add a second application of nonstick spray at this point.
4. When the fruit feels tender to the touch (or a fork slides easily into the flesh), remove the dish from the oven, and transfer the fruit from the dish to a plate or a platter with a rim.

Overnight Roasted Fruit

When partially roasted fruit is left to sit overnight in the turned-off, still-warm oven, it acquires a very different appearance than fruit roasted in the regular way. The latter is lush and colorful looking, especially with the deglazed sauce drizzled on top. The overnight version has its own look—miniaturized and exquisitely reduced to its utter essence. And on the practical side, it's ready to grab and go.

- This method calls for lining the baking dish with foil, which makes short work of cleanup. It also means you won't have the opportunity to deglaze the pan to make a sauce, but the whole reason for doing the roasting overnight is that your mornings are too busy to make a sauce anyway.

YIELD: flexible (see headnotes on opposite page)
PREPARATION TIME: 40 to 50 minutes, plus time to sit

FRUIT YOU CAN ROAST:

Apples

Pears

Underripe bananas

Papayas

Pineapples

Stone fruits (peaches, plums, apricots, cherries)

Grapes

YOU WILL ALSO NEED:

Nonstick spray

1. In the evening, preheat the oven to 375°F. Line a ceramic baking dish with foil, and spray it generously with nonstick spray.
2. Cut the fruit into large chunks. Peel bananas, papayas, and pineapple. Leave other fruit unpeeled. Arrange the pieces peel side down or on their sides in the prepared dish, and place the dish in the oven.
3. After 30 minutes, open the oven, pull out the dish, and use a small metal spatula to loosen any pieces that might have stuck. After the pieces are loosened, just leave them in place. Return the baking dish to the oven, turn the oven off, and leave the baking dish in there overnight.
4. In the morning you will have a wonderful result: beautiful, small pieces of fruit that are tender, chewy, and sweet—about halfway dried, but still moist.

 A NICE LITTLE SAUCE

Roasted fruit usually leaves behind a glaze of flavorful juices in the baking dish. You can retrieve this delicious coating and turn it into a nice little sauce for the fruit.

After removing the fruit, simply pour about ¼ cup fruit juice into the still-hot pan. (Apple juice works best for this, although orange or pineapple juice is also good.) Scrape and swish it around with a wooden spoon to catch all the fruit tidbits that have adhered during the roasting process. Strain the whole thing into a small bowl, and give it a taste. You can leave it as is or season it with a few drops of vinegar and a little sugar or pure maple syrup. Pour this sauce directly over the roasted fruit.

Fruit Crisp or Cobbler

Fruit baked in, on, or under a crunchy, easy-to-prepare topping can be a wonderful breakfast dish. Just add a few spoonfuls of yogurt or crème fraîche, and you have a respectable, filling, and exquisite morning meal.

Crisps and cobblers are very similar. Each consists of a bed of fruit baked under a sweet pastry topping. Fruit crisp is crowned with sweet, buttery crumbs resembling streusel or granola. Fruit cobbler has a less-sweet, biscuitlike "roof," similar in texture to a shortcake. If you like, assemble everything the night before and bake it in the morning.

You can use any combination of fruit. Similar types go well together, like apples with pears or quinces, or a combination of stone fruit (peaches with plums, apricots, or cherries). Accessorize with berries for touches of bright color and tart, contrasting flavor.

- If using frozen berries, don't defrost them first.
- Try rhubarb! Cut it into 1-inch pieces, and double the sugar you add to the fruit.
- If you have any left over and you need to get the topping crisp again, preheat an oven or toaster oven to 300°F, place the crisp or cobbler on a baking tray with foil, and reheat, uncovered, for about 15 minutes. (Don't use a microwave—it will compromise the texture of the topping.)

YIELD: **4 to 6 servings**
PREPARATION TIME: **20 minutes, plus 20 to 25 minutes to bake**

---

5 to 6 cups sliced fruit, peeled if necessary (2½ to 3 pounds)

1 to 2 cups berries, fresh or frozen (optional)

1 to 2 tablespoons fresh lemon juice

1 tablespoon unbleached all-purpose flour

1 to 2 tablespoons sugar

Crisp Topping or Cobbler Topping (recipes follow)

Yogurt or Homemade Crème Fraîche (page 263; optional)

1. Preheat the oven to 400°F if you're making a crisp, and to 425°F if you're making a cobbler.

2. Place the fruit in a medium-sized bowl, and toss with the lemon juice. Sprinkle in the flour and sugar and toss until fairly evenly coated, then transfer the mixture to an ungreased 9- or 10-inch pie pan. Don't clean the bowl.

3. Use the same bowl to make the topping. (Choose between the two topping recipes that follow.) Carefully crumble the topping mixture over the fruit, and pat it into place. Place the pan on a baking tray (to catch any juices that bubble over), and bake in the center of the oven for 20 to 25 minutes, or until brown on top. Cool for 15 minutes before serving. (It will still be plenty hot!)

4. Serve hot, warm, or at room temperature, with a little yogurt or Homemade Crème Fraîche on the side.

Crisp and Cobbler Toppings

CRISP TOPPING

¾ cup rolled oats

¼ cup oat bran

1 tablespoon unbleached
all-purpose flour

⅛ teaspoon salt

2 tablespoons (packed) brown sugar

¼ teaspoon cinnamon

2 to 3 tablespoons minced walnuts
(optional)

3 tablespoons unsalted butter,
melted

COBBLER TOPPING

1 cup unbleached all-purpose flour

2 tablespoons unprocessed wheat
bran

¼ teaspoon salt

1 teaspoon baking powder

⅛ teaspoon baking soda

2 tablespoons granulated sugar

1 to 2 tablespoons (packed) brown
sugar

3 tablespoons unsalted butter,
melted

¼ cup cold buttermilk

1. To make either topping, combine the dry ingredients in the same bowl you used to coat the apples. Use your fingers, if necessary, to mix in the brown sugar.
2. Add the melted butter (and the buttermilk, if you're making the cobbler), and mix with a fork or your hands until uniformly moistened.

 THE TWO THINGS I APPRECIATE MOST ABOUT APPLES

- Apples blend incredibly well with other fruit without dominating the flavor of the finished dish. Thus, you can use apples to fill out recipes featuring other fruit. For example, if you are making a pie or a crisp featuring something more expensive or rare, like raspberries or quince, and you can't get enough of that precious fruit to fill the amount required, add apples to increase the volume. You will still get the benefit of the special fruit's flavor, but the apples will provide the needed bulk.

- Different types of apples blend beautifully with one another. When you combine more than one variety of apple in applesauce or a baked dish, you get wonderful, subtle layers of flavor. This is especially effective when you restrain yourself from using too much cinnamon (a uniquely American fixation, according to an English friend of mine) and instead add a dash of fresh lemon juice.

GRAINS:
CEREALS,
COOKED &
COLD

3

GRAINS: CEREALS, COOKED & COLD

Americans have a unique attachment to commercially prepared breakfast cereal. (For some reason, this very specific passion never developed in any other modern culture that I know of.) And the devotion is fierce! I don't believe it will subside anytime soon. So far be it from me to dissuade you from eating your favorite packaged cereal for breakfast. On the other hand, it's also good to be aware of various options and of ways you can perhaps enhance, if not entirely replace, that bowlful of crunchy familiarity that has virtually defined your mornings since you were in second grade.

This chapter contains a selection of ideas for cooking whole grains, which are the precursor to all of our favorite starchy foods (cereal being only one of many). Although plain, cooked whole grains seem like an obvious choice for a wholesome, convenient breakfast, they are largely overlooked—perhaps because they seem esoteric and hard to find. Now, with the proliferation of large natural food supermarkets around the country, whole grains are slowly becoming more familiar and accessible. Try stocking your cupboard (or better yet, your freezer) with jars of grains, grain flakes, and nuts (possibly already toasted). It's also nice to keep bags of frozen, unsweetened berries on hand, as well as a variety of dried fruit and whatever fresh fruit is in season. That way, you can have the option of preparing cooked whole-grain cereal, homemade granola, or muesli as part of your weekday routine—if not instead of, then in addition to, the boxed cereal you already love. My guess is you will love these other ways of eating grains as well.

A BRIEF HISTORY OF BREAKFAST CEREAL

In the late 19th century, a young physician named John Harvey Kellogg became an early crusader for a simple vegetarian diet. As head of the Western Health Reform Institute in Battle Creek, Michigan, he referred to the place as a "university of health," eventually changing its name to the Battle Creek Sanitarium. His mission was to improve health through lifestyle education (although the word "lifestyle" was about a century short of entering the American vernacular) and enhancing people's awareness of the importance of a sound diet and good nutrition. Kellogg's project became a big success, and it soon grew to encompass a commercial product that became an even bigger hit: a cold breakfast cereal, invented by John Henry himself, called Granola (the original!), and later refined (literally) into Corn Flakes. This innovation triggered a revolution in American breakfast behavior, from which we as a nation have never looked back. That said, let's look back now.

Cereal begins with whole grains.

The road that whole grains must travel from the field to the cereal box to your breakfast bowl is long and somewhat violent, for lack of a better word. An objective look into the production of commercial cold cereal might give you pause the next time you're about to reach for a box of Kix or Rice Krispies. As they are transformed into "cereal," grains are subjected to a series of processes, including roasting, toasting, steaming, flaking, rolling, spraying, and literally being exploded!

Some details: To produce flakes, cereal manufacturers first grind grains into grits or flour and then cook them under pressure, during which time artificial flavoring, vitamins, and minerals are added. The mixture is then dried and flattened under tons of pressure, and the resulting flakes are toasted to bring out color, flavor, and crispness. In some cases, the flakes are also sprayed with hot syrup, which then dries into "sugar coating." Puffed cereals are the result of exposing dried grain pellets to extreme pressure and high temperatures, forcing them to expand until they explode (or, in commercial-speak, "pop"). Other kinds of cereal are shaped by machines that extrude a cooked dough into long ropes that are then cut by high-speed mechanical blades. Little do we realize any of this when we innocently purchase those heat-sealed, brightly decorative cartons lined with moisture-proof paper and filled with America's favorite ready-to-eat food!

Is this to say we should stay away from Corn Flakes and Cheerios? Not at all! I myself really enjoy a bowl of commercially produced breakfast cereal from time to time. It can be fun to eat and a great convenience. (In fact, many top chefs have admitted in private interviews that they eat a bowl of cereal for breakfast.) But I also have some ideas about how to augment that bowl of cereal to give you a more nutritious quick meal. With just a touch or two of enrichment, your authentic American eating experience can give you an energy boost of respectable quality and duration. Consider adding some fresh fruit, unprocessed wheat or oat bran, dried fruit, nuts, leftover whole cooked grains, or wheat germ. And how about pouring on some milk that has been fortified with protein powder (see page 17) or serving a "side" of whole-grain toast spread with peanut butter? I know that John Harvey Kellogg would heartily approve.

The Inside Scoop on Whole Grains

Whole grains are perfect examples of true complex carbohydrates, because they contain the complete, intact package: bran, endosperm, and germ. The outer bran layer holds the fiber (bulk), as well as minerals and protein. The germ, deep inside, is the embryo, which supplies protein, minerals, and vitamins. The endosperm is the whole grain's "storage compartment." Mostly starch, its function is to sustain the seedling until it begins to sprout leaves, which, when mature, will take over the food-producing function so the plant can feed itself.

The carbohydrates we usually end up eating are a refined version of the endosperm, which has the least nutrients—especially after it's been processed—of any part of the original grain. In most commercial breakfast cereals, lost nutrients are added back in during processing—usually in the form of synthetically manufactured vitamins—but the grain is never the same again once it's been broken into and "splintered."

According to many studies, the more intact the grain and the larger the particles, the slower it is metabolized, so the better it is for keeping our blood sugar level steady. For many of us, the idea of eating cooked whole grains—unrefined and straight, not chopped up or made into something else—seems radical and intriguing, even though they're probably the most ancient, basic food. Magazines tell us to eat more of these healthy morsels, citing the many medical studies that now show unequivocally that whole grains are—or should be—the cornerstone of a superior diet. But with our modern lifestyle largely organized, as it is, around processed convenience foods, many of us find changing our habits somewhat challenging, our best intentions notwithstanding.

For one thing, strange though this may sound, we're not used to chewing our food. We've become a "gulp and run" culture, especially during the weekday morning rush that has us grabbing breakfast while heading for the door. And most whole grains are chewy (delightfully so!) and require some participation on the part of the eater. So to include whole grains in our breakfast becomes a time commitment just for the act of eating alone, not to mention the cooking.

If an entire bowlful of whole grains seems a bit intense for you, start with a more gradual plan. Add small amounts of cooked grains to your regular cold or hot cereal, or include some in your muesli (page 52). You can also add cooked grains to many different baked goods (breads, muffins, and coffee cakes) and to pancakes and waffles. I like to add a few spoonfuls of the chewiest grains (barley, rye berries, or spelt, for example) to a steaming bowl of miso soup (page 14). Once you get used to the idea, whole grains will become a more integral part of your breakfast—and other meals as well.

The Basics of Cooking Whole Grains

Cooked whole grains—served individually or in combination with one another—can make wonderful, filling, highly textured hot cereal for breakfast. I recommend that you go to your favorite natural food store and visit the bulk bins, where you'll find many different grains. Buy small amounts of several kinds, and experiment with cooking them some evening when you will be home anyway doing other things.

Preparation is about as basic as it gets: If you can boil water, you can cook whole grains. In fact, boiling the water is all you need to do. After that, the grains basically cook themselves. (Your biggest challenge is to remember they are on the stove.)

Some grains need to cook longer than others, and different types absorb varying amounts of water. But with the exception of couscous and bulgur, which aren't really whole grains and need only to be soaked in hot water, the cooking method is essentially the same across the board.

This is what you do:

- Rinse the grains in a fine-mesh strainer and shake out the water.

- Place the grains in a saucepan of appropriate size; add the prescribed amount of water and a pinch of salt. Bring to a boil, lower the heat to the slowest possible simmer, cover tightly, and cook until all the water is absorbed. Don't peek or stir until the recommended simmering time has passed.

- If any water remains after the grains have become tender, just drain it off. Conversely, if the grains are crunchier than you'd like them, or they're too dry, add a little water (up to ¼ cup) and let them cook up to 5 minutes longer.

- For a fluffy result, lightly comb through the cooked grains with a fork to let steam escape. If you like your grains to be more like a porridge, keep the pot covered after removing it from the heat, and let it sit undisturbed for about 10 minutes before serving.

- All kinds of grains can be cooked in advance and reheated in a microwave or gently on the stovetop with a little extra liquid added. So you can refrigerate cooked grains for up to several days and just reheat them as needed in the morning.

- Various types of cooked grains combine beautifully with one another. For optimal results, cook them separately per their individual requirements, then combine them only after they are done. (The only exception to this is millet and quinoa, which cook together really well. See the chart on the following page.) When mixing different grains, aim for a balance of flavor and texture—for example, combining intense, bitter, chewy types with fluffier, sweeter ones.

- Accoutrements are always welcome! Consider adding any of the following to cooked grains: fresh and/or dried fruit, toasted nuts, seeds, coconut, honey or pure maple syrup, milk or cream, and even a touch of butter.

For details about cooking specific grains, see the chart on the following pages.

 HOW CEREAL GOT ITS NAME

The Roman god Ceres presided over agriculture and grain crops. The word "cereal" comes from Ceres, which, in turn, comes from a linguistic root meaning "to grow," making it an etymological relative of the words "increase," "crescendo," "create," and "accrue." A related linguistic note: The Spanish word for beer is *cerveza* (grain-based beverage), and the Welsh and Irish versions are *cwrw* (koo-roo) and *cuirm* (rhymes with "firm").

Grain Cooking Chart

Here are cooking guidelines for the grains you are most likely to find in your natural food store. Please also refer to "The Basics of Cooking Whole Grains" (preceding page). Note: These proportions will produce fluffy grains that are slightly chewy. (The main exceptions are cracked wheat and amaranth, which become porridgelike when cooked.) For a softer result, add ¼ cup to ½ cup more water, and increase the cooking or soaking time by 5 to 10 minutes.

GRAIN	DESCRIPTION	GRAIN TO WATER RATIO	COOKING TIME	YIELD
OAT GROATS	Sweet, chewy whole grain from which rolled oats are made.	1 cup grains to 2½ cups water	Simmer 40 to 45 minutes	3 cups
BROWN RICE (including basmati)	Slightly sweet and nutty tasting.	1 cup grains to 1½ cups water	Simmer 35 to 45 minutes	3½ cups
WILD RICE	Pleasantly bitter.	1 cup grains to 2½ cups water	Simmer 1¼ hours or until tender	4 cups
PEARL BARLEY	Very chewy and slightly sweet.	1 cup grains to 3 cups water	Simmer 1½ hours or until tender	4 cups
QUINOA	A tiny high-protein, high-calcium grain. Taste is quite bitter and distinctive. Combines well with other grains after cooking.	1 cup grains to 1½ cups water	Simmer 25 to 30 minutes	3 cups
MILLET	Slightly bitter, very high in protein.	1 cup grains to 1½ cups water	Simmer 25 to 30 minutes	3 cups
FLUFFY QUINOA AND MILLET	A wonderful high-protein combination! A rare partnership, in that you can successfully cook these two grains together.	1 cup each quinoa and millet to 3 cups water	Simmer 30 to 35 minutes, then transfer to a pan, spread out, and separate with a fork to let steam escape	6 cups
BUCKWHEAT GROATS (Also known as kasha)	Pungent and nutty.	1 cup grains to 1½ cups water	Simmer 10 minutes	3½ cups
CRACKED WHEAT	Sweet and earthy. (Not really a whole grain, as it is literally cracked. Included here because it makes a great breakfast cereal.)	1 cup grains to 2 cups water	Simmer 10 minutes	3½ cups
AMARANTH	Glutinous and sweet, very nutritious.	1 cup grains to 1¾ cups water	Simmer 25 minutes	2 cups

The following grains stay chewy forever and cook most efficiently if presoaked in cold water for anywhere from 4 to 8 hours (overnight is fine). Drain and rinse, then add fresh water for cooking.

WHEAT BERRIES	Slightly sweet and earthy.	1 cup grains to 2 cups water	Simmer 2 to 2½ hours—longer for hard (red) wheat, shorter for soft (white) wheat	3 cups
SPELT	Slightly sweet and earthy. An ancient form of wheat.	1 cup grains to 1½ cups water	Simmer 50 to 60 minutes	2 cups
KAMUT	Slightly sweet and earthy. Another ancient form of wheat.	1 cup grains to 2½ cups water	Simmer 1¾ hours	2½ cups
RYE BERRIES	Very bitter and intense, and terminally chewy. Best used in baking or combined with other grains.	1 cup grains to 2½ cups water	Simmer 1½ hours	2½ cups

Couscous and bulgur are not really whole grains, but they are regarded as such in many cuisines. They are delicious for breakfast. Both are precooked and need only to soak in boiling water.

QUICK-COOKING COUSCOUS	Slightly sweet and very light. A processed product rather than a whole grain, but utterly delicious nonetheless.	1 cup grains soaked in 1½ cups boiling water for 15 to 20 minutes	No cooking involved	3 cups
BULGUR	Slightly sweet and very nutty.	1 cup grains soaked in 1½ cups boiling water for 30 to 40 minutes	No cooking involved	3½ cups

 EGG-ENRICHED GRAINS

Beaten eggs stirred directly into hot grains will cook practically on contact, and they add instant flavor and richness—and a nice hit of extra protein. This works especially well with freshly cooked brown rice or buckwheat groats (kasha). Add a little extra salt, if desired, and some freshly ground black pepper. A touch of minced scallion will make it even better!

OATMEAL

Oatmeal is the world's humblest superfood.

Oats, the slenderest of all grains, are naturally sweet and very soothing. For people who want to add more whole grains to their diet, oatmeal is a perfect place to begin. Oats are easy to find, inexpensive to buy, simple to cook, and so pleasant to eat! They also happen to be a good source of B vitamins, calcium, protein, and fiber and are known to help regulate blood sugar levels and calm nerves.

The two most commonly available forms of oatmeal are steel-cut (also known as "Irish" or "Scottish") oats, which make a nicely textured cereal, and rolled oats, which cook up to a creamier consistency. Here are instructions for both types of oats. (To cook whole oat groats, see page 46.)

YIELD: Each of these recipes makes 2 servings (easily doubled)
PREPARATION TIME: See individual recipes.

"Regular" Oatmeal   PREPARATION TIME: 6 to 8 minutes

1½ cups water or milk

¼ teaspoon salt

¾ cup rolled oats

2 tablespoons oat bran (optional)

OPTIONAL TOPPINGS

Butter

Brown sugar or pure maple syrup

Fruit syrup (page 246)

Any type of milk or cream

Yogurt or buttermilk

Raisins or other dried fruit

Chopped fresh fruit

Chopped, toasted nuts

Toasted coconut

Ground flax seed

Toasted sunflower or pumpkin seeds

Berry sauce (page 248)

1. Combine everything in a saucepan, and bring to a boil over medium heat.
2. Stir, cover, and lower the heat to a simmer. Cook until thick and tender (about 5 minutes). Serve hot with any of the optional toppings.

 KNOW YOUR OATS

When oats are prepared for human consumption, they are cleaned, toasted, hulled, and, in the case of rolled oats, steamed and flattened with heavy rollers. (Quick-cooking rolled oats are the same, except they're cut into smaller pieces and rolled thinner.) Regular and quick-cooking rolled oats can be used interchangeably for oatmeal cookies and other baked goods, the only difference being that the quick-cooking kind will blend into the batter more readily, and the final product will have a somewhat smoother texture.

Instant oats (the type to which you simply add hot water for a quick breakfast) are a different story. They're cooked and dried before being rolled, which makes them turn gooey when hot water is added. Also, instant oats are often mixed with artificial flavors and a heavy dose of sweeteners. I recommend you stick with rolled oats, which, when you think about it, cook so quickly that they are instant by their very nature.

Steel-Cut Oatmeal

PREPARATION TIME: 15 minutes

2 cups water

¼ teaspoon salt

½ cup steel-cut oats

1. Place the water in a medium-sized saucepan and heat it to a rolling boil. Gradually sprinkle in the oats without slowing the boil.
2. Cook, uncovered, over medium heat (an active boil, not a simmer) for 10 to 12 minutes, or until the oats are tender. Serve hot with any of the toppings listed on the opposite page.

CELTIC OATS

Oats thrive in cold climates and have long been a significant food for both the Irish and the Scottish. In Scotland, proper oat eating is an art. They serve oatmeal hot, as we do, but instead of pouring milk over the top, they place the milk (or cream or buttermilk) in a second bowl next to it, dipping each individual spoonful of hot cereal into the cold milk. It's a time-honored ritual.

Chai Oatmeal

PREPARATION TIME: 15 minutes

Rolled oats simmered in sweet, spice-infused milk make an exquisite breakfast cereal. Green pistachio nuts, sprinkled over the top, look beautiful against the light golden glow provided by the turmeric and saffron.

1½ cups milk

¼ teaspoon salt

¼ teaspoon cinnamon

¼ teaspoon ground coriander

¼ teaspoon ground cardamom

¼ teaspoon ground turmeric

A pinch of saffron (optional)

A drop of vanilla extract (optional)

2 teaspoons light honey

¾ cup rolled oats

2 tablespoons oat bran

OPTIONAL TOPPINGS

Minced pistachio nuts

Yogurt or buttermilk

1. Pour the milk into a medium-sized saucepan. Add the salt and spices, and whisk to blend them in. Place the pan over medium heat.
2. Just before it comes to a boil, lower the heat, and let the milk simmer for about 5 minutes. Stir in the vanilla and honey, and whisk until the honey dissolves.
3. Sprinkle in the oats and oat bran, and stir once or twice. Cover the pan, and leave it over low heat for about 8 minutes, stirring occasionally.
4. When the oatmeal has thickened to your liking, serve it hot, with any of the optional toppings.

Very Crunchy Granola

Granola should be crunchy—very. And here's a recipe that really works! In fact, it's so good, my husband actually asks me to make this less often, because he can't stop eating it.

• If you can't find barley flakes, you can substitute wheat flakes or just use 4 cups rolled oats.

YIELD: 6 to 8 cups
PREPARATION TIME: 10 minutes, plus 35 to 45 minutes to bake

Nonstick spray

3 cups rolled oats

1 cup barley flakes

1 cup oat bran

1 cup sunflower seeds

1 cup chopped almonds

¾ cup canola oil

½ cup light honey or pure maple syrup

1 tablespoon vanilla extract

1 cup soy protein powder

½ teaspoon salt

⅓ cup (packed) brown sugar

1 cup pumpkin seeds (optional, but highly recommended!)

1. Preheat the oven to 325°F. Spray a 13- by 18-inch baking tray with non-stick spray.
2. Combine the oats and barley flakes, bran, sunflower seeds, and almonds in a large bowl.
3. Combine the oil, honey, and vanilla, and pour this mixture into the bowl. Mix thoroughly. (Use your hands, if necessary.)
4. Stir in the protein powder and salt, and mix thoroughly (again, use your hands).
5. Bake for 35 to 45 minutes, or until golden, stirring once or twice during the baking.
6. Crumble in the sugar as soon as the granola comes out of the oven, and let it melt in. Cool it on the tray, and stir in the pumpkin seeds as it cools. Note: The granola will get crunchy as it cools.
7. Store the finished granola in a tightly closed jar in the freezer for maximum freshness. (A batch fits nicely into two or three 1 quart-capacity jars.)

VARIATION   COOL BERRY GRANOLA

After the granola has cooled, add:

• 2 cups sliced fresh strawberries or whole fresh raspberries or blueberries

Stir the berries in gently until the cereal surrounds them like a protective coating. Carefully pack the mixture into jars, close them tightly, and freeze. Remove only as much from the jar as you need, and then return the jar to the freezer. The berries will store beautifully this way and will defrost very quickly in your cereal bowl, after you add milk.

Dry-Roast Granola

Dry-roasting grains, nuts, and seeds on the stovetop gives them a deep, toasty essence with just a hint of smoke. The use of carob powder is unusual; it adds another subtle layer of flavor. This granola is made with no added oil and without any honey or syrup. It's held together by a light coating of brown sugar, which melts into the mixture ever so slightly.

The relatively low yield is due to the need to spread the granola out in the skillet. If the skillet is too crowded, the mixture won't toast properly. If you like, use two skillets, and cook a double batch—or just make it more often!

• If you can't find barley flakes, substitute wheat flakes, or just use 2 cups rolled oats.

YIELD: About 3½ cups
PREPARATION TIME: 25 to 30 minutes

1 cup rolled oats

1 cup barley flakes

½ cup finely chopped nuts (any kind)

½ cup oat bran or unprocessed wheat bran

⅓ cup sunflower seeds

⅓ cup sesame seeds

⅓ cup pumpkin seeds

⅓ cup shredded unsweetened coconut (optional)

5 to 6 tablespoons (packed) light brown sugar

¼ teaspoon salt (rounded measure)

1 tablespoon carob powder

OPTIONAL ADDITIONS

Dried fruit—up to 1 cup

Wheat germ—up to ½ cup

1. Place a large (ideally 10-inch), heavy skillet over medium heat. Add the oats, barley flakes, and nuts, and cook, stirring, for 10 to 15 minutes, or until they smell and look toasty.

2. Add the oat bran, sunflower seeds, sesame seeds, and pumpkin seeds, as well as the coconut, if desired. Keep cooking, stirring frequently, for another 10 minutes or so.

3. Sprinkle in the brown sugar and salt. Continue to cook and stir for about 3 more minutes, or until the sugar melts slightly, coating the other ingredients. Remove from the heat, sprinkle in the carob powder, and toss to distribute it throughout the mixture.

4. Cool to room temperature, and add dried fruit and wheat germ, if desired. (Cut large pieces of fruit into smaller pieces.) Transfer to a clean glass jar with a tight-fitting lid or a zip-style plastic bag. To keep it fresh longer, store it in the freezer.

Muesli

Dr. Max Bircher-Benner, a Swiss physician who died in 1939, advocated a raw food diet. It was a radical idea for his time and remains so even today, although the raw foods philosophy is now gaining wider acceptance. Dr. B.B.'s recipe for muesli went as follows: Soak rolled oats in water for 12 hours, then add a little sweetened condensed milk or a combination of yogurt and honey. Add the juice of half a lemon, some grated unpeeled apple, and ground hazelnuts, walnuts, or almonds. As you can see from this recipe, the basic, original formula remains pretty much unchanged. Some things withstand the test of time.

- If you do the first step in the evening and let it stand overnight, final preparation will be easy the next morning.
- Although muesli is traditionally made with rolled oats, you can also use other kinds of flaked grains (barley, wheat, or rye)—separate or combined.
- The milk in this recipe can be cow's milk, soy milk, rice milk, half-and-half, or cream.
- The nuts and seeds can be raw or lightly toasted.

YIELD: 1 serving (easily multiplied)
PREPARATION TIME: About 15 minutes (2 minutes of work)

---

2 tablespoons rolled oats (or barley, wheat, or rye flakes)

3 tablespoons milk, yogurt, butter-milk, or a berry sauce (page 248)

Half a medium apple, grated

3 tablespoons seeds or ground nuts

2 tablespoons raisins or currants (optional)

OPTIONAL ADDITIONS

Oat bran or unprocessed wheat bran

Fresh lemon juice

Honey or pure maple syrup

Berries (fresh or frozen, defrosted if frozen)

Extra yogurt

1. Combine the rolled oats or grain flakes in a serving bowl with the milk. Let it stand for at least 15 minutes or overnight, covered and refrigerated.

2. Add the remaining ingredients just before serving.

VARIATIONS

REVERSE MUESLI

Put a good amount of yogurt or buttermilk in the bowl first. Add the other ingredients as toppings. (You don't need measurements for this—just do it by feel. And you don't need to do anything the night before.)

COOKED MUESLI

Cooked muesli is an oxymoron, but what the heck. Simply make the basic recipe, adding:

- Up to ½ cup cooked, cooled whole grains, such as oat groats, barley, and wheat berries, or a combination

This variation will give you more nutrition as well as something to really chew on.

Orange-Pecan Skillet Millet

The naturally nutty flavor of millet is greatly enhanced when the grain is sautéed in butter before the cooking liquid is added. In this unusual recipe, the cooking liquid is pure orange juice, spiked with a hint of vanilla. As the millet absorbs the orange juice, it turns a glorious warm, golden yellow color. Toasted pecans are then added, imparting just the right amount of crunch and an even deeper flavor. This is just a totally delightful, surprisingly different bowl of cereal!

- Use a 10-inch skillet with a tight-fitting lid.
- This dish keeps for up to 3 days in a tightly covered container in the refrigerator. Add a little water before reheating it in the microwave or on the stovetop.

YIELD: 3 to 4 servings
PREPARATION TIME: 40 minutes

1 cup millet

1 tablespoon unsalted butter

¼ teaspoon salt

1 teaspoon vanilla extract

2 cups orange juice

½ cup minced pecans,
    lightly toasted

OPTIONAL TOPPINGS

Honey

Milk

1. Place the millet in a fine-mesh strainer and rinse well under running water. Set aside to drain.
2. Place a 10-inch skillet over medium heat and wait about 1 minute. Add the butter and, as it melts, swirl to coat the pan.
3. Sprinkle in the drained millet and the salt, and turn the heat to medium-high. Sauté the millet for 5 minutes, or until it begins to brown slightly and gives off a toasty aroma.
4. Add the vanilla to the orange juice, then slowly pour this mixture into the hot pan, about ½ cup at a time, waiting after each addition for the liquid to begin bubbling.
5. Cover the pan, and reduce the heat to a simmer. Cook undisturbed for 15 minutes, then remove the lid and stir the millet from the bottom of the pan so the grains get redistributed. Replace the lid, and cook for another 15 minutes, or until all the water is absorbed and the millet is tender. Remove the pan from the heat, and fluff the millet with a fork. If the millet is too crunchy for your taste, add about 3 tablespoons water, cover the pan, and let it cook for another 5 to 10 minutes over very low heat.
6. Stir in the pecans, and serve hot or warm—plain or with a little honey and/or milk drizzled on top.

 MARVELOUS MILLET

Humble, inexpensive millet is quite a winner. Brimming with vitamins and minerals (especially B vitamins and phosphorus), it contains the most protein of any of the true cereal grains. It's also nonalkaline, high in fiber, and gluten-free. And perhaps most important of all,, it cooks easily and tastes delicious.

Wild Rice with cherries and hazelnuts

Wild rice has been a staple for the Ojibwa, Chippewa, and Algonquin people for thousands of years. Native Americans in the Great Lakes region still use wild rice in just about everything: cakes, breads, omelets, muffins, casseroles, pancakes, and so on. The dark, robust grain (technically an aquatic grass) is complex, nutty, and pleasantly bitter—and richer in protein, minerals, and B vitamins than wheat, barley, oats, or rye.

When shopping for wild rice, you might notice a light brown "wild rice mix" as well as the more familiar dark variety. This paddy-grown grain is not the same thing as authentic Native American wild rice. It is lighter in color and milder in flavor—and cooks in less time and with less water. If you make this recipe with "wild rice mix," cook it as you would any long-grain brown rice.

- Dried cranberries can be substituted for the cherries.
- Hazelnuts are also known as filberts.

YIELD: 3 or 4 servings
PREPARATION TIME: 1¼ hours (2 minutes of work)

---

1 cup wild rice

2½ cups water

¼ teaspoon salt

Brown sugar or pure maple syrup

½ cup dried cherries

½ cup chopped hazelnuts, lightly toasted

Milk, soy milk, or cream

1. Place the wild rice, water, and salt in a medium-sized saucepan and bring to a boil over medium heat. When it reaches a boil, cover the pot, and lower the heat to a bare simmer. Cook for 1¼ hours, or until all the water is absorbed and the rice is tender and has "butterflied," or burst open. (If the grain has become tender but there is still water left, drain it off.)

2. Remove from the heat, and stir in the sugar or maple syrup and the cherries.

3. Serve hot, topped with chopped hazelnuts and the milk of your choice.

 PRECIOUS WILD RICE

Why is wild rice so expensive? Amazingly, about 20 percent of the world's crop is still hand-picked by Native Americans in canoes, who retain exclusive harvesting rights on the reservations along the shores of the Great Lakes. The crop is an important part of the tribes' economy.

After it is cut, the precious grain is sun-dried, then hulled through an agitation process in a steel drum. This labor of love has been virtually unchanged throughout the centuries, and to this day, true heirloom wild rice grows solely in the northern Great Lakes region. When buying wild rice, look for a "hand-harvested" or "lake-harvested" insignia on the package, which verifies the original organic, foraged variety. By purchasing authentic wild rice, you will be supporting both the economic system of the Native American harvesters (enabling them to produce more) and the crop itself, which is ecologically fragile.

Toasted Barley Flakes with figs

Barley flakes are very similar to rolled oats, but instead of turning soft when they're cooked, they remain separate and chewy, like a pilaf. This is true regardless of how much liquid you add or how long they're cooked. And no amount of reheating will cause them to become mushy, either—barley flakes stay fluffy forever!

- Use a skillet with a tight-fitting lid.
- Some dried fruit is drier than others. For this recipe, really dry figs work best, because they keep their shape most effectively.

YIELD: 3 servings
PREPARATION TIME: About 30 minutes (less than 5 minutes of work, plus intermittent stirring)

1 cup barley flakes

2 cups water

8 to 10 dried figs

¼ teaspoon salt

Milk, soy milk, or cream

Honey (optional)

1. Toast the barley flakes over medium heat in a medium-sized skillet (no oil necessary) for 10 to 15 minutes, stirring intermittently. In the meantime, bring the water to a boil, trim the figs of their stems, and slice them.

2. When the flakes become lightly golden and emit a toasty aroma, add the salt and sliced figs. Pour the boiling water into the skillet, and reduce the heat to low. Cover and cook for 12 to 15 minutes, or until the water is completely absorbed and the flakes are as tender you like them.

3. Serve hot, drizzled with the milk of your choice. Sweeten to taste with honey, if desired. (You might find it sweet enough already from the figs.)

 FIGS ARE POWER FOOD!

In addition to being sensuous and delicious, figs have a surprisingly excellent nutritional profile. With more dietary fiber than dried plums (prunes), figs also contain a significant amount of protein, calcium (more, ounce for ounce, than cow's milk), magnesium, phosphorus, and potassium—a combination unparalleled in the fruit world. Since good fresh figs can be hard to find and are incredibly delicate and perishable—and 85 percent of the crop is dried for the marketplace anyway—stock up on dried figs and eat them often.

Masfouf

Fluffy couscous with crunchy pine nuts and pistachios—and just a hint of sweetness from the dates—makes a lovely Moroccan-style breakfast. This dish becomes even more authentic when served with savory accents, such as olives and olive oil, herbs, and yogurt. (The yogurt rounds this out and really makes it a meal.)

- This dish keeps well in the refrigerator for several days and tastes best at room temperature.
- If you can't find (or afford) the pine nuts, you can make this with just pistachios—or substitute finely chopped walnuts—and it will still come out great.

YIELD: 2 to 3 servings (hard to stop eating!)
PREPARATION TIME: 25 minutes (5 minutes of work)

1 cup quick-cooking couscous

1½ cups boiling water

¼ teaspoon salt

½ cup dates, pitted and sliced

½ cup pine nuts, lightly toasted

½ cup pistachio nuts, lightly toasted

Squeezable lemon wedges

OPTIONAL TOPPINGS

Olives

Extra virgin olive oil (a fruity variety, if possible)

Plain yogurt, seasoned with salt and pepper

Minced fresh chives, parsley, and/or mint

1. Place the couscous in a medium-sized bowl and pour in the hot water. Cover the bowl with a plate, and let it stand for 15 to 20 minutes, or until the water is completely absorbed.
2. Stir in the salt and dates. Cover and let stand until shortly before serving time. (If you're doing this more than several hours ahead of time, cover it tightly and refrigerate until about an hour before you plan to serve it.)
3. Stir in the toasted nuts shortly before serving. Serve at room temperature, with squeezable lemon wedges (which you should definitely use). Pass a selection of toppings, and definitely use these, too!

Anooshavoor: Turkish barley and apricot porridge

I like to make this traditional Turkish dish with apple juice in addition to the usual water. It comes out fruity and slightly tart. Top it with yogurt or milk and lightly toasted sliced almonds, and you'll have a rich-tasting, highly textured breakfast that will keep you satisfied all morning.

The barley is cooked risotto-style, with small amounts of liquid added in increments during a fairly long (but low-maintenance) cooking process. This results in a creamy "sauce" surrounding the chewy cooked grains—a perfect porridge.

YIELD: 3 to 4 servings (easily doubled)
PREPARATION TIME: 2 hours (about 5 minutes of work, plus intermittent attention)

½ cup pearl barley

1 cup water (possibly more)

1½ cups apple juice (possibly more), at room temperature

6 cardamom pods

¼ teaspoon salt

5 or more dried apricots, sliced

1 tablespoon honey

OPTIONAL TOPPINGS

Milk, soy milk, cream, or yogurt

Sliced almonds, lightly toasted

1. Combine the barley and water in a medium-sized saucepan. Bring to a boil, then turn the heat down to a simmer. Cover and simmer over the lowest possible heat for 45 minutes, stirring every 10 minutes or so and checking the water level. (You might need to add a little more water.)

2. Stir in ½ cup of the apple juice. Place the cardamom pods in a teaball, and add this to the pot, along with the salt. Cover and continue to simmer.

3. The total simmering time from the first addition of apple juice will be about 1 hour. During this time, stir the porridge about every 10 minutes, and add two more installments of apple juice, ½ cup each time—one at the 20-minute mark and the other after about 40 minutes. Stir after each addition of apple juice.

4. At the end of the hour, you will end up with a thick porridge. If it seems too thick, thin it with a little more apple juice. Fish out the teaball, and stir in the apricots and honey. Remove from the heat, cover, and let it settle for about 10 minutes, so the apricots can soften and blend into the mixture.

5. Serve hot, warm, at room temperature—or even cold. Top it with milk, cream, or yogurt, and a scattering of lightly toasted sliced almonds.

 ABOUT APRICOTS

The word "apricot" comes from both the Latin *praecoquere* ("to cook or ripen before") and the Spanish-Arabic *al barquq* ("precocious"), referring to the fact that the apricot tree blooms very early each spring.

Good, fresh apricots are a delicacy because they are fragile and don't ship well. The vast majority of the crop is dried, and even though the dried fruit ships well, it is still considered a delicacy, as it takes 6 pounds of fresh fruit to yield just 1 pound dried. In the drying process, the apricots lose only water and vitamin C. The other nutrients (vitamin A, fiber, potassium, iron, magnesium, and copper) not only remain but become concentrated. So dried apricots are a good way to pack in the nutrients!

Old-Fashioned Soft Grits

Both grits and polenta (opposite page) can be served soft and eaten with a spoon as you would any creamy hot cereal—or they can be fried until crisp, and served as a side dish or a snack. Made either way, grits are a particularly good companion for eggs, any style. For an even more comprehensive plateful, melt in some cheese, or combine the grits with amaranth, which is packed with protein and minerals. This will give the meal more nutritional value. (Instructions for cooking amaranth are on page 46. Get the amaranth going before you start the grits—it takes longer and should be freshly cooked and still warm when you add it in.)

- This recipe was designed for quick-cooking grits, the easiest kind to find. But use stoneground grits if you can find them, as they taste better. Cook them in a double boiler in a ratio of 1 part grits to 4 parts water, and increase the cooking time to 30 minutes or even longer, depending on the brand. Salt to taste.

YIELD: 2 to 3 servings (easily multiplied)
PREPARATION TIME: 10 minutes

1½ cups water

½ cup quick-cooking grits

¼ teaspoon salt (possibly more)

Up to 1 cup freshly cooked amaranth (page 46; optional)

OPTIONAL TOPPINGS

Butter

Pure maple syrup

Grated cheddar cheese

Freshly ground black pepper

Fire-Roasted Pepper Salsa (page 254)

1. Set the water to boil in a medium-sized saucepan. Sprinkle the grits and salt into the boiling water. Turn the heat down and simmer, uncovered, for about 6 minutes, or until thickened.
2. Remove from the heat, and add the freshly cooked amaranth right away. Taste and adjust the salt, and serve in a bowl with butter and maple syrup— or next to a savory dish, with grated cheddar, black pepper, and salsa.

VARIATION   CRISPY FRIED GRITS

You make these grits stiffer and then slice and fry them until crisp on the outside but still creamy on the inside. This version will feed 6.

Cook the grits as described in the main recipe, using:

- 1 cup grits
- 2½ cups water
- ¾ teaspoon salt

The mixture will become very stiff. Transfer to a small loaf pan, spreading it in the pan, or just shape it into a mound on a plate. Cool for at least 30 minutes (longer is okay), then slice into large chunks (½ to ¾ inch thick—any shape). To fry, place a skillet over medium heat for several minutes. Pour in enough olive oil to cover the surface of the pan, or melt in some butter. When the oil or butter is hot, add the slabs of grits, and cook on both sides until crisp. (With butter they'll take only about 5 minutes on each side and will be very light colored. With oil, they'll take about twice as long and will turn deep golden and ultra-crisp.) Remove from the pan, sprinkle with extra salt, and serve hot or warm.

Soft Breakfast Polenta

A steaming bowl of bright yellow polenta makes a perfect hot breakfast cereal, compatible with a huge variety of toppings. Serve it with butter, milk, and honey or molasses. Or, for a more colorful treatment, spoon on some Cranberry-Ginger Sauce (page 249) or a berry sauce (page 248). You can also go in a savory direction by adding ricotta or any kind of sliced or grated hard cheese—or crumbled blue cheese—and some toasted walnuts. And for a truly comforting experience, try topping a steaming bowl of polenta with a freshly poached egg and some salt and pepper. It's perfect!

- Polenta will keep for several days in a tightly covered container in the refrigerator. Reheat in a microwave or by mashing it in a bowl and adding hot milk.

YIELD: 3 to 4 servings (a generous 2 cups total)
PREPARATION TIME: 15 to 20 minutes

3 cups water

¼ teaspoon salt (possibly more)

½ cup polenta (coarse cornmeal)

OPTIONAL TOPPINGS

Sweet or savory combinations, as described in the recipe introduction

1. Pour 2 cups of the water into a medium-sized saucepan, add the salt, and bring to a boil. Meanwhile, place the polenta in a bowl with the remaining 1 cup water—cold or at room temperature—and stir until it is completely moistened.

2. When the water boils, turn down the heat to a simmer, and spoon in the wet polenta. It will blend in instantly. Cook over medium-low heat, stirring slowly and often with a wooden spoon, until it turns creamy-thick (about 15 minutes).

3. Serve hot with any combination of toppings.

VARIATION **POLENTA PIECES**

If you make polenta with less water, you get a stiffer result that can be cut into squares, fried, and enjoyed crunchy-style. (See Crispy Southwest Polenta Hash, page 153). This recipe makes about 5 cups of pieces.

Follow the main recipe, but bring only 1¾ cups water to a boil. When you add the wet polenta to the boiling water, it will become thick right away. Keep cooking and stirring over medium-low heat for only about 2 to 3 minutes, then remove it from the stove.

Turn the polenta out onto 2 dinner plates, spreading it into an 8-inch circle, ½ inch thick, on each plate. It will stiffen as it cools. Let it sit for 1 hour, then cut it into ½-inch squares. Separate the pieces, and let them stand for another 30 minutes or longer to dry out.

Fry the pieces until crisp in a hot pan coated with melted butter and/or olive oil. Serve hot, with any savory dish—or as a snack, with any kind of salsa.

You can store the pieces in a tightly covered container in the refrigerator for 4 or 5 days before frying.

Rice Porridge

If you cook rice for a good, long time in a large amount of water, it eventually becomes a creamy porridge with soft grains suspended throughout—almost like a light risotto. Chinese cooks discovered this centuries ago, and rice porridge (also called "jook" or "congee") has long been a traditional Chinese breakfast dish, usually served with meat or fish (fresh or dried) and chiles. Since we Westerners tend to prefer our cereals sweet, I've adapted the recipe accordingly. Savory variations follow.

- You can make this recipe with short-grain brown rice, white or brown basmati rice, or glutinous (sweet) rice. (Note: Basmati rice requires slightly more liquid.)
- Vanilla soy milk (¼ cup or more) can be substituted for both the sweetening and the milk. Add it to the porridge about 40 minutes into the simmering process.

YIELD: About 3 servings
PREPARATION TIME: A few minutes, plus 1¼ hours to simmer

½ cup rice

3 cups water

¼ teaspoon salt (rounded measure)

Honey or light brown sugar

Up to ¼ cup milk (optional)

OPTIONAL TOPPINGS

Chopped, toasted almonds

Dried fruit

Yogurt

1. Combine the rice, water, and salt in a medium-sized saucepan. Bring to a boil, lower the heat to a simmer, and cover the pan.
2. Cook over very low heat for about 1¼ hours, or until it becomes a medium-thick porridge. (The cooking time is quite subjective; you can decide for yourself when it's done.)
3. Sweeten to taste, and stir in the milk. Serve hot—plain or topped with almonds, dried fruit, and/or yogurt.

VARIATION   SAVORY RICE PORRIDGE

You can also take this porridge in a savory direction. Make the main recipe, substituting vegetable broth for the water and adding a few slices of ginger. Omit the sweetener and the milk.

During the last 5 minutes of cooking, you can stir in:

- 1 or 2 beaten eggs
- Chopped spinach (a handful or two)

Garnish with any of the following:

- Minced scallions
- Crushed red pepper
- Cooked sweet potato, diced
- Leftover cooked vegetables
- Diced tofu
- Crumbled nori (or another sea vegetable)

Amazing Amaranth Wafers

Crunchy on the outside (as though coated with infinitesimal popcorn) and creamy on the inside, these little cakes, made purely from cooked amaranth, are truly surprising! Take a few to work with you for a terrific portable breakfast or midmorning snack. They don't lose their texture as they cool—or even after being stored—and they taste delicious at any temperature. You can eat them plain, with just a little salt, or drizzled with syrup. They also go well with savory condiments.

- High-oleic safflower oil (page 155) can be heated safely to a very high temperature, which gets the wafers really crisp. If you don't have this kind of oil on hand, you can sauté the wafers in canola oil at a lower temperature. They'll still be good, although not as crisp.
- Store the wafers for up to a week in a tightly covered container in the refrigerator, and reheat in a toaster oven or in a hot frying pan that has been sprayed lightly with nonstick spray. They will virtually spring back to life when reheated!

YIELD: **About 3 servings (1 dozen wafers)**
PREPARATION TIME: **25 minutes**

---

1 cup cooked amaranth, cooled
 (page 46)

High-oleic safflower oil for frying

Salt

OPTIONAL TOPPINGS

Pure maple syrup

Chipotle Cream (page 256)

Salsa (pages 250 to 255)

1. Scoop up the cooked amaranth, about 1½ tablespoons at a time, and form it into small (2-inch diameter), flat, waferlike disks with your hands. (It's easiest to do this if you wet your palms.)
2. Place a skillet over medium heat for about 2 minutes. Add enough oil to cover the bottom of the pan in a thin layer, and wait about 20 seconds for the oil to get hot. Add the wafers, and fry for about 10 minutes on each side (possibly even longer), until brown and crisp. Transfer to a plate lined with paper towels, and cool for a few minutes. Sprinkle lightly with salt.
3. Serve hot or warm, with the toppings of your choice.

 AMARANTH IS A BRILLIANT GRAIN

Amaranth is one of the few foods that is edible as both a vegetable and a grain. (The vegetable comes in the form of the leafy greens, which can be cooked as you would collard greens or spinach.) The vitamin-packed grain is higher in protein than beans, has more fiber than wheat or soybeans, and is exceptionally rich in the amino acid lysine (rare in the plant world). Amaranth also contains more calcium and magnesium than milk and four times the iron of brown rice. Factoring in how good it tastes, how easy it is to cook, and its reasonable price, one is left wondering why this humble, superior grain isn't better known and more widely used. So spread the word!

4

MUFFINS, BISCUITS, BREADS & BUNS

CONTENTS

MUFFINS, BISCUITS, BREADS & BUNS

The smell of good bread baking, like the sound of lightly flowing water,
is indescribable in its evocation of innocence and delight.

—M. F. K. Fisher

Bread, in one form or another, is something just about anyone can happily relate to first thing in the day. Even those of us who are not breakfast eaters can usually cozy up to a piece of toast. In fact, bread is *the* common breakfast denominator among the various cultures around the world. And in many places, a simple breakfast of just bread and coffee, tea, or chocolate is the standard. If your daily breakfast fits this pattern, and you don't really want to change your routine but you'd like whatever it is you dunk in your morning coffee to be even a *little* more nourishing, here's an idea: *Make that bread count.* Let it be *real* food.

Many of the recipes in this chapter are subtly enhanced with extra ingredients to increase their nutritional value, so they won't be just empty calories and your energy won't come crashing down by 10:45 a.m. The word "subtle" is important here, because I know you want your bread to be tender and delicious as well as "meaningful" and satisfying. (Don't you wish everything could fit this description? But these recipes really do.)

A LOGISTICAL NOTE

You can easily have freshly baked muffins, quick breads, biscuits, or scones for breakfast if you get the ingredients ready the night before. In the evening, prepare both the wet and dry mixtures for muffins or quick breads, and place them in separate, covered bowls or containers, refrigerating anything that might spoil. (For scones, make the entire batter the night before and refrigerate it. For biscuits, roll and cut them out, and refrigerate them overnight on the baking tray.) In the morning, simply preheat the oven, put the muffin or quick bread batter together, spoon it into the pan (or, in the case of scones, just scoop the batter onto the tray), and bake. And remember that, even though fresh-baked, still-warm breakfast breads are very exciting, they also taste wonderful on the second day and thereafter, sliced into halves or thirds, and toasted—if they've been stored properly. So consider baking several batches (a variety) on a Sunday afternoon—say, once a month—and, after they've cooled, store them in zip-style plastic bags in the freezer. Then you can defrost and toast them individually—a tremendous convenience and quality-of-life enhancement for busy mornings!

Some Thoughts About Toast

What is it about toast? It's the plainest, most accessible comfort food, complete with healing properties, "tea and toast" being second only to chicken soup as the universal delectable palliative. The word "toast" comes from an ancient root—shared with "tostada" and "thirst," among other words—meaning "to dry." And sometimes I think it's the very dryness of toast that makes it such a cozy food, allowing it to readily soak up melted butter, hot milk, or cappuccino, and carrying us into simple transcendence on a daily basis. When my grandmother made cinnamon toast (which, for some mysterious, wonderful reason, she would cut into three strips instead of in half), I would have a miniature religious experience, right on the spot. Just think for a moment how we can move small worlds, even for just a moment, with a warmed-up, dried-out slice of bread!

A FEW TOAST TIPS

- Good bread, fresh or "day-old," makes good toast. Bad bread makes bad toast. It's that simple.

- If you use a toaster oven or a broiler to make toast, you can watch over the process more closely than if you use a toaster. Plus, you can toast thicker slices or oddly shaped pieces (like split muffins or scones), and you can melt cheese or sugar on top as well.

- To add fiber to the toast experience, lightly mash some fresh, ripe fruit—especially berries—and spread it on top. This is a good replacement for sugary jams and jellies.

- Don't forget that trusty standby, peanut butter. It makes a wonderful toast spread! Also consider using almond butter or cashew butter—or a mixture. Sliced bananas or nectarines pressed into the top will make it deluxe.

- Keep *sliced* artisan bread, homemade muffins, and bagels in your freezer, so they're ready to toast in a hurry. No defrosting necessary.

- For a quick, hearty breakfast, reheat the vegetables from last night's dinner and heap them onto a fresh piece of toast.

 MY FAVORITE TOAST STORY

A journalist friend of mine called one day, very excited. Not only had she lined up a personal interview with Julia Child, but Julia had actually invited the interviewer to her home for the occasion! When my friend arrived, Julia insisted on feeding her—offering not some exotic tart or soufflé, as you might expect, but plain hot, buttered toast, lovingly and simply prepared. This humble, authentic gesture made more of an impression than anything that got said that morning.

 CRUNCHY CINNAMON TOAST

Grind some soy nuts (about ⅓ cup) to a fine powder in an electric spice grinder. Mix them with 1 teaspoon cinnamon and 2 tablespoons turbinado sugar or brown sugar crystals. Toast and butter up to 4 slices of your favorite bread, then spoon on a thick layer of this mixture. Broil until the topping melts, watching carefully so it doesn't burn. Cool for a minute or so before serving. You'll have enough topping for 4 slices of toast.

Do you know on this one block you can buy croissants in five different places? There's one store called Bonjour Croissant. It makes me want to go to Paris and open a store called Hello Toast.

—Fran Leibowitz

A Few Words About Muffins

Muffins are a uniquely North American breakfast food. In the late 19th and early 20th centuries, the discovery of chemical leavening agents (baking powder and baking soda) and the development of the modern oven made it possible for home bakers to produce early versions of what later became known as muffins. Often made from whole wheat flour and bran, these miniature, round breads were considered "health food" long before the term was officially coined. Over the years, this notion of muffins being a healthy breakfast choice has stuck, but unfortunately, it has become somewhat of a myth. A closer look at most commercially produced muffins blows their cover, revealing them to be little more than glorified (and often enormous) cupcakes, largely devoid of fiber and other nutrients. In other words, they're not a very healthy choice at all, but rather a fantasy that allows us to feel good about scarfing down a big, sweet treat.

Now for the good news: You can have it both ways! It's been my very enjoyable challenge to create a selection of nutritionally respectable muffins that will also answer your yearning for something cakelike and sweet for breakfast. I've had a lot of fun coming up with muffin categories that include whole grain, corn variations, fruit-based and vegetable-based muffins, and even a selection of ricotta muffins that are out of this world. These muffins can become a mainstay in your household—not only for breakfast but for lunch treats and afternoon snacks as well.

USING SOY PROTEIN POWDER

Fluffy, beige, and somewhat sweet, soy protein powder is 80 to 90 percent pure soy isolate, packing in about 25 grams of soy protein (and sometimes some calcium) per ounce. (Note that soy protein powder is not the same thing as soy flour, which is made from ground soybeans.) Unless otherwise specified, you can use soy protein powder in place of up to half the flour in all these muffin recipes. The result is delicious yet slightly more crumbly and denser in texture than muffins made with flour only. Look for soy protein powder in the bulk bins at natural food stores.

USING WHOLE WHEAT PASTRY FLOUR

A very finely milled whole wheat pastry flour is available in the bulk bins of many natural food stores, and it is interchangeable with the unbleached all-purpose flour in the muffin recipes that follow. Be sure it says "*pastry* flour" on the label, and feel it with your fingers to be sure it is soft and silky. Regular whole wheat flour, which is coarse and heavy, will not work.

Buttermilk Bran Muffins

After years of searching for a bran muffin I could truly adore and not just eat dutifully, I'm pleased to report that my quest has come to a happy conclusion in this recipe.

- The range of sugar allows you to make these sweeter or not, according to your taste.
- For protein powder and whole wheat flour options, see the previous page.
- Canola oil can be substituted for some or all of the butter.
- The optional raisin bran cereal will increase the yield somewhat and will produce a sweeter muffin with a crisper top.

YIELD: 12 to 14 muffins
PREPARATION TIME: 10 minutes, plus 20 to 25 minutes to bake

Nonstick spray

2 cups unbleached all-purpose flour

½ teaspoon salt (rounded measure)

1 tablespoon baking powder

¼ teaspoon baking soda

6 to 8 tablespoons granulated sugar

½ cup (packed) light brown sugar

2 cups unprocessed wheat bran

3 to 4 cups raisin bran cereal (optional)

2 cups buttermilk

2 large eggs

½ cup (1 stick) unsalted butter, melted

1. Preheat the oven to 375°F. Lightly spray 12 standard (2½-inch-diameter) muffin cups with nonstick spray.
2. Combine the flour, salt, baking powder, baking soda, and granulated sugar in a medium-sized bowl. Crumble in the brown sugar, rubbing it with your fingers to break up any clumps. Stir in the bran and the optional raisin bran cereal until the mixture is thoroughly blended.
3. Measure the 2 cups buttermilk into a 4-cup liquid measure. Add the eggs and beat gently with a fork or a small whisk until smooth.
4. Slowly pour this mixture, along with the melted butter, into the dry ingredients. Using a spoon or a rubber spatula, stir from the bottom of the bowl until the dry ingredients are all moistened. Don't overmix; a few lumps are okay.
5. Spoon the batter into the prepared muffin cups. For smaller muffins, fill the cups about four-fifths full. For larger muffins, fill them up to the top. If you have extra batter, spray one or two additional muffin cups with nonstick spray and fill with the remaining batter.
6. Bake in the middle of the oven for 20 to 25 minutes, or until lightly browned on top and a toothpick inserted into the center comes out clean. Remove the pan from the oven, then remove the muffins from the pan and place them on a rack to cool. Wait at least 30 minutes before serving.

VARIATIONS   For each variation, follow the main recipe with these adjustments.

CRANBERRY-APPLE-WALNUT BRAN MUFFINS

Stir into the batter in step 4:

- 2 cups peeled, minced Granny Smith apples
- ⅔ cup minced walnuts, lightly toasted
- 1 cup dried cranberries

APRICOT-ALMOND BRAN MUFFINS

Stir into the batter in step 4:

- 1 cup minced almonds, lightly toasted
- 1 cup dried apricots, cut into pieces the size of raisins

Buttermilk-Barley Muffins with cashews and sesame seeds

If you like your muffins multitextured and layered with contrasting flavors, this recipe is for you. Chewy barley, crunchy, toasty cashews and sesame seeds, and tart buttermilk are a great team, and the result is just filling enough to get you through the morning. An additional benefit: Barley is a good source of folate (folic acid), a very important B vitamin.

- Cook the barley well ahead of time. (Guidelines are on page 46.)
- If you are using leftover cooked barley and it has been salted, reduce the amount of salt in the muffins accordingly.
- For protein powder and whole wheat flour options, see page 68.
- Canola oil can be substituted for some or all of the butter.

YIELD: 10 to 12 medium-sized muffins
PREPARATION TIME: 15 minutes, plus 20 to 25 minutes to bake

Nonstick spray

2 cups unbleached all-purpose flour

¾ teaspoon salt

1½ teaspoons baking powder

⅛ teaspoon baking soda

2 tablespoons (packed) light brown sugar

1½ cups cooked pearl barley

¼ cup lightly toasted sesame seeds

¼ cup minced cashews, lightly toasted

¾ cup buttermilk

¼ cup pure maple syrup

1 large egg

1½ teaspoons vanilla extract

4 tablespoons (½ stick) unsalted butter, melted

1. Preheat the oven to 400°F. Lightly spray 10 standard (2½-inch-diameter) muffin cups with nonstick spray.
2. Place the flour, salt, baking powder, baking soda, and brown sugar in a medium to large bowl. Break up any little clumps of sugar with your fingers, then stir until thoroughly combined.
3. Add the barley, and use a fork or your fingers to separate and distribute the grains throughout the flour. Stir in the sesame seeds and cashews.
4. Measure the ¾ cup buttermilk into a 2-cup liquid measure. Add the maple syrup, egg, and vanilla, and beat gently with a fork or a small whisk until smooth.
5. Slowly pour this mixture into the dry ingredients, adding the melted butter at the same time. Using a spoon or a rubber spatula, stir from the bottom of the bowl until the dry ingredients are all moistened. Don't overmix; a few lumps are okay.
6. Spoon the batter into the prepared muffin cups. For smaller muffins, fill the cups about four-fifths full. For larger muffins, fill them up to the top. If you have extra batter, spray one or two additional muffin cups with nonstick spray and fill with the remaining batter.
7. Bake in the middle of the oven for 20 to 25 minutes, or until lightly browned on top and a toothpick inserted into the center comes out clean. Remove the pan from the oven, then remove the muffins from the pan and place them on a rack to cool. Wait at least 30 minutes before serving.

Spiced Basmati-Almond Muffins

My own version of a "fusion" baked good combines Indian-style grains and spices baked into a very American-style muffin. Not surprisingly, I recommend serving these with Cucumber-Mint Lassi (page 16) or Chai-Spiced Milk (page 17).

- Cook the rice well ahead of time. (Guidelines are on page 46.)
- If you are using leftover cooked rice and it has been salted, reduce the amount of salt in the muffins accordingly.
- For protein powder and whole wheat flour options, see page 68.
- Canola oil can be substituted for some or all of the butter.

YIELD: 12 to 14 muffins
PREPARATION TIME: 15 minutes, plus 20 to 25 minutes to bake

Nonstick spray

2 cups unbleached all-purpose flour

1 teaspoon salt

1½ teaspoons baking powder

¼ teaspoon baking soda

1 teaspoon cinnamon

1 teaspoon ground coriander

1 teaspoon powdered ginger

½ teaspoon ground cardamom

½ teaspoon ground fennel

½ teaspoon allspice or cloves

2 teaspoons grated orange zest

⅔ cup (packed) light brown sugar

1½ cups cooked brown basmati rice, cooled

¾ cup minced almonds, lightly toasted

1½ cups buttermilk

2 large eggs

1 tablespoon vanilla extract

1 tablespoon fresh lemon juice

4 tablespoons (½ stick) unsalted butter, melted

1. Preheat the oven to 400°F. Lightly spray 12 standard (2½-inch-diameter) muffin cups with nonstick spray.
2. Combine the flour, salt, baking powder, baking soda, spices, and orange zest in a medium-sized bowl.
3. Crumble in the brown sugar, rubbing it with your fingers to break up any clumps. Add the rice, and use a fork or your fingers to distribute it throughout. Stir in the almonds.
4. Measure the 1½ cups buttermilk into a 4-cup liquid measure. Add the eggs, vanilla, and lemon juice, and beat gently with a fork or a small whisk until smooth.
5. Slowly pour this mixture, along with the melted butter, into the dry ingredients. Using a spoon or a rubber spatula, stir from the bottom of the bowl until the dry ingredients are all moistened. Don't overmix; a few lumps are okay.
6. Spoon the batter into the prepared muffin cups. For smaller muffins, fill the cups about four-fifths full. For larger muffins, fill them up to the top. If you have extra batter, spray one or two additional muffin cups with nonstick spray and fill with the remaining batter.
7. Bake in the middle of the oven for 20 to 25 minutes, or until lightly browned on top and a toothpick inserted into the center comes out clean. Remove the pan from the oven, then remove the muffins from the pan and place them on a rack to cool. Wait at least 30 minutes before serving.

Toasted Oatmeal–Oat Bran Muffins

Highly textured and very tasty, these muffins are like a portable bowl of oatmeal, only better. Buttermilk, eggs, nuts, and oat bran provide extra protein and fiber to help propel you through the day. For an additional energy boost, and to keep the edge off your appetite even longer, try spreading these crunchy muffins with almond butter after you split and toast them.

- The range of sugar allows you to make these sweeter or not, according to your taste.
- You can toast the oats and nuts (step 1) up to several days ahead. Store the finished mixture in an airtight container in the refrigerator.
- For protein powder and whole wheat flour options, see page 68.
- Canola oil can be substituted for some or all of the butter.

YIELD: 8 to 10 muffins

PREPARATION TIME: 15 minutes to prepare the oat-nut mixture (can be done ahead), then 10 minutes of work, plus 20 to 25 minutes to bake

---

Nonstick spray

1 cup rolled oats

⅓ cup oat bran

⅓ cup minced walnuts or pecans

6 tablespoons (packed) light brown sugar

1 to 2 tablespoons granulated sugar (optional)

1½ cups unbleached all-purpose flour

¾ teaspoon salt

1½ teaspoons baking powder

⅛ teaspoon baking soda

1 cup buttermilk

2 large eggs

1 tablespoon vanilla extract

4 tablespoons (½ stick) unsalted butter, melted

¼ cup raisins (optional)

⅓ cup dried cherries or cranberries (optional)

1. Spray a medium-sized skillet (preferably cast iron) with nonstick spray, and place it on the stove over medium-low heat. Add the oats, oat bran, and nuts, and toast them, stirring frequently, until they give off a pleasant aroma and have turned light golden brown. This takes a good 15 to 20 minutes. At a certain point, this mixture could suddenly begin to burn on the bottom, so watch it carefully and stir often. Add the brown sugar and the optional granulated sugar at the very end and stir until it melts slightly. Set aside to cool.

2. Preheat the oven to 400°F. Lightly spray 8 standard (2½-inch-diameter) muffin cups with nonstick spray.

3. Combine the flour, salt, baking powder, and baking soda in a medium-sized bowl. Add the toasted oat-nut mixture and stir until well blended.

4. Measure the 1 cup buttermilk into a 2-cup liquid measure. Add the eggs and vanilla, and beat gently with a fork or a small whisk until smooth.

5. Slowly pour this mixture, along with the melted butter and optional dried fruit, into the dry ingredients. Using a spoon or a rubber spatula, stir from the bottom of the bowl until the dry ingredients are all moistened. Don't overmix; a few lumps are okay.

6. Spoon the batter into the prepared muffin cups. For smaller muffins, fill the cups about four-fifths full. For larger muffins, fill them up to the top. If you have extra batter, spray one or two additional muffin cups with nonstick spray and fill with the remaining batter.

7. Bake in the middle of the oven for 20 to 25 minutes, or until lightly browned on top and a toothpick inserted into the center comes out clean. Remove the pan from the oven, then remove the muffins from the pan and place them on a rack to cool. Wait at least 30 minutes before serving.

Crunchy Millet Muffins

Millet goes directly into these muffins au naturel—*with no prior cooking or soaking. The result is a playful and surprisingly delicate crunchiness guaranteed to wake you up if your cup of coffee failed to do the trick.*

- For protein powder and whole wheat flour options, see page 68.
- Canola oil can be substituted for some or all of the butter.

YIELD: 8 to 10 muffins
PREPARATION TIME: 10 minutes, plus 20 to 25 minutes to bake

Nonstick spray

2 cups unbleached all-purpose flour

½ teaspoon salt

1½ teaspoons baking powder

¾ teaspoon cinnamon

¾ cup uncooked millet

⅓ cup (packed) light brown sugar

1 cup milk

1 large egg

1½ teaspoons vanilla extract

4 tablespoons (½ stick) unsalted
   butter, melted

1. Preheat the oven to 375°F. Lightly spray 8 standard (2½-inch-diameter) muffin cups with nonstick spray.
2. Combine the flour, salt, baking powder, and cinnamon in a medium-sized bowl. Add the millet, then crumble in the brown sugar and mix with a fork or your fingers until thoroughly blended.
3. Measure the 1 cup milk in a 2-cup liquid measure. Add the egg and vanilla, and beat gently with a fork or a small whisk until smooth.
4. Slowly pour this mixture, along with the melted butter, into the dry ingredients. Using a spoon or a rubber spatula, stir from the bottom of the bowl until the dry ingredients are all moistened. Don't overmix; a few lumps are okay.
5. Spoon the batter into the prepared muffin cups. For smaller muffins, fill the cups about four-fifths full. For larger muffins, fill them up to the top. If you have extra batter, spray one or two additional muffin cups with nonstick spray and fill with the remaining batter.
6. Bake in the middle of the oven for 20 to 25 minutes, or until lightly browned on top and a toothpick inserted into the center comes out clean. Remove the pan from the oven, then remove the muffins from the pan and place them on a rack to cool. Wait at least 30 minutes before serving.

Wild Rice and Quinoa Muffins with cranberries

Color, texture, fiber, flavor—it's all here! Did I mention protein? Quinoa is a champion in this department, and I've stuffed as much of it into these muffins as would fit. With sweetness from the brown sugar, a very pleasant earthiness from the grains, and tart dried cranberries throughout, these complex muffins are unbelievably satisfying.

- The range of sugar allows you to make these sweeter or not, according to your taste.
- Cook the grains well ahead of time. (Guidelines are on page 46.)
- If you are using leftover cooked grains and they have been salted, reduce the salt accordingly.
- For protein powder and whole wheat flour options, see page 68.
- Canola oil can be substituted for some or all of the butter.

YIELD: 10 to 12 muffins
PREPARATION TIME: 10 minutes of work (once the grains are cooked), plus 20 to 25 minutes to bake

---

Nonstick spray

2 cups unbleached all-purpose flour

¾ teaspoon salt

1½ teaspoons baking powder

⅓ cup (packed) light brown sugar

2 to 3 tablespoons granulated sugar (optional)

1¼ cups cooked wild rice

1¼ cups cooked quinoa

⅔ cup dried cranberries

1 cup milk

1 large egg

1½ teaspoons vanilla extract

4 tablespoons (½ stick) unsalted butter, melted

1. Preheat the oven to 400°F. Lightly spray 10 standard (2½-inch-diameter) muffin cups with nonstick spray.
2. Place the flour, salt, baking powder, and brown sugar in a medium to large bowl. Break up any little clumps of sugar with your fingers, and then stir the mixture until thoroughly combined. Stir in the granulated sugar, if you like your muffins on the sweet side.
3. Add the cooked grains, using a fork or your fingers to separate and distribute them throughout. Stir in the dried cranberries.
4. Measure the 1 cup milk into a 2-cup liquid measure. Add the egg and vanilla, and beat gently with a fork or a small whisk until smooth.
5. Slowly pour this mixture into the dry ingredients, adding the melted butter at the same time. Using a spoon or a rubber spatula, stir from the bottom of the bowl until the dry ingredients are all moistened. Don't overmix; a few lumps are okay.
6. Spoon the batter into the prepared muffin cups. For smaller muffins, fill the cups about four-fifths full. For larger muffins, fill them up to the top. If you have extra batter, spray one or two additional muffin cups with nonstick spray and fill with the remaining batter.
7. Bake in the middle of the oven for 20 to 25 minutes, or until lightly browned on top and a toothpick inserted into the center comes out clean. Remove the pan from the oven, then remove the muffins from the pan and place them on a rack to cool. Wait at least 30 minutes before serving.

Wheat-Free Muffins

Just about any grain can be ground into flour, and each has its own distinct personality and flavor. You can buy many kinds of flour at natural foods stores, usually in 2-pound bags. Store them in an airtight container in a cool, dry place—ideally the freezer—to keep the flour fresh.

Most "alternative" (nonwheat) flours need to be combined with at least some wheat flour, so the final product will hold together and feel good in the mouth. This is because only wheat flour contains sufficient gluten-forming proteins to give coherent structure and texture to the result. That said, sometimes you can get away with leaving the wheat flour out—and I know this is important for those of you with wheat allergies. These wheat-free muffins are a case in point. They have a lovely flavor and a texture that is much more delicate and crumbly (almost powdery, in a nice kind of way) than "regular" muffins.

- Canola oil can be substituted for some or all of the butter.
- Don't try splitting and toasting these, as they are too crumbly. It's better to just reheat them, whole, in a toaster oven.

YIELD: About 8 muffins
PREPARATION TIME: 10 minutes, plus 20 to 25 minutes to bake

Nonstick spray

1 cup rice flour

½ cup millet or barley flour

½ cup oat flour

½ teaspoon salt

1 teaspoon baking powder

¾ cup milk

¼ cup pure maple syrup or light honey

1 large egg

1 teaspoon vanilla extract

4 tablespoons (½ stick) unsalted butter, melted

1. Preheat the oven to 375°F. Lightly spray 8 standard (2½-inch-diameter) muffin cups with nonstick spray.
2. Combine the flours in a medium-sized bowl with the salt and baking powder.
3. Measure the ¾ cup milk into a 2-cup liquid measure, and add the maple syrup or honey. Add the egg and vanilla, and beat gently with a fork or a small whisk until smooth.
4. Slowly pour this mixture into the dry ingredients, along with the melted butter. Using a spoon or a rubber spatula, stir from the bottom of the bowl until the dry ingredients are all moistened. Don't overmix; a few lumps are okay.
5. Spoon the batter into the prepared muffin cups. For smaller muffins, fill the cups about four-fifths full. For larger muffins, fill them up to the top. If you have extra batter, spray one or two additional muffin cups with nonstick spray and fill with the remaining batter.
6. Bake in the middle of the oven for 20 to 25 minutes, or until lightly browned on top and a toothpick inserted into the center comes out clean. Remove the pan from the oven, then remove the muffins from the pan and place them on a rack to cool. Wait at least 30 minutes before serving.

Basic Corn Muffins

One of the first things I learned to bake all by myself was a plain corn muffin from small boxes of muffin mix that my mother would buy for 10 cents apiece. Even though it wasn't "from scratch," the experience was deeply authentic to me, and I adored the results. Plain corn muffins have occupied a special place in my culinary heart ever since.

- Use a fine grade of cornmeal (not the coarser polenta) for best results.
- For protein powder and whole wheat flour options, see page 68.
- Canola oil can be substituted for some or all of the butter.

YIELD: 8 to 10 muffins
PREPARATION TIME: 10 minutes, plus 20 to 25 minutes to bake

Nonstick spray

1¼ cups unbleached all-purpose flour

1¼ cups cornmeal

½ teaspoon salt (slightly rounded measure)

1½ teaspoons baking powder

3 to 4 tablespoons sugar

1¼ cups milk

2 large eggs

4 tablespoons (½ stick) unsalted butter, melted

1. Preheat the oven to 400°F. Lightly spray 8 standard (2½-inch-diameter) muffin cups with nonstick spray.
2. Combine the flour, cornmeal, salt, baking powder, and sugar in a medium-sized bowl.
3. Measure the 1¼ cups milk into a 2-cup liquid measure. Add the eggs, and beat gently with a fork or a small whisk until smooth.
4. Slowly pour this mixture, plus the melted butter, into the dry ingredients. Using a spoon or a rubber spatula, stir from the bottom of the bowl until the dry ingredients are all moistened. Don't overmix; a few lumps are okay.
5. Spoon the batter into the prepared muffin cups. For smaller muffins, fill the cups about four-fifths full. For larger muffins, fill them up to the top. If you have extra batter, spray one or two additional muffin cups with nonstick spray and fill with the remaining batter.
6. Bake in the middle of the oven for 20 to 25 minutes, or until lightly browned on top and a toothpick inserted into the center comes out clean. Remove the pan from the oven, then remove the muffins from the pan and place them on a rack to cool. Wait at least 30 minutes before serving.

VARIATION **SAVORY CORN MUFFINS**

Follow the main recipe with these adjustments.

You can add one, some, or all of the following with the liquid in step 4:

- 1 cup corn kernels (fresh or frozen, defrosted if frozen)
- ½ cup minced green chiles (canned or fresh)
- 1 cup (packed) grated jack cheese
- ⅓ cup minced scallions or chives

Orange-Cherry Corn Muffins

You will love these elegant muffins. In addition to being perfect for breakfast, they're also great for lunch or afternoon tea.

- The range of sugar allows you to make these sweeter or not, according to your taste.
- Remember to grate the orange zest before squeezing the juice.
- Use a fine grade of cornmeal (not the coarser polenta) for best results.
- For protein powder and whole wheat flour options, see page 68.
- Canola oil can be substituted for some or all of the butter.

YIELD: 8 to 10 muffins
PREPARATION TIME: 15 minutes, plus 20 to 25 minutes to bake

Nonstick spray

1 cup unbleached all-purpose flour

1 cup cornmeal

½ teaspoon salt

1½ teaspoons baking powder

⅛ teaspoon baking soda

⅓ to ½ cup sugar

1 tablespoon grated orange zest

½ cup orange juice

½ cup buttermilk

1 large egg

½ teaspoon vanilla extract

4 tablespoons (½ stick) unsalted butter, melted

1½ cups cherries (fresh or frozen, undefrosted), pitted and sliced, or 1 cup dried cherries

1. Preheat the oven to 400°F. Lightly spray 8 standard (2½-inch-diameter) muffin cups with nonstick spray.
2. Combine the flour, cornmeal, salt, baking powder, baking soda, sugar, and orange zest in a medium-sized bowl.
3. Measure the orange juice and buttermilk into a 2-cup liquid measure. Add the egg and vanilla, and beat gently with a fork or a small whisk until smooth.
4. Slowly pour this mixture, plus the melted butter, into the dry ingredients. Using a spoon or a rubber spatula, stir from the bottom of the bowl. When it is almost all mixed, add the cherries, then complete the mixing with a few swift strokes until the dry ingredients are all moistened. Don't over-mix; a few lumps are okay.
5. Spoon the batter into the prepared muffin cups. For smaller muffins, fill the cups about four-fifths full. For larger muffins, fill them up to the top. If you have extra batter, spray one or two additional muffin cups with non-stick spray and fill with the remaining batter.
6. Bake in the middle of the oven for 20 to 25 minutes, or until lightly browned on top and a toothpick inserted into the center comes out clean. Remove the pan from the oven, then remove the muffins from the pan and place them on a rack to cool. Wait at least 30 minutes before serving.

VARIATIONS   For each variation, follow the main recipe with these adjustments.

ORANGE-CRANBERRY CORN MUFFINS

Increase the sugar to ⅔ cup, and omit the vanilla extract. Replace the cherries with:

- 2 cups chopped fresh cranberries

RASPBERRY CORN MUFFINS

Increase the sugar to ⅔ cup. The orange zest is optional. Omit the vanilla extract.

Replace the cherries with:

- 1½ cups raspberries (fresh or frozen, undefrosted)

Black Bean and Salsa Corn Muffins

Corn muffins are switch-hitters, able to go in a sweet or savory direction with ease. In this unusual treatment, they go both ways at once! It seems contradictory, but it really works. Be encouraged by the fact that you don't need to go through the lengthy process of soaking and cooking the black beans ahead of time. Just open a can.

About those canned beans: This recipe will use most, but not all, of a 15-ounce can. Store the extra beans in a small, tightly covered container in the refrigerator, and use them in scrambled eggs, salads, Mexican Home Fries (page 148), or Crispy Southwest Polenta Hash (page 153). Rinse and thoroughly drain the beans before using.

Here's a nice way to serve these muffins: Cut them in half and toast them. Then place each half on the tray of a toaster oven, and sprinkle lightly with grated jack cheese. Heat or broil until the cheese melts. Serve right away.

- Use a fine grade of cornmeal (not the coarser polenta) for best results.
- For protein powder and whole wheat flour options, see page 68.
- You can use your favorite commercial brand of fresh salsa, or make your own (pages 250 to 255).

YIELD: 8 to 10 muffins
PREPARATION TIME: 10 minutes, plus 30 minutes to bake

Nonstick spray

1 cup unbleached all-purpose flour

1 cup cornmeal

¾ teaspoon salt

1½ teaspoons baking powder

⅛ teaspoon baking soda

3 tablespoons sugar

½ cup sour cream

½ cup tomato-based salsa
  (your favorite)

¼ cup milk

2 tablespoons olive oil

1 large egg

1¼ cups cooked black beans,
  rinsed and thoroughly drained

1. Preheat the oven to 400°F. Lightly spray 8 standard (2½-inch-diameter) muffin cups with nonstick spray.

2. Combine the flour, cornmeal, salt, baking powder, baking soda, and sugar in a medium-sized bowl.

3. Measure the sour cream, then the salsa, milk, and olive oil into a 2-cup liquid measure. Add the egg, and beat gently with a fork or a small whisk until smooth.

4. Slowly pour this mixture into the dry ingredients, along with the beans. Using a spoon or a rubber spatula, stir from the bottom of the bowl until the dry ingredients are all moistened. Don't overmix; a few lumps are okay.

5. Spoon the batter into the prepared muffin cups. For smaller muffins, fill the cups about four-fifths full. For larger muffins, fill them up to the top. If you have extra batter, spray one or two additional muffin cups with nonstick spray and fill with the remaining batter.

6. Bake in the middle of the oven for about 30 minutes, or until lightly browned on top and a toothpick inserted into the center comes out clean. (Be sure they're really baked through. Even more than other kinds of muffins, these don't taste good underdone.) Remove the pan from the oven, then remove the muffins from the pan and place them on a rack to cool. Wait at least 30 minutes before serving.

Buttermilk Blueberry Muffins

I've always thought of blueberry muffins as being somewhat bland, lacking that elusive perkiness needed to awaken the palate. Believing strongly that breakfast food should wake you up and not put you back to sleep, I experimented with adding buttermilk (spunky and tart) and an enthusiastic dose of grated lemon zest to make the blueberries' flavor pop. It worked!

- The range of sugar allows you to make these sweeter or not, according to your taste.
- Remember to grate the lemon zest before squeezing the juice.
- For protein powder and whole wheat flour options, see page 68.
- Canola oil can be substituted for some or all of the butter.

YIELD: About 10 muffins
PREPARATION TIME: 10 minutes, plus 20 to 25 minutes to bake

Nonstick spray

2½ cups unbleached all-purpose flour

¾ teaspoon salt

1½ teaspoons baking powder

¼ teaspoon baking soda

½ to ⅔ cup sugar

1 tablespoon grated lemon zest

1½ cups buttermilk

2 tablespoons fresh lemon juice

1 large egg

1 tablespoon vanilla extract

4 tablespoons (½ stick) unsalted butter, melted

1½ cups blueberries (fresh or frozen, undefrosted)

1. Preheat the oven to 375°F. Lightly spray 10 standard (2½-inch-diameter) muffin cups with nonstick spray.
2. Combine the flour, salt, baking powder, baking soda, sugar, and lemon zest in a medium-sized bowl.
3. Measure the 1½ cups buttermilk into a 4-cup liquid measure. Add the lemon juice, egg, and vanilla, and beat gently with a fork or a small whisk until smooth.
4. Slowly pour this mixture, along with the melted butter, into the dry ingredients. Using a spoon or a rubber spatula, stir from the bottom of the bowl until the dry ingredients are all moistened. Carefully fold in the blueberries at the very end. Don't overmix; a few lumps are okay.
5. Spoon the batter into the prepared muffin cups. For smaller muffins, fill the cups about four-fifths full. For larger muffins, fill them up to the top. If you have extra batter, spray one or two additional muffin cups with nonstick spray and fill with the remaining batter.
6. Bake in the middle of the oven for 20 to 25 minutes, or until lightly browned on top and a toothpick inserted into the center comes out clean. Remove the pan from the oven, then remove the muffins from the pan and place them on a rack to cool. Wait at least 30 minutes before serving.

 BAKING WITH BLUEBERRIES

When frozen blueberries bleed into baked goods, it's usually because they were defrosted before being added to the batter. Always add the berries to the batter while still frozen, and stir them in at the last minute. Fresh blueberries won't bleed out their juices unless the skins are broken, so if using fresh berries, mix them gently.

Pumpkin Muffins

You don't need to wait for autumn to celebrate the spirit of the harvest. Create your own holiday season any time of year with these golden muffins.

For a touch of texture, and to give more of an intriguing bitter edge to the muffins, coarsely chop the orange zest rather than grating it. The easiest way to do this is to shave off the outermost peel with a vegetable peeler and then to chop the shavings into smaller pieces with a sharp knife.

- The range of sugar allows you to make these sweeter or not, according to your taste.
- Cooked sweet potato or winter squash can be substituted for the pumpkin.
- For protein powder and whole wheat flour options, see page 68.
- Canola oil can be substituted for some or all of the butter.

YIELD: 8 to 10 muffins
PREPARATION TIME: 15 minutes, plus 20 to 25 minutes to bake

Nonstick spray

2 cups unbleached all-purpose flour

½ teaspoon salt (rounded measure)

1½ teaspoons baking powder

1½ teaspoons cinnamon

1 teaspoon ground ginger

¼ teaspoon allspice

3 to 4 tablespoons granulated sugar

1 tablespoon chopped orange zest

⅓ cup (packed) dark brown sugar

1 cup mashed pumpkin

1 large egg

½ cup milk

1 tablespoon vanilla extract

4 tablespoons (½ stick) unsalted butter, melted

1. Preheat the oven to 400°F. Lightly spray 8 standard (2½-inch-diameter) muffin cups with nonstick spray.
2. Combine the flour, salt, baking powder, spices, granulated sugar, and orange zest in a medium-sized bowl. Crumble in the brown sugar and mix with a fork or your fingers until thoroughly blended.
3. Measure the pumpkin into a second medium-sized bowl. Add the egg, milk, and vanilla, and beat with a fork or a whisk until smooth.
4. Slowly pour this mixture, along with the melted butter, into the dry ingredients. Using a spoon or a rubber spatula, stir from the bottom of the bowl until the dry ingredients are all moistened. Don't overmix; a few lumps are okay.
5. Spoon the batter into the prepared muffin cups. For smaller muffins, fill the cups about four-fifths full. For larger muffins, fill them up to the top. If you have extra batter, spray one or two additional muffin cups with nonstick spray and fill with the remaining batter.
6. Bake in the middle of the oven for 20 to 25 minutes, or until lightly browned on top and a toothpick inserted into the center comes out clean. Remove the pan from the oven, then remove the muffins from the pan and place them on a rack to cool. Wait at least 30 minutes before serving.

Carrot-Currant Muffins

Make these pretty orange-and-black speckled muffins for an already-special morning (like a birthday) or to make an otherwise ordinary morning become *special (like a Thursday in March). These muffins are like having carrot cake for breakfast, only tidier—and healthier, because the flavor and fiber are there, but not the huge amount of fat.*

A food processor fitted with the fine grating attachment will make short work of preparing the carrots. You can do this up to several hours ahead of time if you store the grated carrot in an airtight container in the refrigerator until just before use.

- For protein powder and whole wheat flour options, see page 68.
- Try substituting zucchini for the carrot, for a pretty green variation.
- Canola oil can be substituted for some or all of the butter.

YIELD: **8 to 10 muffins**
PREPARATION TIME: **20 minutes, plus 20 to 25 minutes to bake**

Nonstick spray

2 cups unbleached all-purpose flour

½ teaspoon salt

1½ teaspoons baking powder

½ teaspoon cinnamon

⅛ teaspoon allspice

⅓ cup (packed) light brown sugar

2 tablespoons granulated sugar (optional)

1 cup (packed) finely grated carrot

1 tablespoon grated lemon zest

3 tablespoons fresh lemon juice

½ cup currants

½ cup milk

1 large egg

2 teaspoons vanilla extract

4 tablespoons (½ stick) unsalted butter, melted

1. Preheat the oven to 400°F. Lightly spray 8 standard (2½-inch-diameter) muffin cups with nonstick spray.
2. Combine the flour, salt, baking powder, and spices in a medium-sized bowl. Crumble in the brown sugar, rubbing it in a bit with your fingers until the mixture is thoroughly blended. Stir in the granulated sugar, if you like your muffins on the sweet side.
3. Place the grated carrot in a second bowl. Add the lemon zest, lemon juice, and currants, and mix with a fork. Use the fork to beat in the milk, egg, and vanilla. Slowly pour this mixture, along with the melted butter, into the dry ingredients. Using a spoon or a rubber spatula, stir from the bottom of the bowl until the dry ingredients are all moistened. Don't overmix; a few lumps are okay.
4. Spoon the batter into the prepared muffin cups. For smaller muffins, fill the cups about four-fifths full. For larger muffins, fill them up to the top. If you have extra batter, spray one or two additional muffin cups with nonstick spray and fill with the remaining batter.
5. Bake in the middle of the oven for 20 to 25 minutes, or until a toothpick inserted into the center comes out clean. Remove the pan from the oven, then remove the muffins from the pan and place them on a rack to cool. Wait at least 30 minutes before serving.

Ginger-Pear Muffins

Studded with tiny pieces of sweet pear and even tinier bits of crystallized ginger—and laced throughout with gentle heat from grated fresh ginger—these muffins are quite heavenly.

Ripe, fresh pears are ideal for this recipe, but the canned-in-juice variety, drained well, can be your fallback. Be sure to peel the pears if they are fresh, and cut them into very small pieces (say, the size of a raisin) so their lovely, subtle flavor will be distributed well. Similarly, the crystallized ginger will also blend in better if cut really small.

- The range of sugar allows you to make these sweeter or not, according to your taste.
- Remember to grate the lemon zest before squeezing the juice.
- For protein powder and whole wheat flour options, see page 68.
- Canola oil can be substituted for some or all of the butter.

YIELD: 8 to 10 muffins
PREPARATION TIME: 15 minutes, plus 20 to 25 minutes to bake

Nonstick spray

1 cup finely chopped ripe pear
(fresh or canned, peeled if fresh)

1 tablespoon fresh lemon juice

2 cups unbleached all-purpose flour

½ teaspoon salt

1½ teaspoons baking powder

⅓ to ½ cup sugar

1 tablespoon grated lemon zest

⅓ cup very finely minced
crystallized ginger

1 cup buttermilk

1 large egg

1 to 3 teaspoons grated fresh ginger

1 teaspoon vanilla extract

4 tablespoons (½ stick) unsalted
butter, melted

1. Preheat the oven to 375°F. Lightly spray 8 standard (2½-inch-diameter) muffin cups with nonstick spray.
2. Place the chopped pear in a shallow dish, drizzle with the lemon juice, and set aside.
3. Combine the flour, salt, baking powder, sugar, and lemon zest in a medium-sized bowl. Stir in the minced crystallized ginger, then comb through the mixture with your fingers to seek out any larger pieces. Cut them into even smaller pieces with scissors. (This is far easier to do when they are coated with flour. Ideally, each bit of ginger should end up about the size of a rolled oat flake.)
4. Measure the 1 cup buttermilk into a 2-cup liquid measure. Add the egg, fresh ginger, and vanilla, and beat gently with a fork or a small whisk until smooth.
5. Slowly pour this mixture, along with the melted butter, into the dry ingredients. Using a spoon or a rubber spatula, stir from the bottom of the bowl until the dry ingredients are all moistened. Don't overmix; a few lumps are okay.
6. Spoon the batter into the prepared muffin cups. For smaller muffins, fill the cups about four-fifths full. For larger muffins, fill them up to the top. If you have extra batter, spray one or two additional muffin cups with non-stick spray and fill with the remaining batter.
7. Bake in the middle of the oven for 20 to 25 minutes, or until lightly browned on top and a toothpick inserted into the center comes out clean. Remove the pan from the oven, then remove the muffins from the pan and place them on a rack to cool. Wait at least 30 minutes before serving.

Pineapple-Coconut Muffins with crystallized ginger

Crystallized ginger, which is like a cross between a dried fruit and a candy, shares the spotlight with pineapple and coconut in these spunky muffins. The result is a real waker-upper! Serve them with cream cheese for a peak experience. You might need these often to make ordinary days feel special, so stock up that freezer.

- For protein powder and whole wheat flour options, see page 68.
- Canola oil can be substituted for some or all of the butter.

YIELD: About 10 muffins
PREPARATION TIME: 15 minutes, plus 20 to 25 minutes to bake

Nonstick spray

2½ cups unbleached all-purpose flour

¾ teaspoon salt

1½ teaspoons baking powder

2 tablespoons sugar

1 teaspoon powdered ginger

1½ cups shredded sweetened coconut

¼ cup finely minced crystallized ginger

⅔ cup coconut milk (regular or lowfat)

1 cup plus 2 tablespoons canned crushed pineapple packed in juice, undrained

1 large egg

1 tablespoon vanilla extract

3 tablespoons unsalted butter, melted

1. Preheat the oven to 400°F. Lightly spray 10 standard (2½-inch-diameter) muffin cups with nonstick spray.
2. Combine the flour, salt, baking powder, sugar, powdered ginger, and coconut in a medium-sized bowl.
3. Add the minced crystallized ginger and stir it around until coated. Then comb through the mixture with your fingers, picking up random pieces of ginger and snipping them into even smaller pieces with scissors. The ginger should be in really tiny bits, each about the size of a currant.
4. Measure the ⅔ cup coconut milk into a 4-cup liquid measure, then add the pineapple with its juice and the egg and vanilla. Beat gently with a fork or a small whisk until smooth.
5. Slowly pour this mixture, along with the butter, into the dry ingredients. Using a spoon or a rubber spatula, stir from the bottom of the bowl until the dry ingredients are all moistened. Don't overmix; a few lumps are okay.
6. Spoon the batter into the prepared muffin cups. For smaller muffins, fill the cups about four-fifths full. For larger muffins, fill them up to the top. If you have extra batter, spray one or two additional muffin cups with nonstick spray and fill with the remaining batter.
7. Bake in the middle of the oven for 20 to 25 minutes, or until lightly browned on top and a toothpick inserted into the center comes out clean. Remove the pan from the oven, then remove the muffins from the pan and place them on a rack to cool. Wait at least 30 minutes before serving.

Chocolate Ricotta Muffins

For me, this recipe has become a great option for breakfast, lunchbox, and after-school snack—sometimes all in the same day. My children love the deep, chocolaty flavor, and I love the rich wholesomeness of the ricotta and the milk. I often substitute soy protein powder for some of the flour, which makes me even happier (and which the kids don't seem to notice).

- These taste best made with whole-milk ricotta, but the lowfat variety is good as well.
- For protein powder and whole wheat flour options, see page 68.
- Canola oil can be substituted for some or all of the butter.

YIELD: **12 to 14 muffins**
PREPARATION TIME: **10 minutes, plus 20 to 25 minutes to bake**

Nonstick spray

2⅓ cups unbleached all-purpose flour

¾ teaspoon salt

2 teaspoons baking powder

6 to 8 tablespoons unsweetened cocoa

1 cup sugar

1 cup semisweet chocolate chips

1 cup ricotta cheese

2 large eggs

1⅓ cups milk

1 tablespoon vanilla extract

4 tablespoons (½ stick) unsalted butter, melted

1. Preheat the oven to 350°F. Lightly spray 12 standard (2½-inch-diameter) muffin cups with nonstick spray.
2. Combine the flour, salt, baking powder, cocoa, sugar, and chocolate chips in a medium-sized bowl.
3. Place the ricotta in a second medium-sized bowl, and add the eggs one at a time, beating well with a medium-sized whisk after each addition. Add the milk and vanilla, and whisk until thoroughly blended.
4. Pour the ricotta mixture, along with the melted butter, into the dry ingredients. Using a spoon or a rubber spatula, stir from the bottom of the bowl until the dry ingredients are all moistened. Don't overmix; a few lumps are okay.
5. Spoon the batter into the prepared muffin cups. For smaller muffins, fill the cups about four-fifths full. For larger muffins, fill them up to the top. If you have extra batter, spray one or two additional muffin cups with nonstick spray and fill with the remaining batter.
6. Bake in the middle of the oven for 20 to 25 minutes, or until lightly browned on top and a toothpick inserted into the center comes out clean. Remove the pan from the oven, then remove the muffins from the pan and place them on a rack to cool. Wait at least 30 minutes before serving.

Cherry-Vanilla Ricotta Muffins

Imagine a muffin that took Italian cheesecake lessons. In all seriousness, that's what these taste like.

- The range of sugar allows you to make these sweeter or not, according to your taste.
- These muffins taste best made with whole-milk ricotta, but the lowfat variety is good as well.
- Remember to grate the lemon zest before squeezing the juice.
- For protein powder and whole wheat flour options, see page 68.
- Canola oil can be substituted for some or all of the butter.

YIELD: 8 to 10 muffins
PREPARATION TIME: 15 minutes, plus 20 to 25 minutes to bake

Nonstick spray

2 cups unbleached all-purpose flour

½ teaspoon salt

1½ teaspoons baking powder

⅛ teaspoon baking soda

1 tablespoon grated lemon zest

½ to ⅔ cup sugar

1 cup ricotta cheese

1 cup buttermilk

2 large eggs

1 tablespoon fresh lemon juice

1 tablespoon plus ½ teaspoon vanilla extract

4 tablespoons (½ stick) unsalted butter, melted

1½ cups cherries (fresh or frozen, undefrosted), pitted and sliced, or 1 cup dried cherries

1. Preheat the oven to 350°F. Lightly spray 8 standard (2½-inch-diameter) muffin cups with nonstick spray.
2. Combine the flour, salt, baking powder, baking soda, lemon zest, and sugar in a medium-sized bowl.
3. Place the ricotta in a second medium-sized bowl, and beat in the buttermilk. Add the eggs, one at a time, beating well with a medium-sized whisk after each addition. Beat in the lemon juice and vanilla.
4. Pour the ricotta mixture, along with the melted butter and the cherries, into the dry ingredients. Using a spoon or a rubber spatula, stir from the bottom of the bowl until the dry ingredients are all moistened. Don't overmix; a few lumps are okay.
5. Spoon the batter into the prepared muffin cups. For smaller muffins, fill the cups about four-fifths full. For larger muffins, fill them up to the top. If you have extra batter, spray one or two additional muffin cups with nonstick spray and fill with the remaining batter.
6. Bake in the middle of the oven for 20 to 25 minutes, or until lightly browned on top and a toothpick inserted into the center comes out clean. (The baking time will be slightly longer if you are using frozen cherries, as they give off more liquid.) Remove the pan from the oven, then remove each muffin from the pan and place on a rack to cool. Wait at least 30 minutes before serving.

VARIATIONS   For each variation, follow the main recipe with these adjustments.

LEMON RICOTTA MUFFINS

In step 2, use up to:

- 2 tablespoons grated lemon zest

Decrease the vanilla extract to 1 tablespoon, and omit the cherries.

POPPY SEED RICOTTA MUFFINS

Add to the dry mixture in step 2:

- ¼ cup poppy seeds

Omit the cherries. You will get a slightly lower yield with this variation.

Savory Dill Ricotta Muffins

For a change of pace, these muffins have a focus that is more savory than sweet. Buttermilk gives these a tartness, fresh herbs add a subtle earthy quality, and there's just enough sugar to smooth the edges. Top them with cream cheese, thin slices of cucumber, sliced ripe tomatoes, and, if you are so inclined, smoked salmon.

- These taste best made with whole-milk ricotta, but the lowfat variety is good as well.
- For protein powder and whole wheat flour options, see page 68.
- Canola oil can be substituted for some or all of the butter.

YIELD: 8 to 10 muffins
PREPARATION TIME: 10 minutes, plus 20 to 25 minutes to bake

Nonstick spray

2 cups unbleached all-purpose flour

½ teaspoon salt (rounded measure)

1½ teaspoons baking powder

⅛ teaspoon baking soda

4 to 5 tablespoons sugar

3 tablespoons minced fresh dill

2 tablespoons minced fresh chives (if available)

1 cup ricotta cheese

1 cup buttermilk

2 large eggs

4 tablespoons (½ stick) unsalted butter, melted

1. Preheat the oven to 350°F. Lightly spray 8 standard (2½-inch-diameter) muffin cups with nonstick spray.
2. Combine the flour, salt, baking powder, baking soda, sugar, and herbs in a medium-sized bowl.
3. Place the ricotta in a second medium-sized bowl, and beat in the buttermilk. Add the eggs, one at a time, beating well with a medium-sized whisk after each addition.
4. Pour the ricotta mixture, along with the melted butter, into the dry ingredients. Using a spoon or a rubber spatula, stir from the bottom of the bowl until the dry ingredients are all moistened. Don't overmix; a few lumps are okay.
5. Spoon the batter into the prepared muffin cups. For smaller muffins, fill the cups about four-fifths full. For larger muffins, fill them up to the top. If you have extra batter, spray one or two additional muffin cups with nonstick spray and fill with the remaining batter.
6. Bake in the middle of the oven for 20 to 25 minutes, or until lightly browned on top and a toothpick inserted into the center comes out clean. Remove the pan from the oven, then remove the muffins from the pan and place them on a rack to cool. Wait at least 30 minutes before serving.

Vanilla Ricotta Muffins

Subtle and soothing, these muffins are like an old-fashioned comfort food that you can either eat fresh or pull from the freezer, defrost in the microwave, toast and butter, and then carry with you as you run out the door. Comfort, nourishment, and modern convenience are all rolled into one little handheld treat!

- These taste best made with whole-milk ricotta, but the lowfat variety is good as well.
- For protein powder and whole wheat flour options, see page 68.
- Canola oil can be substituted for some or all of the butter.

YIELD: 8 to 10 muffins
PREPARATION TIME: 10 minutes, plus 20 to 25 minutes to bake

Nonstick spray

1½ cups unbleached all-purpose flour

½ cup dry milk powder

½ teaspoon salt

1½ teaspoons baking powder

½ cup granulated sugar

¼ teaspoon cinnamon

A pinch (or a few grates) of nutmeg

2 tablespoons (packed) light brown sugar

1 cup ricotta cheese

½ cup milk

2 large eggs

1 tablespoon vanilla extract

4 tablespoons (½ stick) unsalted butter, melted

1. Preheat the oven to 350°F. Lightly spray 8 standard (2½-inch-diameter) muffin cups with nonstick spray.
2. Combine the flour, powdered milk, salt, baking powder, granulated sugar, and spices in a medium-sized bowl. Crumble in the brown sugar, rubbing it with your fingers to break up any clumps. Stir until thoroughly blended.
3. Place the ricotta in a second medium-sized bowl, and beat in the milk. Add the eggs, one at a time, beating well with a medium-sized whisk after each addition. Stir in the vanilla.
4. Pour the ricotta mixture, along with the melted butter, into the dry ingredients. Using a spoon or a rubber spatula, stir from the bottom of the bowl until the dry ingredients are all moistened. Don't overmix; a few lumps are okay.
5. Spoon the batter into the prepared muffin cups. For smaller muffins, fill the cups about four-fifths full. For larger muffins, fill them up to the top. If you have extra batter, spray one or two additional muffin cups with nonstick spray and fill with the remaining batter.
6. Bake in the middle of the oven for 20 to 25 minutes, or until lightly browned on top and a toothpick inserted into the center comes out clean. Remove the pan from the oven, then remove the muffins from the pan and place them a rack to cool. Wait at least 30 minutes before serving.

VARIATION   **MAPLE-WALNUT RICOTTA MUFFINS**

Follow the main recipe with these adjustments.

Decrease the granulated sugar to 3 tablespoons, and omit the brown sugar. Add to the flour mixture in step 2:

- ½ cup minced walnuts, lightly toasted

Reduce the milk to ¼ cup. Add to the ricotta mixture in step 3:

- ¼ cup pure maple syrup
- 1½ teaspoons maple extract

Pumpkin–Chocolate Chip Protein Bread

With vitamins and fiber from the pumpkin, staying power from the protein powder, and mood enhancement from the chocolate, you're all set!

I love feeding this bread to my family on rushed mornings, confident that they're being fueled by more than just carbohydrates. Protein quick breads are made the same way as the regular kind—they just need a little extra time in the oven. They come out with a wonderful double texture: crisp on the outside and moist on the inside.

- For information about soy protein powder, see page 68.
- Cooked sweet potato or winter squash can be substituted for the pumpkin.
- Freeze individual slices, wrapped in a heavy zip-style plastic bag, and then defrost as needed. Toasting is optional.

YIELD: 1 standard-sized loaf
PREPARATION TIME: 10 minutes, plus 45 minutes to 1 hour to bake

Nonstick spray

1 cup unbleached all-purpose flour

1 cup soy protein powder

1 teaspoon salt

2 teaspoons baking powder

½ cup sugar

1 cup semisweet chocolate chips

1 can (15 ounces) pumpkin (2 cups)

2 large eggs

2 teaspoons vanilla extract

3 tablespoons unsalted butter, melted (optional)

1. Preheat the oven to 350°F (325°F for a glass pan). Lightly spray a standard-sized loaf pan with nonstick spray.
2. Place the flour, protein powder, salt, baking powder, and sugar in a medium-sized bowl, and stir until thoroughly combined. Stir in the chocolate chips.
3. In a second bowl, combine the pumpkin, eggs, vanilla, and optional melted butter, and stir with a whisk or a fork until uniform.
4. Add the pumpkin mixture to the dry ingredients, and stir from the bottom of the bowl until everything is thoroughly blended. The batter will be stiff.
5. Transfer the batter to the prepared pan, patting it into place with a dinner knife and shaping it so that it is gently mounded in the center. Bake in the center of the oven for 45 minutes (for a damper, more puddinglike bread) to 1 hour (for a drier loaf). Cool in the pan for about 10 minutes, then rap the pan sharply to remove the bread, and cool it on a rack for at least another 20 minutes before slicing.

VARIATIONS   For each variation, follow the main recipe with these adjustments.

BANANA–CHOCOLATE CHIP PROTEIN BREAD

Replace the pumpkin with:

- 2 cups mashed ripe banana

Add with the vanilla extract in step 3:

- ¼ teaspoon almond extract

APPLESAUCE–CHOCOLATE CHIP PROTEIN BREAD

Add to the dry ingredients in step 2:

- ½ teaspoon cinnamon

Replace the pumpkin with:

- 2 cups unsweetened applesauce

Zucchini-Pecan Protein Bread

Even though zucchini is a summer squash, it is generally available year round. So not only is this delicious, green-speckled treat never out of style, it's never out of season either. If you can't get your children to eat their vegetables in the usual way, here is a back door.

- For information about soy protein powder, see page 68.
- Use the medium grating attachment of a food processor to make short work of preparing the zucchini.
- Freeze individual slices, wrapped in a heavy zip-style plastic bag—and then defrost as needed. Toasting is optional.

YIELD: **1 standard-sized loaf**
PREPARATION TIME: **20 minutes, plus 1 hour to bake**

Nonstick spray

2 cups (packed) grated zucchini (about ⅔ pound)

¾ teaspoon salt

1 cup unbleached all-purpose flour

1 cup soy protein powder

2 teaspoons baking powder

⅛ teaspoon baking soda

½ cup sugar

½ teaspoon cinnamon

¼ teaspoon nutmeg

⅔ cup buttermilk

2 large eggs, beaten

2 teaspoons vanilla extract

3 tablespoons unsalted butter, melted

½ cup chopped pecans

½ cup currants

1. Preheat the oven to 350°F (325°F for a glass pan). Lightly spray a standard-sized loaf pan with nonstick spray.
2. Place the grated zucchini in a colander in the sink, and sprinkle with ¼ teaspoon of the salt. Stir it around with a fork to distribute the salt, then let it stand for 10 minutes or longer.
3. Place the flour, protein powder, baking powder, baking soda, sugar, and spices in a medium-sized bowl, along with the remaining ½ teaspoon salt. Stir until thoroughly combined.
4. Squeeze out all excess liquid from the zucchini, and transfer it to a second bowl. Add the buttermilk, eggs, vanilla, and melted butter, and stir with a whisk or a fork until uniform.
5. Add the zucchini mixture to the dry ingredients, along with the pecans and currants. Stir from the bottom of the bowl until everything is thoroughly blended. The batter will be stiff.
6. Transfer the batter to the prepared pan, spreading it into place with a dinner knife and shaping it so that it is gently mounded in the center. Bake in the center of the oven for 1 hour, or until it feels solid and springs back when pressed firmly in the center. Cool in the pan for about 10 minutes, then rap the pan sharply to remove the bread, and cool it on a rack for at least another 20 minutes before slicing.

 THE BISCOTTI TREATMENT

Both this bread and the one on the previous page are very dense and moist—almost like sliceable puddings. If you prefer the breads to be drier, follow up with what I call the Biscotti Treatment: After the loaf cools, cut it into ¾-inch slices, and bake the slices on a baking tray coated with nonstick spray at 350°F for about 15 minutes. Cool the rebaked slices on a rack. The result is like a slice of soft cookie-cake.

Wildly Fruity Soda Bread

If you have never baked bread before, this cross between a big scone and a quick bread is the perfect place to start. It offers the best of both worlds: a resilient batter, verging on a dough, and a very tender result. Proceed with confidence!

Serve this bread with butter or, for a special treat, with an extraordinary dairy product, like clotted cream or fromage blanc, *if available. For those of you with a morning sweet tooth, this rather tart bread presents the perfect excuse to open that gift jar of exquisite preserves or marmalade you've been saving.*

- Leftover cooked grains lend a delightful chewiness and some good nutrition to this sturdy bread. I recommend brown rice, wild rice, millet, and especially barley. You can experiment here. For grain-cooking guidelines see page 46.

YIELD: 10 to 12 servings
PREPARATION TIME: 20 minutes, plus 30 to 35 minutes to bake

Nonstick spray

1 cup unbleached all-purpose flour

½ cup oat bran

½ cup cornmeal

½ teaspoon salt

¾ teaspoon baking powder

½ teaspoon baking soda

1½ teaspoons grated orange zest

1½ tablespoons brown sugar

¼ cup currants or golden raisins

¼ cup dried cranberries

¾ cup chopped tart apple
  (1 small to medium apple)

¼ cup minced prunes

1 cup cooked whole grains
  (optional)

¾ cup buttermilk

1 large egg

2 tablespoons unsalted butter,
  melted

1. Preheat the oven to 350°F (325°F for a glass pan). Lightly spray an 8- or 9-inch pie pan with nonstick spray.
2. Combine the flour, oat bran, cornmeal, salt, baking powder, baking soda, and orange zest in a medium-sized bowl. Add the brown sugar, rubbing it in with your fingers until the mixture is uniform. Stir in the fruit and optional grains.
3. Measure the ¾ cup buttermilk into a 2-cup liquid measure. Add the egg, and beat gently with a fork or a small whisk until well blended. Slowly pour this mixture into the dry ingredients, adding the melted butter at the same time. Using a spoon or a rubber spatula, stir and mash the mixture, intermittently scraping from the bottom of the bowl, until the dry ingredients are all moistened. Don't overmix; a few lumps are okay.
4. Transfer the dough to the prepared pan. Use a rubber spatula and/or your hands to shape the dough into a smooth mound. (If using your hands, lightly flour or wet them first for easier handling.)
5. Bake in the middle of the oven for 30 to 35 minutes, or until a knife inserted into the center comes out clean and the bread is golden on top. Remove to a rack to cool, then wait at least 15 minutes before slicing; otherwise it will seriously crumble.

Simplest Buttermilk Biscuits

Sometimes "flaky" is a good adjective, and these biscuits are a perfect example. Working the dough quickly with cold ingredients (butter and buttermilk) prevents the gluten in the flour from developing, yielding a very light biscuit. A food processor makes this truly fast and easy. (If you don't have a food processor, it is possible to cut the butter into the flour mixture with two forks. Work as quickly as you can, to keep the ingredients cold.)

You can eat these sooner than you can many of the other baked goods in this chapter. Just give them about 5 minutes on the cooling rack, then dig in!

• Biscuits freeze very well if wrapped in a heavy zip-style plastic bag. After defrosting, reheat or lightly toast them in a toaster oven.

YIELD: 8 to 10 medium-sized biscuits
PREPARATION TIME: 15 minutes, plus 12 to 15 minutes to bake

Nonstick spray

2 cups unbleached all-purpose flour

½ teaspoon salt

2 teaspoons baking powder

¼ teaspoon baking soda

1 tablespoon sugar (optional)

6 tablespoons cold unsalted butter

⅔ cup cold buttermilk

1. Preheat the oven to 400°F. Lightly spray a baking tray with nonstick spray.
2. Place the flour, salt, baking powder, baking soda, and optional sugar in a food processor fitted with the steel blade. Process briefly to combine them.
3. Cut the butter into thin slices and distribute them on top of the dry mixture. Using several long pulses, process until the butter is uniformly cut into the dry ingredients and the mixture resembles a coarse meal.
4. With the food processor running, pour the buttermilk directly through the feed tube and into the dough. As soon as the mixture holds together (after about 3 or 4 seconds), turn off the machine.
5. Roll or pat the dough into an 8-inch circle, ¾ inch thick. Cut free-form biscuits with a knife or, to be more traditional, with a glass. I like to use a glass that has a 2½-inch-diameter rim.
6. Bake in the center of the oven for 12 to 15 minutes, or until deep golden brown on the bottom and light golden brown on top. Cool on a rack for 5 minutes before serving.

(VARIATIONS) For each variation, follow the main recipe with these adjustments.

BUTTERMILK-BRAN BISCUITS

Reduce the flour to 1½ cups, and add to the dry mixture in step 2:

• ½ cup oat bran or unprocessed wheat bran

Reduce the buttermilk to ½ cup. The yield will be slightly lower (6 to 7 biscuits), and the baking time will be slightly longer (15 to 20 minutes).

PROTEIN POWDER BISCUITS

For information about soy protein powder, see page 68.

Reduce the flour to 1 cup, and add to the dry mixture in step 2:

• 1 cup soy protein powder

Reduce the salt slightly to a *scant* ½ teaspoon. The yield will be slightly lower (7 to 8 biscuits).

Bran Scones

Rather than calling for hand mixing, rolling, and cutting—steps that often scare people away from attempting home-baked scones—my technique is quick and user-friendly. You can mix the batter in a food processor and then make free-form scones by scooping batter directly out of the work bowl and onto the baking tray, with minimal handling and no fuss.

• Scones freeze very well if wrapped in a heavy zip-style plastic bag. After defrosting, reheat or lightly toast them in a toaster oven.

YIELD: 6 large scones or 8 smaller ones
PREPARATION TIME: 10 minutes, plus 20 minutes to bake

Nonstick spray

2 cups unbleached all-purpose flour

½ cup unprocessed wheat bran

2 teaspoons baking powder

⅛ teaspoon baking soda

½ teaspoon salt

¼ cup sugar

1 teaspoon grated lemon zest

6 tablespoons cold unsalted butter

⅔ cup cold buttermilk

1 large egg

1 teaspoon vanilla extract

½ cup currants or golden raisins

1. Preheat the oven to 375°F. Lightly spray both a baking tray and a ⅓-cup measure with nonstick spray.
2. Place the flour, bran, baking powder, baking soda, salt, sugar, and lemon zest in a food processor fitted with the steel blade. Process briefly to combine them.
3. Cut the butter into thin slices and distribute them on top of the dry mixture. Using several long pulses, process until the butter is uniformly cut into the dry ingredients, and the resulting mixture resembles a coarse meal.
4. Pour the ⅔ cup buttermilk into a 2-cup liquid measure. Add the egg and vanilla, and beat gently with a fork or a small whisk until well blended. Stir in the currants or raisins.
5. With the food processor running, pour the buttermilk mixture directly through the feed tube and into the dough. As soon as the batter comes together (after about 2 seconds), turn off the machine.
6. Remove the food processor blade. Use the sprayed ⅓-cup measure (from step 1) to reach into the work bowl and lift out a hunk of batter, then shake it out onto the prepared baking tray. Continue this process until you have 6 or 8 hunks of batter, arranged several inches apart on the tray.
7. Bake in the center of the oven for 20 minutes, or until golden brown spots appear all over. Cool on a rack for at least 15 minutes before serving.

VARIATIONS   For each variation, follow the main recipe with these adjustments.

FRUIT SCONES

In addition to the currants or golden raisin, add:

• Up to ⅓ cup chopped dried fruit (such as apricots, prunes, peaches, or pineapple)

GINGER-OAT SCONES

Replace the wheat bran with oat bran, and add to the dry mixture in step 2:

• ⅓ cup rolled oats
• ½ cup minced crystallized ginger

Corn Scones

The range of sugar in this recipe is quite wide, allowing you to make these scones more or less sweet, depending on your taste (and depending on the amount of exotic marmalade you may or may not anticipate heaping on top). If you prefer a savory version, see the Chile-Cheese Corn Scones variation that follows.

• Use a fine grade of cornmeal (not the coarser polenta) for best results.

YIELD: 6 large scones or 8 smaller ones
PREPARATION TIME: 10 minutes, plus 20 minutes to bake

Nonstick spray

1 cup unbleached all-purpose flour

1 cup cornmeal

2 teaspoons baking powder

⅛ teaspoon baking soda

½ teaspoon salt

3 to 5 tablespoons sugar

6 tablespoons cold unsalted butter

⅔ cup cold buttermilk

1 large egg

1. Preheat the oven to 375°F. Lightly spray both a baking tray and a ⅓-cup measure with nonstick spray.
2. Place the flour, cornmeal, baking powder, baking soda, salt, and sugar in a food processor fitted with the steel blade. Process briefly to combine them.
3. Cut the butter into thin slices and distribute them on top of the dry mixture. Using several long pulses, process until the butter is uniformly cut into the dry ingredients, and the resulting mixture resembles a coarse meal.
4. Pour the ⅔ cup buttermilk into a 2-cup liquid measure. Add the egg, and beat gently with a fork or a small whisk until well blended.
5. With the food processor running, pour the buttermilk mixture directly through the feed tube and into the dough. As soon as the batter comes together (after about 2 seconds), turn off the machine.
6. Proceed to form and bake scones exactly as described in steps 6 and 7 in the Bran Scones recipe on the opposite page.

VARIATIONS   For each variation, follow the main recipe with these adjustments.

CRANBERRY OR CHERRY CORN SCONES

In step 4, add:

• ½ cup dried cranberries or cherries

CORN-BERRY SCONES

In step 2, add up to:

• 1 tablespoon orange zest, chopped or grated

Replace the currants with:

• 1 cup blueberries, blackberries, or raspberries (fresh or frozen, undefrosted)

CHILE-CHEESE CORN SCONES

In step 2, use the lesser amount of sugar, and add:

• 1 tablespoon pure ground chile powder
• ⅓ cup minced green chiles (fresh or canned)
• 1 cup (packed) grated jack cheese

Replace the currants with:

• ½ cup corn kernels (fresh or frozen, defrosted if frozen)

A Few Words About Yeasted Breads

I love to work with yeasted dough, enjoying the process as much as I do the results. Yet this is the area of baking that seems to scare people the most (along with pie crust, which is discussed on page 139). Some folks assume that yeasted dough is a lot of work (it isn't) or that it's temperamental (it's not). I'm hoping, with the following recipes, to make this realm of baking more approachable to you all. But first, a pep talk.

Please don't be intimidated by yeasted dough! Let me dispel the two most common myths.

MYTH 1: YEASTED DOUGH IS TIME-CONSUMING

Yeasted dough needs at least one (and often two) rising periods. In this respect, it takes longer than batters that you just throw together and bake. However, the actual work required to put together and "handle" a yeasted dough is only about 15 minutes, on average. Plan your baking project for an afternoon or evening when you will be home anyway, doing other things. Gratification only *seems* delayed. In the meantime, a lovely physical and spiritual relationship develops between you and the dough, and that has its own tangible and intangible rewards.

MYTH 2: YEASTED DOUGH IS TEMPERAMENTAL

Yeast is sensitive to one factor: heat, which is the only thing that kills it. (When all goes well, the yeast in the dough dies only at the very end of the process—in the oven—after performing its function.) If you avoid getting the dough too hot before baking time, it should be fine. The best gauge is to be sure the liquid in which you proof the yeast is no warmer than your body temperature—which means that the liquid should feel utterly neutral in temperature when you drip a little on your wrist.

Buy yeast in bulk, if you can, and store it in a heavy zip-style plastic bag in the freezer. You can also buy yeast in packets, which should be stored in the refrigerator or the freezer. For maximum results, pay attention to the expiration date.

In all other ways, yeasted dough is actually very resilient, easy, and forgiving. It stretches and flexes and tastes delicious with a huge range of seasonings, additions, special touches, and fillings. You can freeze it—baked or unbaked—and, once it comes back to room temperature, it will behave exactly as if it were freshly made.

 THE DISCOVERY OF YEAST

No one knows exactly when people began baking yeasted bread, but the ancient Egyptians are generally credited with being the first to do so. If you think about it, there must have been leavened bread in ancient Egypt, because the Israelites had to flee without waiting for their bread to rise. According to legend, about five thousand years ago (give or take a century or two), an Egyptian baker left his bread dough out overnight. Yeast spores invaded it, unbeknownst to the baker, who, needless to say, had never heard of yeast spores. By the next morning, the dough had puffed up to twice its original volume. Undaunted, the baker just punched it down, kneaded and shaped it, and put it into the oven. The resulting bread, chewy and light, caused a sensation. Word spread, and leavened bread became the greatest thing since . . . I can't say "since sliced bread," as effective bread-slicing tools probably hadn't been perfected yet.

In the following pages you'll find recipes for yeasted flatbreads, which can be baked in the oven or on the stovetop. You'll also find a wonderful smooth, rich babka dough that serves as the basis for filled coffee cakes and sweet buns (including the classics, cinnamon buns and sticky buns). For a heartier, whole-grain experience, try the Whole-Grain Rye-Raisin Rolls and Everything Bread, which provide great texture adventures that will keep you satisfied for hours.

About Yeasted Flatbreads

Tortillas, pitas, nan, injera, mu-shu, pizza bianca, focaccia, crackers, matzoh—the most versatile breads are the flatbreads, made with or without yeast. They've been used for millennia—and in countless cultures—as utensils for scooping up all sorts of food. Their enduring popularity, now that we've had silverware for a few centuries, is a testament to how delightful flatbreads are on their own merits.

My favorite flatbread is made from a very soft yeasted dough. It's tender and flexible, with great potential for both crispness and softness, depending on how thin it is rolled and how long it is baked. You can stud the dough with tasty accoutrements, like nuts or olives, or leave it plain, so it can be wrapped around cheese or vegetables or scrambled eggs— or anything else you can think of. You can serve flatbread by itself, fresh and warm, or brushed with butter or olive oil. You can also use it as a scoop for any delicious sauce (like Creamy Tahini Sauce, page 256) or melt some cheese on top for lunch or for a midmorning snack.

Here's a rundown of some of the many ways you can augment and accessorize fresh flatbread:

ADD HERBS, SEEDS, OR SEASONINGS

- Mix minced scallions and fresh herbs directly into the dough. If you're using the food processor method (page 96), process a few handfuls of fresh herbs right into the flour.
- Knead dried herb and spice blends (page 260) into the dough and/or sprinkle them onto the bread before or after baking.
- For a deep, pungent flavor, try mixing some whole cumin seed, sesame seed, and/or minced garlic into the dough.
- A *sabsi* (fresh herb) sandwich is traditional in central Asian cuisines. Just wrap a soft, freshly baked flatbread around a bouquet of fresh mint, parsley, basil, and chives.

ADD NUTS

Don't toast the nuts first. They will toast during the baking process, and you don't want them to get too dark.

- Knead pine nuts right into the dough.
- Press coarsely chopped cashews or walnuts into the rolled-out dough as a built-in topping.

ADD TOPPINGS

Sprinkle toppings on freshly baked flatbread while it's still hot, or let it cool down a bit and use it to dip, mop, or scoop any of the following:

- Extra virgin olive oil
- Coarse salt
- Cracked pepper
- Pitted olives, coarsely chopped (olives can also be pressed into the dough before it's baked)
- Goat cheese or crumbled feta cheese
- Finely minced onions, cooked until very soft in olive oil and butter

Turn the page to get started on your flatbread adventure!

Basic Yeasted Flatbread

I have a special relationship with this recipe and with the variations on the following pages. In fact, I make these breads so often they've become a staple in my busy household. I almost always have some dough in the refrigerator, and I just tear off a handful, roll it out, and cook it on a hot griddle (or bake it into pizza) whenever my kids get hungry. They never tire of it!

- Please read "About Yeasted Flatbreads" (preceding page) to get an overview and some ideas for enhancing this dough.
- The dough comes together very easily, requiring little, if any, kneading and minimal rising time.
- You can bake the breads in the oven or cook them on the stovetop. Each method takes about 10 minutes after preheating. Keep finished ones warm by wrapping them tightly in foil.
- The dough can be refrigerated in an airtight container or plastic bag for a day or two before being shaped and baked. It may acquire a slight sourdough flavor, which is actually quite nice.

YIELD: **Eight 7- to 8-inch flatbreads**
PREPARATION TIME: **10 minutes, plus about 1¾ hours to rise and bake**

1 cup wrist-temperature water

1¼ teaspoons yeast (half a package)

1 tablespoon olive oil or unsalted butter, melted (plus extra for brushing the breads)

¾ teaspoon salt

2¼ cups unbleached all-purpose flour, plus more for handling the dough

Nonstick spray

Butter for the griddle (optional)

Cornmeal (optional)

Coarse salt (optional)

1. Place the water in a medium-sized bowl. Sprinkle in the yeast, and let it stand for 5 minutes. Stir in the olive oil or melted butter and the salt.
2. Add 1 cup of the flour, whisking until it is incorporated. Switch to a wooden spoon, and mix in the remaining flour. Lightly flour your hand and knead the dough, still in the bowl, for a minute or two, or until the dough is smooth. (It will be quite soft.)
3. Gently lift the dough, spray the bowl underneath it with nonstick spray, and then put the dough back down. Lightly spray its top surface with nonstick spray as well. Cover the bowl with a clean tea towel, and leave it in a warm place for about 1½ hours, or until doubled in bulk.
4. When the dough has risen, lightly flour your fist, punch down the dough, and turn it out onto a clean, floured work surface. The dough will be very soft and slightly wet. Use a knife or kitchen scissors to cut the dough into 8 equal pieces, then briefly shape each piece into a ball with your hands. Let the balls rest for 5 minutes.

 FOOD PROCESSOR METHOD

You can make the flatbread dough in a food processor. This really saves time!

1. Place the water in a measuring cup, and sprinkle in the yeast. After 5 minutes, add the olive oil or melted butter.
2. Place all the flour and the salt in a food processor fitted with the steel blade, and turn on the machine. Whisk the liquid mixture from the bottom, then pour it in through the feed tube all at once, while the motor is running. The dough will come together quickly. As soon as it does, turn off the machine. Turn the dough out on a floured surface, knead briefly, and then transfer to a bowl. Proceed with step 3 of the main recipe.

FRESHLY BAKED BREAD ON WORK MORNINGS

Fortify your soul and warm your hands with freshly baked bread as you run out the door! How? Freeze the unbaked, rolled-out flatbreads, and then pull them out one at a time to bake or cook on a griddle in just minutes, without defrosting them first.

To freeze, line a plate with plastic wrap and place a rolled-out, unbaked flatbread on top. Lay a piece of plastic wrap on top of the bread, and continue layering plastic wrap and rolled-out breads. Seal the whole thing in a heavy zip-style plastic bag, and place it in the freezer for about 45 minutes. Remove the plate and plastic wrap, put the separately frozen breads back in the bag, seal it up, and return it to the freezer. They will keep for a month or longer, and you can bake them as needed, one at a time, straight from the freezer. Just follow step 6, baking or cooking the frozen breads as if the dough were freshly made. (Hint: Begin preheating the griddle or oven when you wake up.) Because the breads are so thin, the fact that they are frozen does not increase their cooking time.

5. Generously flour a rolling pin and the work surface, and without kneading or handling the "rested" balls, roll each one into a very thin circle 7 to 8 inches in diameter. The breads are now ready to cook on a griddle or bake.

6. GRIDDLE METHOD: Preheat a griddle or a heavy skillet (ideally cast iron) over medium heat for a good 5 minutes, then spray it lightly with nonstick spray. You can also melt in some butter. Lay the breads flat on the hot griddle, and cook for 3 to 4 minutes, or until golden spots appear on the bottom surface. Brush with a little olive oil or melted butter, turn the breads over, and cook for 2 to 3 minutes on the second side.

   OVEN METHOD: Preheat the oven to 450°F. Spray a baking tray with non-stick spray or sprinkle it lightly with cornmeal or flour. Lay the breads flat on the tray, and bake for about 5 minutes. Turn them over and bake for 5 minutes more, or until golden brown in spots but still supple.

7. Brush the tops with olive oil or melted butter, and sprinkle with a little coarse salt, if desired. Serve hot or warm.

Quinoa and Soy Flatbread

You can vary the basic flatbread recipe on the previous pages to include quinoa flour and soy protein powder, which give the bread a complex, toasty flavor and greater protein content. This version makes a dense, spongy dough that will not rise as much. However, it will roll out just as thin as the regular dough, and the final product will be just as tender.

- Please read "About Yeasted Flatbreads" (page 95) and the Basic Yeasted Flatbread recipe (page 96) to get an overview and some serving ideas.
- For information about protein powder, see page 68. Soy flour can be substituted for up to half of the protein powder.

YIELD: Eight 7- to 8-inch flatbreads
PREPARATION TIME: 10 minutes, plus about 1¾ hours to rise and bake

1½ cups wrist-temperature water

1¼ teaspoons yeast (half a package)

1 tablespoon sugar

1 tablespoon olive oil or unsalted butter, melted (plus extra for brushing the breads)

¾ teaspoon salt

½ cup quinoa

½ cup soy protein powder

1 cup unbleached all-purpose flour, plus more for handling the dough

Nonstick spray

Butter for the griddle (optional)

Cornmeal (optional)

Coarse salt (optional)

1. Place the water in a medium-sized bowl. Sprinkle in the yeast and sugar, and let it stand for 5 minutes. Stir in the olive oil or melted butter and the salt.
2. Place the quinoa in an electric spice grinder or a blender, and grind to a fine powder. Measure out half of this quinoa flour and whisk it into the water mixture, along with the protein powder. Add the all-purpose flour and mix it in, first with a spoon and then with your hand. Lightly flour your hand, and knead the dough directly in the bowl for a minute or two, or until the dough is smooth. (It will be quite spongy.)
3. Continue with step 3 of the recipe for Basic Yeasted Flatbread (preceding pages).

> **VARIATION** · **MILLET, QUINOA, AND SOY CRACKERBREAD**
>
> This variation makes 8 slightly larger (8- to 10-inch) flatbreads. Prepare the main recipe on this page. Preheat the oven to 475°F. Have ready:
>
> - 1 cup Fluffy Quinoa and Millet (page 46)
>
> During step 4 (page 96), briefly knead 2 tablespoons of the cooked grain mixture into each ball of dough. Also knead in a little extra flour if the dough becomes too sticky. (The cooked grains will slightly increase the moisture content.)
>
> Roll each ball into a very thin circle 8 to 10 inches in diameter. Bake in the center of the oven (on a baking tray lightly sprayed with nonstick spray) for 8 to 10 minutes, or until brown and crisp around the edges.

Yogurt Nan

Nan, sometimes spelled naan, is the traditional flatbread of almost every country in the huge region stretching from India through central Asia. Authentic nan is made by slapping a circle of soft, leavened dough directly onto the inner wall of a hot clay oven known as a tandoor oven, where the bread puffs up and acquires a smoky oven flavor and a terrific crust. The bread is then carefully peeled off the oven wall with a long metal rod and served hot. I assume that you don't have such a setup in your kitchen, so try baking these in the oven on a pizza stone or on the stovetop in a cast-iron skillet to infuse the bread with similar character.

- Whole-milk yogurt is best for this dough, but lowfat yogurt will also work.
- Please read "About Yeasted Flatbreads" (page 95) and the Basic Yeasted Flatbread recipe (page 96) to get an overview and some serving ideas.

YIELD: Eight 7- to 8-inch flatbreads
PREPARATION TIME: 10 minutes, plus about 1¾ hours to rise and bake

---

¼ cup wrist-temperature water

1¼ teaspoons yeast (half a package)

A pinch of sugar

1 cup plain yogurt

1 tablespoon olive oil or unsalted butter, melted (plus extra for brushing the breads)

¾ teaspoon salt

2 cups plus 2 tablespoons unbleached all-purpose flour, plus more for handling the dough

Nonstick spray

Butter for the griddle (optional)

Cornmeal (optional)

Coarse salt (optional)

1. Place the water in a medium-sized bowl. Sprinkle in the yeast and sugar, and let it stand for 5 minutes. Add the yogurt, olive oil or melted butter, and salt, and whisk until smooth.
2. Continue with step 2 of the recipe for Basic Yeasted Flatbread (pages 96 and 97).

Babka Dough

Babkas are remarkably versatile yeasted coffee cakes that can literally embrace countless enhancements and fill-
ings. Once you've made the dough and the filling of your choice, simply roll them together, let it rise, and bake it
to perfection. Here's the basic dough recipe, followed by recipes for my three favorite fillings. Instructions for
assembling a babka are on page 104.

- Whole-milk yogurt is best for this dough, but lowfat yogurt will also work.
- The instructions call for hand mixing, but you can mix the dough in an electric mixer with the dough hook attachment, if you prefer.
- To save on labor, make a double batch and freeze half the dough for a future adventure. (This is especially easy if you use an electric mixer with the dough hook attachment.)
- To give the dough a mild sourdough flavor, refrigerate it for at least 2 days before using. See the refrigeration instructions in the box on the opposite page.

YIELD: Dough for 1 large babka or 1 batch of buns (pages 105 through 107)
PREPARATION TIME: 15 minutes, plus about 1 hour to rise

¼ cup wrist-temperature water

1¼ teaspoons yeast (half a package)

3 tablespoons sugar

1¼ teaspoons salt

½ cup plain yogurt

1 large egg, beaten

3 tablespoons unsalted butter, melted

About 2⅓ cups unbleached all-purpose flour

Nonstick spray

1. Place the water in a medium to large bowl. Sprinkle in the yeast, and let it stand for about 5 minutes.
2. Whisk the sugar, salt, yogurt, egg, and melted butter into the yeast mixture.
3. Add 2 cups of the flour, 1 cup at a time, beating after the first addition with a large whisk and after the second with a wooden spoon. Add approximately ⅓ cup more flour, mixing it in with your hands. As the dough comes together, you might need to add tiny amounts of additional flour—or nonstick spray—to both your hand and the dough to prevent sticking. (Keep the flour to a minimum so the dough can remain soft.)
4. Knead the dough, still in the bowl, until all the flour is incorporated. You should end up with a soft, smooth, slightly sticky dough.
5. Lift the dough and spray the bowl underneath with nonstick spray. Then set the dough back in the bowl, and spray the top with nonstick spray. Cover the bowl with a clean tea towel, and leave it in a warm place to rise for an hour or longer, until it has increased in bulk by 50 to 75 percent. Proceed with filling and assembling the babka or buns (pages 105 through 107). Note: At this point, you can also refrigerate or freeze the dough for later use. Instructions are on the opposite page.

VARIATION   PROTEIN-ENRICHED BABKA DOUGH

This variation, made with protein powder and soy and quinoa flours, is quite delicious! Use it just as you would the basic dough. The results will be denser and more compact and might just leave you feeling satisfied for longer.

For information about soy protein powder, see page 68. To make your own quinoa flour, simply grind quinoa for a few seconds in an electric spice grinder or a blender.

Follow steps 1 and 2 of the main recipe, replacing the yogurt with milk and reducing the salt to ½ teaspoon. Beat into the yeast mixture:

- ½ cup soy flour
- ½ cup soy protein powder

It will look and feel more like a batter than a dough at this point. Then stir and knead in:

- ½ cup quinoa flour
- ½ cup unbleached all-purpose flour

The mixture will become more doughlike as the flour is incorporated. Proceed with step 4 of the main recipe.

TO REFRIGERATE OR FREEZE BABKA DOUGH

If you want to make babka dough that you can assemble and bake at another time, punch down the risen dough and knead it briefly. Transfer it to a heavy-duty zip-style plastic bag or a lidded container at least twice as large as the dough. If using a plastic bag, press out any air, then tightly seal the bag, leaving as much deflated space inside as possible. (The dough will continue to rise when it is cold, although this will happen very slowly.) If using a plastic container, spray the inside surface and the lid with nonstick spray, and make sure the lid fits tightly.

- REFRIGERATE the dough for up to 4 days, during which time it will acquire a slightly sour flavor. (This is great for sourdough aficionados!)

- FREEZE the dough for up to a month. Defrost it thoroughly in the bag or container before using. The dough will become slightly wet as it returns to room temperature. Knead in a little extra flour, if necessary, but keep the flour to a minimum so the dough will stay soft.

MY THREE FAVORITE BABKA FILLINGS

Satisfaction guaranteed! Use these filling recipes, or create your own. Rule of thumb: You can fill a babka with just about anything you desire, as long as it fits, makes "taste sense," and is tightly sealed inside the dough.

• The Babka Dough recipe is on page 100. The method for assembling and baking the babka is on page 104.

YIELD: Each makes enough for 1 babka (page 104)
PREPARATION TIME: Varies according to recipe

Chocolate Babka Filling PREPARATION TIME: 5 minutes

You can make this a pure chocolate affair or augment it with some or all of the optional enhancements. It's wonderful all ways!

3 tablespoons unsweetened cocoa

5 tablespoons sugar

1½ tablespoons unsalted butter, softened or melted, for spreading on the dough

1 cup semisweet chocolate chips

OPTIONAL ADDITIONS

Cinnamon (up to 1 teaspoon)

Shredded unsweetened coconut (up to ½ cup)

Minced or ground nuts (up to ½ cup)

1 tablespoon grated orange zest

Minced dried fruit (up to ½ cup)

1. Combine the cocoa and sugar in a small bowl.
2. Form the Babka Dough into a rectangle, as directed on page 104, steps 1 and 2. Spread the softened or melted butter over the dough, leaving a half-inch border all around the edges. Sprinkle the cocoa mixture over the butter. (If you have extra, save it for the top.) Scatter the chocolate chips—and any optional additions—over the cocoa.
3. Roll up the dough and finish the babka as directed on page 104, steps 3 through 6. Sprinkle any leftover cocoa mixture over the top before baking.

Frangipane Babka Filling

PREPARATION TIME: 10 minutes

Frangipane is an almond cream. In this recipe, the creaminess comes from eggs. The optional dried cherries make it truly deluxe.

1 cup whole almonds

2 tablespoons unbleached
    all-purpose flour

¼ cup granulated sugar

¼ teaspoon salt (scant measure)

¼ cup (packed) brown sugar

½ teaspoon vanilla extract

¼ teaspoon almond extract

2 large eggs, beaten

1 cup dried sour cherries (optional)

1. Place the almonds, flour, granulated sugar, and salt in a food processor fitted with the steel blade. Process until everything combines into a powder. Transfer to a bowl.
2. Add the remaining ingredients, and mix until thoroughly combined.
3. Use as the filling for a babka, as directed on the following page, step 3.

Poppy Seed Babka Filling

PREPARATION TIME: 10 minutes, plus 1 hour to stand

In this traditional East European mixture, poppy seeds, sugar, citrus, and vanilla are folded into cream cheese—and the result is rich, bittersweet, and slightly crunchy.

This filling needs to rest for about an hour for the flavors to meld. Make it right after you make the dough, so it can stand while the dough rises.

¾ cup cream cheese, softened

⅓ cup poppy seeds

¼ cup sugar

⅛ teaspoon salt

2 tablespoons unbleached
    all-purpose flour

2 tablespoons grated orange zest
    and/or lemon zest

1 teaspoon vanilla extract

1 large egg, beaten

1. Place the cream cheese in a small to medium bowl, and add the poppy seeds, sugar, salt, flour, and zest. Mash with a fork until well combined.
2. Add the vanilla and egg, and mix thoroughly. Let the filling stand at room temperature for about an hour.
3. Use as the filling for a babka, as directed on the following page, step 3.

How to Assemble and Bake a Babka

Once you've made the babka dough and your chosen filling, you're ready to put it all together. (The dough and filling recipes are on the preceding four pages.)

- The assembled, unbaked babka can be frozen—right on the baking tray—for several days. Wrap and seal the whole tray in a heavy plastic bag. To bake, place the tray in the preheated oven without defrosting the babka first. This really works!
- You can also freeze the baked babka in *slices,* so you can defrost and enjoy individual servings. (If wrapped airtight in a heavy plastic bag, they will keep in the freezer for a month.)

YIELD: **16 servings (1 large babka)**
PREPARATION TIME: **About 15 minutes (once Babka Dough and filling are made), plus about 1¾ hours to rise and bake**

Nonstick spray

Babka Dough (page 100)

Flour for handling the dough
(as needed)

Babka filling of your choice
(preceding pages)

1 medium egg, beaten (optional)

1. Lightly spray a baking tray and a clean work surface with nonstick spray, and set the tray aside. Lightly spray your fist with nonstick spray as well, and punch down the risen dough. Transfer it to the prepared work surface, and let the dough rest for about 5 minutes.

2. Without handling or kneading, gently stretch the rested dough into a rectangle approximately 10 by 16 inches. If it's too sticky to handle, add a little nonstick spray to your hands or a very light sprinkling of flour to the dough.

3. Spread or sprinkle your chosen filling liberally over the rectangle, leaving a half-inch border of dough all around the edges. Slowly roll up the dough on the long side, gently pulling and stretching the dough over the filling. Pinch the seam tightly closed.

4. Carefully transfer the filled "log" to the prepared baking tray, seam side down. (Curve the babka, if necessary, to make it fit.) Leave it in a warm place for about 1 hour. It will rise only slightly. During this time, preheat the oven to 350°F.

5. Bake in the center of the oven for 35 to 40 minutes, or until the babka is lightly browned on the edges and feels hollow when gently squeezed or thumped. (For a lovely golden crust, you can brush the top with beaten egg 15 minutes into the baking.)

6. Remove the tray from the oven, and transfer the babka to a rack to cool for at least 30 minutes before serving.

Lemon-Glazed Rosemary/Lavender Raisin Buns

Sweet raisins, an intense dose of lemon zest, and the otherworldly, aromatic presence of rosemary and lavender make these buns a great reason to get out of bed in the morning. The finishing touch is an exquisite lemon glaze, which, although barely visible, gives a startling hit of additional flavor.

These buns freeze well and defrost very quickly. Toasting is unnecessary and may cause the raisins and glaze to burn.

- Prepare the lemon zest before juicing the lemons: Shave off the outermost peel with a vegetable peeler, then chop the shavings into smaller pieces with a sharp knife.
- You can use fresh or dried rosemary leaves. If using fresh, be sure to chop them into tiny pieces.
- If you are lucky enough to have access to fresh lavender, you can use the leaves and/or the flowers, also finely chopped. Dried lavender will also work.

YIELD: **16 medium-sized buns**
PREPARATION TIME: **15 to 20 minutes of intermittent work (once Babka Dough is made),**
plus about 1¼ hours to rise and bake

Nonstick spray

½ cup golden raisins

¼ cup fresh lemon juice

Babka Dough (page 100)

1 tablespoon unsalted butter, softened

3 tablespoons chopped lemon zest

1½ tablespoons crumbled rosemary and/or lavender

LEMON GLAZE

½ cup powdered sugar

1 tablespoon fresh lemon juice

1. Lightly spray two 8- or 9-inch round cake pans or a baking tray—plus a clean, dry work surface—with nonstick spray.
2. Place the raisins and lemon juice in a small bowl, and heat together in a microwave oven for about 40 seconds. Remove and set aside.
3. Spray your fist lightly with nonstick spray, punch down the risen dough, and transfer it to the prepared work surface. Let the dough rest for about 5 minutes, then without further handling, gently stretch it into a rectangle approximately 10 by 16 inches. If the dough is too sticky to handle, add a little nonstick spray to your hands. Use a rubber spatula to spread the dough with the softened butter, leaving a ½-inch border around the edge.
4. Sprinkle the buttered area with the chopped lemon zest, crumbled herbs, and plumped raisins. Roll the dough up into a firm log, and pinch the seam tightly closed.
5. Cut the log into 16 equal slices, and stand them on end about 2 inches apart in the prepared pans or on the tray. Cover the pans or tray loosely with a clean tea towel, and let stand in a warm place for about 1 hour. The buns will increase in bulk by 50 to 75 percent. During this time, preheat the oven to 350°F.
6. Place the pans or tray in the center of the preheated oven and bake for 15 to 20 minutes, or until the buns are lightly browned on the edges and sound hollow when thumped. Transfer the hot buns to a plate or a platter.
7. To make the glaze, sift the powdered sugar into a small bowl, and stir in the lemon juice. Use a small spoon to drizzle some of this mixture onto each bun. It will be thin and subtle—barely visible—but will coat the buns, soaking in slightly. Wait about 20 minutes before serving.

Cinnamon Buns

Cinnamon buns are the first stop on the road to sticky buns (opposite page), but they are so good on their own, you may choose to go no further.

- Soy nuts (the kind sold as a snack in the bins at the natural food store) add texture and some protein to the filling. Grind them to a fine powder in an electric spice grinder or a blender.

YIELD: 16 medium-sized buns
PREPARATION TIME: 15 to 20 minutes of intermittent work (once Babka Dough is made),
plus about 1¼ hours to rise and bake

Nonstick spray

Babka Dough (page 100)

1 tablespoon unsalted butter, softened

1 teaspoon cinnamon

2 tablespoons sugar

2 to 3 tablespoons ground soy nuts (optional)

1. Lightly spray two 8- or 9-inch round cake pans or a baking tray—plus a clean, dry work surface—with nonstick spray. If you'll be making Sticky Buns (see the next recipe), use cake pans rather than a baking tray.

2. Spray your fist lightly with nonstick spray, punch down the risen dough, and transfer it to the prepared work surface. Let the dough rest for about 5 minutes, then without further handling, gently stretch it into a rectangle approximately 10 by 16 inches. If the dough is too sticky to handle, add a little nonstick spray to your hands.

3. Use a rubber spatula to spread the dough with the softened butter, leaving a ½-inch border around the edge.

4. Place the cinnamon, sugar, and ground soy nuts in a small bowl, stir until thoroughly combined, and sprinkle this mixture liberally over the buttered area. Roll up the dough on the long side into a firm log, and pinch the seam tightly closed.

5. Cut the log into 16 equal slices, and stand them on end about 2 inches apart in the prepared pans or on the tray. (If you have leftover cinnamon sugar, you can fill the crevices of the buns with it. Focus this process on the end pieces, which tend to get shortchanged on the filling.)

6. Cover the pans or tray loosely with a clean tea towel, and let stand in a warm place for about 1 hour. The buns will increase in bulk by 50 to 75 percent. During this time, preheat the oven to 350°F.

7. After the buns have risen, gently lift each one, and spray the pan or tray directly underneath with a little additional nonstick spray. Place the pans or tray in the center of the oven, and bake for 15 to 20 minutes, or until the buns are lightly browned on the edges and they feel light and hollow when squeezed or thumped. Remove them from the oven.

8. Use tongs to gently lift and invert each bun onto a rack or a plate. (Some of the cinnamon sugar might have leaked out the bottom of the buns and caramelized onto the baking surface, creating a delicious crust. Scrape this up and spread it back onto the buns while they're still hot. It's the best part!) Cool for about 20 minutes before serving.

Sticky Buns

If you prefer cinnamon buns to be voluptuously drenched in nut-studded syrup, this recipe is for you. Treat yourself to these on a morning when you know you've got a full, busy schedule ahead of you. Talk about stoked! That word was invented by someone who had sticky buns for breakfast.

- The syrup is very hot when it first comes out of the oven. Please be careful, and keep children away until it cools to a comfortable temperature.

YIELD: 16 medium-sized buns
PREPARATION TIME: 15 to 20 minutes of intermittent work (once Cinnamon Buns are made), plus about 1¼ hours to rise and bake

10 tablespoons (1 stick plus 2 tablespoons) unsalted butter

1 cup (packed) brown sugar

¾ cup light corn syrup or pure maple syrup

¾ cup pecans and/or walnuts, coarsely chopped

Cinnamon Buns (preceding recipe), prepared through step 4

Nonstick spray

1. Place the butter in a small to medium saucepan and slowly melt it over low heat. Add the brown sugar, stirring until the sugar melts.

2. As soon as the sugar is liquefied, add the syrup, continuing to stir over low heat for just a few seconds longer, until the syrup is incorporated and the mixture is uniform. Remove from the heat right away—don't let it cook further. (If it comes to a boil, it will start turning into candy, which tastes good but wouldn't serve our purpose here.)

3. Divide the syrup between the two prepared cake pans. Divide the chopped pecans and/or walnuts between the pans as well, sprinkling them directly into the syrup.

4. Cut the rolled Cinnamon Bun log into 16 equal slices, and stand them on end, about 2 inches apart, in the pans, on top of the nuts and syrup. Cover the pans loosely with a clean tea towel, and let stand in a warm place for about 1 hour. The buns will increase in bulk by 50 to 75 percent. During this time, preheat the oven to 350°F.

5. Bake in the center of the oven for 15 to 20 minutes, or until the tops and edges of the buns turn golden brown. During this time, spray a serving platter with nonstick spray. This will keep the finished buns from sticking to the plate.

6. When the buns come out of the oven, use tongs to gently lift and invert each one onto the sprayed platter. Spoon the extra syrup over the tops of the buns. (Don't worry if it runs over and puddles on the plate. This will be fun to eat when it cools.) Wait at least 20 minutes before serving. Sticky buns taste best if eaten within about 2 hours of baking.

Whole-Grain Rye-Raisin Rolls

Whole rye is a rich source of "high water bonding–capacity fiber." Translated into the vernacular, this means that rye-based breads have a tendency to make us feel fuller and more satisfied than we might after eating other types of breads. Yet filling though these rolls are, you'll be surprised by their lightness and subtle chewiness. Eat them plain, or make them into petite sandwiches, spread with nut butter and jam or stuffed with a little cheese.

- Cook the rye berries well ahead of time. (Guidelines are on page 47.)
- If you'd like the finished rolls to have a lovely, rich sheen, give them the egg yolk wash. It's a very special touch. You can use the whites to make Scrambled Egg Whites (page 122).

YIELD: 18 to 20 medium-sized rolls
PREPARATION TIME: 30 minutes of intermittent work, plus about 2½ hours to rise and bake

1½ cups wrist-temperature water

2½ teaspoons yeast (1 package)

3 tablespoons molasses

3 cups rye flour

About 4 cups unbleached all-purpose flour, plus more for handling the dough

2 tablespoons pure maple syrup

2 teaspoons salt

2 tablespoons unsalted butter, melted or softened

1½ cups cooked whole rye berries

¾ cup (packed) raisins

Nonstick spray

Cornmeal

OPTIONAL EGG WASH

2 egg yolks

1 tablespoon cold water

1. Place the water in a large bowl and sprinkle in the yeast. Add 1 drop of the molasses and let stand 5 minutes.

2. Add 1 cup each of the rye flour and all-purpose flour, and beat with a whisk until all the flour is absorbed. Cover with a clean tea towel, and let the dough rise for about 30 minutes.

3. Add the remaining molasses along with the maple syrup, salt, and butter, and beat with a whisk until these ingredients are incorporated. Switch to a wooden spoon, and stir in the cooked whole rye berries and the raisins. Add the remaining 2 cups rye flour, 1 cup at a time, stirring well after each addition.

4. When you've added all of the rye flour, begin adding the remaining 3 cups all-purpose flour, 1 cup at a time, mixing well after each. At some point, you will need to graduate from the wooden spoon to mixing with your hand. Keep adding flour and mixing until you have a uniform dough.

5. Lightly flour a clean, dry surface, turn the dough out onto it, and knead it for about 3 minutes, or until it starts to feel smooth and elastic. If your kitchen is humid, you might need to add a little extra flour to achieve the right texture. The dough should be soft and supple but not sticky—ideally, it should feel similar to your earlobe.

6. Clean out the bowl (wash and dry it, or just wipe it out), and spray it with nonstick spray. Return the kneaded dough to the bowl, and spray the top of the dough with nonstick spray. Cover the bowl with a clean tea towel, and let it stand in a warm place for about 1½ hours, or until the dough

rises by about 50 to 75 percent. (It doesn't have to double in bulk.)

7. Generously sprinkle a baking tray with cornmeal. Lightly spray the work surface with nonstick spray, punch down the dough, and turn it out onto the work surface. Without further kneading, cut the dough into 18 to 20 equal pieces. Pushing with the palm of your hand against the work surface, roll each piece into a small, tight ball. Place the rolls on the prepared tray, cover them with the towel, and leave them in a warm place for about 30 minutes. (The rolls will increase in size only slightly.) During this time, preheat the oven to 350°F.

8. To give the rolls an egg wash, place the egg yolks in a small bowl and beat with a fork until smooth, adding the cold water as you go. Brush this glaze over the top surface of the unbaked rolls, then place the tray in the center of the oven. Bake for 20 to 25 minutes, or until they are golden brown all over and give off a hollow sound when thumped. Transfer to a rack immediately, and allow them to cool for at least 20 minutes before serving.

FRESH-BAKED ROLLS FOR BREAKFAST

To enjoy fresh-baked rolls in the morning, make the recipe through step 7 up to 2 days ahead of time. Wrap and seal the tray of unbaked rolls in a large plastic bag (such as a medium-sized garbage bag), and refrigerate. In the morning, just preheat the oven and bake the rolls straight out of the refrigerator. You can also freeze the baked rolls for up to a month if they're sealed, airtight, in a heavy zip-style plastic bag.

RYE'S ROOTS

Why is rye bread traditional in almost all the cold regions of northern and eastern Europe? Because the grain comes from a wild, feisty plant that survives well in severe climates. Most likely brought to the New World by Dutch and German settlers (and first planted in Nova Scotia), rye became widely cultivated in America, not because the grain itself, or breads made from it, were so popular, but rather because rye *whiskey* became all the rage. To this day, whiskey production remains rye's primary purpose in North America.

Everything Bread

Literally filled to capacity with cooked whole grains, sunflower seeds, and raisins, this bread is truly like having a bowl of cooked cereal and a big piece of toast all rolled into one.

Any cooked grains will work for this recipe. My favorite combination is oat groats, wild rice, and quinoa. The groats are chewy and somewhat sweet, and the other two are pleasantly bitter, which gives them a meaningful relationship with the raisins.

- Cook the grains well ahead of time. (Guidelines are on page 46.)
- Heat the milk in advance, so it will have time to cool to room temperature.
- You can substitute homemade quinoa flour for up to 1 cup of the flour. Just grind 1 cup quinoa in an electric spice grinder or a blender until it becomes a fine meal, and proceed.
- If you slice the bread and then freeze the slices in a heavy, zip-style plastic bag, you can defrost and toast individual slices as desired.

YIELD: 1 large loaf or 2 smaller ones
PREPARATION TIME: 30 minutes of intermittent work, plus about 2¾ hours to rise and bake

---

1½ cups milk (soy milk will also work)

2½ teaspoons yeast (1 package)

1 tablespoon honey or pure maple syrup

2 tablespoons canola oil or unsalted butter, softened or melted

2¼ teaspoons salt

About 4 cups unbleached all-purpose flour, plus more for handling the dough

3 cups cooked whole grains

1 cup sunflower seeds

1 cup (packed) raisins

Nonstick spray

Cornmeal

Additional canola oil or melted butter (optional)

1. (Do this ahead of time.) Gradually heat the milk in a small saucepan until it becomes very hot but is not yet boiling. Remove the pan from the heat, and set it aside to cool to wrist temperature.

2. When the milk has cooled to a temperature no warmer than your wrist, sprinkle in the yeast and let it stand for 5 minutes.

3. Stir in the honey or syrup, oil, and salt. Add 1 cup of the flour, and beat with a whisk until it is incorporated. Switch to a wooden spoon, and stir in the cooked grains, sunflower seeds, and raisins.

4. Add the remaining flour, 1 cup at a time, mixing well after each addition. At some point, you will need to graduate from the wooden spoon to mixing with your hand. Keep adding flour and mixing until you have a uniform dough. The grains will appear to be bursting out of the dough, but don't worry. They'll stay in there.

5. Lightly flour a clean, dry surface. Turn the dough out onto it, and knead for about 3 minutes, or until the dough starts to feel smooth and elastic. If your kitchen is humid, you might need to add a little extra flour to achieve the right texture. The dough should be soft and supple but not sticky—ideally, it should feel similar to your ear lobe.

6. Clean out the bowl (wash and dry it, or just wipe it out), and spray it with nonstick spray. Return the kneaded dough to the bowl, and spray the top of the dough with nonstick spray. Cover the bowl with a tea towel, and let it stand in a warm place for about 1½ hours, or until the dough rises by about 50 to 75 percent. (It doesn't have to double in bulk.)

SUNFLOWER SEEDS: THE FRUIT OF THE GREAT FLORAL DISC

Native to the Americas—and prominent in Native American cuisine, religion, and folklore—the sunflower has been raised for its rich, nourishing seeds for centuries. With flowers ranging up to 2 feet in diameter, a single plant can produce hundreds of kernels per season. Each kernel holds a powerful seed containing superior nutritional attributes, including high-quality protein, healthful unsaturated fat, significant amounts of vitamins A and D, more B vitamins than an equivalent amount of wheat germ, and vitamins E and K. Of course, because sunflower seeds are tiny, one has to eat quite a few of them to reap the benefits. Try toasting the seeds and then pressing a small handful onto a piece of freshly buttered bread as a crunchy topping. Or grind the seeds into a butter in the blender, like peanut butter, and use it as a spread. It's tremendously good for you!

7. Generously sprinkle a baking tray with cornmeal. Lightly flour the work surface, punch down the dough, and turn it out onto the work surface. Knead the dough for about 5 minutes, adding only as much flour as you absolutely need to prevent the dough from sticking. Form the dough into a large round or oval loaf (or 2 smaller ones), and transfer to the prepared baking tray. Cover loosely with the tea towel and set in a warm place to rest for 35 to 40 minutes. During this time, preheat the oven to 350°F.

8. If you prefer a softer crust, brush the top surface of the bread with a little oil or melted butter. Bake in the center of the oven for 40 minutes (for 1 large loaf) or 35 minutes (for 2 smaller loaves), or until the bread is lightly browned all over and gives off a hollow sound when thumped. (For a softer crust, you can cover the bread loosely with a piece of foil about halfway through the baking.) Transfer the bread to a rack as soon as it comes out of the oven, and let it cool for at least 30 minutes before slicing.

5

EGGS, TOFU, SCRAMBLES, QUICHES & SOUFFLÉS

CONTENTS

EGGS, TOFU, SCRAMBLES, QUICHES & SOUFFLÉS

A hen is only an egg's way of making another egg.
—Samuel Butler

Building upon Mr. Butler's egg-centric statement, I want to make a case for eggs. An egg is a glorious thing: inexpensive, quick to prepare, delicious, satisfying, and a good keeper. To me, eggs are a wonderful reminder of the genius of nature—so basic and accessible and so nutritionally rich.

Eggs have very high "nutrient to calorie" ratio, providing high-quality protein, all of the vitamins except C, lutein and zeaxanthin (good for eye health), choline (good for brain function and fetal development), and many other important minerals, including iron and zinc. And eggs contain these chemicals in a highly "bioavailable" form, so we can absorb nutrients more easily from eggs than from vegetables or other foods.

Despite the fact that eggs are so healthful, in recent years they have been stigmatized as being "too high in cholesterol" and have thus fallen out of general nutritional favor. However, the latest research shows that eating cholesterol-rich food does not significantly increase blood cholesterol levels in most people. According to Walter C. Willett, M.D., Dr. P.H., chair of the Harvard School of Public Health's department of nutrition, "No research has ever shown that people who eat more eggs have more heart attacks than people who eat few eggs." Different people react differently to dietary cholesterol, and most can handle cholesterol intake within the normal range. This means that healthy folks with decent eating habits and reasonably active lifestyles can happily and safely enjoy an egg breakfast quite often without worry.

I strongly encourage you to include eggs in your breakfast plans on a regular basis. This doesn't mean you have to make a showy omelet or a fussed-over soufflé or create a groaning plateful fit for a lumberjack, although you certainly can. Sometimes just a simple fried egg and a piece of toast can be the most satisfying breakfast imaginable. This chapter offers a broad range of egg options, from basic and plain to puffed up and spectacularly enhanced. And for those of you who want to enjoy a savory, high-protein breakfast but prefer to keep your diet lower on the food chain, I've included a versatile and foolproof recipe for scrambled tofu—interchangeable with scrambled eggs—that can be a springboard for many delicious variations.

Some Egg Pointers

HOW TO SHOP FOR EGGS

Eggs are classified according to freshness and condition. Buy eggs that are graded AA or A to ensure the highest quality. And my mother taught me this little trick: Before you buy a carton of eggs, open it up and gently wiggle each egg to be sure it isn't stuck in place. This lets you know the shells are intact—an important indicator of freshness.

Once you get eggs home from the store, you can check on their freshness by placing them in a bowl of water. The freshest eggs will lie flat in the bottom of the bowl. Older, less fresh eggs will "stand up" but still stay in the bottom of the bowl, perhaps bobbing a little. (If an egg floats up to the surface, it is rotten and you should throw it away. This is a very rare occurrence.)

THE MYTH OF BROWN EGGS

Many people assume that brown eggs are more virtuous (or at least more nutritious) than their white counterparts. But in fact, an egg's hue is determined by the color of the mother hen's ears (no kidding!) and nothing more.

HOW TO STORE EGGS

The American Egg Board discourages storing eggs in the built-in egg compartment of the refrigerator door. Instead they advise keeping eggs in the body of the refrigerator *in their carton,* where they will stay cold and vertical—and where they will be protected from the jarring motion of the door being opened and closed.

WHICH EGGS TO USE FOR WHAT?

Fresh eggs are the ones to poach or fry, but don't hard-boil them, or they'll be miserable to peel. Hard-boil only older eggs, which will peel beautifully if done right. (See the opposite page.) Note that the age of the eggs is not important if you are planning to scramble them or use them for baking.

 NEW AGE EGG GLOSSARY

Once upon a time an egg was just an egg—larger or smaller perhaps, but still just an egg. These days, eggs have résumés. Here's a quick walk-through.

ORGANIC EGGS	The hens have been fed certified organically grown grain (no pesticides, fungicides, herbicides, antibiotics, or commercial fertilizers).
VEGETARIAN EGGS	The hens have not been fed anything containing meat or fish, or their by-products.
FREE-RANGE EGGS	Rather than being confined to cages, the hens have been allowed to roam around and scratch for food, so their diet is more varied and they've gotten more exercise.
FERTILE EGGS	The eggs are laid after the hen has mated with a rooster, so theoretically these eggs could hatch into chicks. There is no proven benefit to consuming fertile eggs, although it sounds exotic.
ENHANCED EGGS	The hens have been fed an enriched diet that improves the nutritional profile of the eggs. This usually translates as increased DHA, omega-3 fatty acids, and vitamin E and/or an altered and improved ratio of unsaturated to saturated fat. These eggs cost more, but I think they are worth it. I buy them.

How to Boil an Egg

People tend to be very particular about their boiled eggs, with deeply emotional preferences—usually dating back to early childhood—as to how firm or soft the whites and yolks must (or must not) be. Even though it sounds pedestrian, boiling eggs to just the right degree is not that easy, mostly because you can't see the progress of the cooking until you open the shell, by which time it is too late to change anything. I've tried to cover all the bases here, so you can predict with some certainty what you will find when you break into your precious boiled egg.

SOFT- OR MEDIUM-BOILED EGGS

• Temper the eggs by placing them in a bowl of very warm tap water for a few minutes.

• Put a potful of water on to boil. It should be large enough to accommodate all the eggs you intend to boil without crowding. When the water reaches a boil, reduce the heat to very low, and use a spoon to lower the eggs into the simmering water.

• Begin timing the cooking when the eggs go into the water.

The following times apply to large eggs. Shave off a few seconds for medium-sized eggs, and add a few for extra-large ones.

3- TO 3½-MINUTE EGG	The egg is cooked enough to eat safely, but the white is still mostly runny.
4-MINUTE EGG	The white is barely set and the yolk is runny.
5-MINUTE EGG	The white is firmly set and the yolk is cooked but soft.

HARD-BOILED EGGS

• In a hard-boiled egg, the white and yolk are both firm.

• Be sure the eggs you begin with are not too fresh—otherwise, they will be difficult to peel.

• Place the eggs in a pot and fill with cold water to cover. Bring it to a boil, then immediately lower the heat to a simmer. Cook very gently for 1 minute, then remove the pot from the heat and let it stand for 15 minutes. Drain and refresh the eggs under cold running water.

HOW TO EAT A SOFT- OR MEDIUM-BOILED EGG

Place the egg in an egg cup, and slice off the top ½ inch with a very sharp knife. (There's also such a thing as "egg scissors" designed for just this purpose—use them if you have them.) Sprinkle in some salt and pepper, and eat the egg from the shell with a small spoon. For a more sensual experience, dunk triangles of buttered toast into the creamy yolk.

HEAVENLY EGG TARTINE

Baguettes—split, toasted, and buttered—are called *tartines* in France, and of course calling them this makes them all the more delicious. To make an egg tartine, drizzle a split, toasted baguette with extra virgin olive oil, and if desired spread on a little mayonnaise. Press thick slices of fresh, warm hard-boiled egg onto the bread, alternating with slices or small wedges of fresh tomato. Sprinkle with coarse salt and pepper, and eat it over a plate to catch the pieces and juices that will invariably fall and drip off as you eat.

How to Poach an Egg

A perfectly cooked poached egg on toast is a time-honored breakfast classic. You can also get creative and explore other bedding options besides toast: Try serving poached eggs on a bowlful of soft, hot polenta (page 59) or on top of cooked grains, mashed potatoes, or any kind of cooked vegetables. (Classic Creamed Spinach, page 171, comes to mind.) And poached eggs on Fried Green Tomatoes (page 169) or on steamed artichoke bottoms can be a real treat! The possibilities are endless.

- To poach up to 3 large eggs, fill an 8-inch nonstick omelet or crêpe pan with 2 cups water. Add 1½ teaspoons vinegar and ½ teaspoon salt and bring it to a boil, then lower the heat to a very slow simmer. (If you're poaching more than 3 eggs, fill a 10-inch sauté pan with 4 cups water and double the amounts of vinegar and salt.)

- Use cold, fresh eggs. Break each one into a saucer and then slide it into the simmering water.

- If the eggs cling to the bottom of the pan, gently nudge them with a rubber spatula until they let go. You can also push the whites toward the yolks to help them hold their shape. Don't worry if a yolk accidentally breaks—it will seal itself up again.

- Simmer until the whites are firm, then use a slotted spoon to remove the eggs and place them on a clean, folded towel to dry briefly before serving. (If you prefer, you can dip the eggs in a bowl of warm water first, to rinse off the vinegar flavor.)

- Poached eggs can be made ahead of time—they store and reheat surprisingly well. To store them, place the eggs in a bowl of ice water as soon as they're cooked. Keep them, water and all, in a closed container in the refrigerator for several days. To reheat, use a strainer or slotted spoon to dunk the eggs in simmering water for about half a minute. Then briefly dry them on a towel and serve.

EGGS BENEDICT

This classic brunch dish has just four components:

- Toasted English muffins
- Pan-fried Canadian bacon, "veggie" or real
- Poached eggs
- Hollandaise Sauce (page 265)

For each serving, place a toasted English muffin on a plate, topping each half with a slice of the meat—or "meat." Lay a freshly poached egg on top of each muffin half, and spoon on a little Hollandaise Sauce. That's all there is to it!

CODDLED EGGS

Like poached eggs, a coddled egg is cooked out of its shell and in simmering water. The difference is that it is literally coddled in a small container, which, not surprisingly, is called a "coddler." Traditional British coddlers are decorative little cups made of porcelain. They have a screw-on top, so you can put in the egg—plus a touch of butter or cream and a little salt and pepper—close up the coddler, and then lower it into simmering water. Cook for several minutes, or until the egg is done to your liking. Eat the egg directly from the coddler with a little spoon, or with toast fingers. You will feel quite elegant.

How to Fry an Egg

There is something just so familiar about a plain fried egg. Less familiar, perhaps, is a precise method for frying eggs "to specification" and with control over the process. Here are the basic guidelines.

• Place a heavy nonstick pan over medium-low heat for about 1 minute. Have a tight-fitting cover handy.

• Lightly spray the pan with nonstick spray, and add a little butter or olive oil. When the butter melts and begins to sizzle—or the olive oil is hot—swirl to coat the pan.

• Crack each egg into a saucer. (This is your insurance policy: If some shell gets in you can safely remove it, and if the yolk breaks you can use the egg for something else.)

• Slide each egg into the pan, making sure there is room for the egg to sit in its own spot. Sprinkle the egg(s) lightly with salt and pepper, and keep the heat at medium-low.

SUNNY-SIDE UP	(The yolk is set on the bottom but remains creamy. The white is firm and light golden on the bottom.) Cover the pan and cook for 3 to 5 minutes.
OVER EASY	(The yolk remains creamy but becomes covered by a cooked film of egg white.) Begin cooking the eggs as you would for sunny-side up, but after about 3 minutes, gently flip the eggs over and cook just briefly on the second side.
STEAM-BASTED FRIED EGGS	(Similar to eggs over easy, but turning is unnecessary.) Begin cooking the eggs as you would for sunny-side up. After 2 minutes (or when the edges turn white) add 1 teaspoon water per egg, directly to the exposed surface of the pan. Quickly replace the cover to hold in the steam, and cook until the whites are completely set and the yolks begin to thicken but are not hard (about 1½ minutes longer.)

 PORTABLE FRIED EGGS

Fried eggs are a great choice when you are in a hurry but really must eat something substantial to get through the morning. Get your toast started first (or begin warming a tortilla in a toaster oven), and then fry your eggs. Pack the eggs into a sandwich or a wrap—perhaps adding a touch of salsa—and take your fresh, hot breakfast with you as you head out the door.

How to Scramble an Egg

You may already be perfectly happy with your scrambled eggs. If you are, that's great. Turn the page and look for some other ideas. But if you aren't satisfied, and you would like a creamier, more ethereal result, here are some pointers you might find helpful. The best scrambled eggs can be summed up as follows: large, soft curds. Here's how to achieve them:

- If possible, break the eggs into a bowl about an hour ahead of time. Cover the bowl and let the eggs come to room temperature. This is not essential, but it does improve their final texture.
- Beat the eggs with a fork or a small whisk, adding pinches of salt and pepper. Don't overbeat them or they will become stringy and tough. They just need to be relatively smooth.
- Scramble a maximum of 3 large eggs at a time if using an 8-inch pan, and no more than 6 eggs at a time in a 10-inch pan.
- Warm a heavy, nonstick pan over medium heat for about 3 minutes before you begin, and keep the heat at medium—no higher—throughout the cooking process.
- Lightly spray the pan with nonstick spray, then melt in a little butter and swirl to coat the pan.
- Quickly pour in the beaten eggs. As the eggs begin to set, push the curds from the bottom to one side, allowing uncooked egg to flow into contact with the pan. Stop and let them puff for a few seconds, then keep piling the curds to the side. Allowing the eggs to puff before gently pushing the curds to one side produces large, soft curds.
- When the eggs are almost—but not completely—set, remove the pan from the heat and transfer the eggs to a plate. They will finish cooking there from their own heat.

Enriching Scrambled Eggs

"So what's the verdict? Should I or shouldn't I put milk in my scrambled eggs?" Amazingly, this is one of the first things almost everyone asks me when I mention that I've been writing a breakfast book. Here comes the answer to that question, along with other clarifications and musings on the lovely, wholesome, bright yellow subject of scrambled eggs.

- MILK is controversial. Some people say it makes the eggs creamy. Others believe it toughens the eggs, because the proteins in the milk coagulate from exposure to the heat. So I'm throwing the decision back to you. Add a little milk if you like.
- HEAVY CREAM is a great solution! Just a tiny splash can make your scrambled eggs voluptuous. In fact, the addition of any kind of creamy fat can take scrambled eggs over the top. Consider small touches of mayonnaise or cream cheese. (You can use a blender—just a few short pulses—to mix the cream cheese into the eggs.)
- RICOTTA CHEESE makes scrambled eggs fluffy. Beat in 1 tablespoon per large egg.
- WATER will make scrambled eggs puff as it turns to steam during the cooking process. Add 1 tablespoon water per large egg.

You can also add none of the above and just scramble your eggs straight. That's how I do mine.

Augmenting Scrambled Eggs

Scrambled eggs are a great vehicle for adding more vegetables and fresh herbs—and even additional protein—to your diet.

FRESH HERBS

Beat the eggs as usual, and stir in a handful of coarsely (or finely) chopped fresh herbs. You can cut them into big pieces with scissors if you like. It's nice to use a combination of aromatics, like flat-leaf parsley, thyme, cilantro, basil (these last two are strong, so go easy), minced scallions, chives, and so on. Somehow the eggs can hold a lot of herbs without tasting grassy.

ARUGULA OR SPINACH

Coarsely chop a handful or two of clean, dry arugula or spinach leaves and add them to the eggs before they go into the pan.

CHOPPED BROCCOLI, ONION, SCALLION, ZUCCHINI, ASPARAGUS, STURDIER GREENS (KALE, COLLARDS, ETC.)

Get the pan very hot, and flash-cook a handful or two of chopped vegetables, with a dash of salt, in olive oil over medium-high heat. When the vegetables are tender-crisp, turn them out onto a plate. Wipe the pan clean, let it cool down, and then return it to the stove, this time over medium heat. Proceed to make scrambled eggs, adding the vegetables back in when the eggs are about halfway done.

TOUCHES OF SMOKY-FLAVORED PROTEIN

Minced smoked salmon or crumbled "veggie bacon" are a terrific accent for scrambled eggs, especially if you also add a handful of minced scallions or chives. Mix all of it directly into the eggs before pouring them into the pan.

THE WORLD'S CREAMIEST SCRAMBLED EGGS

For the creamiest curds imaginable, use a double boiler—or a regular pan over very low heat—and stir constantly. This will take up to 20 minutes, depending on how many eggs you're cooking and the size of the pan. My solution to the possible tedium: Invite a friend to visit with you while you cook eggs this way for the two of you on a rainy Sunday morning. And put on some background music. It's an act of devotion that's ultimately quite relaxing. And the eggs are to die for!

Scrambled Egg Whites

Although it has been shown that eating whole eggs is perfectly healthful for most people (page 115), there are still those of us who prefer the option of egg whites only. Scrambled egg whites are quite delicious in their own understated way. Be prepared to use more eggs than you normally would (about 3 to 4 large eggs per serving) in order to get enough volume.

- How to use all those unemployed yolks? You can brush them onto loaves of unbaked bread for a rich, shiny crust (page 108) or use them in Roasted Garlic Aïoli (page 264) or in Hollandaise (page 265).
- Separate the eggs while they are still cold. Place the egg whites in a medium to large bowl, cover it with plastic wrap, and let them come to room temperature. (This is easily accomplished by letting them sit out overnight.)

YIELD: 2 servings (easily multiplied)
PREPARATION TIME: 5 minutes or less

---

6 to 8 egg whites, at room temperature

A few pinches of salt

A pinch of turmeric (optional, for color)

Nonstick spray

A little butter

1. Have the egg whites ready in a bowl. Place a medium-sized nonstick skillet over medium heat and wait several minutes.
2. While the pan is heating, add the salt and the turmeric, if desired, to the egg whites, and beat with a whisk until small bubbles form all over the surface. (You can also beat the egg whites longer—until they form soft peaks, like a meringue. This yields a drier, fluffier result.)
3. Spray the hot pan with nonstick spray, and melt in a little butter. When the pan is hot enough to sizzle a bread crumb, add the egg whites, and scramble them as you would whole eggs. The whites will cook extremely fast, especially if they have been beaten only a little. (If they've been beaten to soft peaks, they will take longer.)
4. When they seem done to your liking, transfer the egg whites to 2 plates and serve right away.

FREEZING EGGS

You can't freeze whole eggs in the shell, but you can freeze uncooked egg whites and yolks if they have been separated. Egg whites will keep in the freezer for up to a year. When fully thawed, they should beat up to the same volume as fresh whites, and you can use them as you would fresh ones. Yolks can be frozen for a month or two and, when defrosted, make a lovely glaze for home-baked bread.

Freeze individual egg whites and yolks in ice cube trays, then turn out the "egg cubes" and combine them in a zip-style plastic bag. (This saves having to measure.) Thaw whites and yolks overnight in separate tightly covered containers in the refrigerator. Once defrosted, they will keep in the refrigerator for 2 to 3 days.

Scrambled Tofu

I've discovered the secret to making soft, puffy scrambled tofu that comes out every bit as tender as real scrambled eggs: silken tofu. Unlike other forms of tofu, this terrific product is seamless and has absolutely no grittiness.
There's a second secret at work here as well: A double cooking process—boiling followed by frying—firms up the tofu just the right amount and prevents it from disintegrating into crumbs as it gets fried. Instead, it fluffs up into the most convincing scrambled egg impersonation yet.

- Silken tofu comes in small vacuum-packed boxes and is available in supermarkets, Asian groceries, and natural food stores. Usually it is stored with other Asian items on the grocery shelf—not in the refrigerator.
- The tofu can be boiled up to several days ahead of time and stored in a tightly covered container in the refrigerator. It can go directly from the refrigerator into the hot frying pan.

YIELD: 1 to 2 servings (easily multiplied)
PREPARATION TIME: 15 minutes

1 box (12 ounces) silken tofu

Nonstick spray

Olive oil or butter

A large pinch of salt

Freshly ground black pepper

1. Cut open the box of tofu, and slide its contents into a medium-sized saucepan. Add water to cover, and bring to a boil. Simmer for 10 minutes, then drain in a fine-mesh strainer. Transfer to a plate, and use a dinner knife to cut the tofu into pieces the size of large cottage cheese curds.
2. Place an 8-inch nonstick crêpe or omelet pan over medium heat and wait several minutes. Spray it lightly with nonstick spray, and add a little olive oil or butter. Wait about 10 seconds, then swirl to coat the pan.
3. Add the tofu pieces, salt, and a light sprinkling of pepper, and sauté over medium heat for about 8 minutes, or until the tofu is light golden brown.
4. Transfer to a plate and serve right away.

SCRAMBLED TOFU PLUS

Like scrambled eggs, Scrambled Tofu can be expanded and augmented in many ways. You can add it to vegetables (see Flash-Cooked Vegetables, page 174) or dress it up with minced scallions, "veggie bacon," Basic Guacamole (page 257), or salsa (pages 250 to 255). Enjoy it on—or with—toast or wrapped in a warm flour tortilla. And don't forget that Scrambled Tofu doesn't necessarily need to *replace* scrambled eggs—they are actually very good combined. The tofu lightens up the eggs and fortifies them with wholesome soy, and the eggs lend credibility to the tofu, making this a good vehicle for gently converting the tofu-phobic among us.

Green Chile–Tortilla Scramble

A relatively long cooking process over strong heat—plus the addition of just a few choice seasonings—will transform green chiles and tortilla strips into an intense backdrop for scrambled eggs. My favorite garnish for this is a scattering of variously colored cherry tomatoes, which make it look every bit as compelling as it smells.

- Different chile powders have quite a range of flavor and heat. I use a very strong New Mexico chile powder; therefore I add only a little. You can adjust the amount of the chile powder to taste, depending on the type you are using.
- By "minced green chiles" I mean any combination of anaheims, poblanos, and jalapeños—all of which have a range of heat. For a milder flavor, remove and discard the seeds. (Wash your hands after handling these or any other hot peppers.) You can also substitute canned green chiles.

YIELD: **6 servings**
PREPARATION TIME: **25 minutes**

2 corn tortillas

1½ tablespoons olive oil

1 heaping cup minced onion

1 cup minced green chiles

½ teaspoon pure ground chile powder

¼ teaspoon salt

2 teaspoons minced garlic

1 cup cooked pinto beans (optional)

6 large eggs

OPTIONAL TOPPINGS

Cherry tomatoes

Grated jack cheese

Basic Guacamole (page 257)

Salsa (pages 250 to 255)

1. Cut the tortillas into small, thin strips about ½-inch wide with a knife or scissors, and set aside.
2. Place a 10-inch skillet or sauté pan over medium heat. After several minutes, add 1 tablespoon of the olive oil, wait about 10 seconds, then swirl to coat the pan. Turn the heat up to medium-high, add the onion, and sauté for 5 minutes.
3. Stir in the chiles, chile powder, and salt, and sauté for another 5 minutes, keeping the heat at medium-high.
4. Add a little more olive oil (about 1½ teaspoons), plus the garlic and tortilla strips. Cook and stir over medium-high heat for another 10 minutes, or until the vegetables are very tender and the tortillas turn a deep golden brown. Gently stir in the beans, if desired. Keep the pan hot.
5. Break the eggs into a bowl and beat until smooth. Pour them into the hot pan, and scramble them into the vegetable-tortilla mixture. This will go quite quickly. Remove the pan from the heat when the eggs are mostly set but still moist. (They will continue cooking from their own heat, and we want to prevent them from becoming dry.)
6. Serve hot, topped with cherry tomatoes, a light sprinkling of grated cheese, if desired, and/or additional toppings of your choice.

VARIATIONS   For each variation, follow the main recipe with these adjustments.

GREEN CHILE–TORTILLA TOFU SCRAMBLE

Replace the scrambled eggs with:

- A triple batch of Scrambled Tofu (preceding page)

Add it directly to the vegetable-tortilla mixture after step 4, and proceed with step 6.

POACHED OR FRIED EGGS OVER GREEN CHILES AND TORTILLAS

Prepare the main recipe through step 4. Divide the sautéed mixture among 2 or 3 serving plates. Top with:

- 3 to 6 fried or poached eggs
- Any of the optional toppings

Greek Scramble

A bright green quartet of fresh herbs (mint, scallions, parsley, and oregano) teams up with freshly cooked spinach to infuse scrambled eggs with Mediterranean soul. Laced throughout with crumbled feta—which is as much a seasoning as it is a cheese—this dish needs no salt. Just grind in a generous amount of black pepper and you're good to go.

I like to serve this dish with thin slices of freshly toasted sourdough walnut bread.

- A mini-food processor makes short work of mincing the herbs.
- If you can't find fresh oregano, substitute ½ teaspoon dried oregano.

YIELD: 4 servings
PREPARATION TIME: 15 minutes

6 to 8 large eggs

3 tablespoons minced fresh mint

1 tablespoon minced flat-leaf parsley

1 teaspoon minced fresh oregano

2 tablespoons minced scallion

Freshly ground black pepper

1 tablespoon olive oil

2 cups (packed) spinach

1 cup crumbled feta

1 cup diced ripe tomatoes or halved cherry tomatoes

1. Break the eggs into a medium-sized bowl and beat with a whisk until smooth. Stir in the herbs and scallion, and grind in a good amount of black pepper.
2. Place a 10-inch skillet or sauté pan over medium heat. After several minutes, add the olive oil, wait about 10 seconds, then swirl to coat the pan. Turn the heat up to medium-high, add the spinach, and sauté for 2 to 3 minutes, or until the spinach has wilted and turned a deep green.
3. With the heat still at medium-high, pour the eggs into the pan, scrambling them slowly. As the eggs begin to set, push the curds from the bottom to one side, allowing uncooked egg to flow into contact with the pan. The spinach will blend into the eggs.
4. When the eggs are mostly set but still slightly wet, sprinkle in the crumbled feta. Continue scrambling slowly, allowing the cheese to melt slightly into the eggs. After about a minute, stir in the tomatoes.
5. Cook for just a few seconds longer, or until the eggs are done to your liking. Serve right away.

Spring or Summer Frittata with scallions, roasted garlic, zucchini, and crumbly cheese

A frittata is a thick Italian omelet—sturdy and adaptable—and full of vegetables, herbs, and cheese. Here's a basic recipe that can change with the seasons, so feel free to improvise according to what is fresh at the market.

Frittatas are very convenient in that, unlike most other egg dishes, they can be made ahead and either reheated or served at room temperature, so you can avoid the hassle of last-minute preparations. Try taking a wedge of frittata with you as your commute item or for a midmorning meal at your desk—it's very portable.

- A frittata will keep for up to a week if stored in an airtight container in the refrigerator, and it reheats beautifully in a microwave.

YIELD: 4 to 6 servings
PREPARATION TIME: 30 minutes

---

2 to 3 tablespoons olive oil

2 small zucchini, thinly sliced

½ teaspoon salt

2 teaspoons minced garlic

8 large eggs

6 medium scallions, minced
(both white and green parts)

1 or 2 handfuls minced parsley

Freshly ground black pepper

1 cup ricotta salata or feta

OPTIONAL ADDITIONS

Fresh peas, lightly steamed

Minced fresh herbs (dill, savory, and/or basil)

Halved cherry tomatoes

Lightly toasted pine nuts

1. Place a 10-inch skillet with an ovenproof handle over medium heat for about 2 minutes. Add 1 tablespoon of the olive oil, wait about 10 seconds, then swirl to coat the pan. Add the zucchini and sauté for about 5 minutes, or until just tender. Stir in the salt and garlic, cook for about 1 minute longer, and remove from the heat.

2. Break the eggs into a large bowl and beat well with a whisk. Add the sautéed vegetables, scallions, and minced parsley. (You can also stir in the optional additions at this time.) Grind in some black pepper, crumble in the cheese, and stir until blended. Clean and dry the skillet and return it to the stove over medium heat. Preheat the broiler.

3. When the skillet is hot again, add the remaining 1 to 2 tablespoons olive oil, wait about 30 seconds, and swirl to coat the pan. Pour in the vegetable-egg mixture and let it cook undisturbed over medium heat for 3 to 4 minutes, or until the eggs are set on the bottom.

4. Transfer the skillet to the preheated broiler, and broil for about 3 minutes, or until the frittata is firm in the center. Remove the pan from the broiler, and run a rubber spatula around the edge to loosen the frittata. Slide or invert it onto a large, round plate, and serve hot, warm, or at room temperature, cut into wedges.

VARIATIONS   For each variation, follow the main recipe with these adjustments.

FRITTATA WITH ASPARAGUS OR GREEN BEANS

Replace the zucchini with:

- 2 cups asparagus tips or slender green beans

PARMESAN-CRUSTED FRITTATA

For a lovely cheese crust, sprinkle:

- ⅓ cup grated parmesan

over the top about halfway through the broiling.

Autumn or Winter Frittata with red onion, red potato, ruby chard, and goat cheese

Ruddy late-season vegetables make a beautiful frittata, speckled with touches of reddish purple. The many variations that follow enable you to make this as complex as you desire.

• See the introduction to the Spring or Summer Frittata (opposite page) for hints on storing and serving a frittata.

YIELD: 4 to 6 servings
PREPARATION TIME: 30 minutes

2 large stalks ruby chard

2 to 3 tablespoons olive oil

2 cups sliced red onion

2 cups thinly sliced red potato (scrubbed but not peeled)

1 teaspoon salt

2 teaspoons dried rosemary

2 teaspoons minced garlic

8 large eggs

Freshly ground black pepper

4 ounces goat cheese

1. Remove and mince the chard leaves, and cut the stems in ½-inch pieces. Keep the leaves and stems in separate containers, and set aside.
2. Heat 1 tablespoon of the olive oil in a 10-inch skillet with an ovenproof handle, and add the onion, potato, ½ teaspoon of the salt, and the rosemary. Sauté for about 5 minutes over medium heat, then cover and cook for about 10 minutes, stirring intermittently, or until the potato slices are tender.
3. Stir in the chard stems, and sauté for about 2 minutes more. Add the chard leaves and the garlic, and sauté for another minute, or until the leaves are wilted but still bright green. Remove the pan from the heat.
4. Break the eggs into a very large bowl, add the remaining ½ teaspoon salt, and beat well with a whisk. Add the vegetables, grind in some black pepper, and crumble in the goat cheese. Stir until everything is fairly evenly distributed. Clean and dry the skillet and return it to the stove over medium heat. Preheat the broiler.
5. Continue with steps 3 and 4 of the preceding recipe.

VARIATIONS Follow the main recipe, adding any of the following in any combination—as much as will fit.

Add in step 2:
• Chopped broccoli
• Chopped cauliflower
• Pinches of marjoram or sage

Add in step 3:
• Other leafy greens, chopped
• Sliced bell pepper

Add in step 4:
• Mashed roasted garlic (Roasted Garlic Aïoli, page 264, steps 1 and 2)
• Sliced dried tomatoes
• Chopped, toasted walnuts

About Omelets

If you enjoy making omelets your way and you're happy with how they turn out—and you don't intend to cook them professionally—there's no need to bother with the particulars outlined below. On the other hand, if you want to become a master of *la technique française*, impressing people far and wide with the flawless, tender masterpieces that emerge—seemingly effortlessly—from your modest frying pan, read on.

> *There is only one infallible recipe for the perfect omelet: Your own.*
>
> —Elizabeth David

Elizabeth David, the venerable culinary author, tells the story of the most famous omelet maker of all time, a certain Madame Poulard of the Hôtel de la Tête d'Or in Mont Saint-Michel. Her omelets were a destination to crowds of tourists from all over France. People could only guess as to her omelet-making secret. There were rumors that she raised an exclusive breed of chickens and/or used a customized omelet pan. Some decided that she sneaked a little foie gras into the beaten eggs to enrich them. Eventually someone decided to write her a letter and simply ask her. This was her reply:

> *Monsieur Viel,*
>   *Here is the recipe for the omelet: I break some good eggs in a bowl. I beat them well,*
> *I put a good piece of butter in the pan, I throw the eggs into it, and I shake it constantly.*
> *I am happy, Monsieur, if this recipe pleases you.*
>
>   *Annette Poulard*

What are we to conclude? Precisely that there is no particular mystery behind a good omelet. Sheila Lukins and Julee Rosso sum it up this way in *The Silver Palate Cookbook*:

> *At the bottom line, an omelet is nothing more than eggs, butter, and body English.*

(Or, in the case of Madame Poulard, body *French*.)

 TWO FASCINATING MORSELS OF OMELET HISTORY

- Omelets are believed to have been invented by the Romans, who were the first to break the ancient taboo against eating eggs—a practice condemned in primitive times because it was seen as destroying a chicken (though the reasoning behind this eludes me). The first known omelet recipe is said to have been recorded by the Roman epicure Apicius, and it was apparently made from eggs, honey, and black pepper. It sounds rather good!

- The *Guinness Book of World Records* lists Howard Helmer as the record holder for making the most omelets in a 30-minute span. Howard landed 427 quality omelets, using a six-burner stove. His method? The traditional French technique, plain and simple, that I describe here. You will probably never need to cook omelets in this quantity or with a stopwatch ticking, but it is nevertheless reassuring to know that the method really works.

How to Make an Omelet

Omelets are the most humbling reminder of how the simplest dishes can sometimes be the most difficult to prepare well. Quality ingredients are essential, of course, but technique is also very important. Here is the lowdown on the classic French method:

- An omelet pan must have rounded, sloping shoulders and be the right size for the number of eggs you are cooking. If the pan is too small, the omelet will be overly thick and difficult to cook through without becoming tough. If the pan is too large, you risk producing an omelet that is excessively thin and dry. I use an 8-inch pan for 2 medium-sized eggs and a 10-inch pan for 3 to 4 medium-sized eggs. If I want a larger quantity, I simply make more omelets, not larger ones.

- Use a good, heavy, nonstick pan.

- Have all the ingredients ready and at room temperature before you begin.

- Don't beat the eggs for too long or they will become thin and tough when cooked. Thirty seconds of beating with a fork is usually enough. If you like, you can mix the eggs with a little water (1 tablespoon per egg) to make them lighter and more tender.

- Heat the skillet slowly over medium heat until a tablespoon of butter will melt immediately. Don't let the butter get too hot. It should sizzle and then settle down, but not brown. And don't skimp on the butter, even if you are using a non-stick pan. Tilt the pan in all directions to distribute the butter, then pour in the egg mixture, keeping the heat at medium.

- As the eggs begin to set at the edges, carefully push the cooked portion toward the center of the pan with a small spatula. At the same time tilt the pan, allowing any remaining raw egg to fill the spaces. If you're using a filling, spoon it onto half the omelet as soon as the eggs stop flowing. The egg mixture should still be moist, as it will continue cooking when removed from the pan, and you don't want it to overcook and become leathery. Use the spatula to fold the omelet in half, and slide or flip it onto the waiting plate.

- In a perfect world you will have remembered to warm the serving plate ahead of time in the microwave. Although not essential, this is a very nice touch.

- As with many of the dishes in your breakfast repertoire, don't confine your omelet making to breakfast. An omelet makes a fine, quickly prepared meal any time of the day or evening. In fact, the French don't serve omelets for breakfast at all but consider them classic light fare for lunch or dinner.

- Ideas for omelet fillings are on the following page.

A few words of encouragement before you begin: In her classic 19th-century treatise *The Omelet Book,* Narcissa G. Chamberlain reminds us that in addition to quality ingredients, the making of a successful omelet requires "practice, practice, practice and a generous dash of self-confidence." To these I would add two more qualities: a sense of humor and a willingness to end up with scrambled eggs.

OMELET FILLINGS

A well-crafted omelet is a golden, buttery delight unto itself, so I like to fill my creations with a very light hand, if at all. When contemplating an omelet filling, keep in mind that you don't want to overwhelm the eggs—and you don't want to weigh them down with a filling that is too copious or too heavy. A good rule of thumb is to add approximately ¼ cup of filling ingredients per 2-egg omelet, or ⅓ cup at the very most. Small touches go a long way.

Here are some combinations that go well together inside an omelet. (I'm sure you will also come up with your own ideas as well.) Get everything ready—and cooked, if that is part of the plan—before you begin the omelet. And put your bread in the toaster ahead of time, too. Remember, from start to finish, a 2-egg omelet takes less than 3 minutes if made correctly.

QUICK VEGETABLE-CHEESE OMELETS

Just about any freshly cooked vegetable can go into an omelet. And it can be done very quickly, since such a small amount is required. A few strokes of the knife, a quick "flash" in a hot pan with perhaps a dash of salt and a sprinkling of minced scallions, and the vegetable is ready. If you use the omelet pan for this, just dump out the hot vegetables, wipe out the pan, and return it to the heat to make the omelet. Pair your freshly cooked vegetable with a favorite cheese.

ASIAN OMELET

Heat a small skillet (the omelet pan itself is fine) and add a little Chinese sesame oil. Add sliced fresh shiitake mushrooms and a pinch of salt, and sauté until done to your liking. Add this to the omelet, along with some minced scallion (including the greens) and fresh bean sprouts. Drizzle the finished omelet with a little more Chinese sesame oil.

GREEN GODDESS OMELET

Add a combination of finely minced fresh herbs (parsley, chives, dill, basil, marjoram, thyme, savory) directly to the beaten eggs. Make this into a beautiful green omelet—no filling necessary!

ROASTED PEPPER AND GOAT CHEESE OMELET

Spoon some Fire-Roasted Pepper Salsa (page 254) onto your omelet, and crumble in some goat cheese.

ONION-LEMON OMELET WITH GRUYÈRE

Spread a little Caramelized Onion and Lemon Marmalade (page 258) on your omelet, and sprinkle it with grated gruyère.

RICOTTA OMELET WITH FRUIT

Roasted Fruit (page 36) or Caramelized Fruit (page 27) make a lovely omelet filling with a spoonful or two of ricotta cheese spread in a thin layer.

LEFTOVER OMELET

Omelets also provide a great opportunity to do justice to leftovers. In fact, think ahead and cook extra vegetables at dinnertime to have for your eggs the following morning.

Cheddar-Shirred Eggs

Baked (shirred) eggs are a good solution for when you want to feed more than just one or two people. This rich-tasting recipe goes very well with almost any dish in the "Potatoes, Beans, Tempeh & Hashes" chapter, and it is gloriously enhanced by Roasted Herbes de Provence Tomatoes (page 168) served on the side.

It works best to bake the eggs in individual 6-ounce ramekins or custard cups—or in small gratin dishes (1-cup capacity, 5 inches in diameter) and to serve them directly from the oven on liner plates.

YIELD: 4 to 8 servings (8 baked eggs)
PREPARATION TIME: 5 minutes, plus 20 minutes to bake

Nonstick spray

A little butter (optional)

8 large eggs

Salt and pepper

¼ pound sharp cheddar, thinly sliced

OPTIONAL TOPPINGS

Bread crumbs

Cayenne or paprika

1. Preheat the oven to 350°F. Lightly spray 8 ramekins or custard cups or 4 gratin dishes with nonstick spray. You can also place a small piece of butter in each cup and melt it in the microwave. Place the prepared containers on a baking tray.

2. Break an egg into a saucer and slide it into a prepared container. Repeat with the remaining eggs, placing 1 egg in each custard cup or ramekin or 2 eggs in each gratin dish. Sprinkle each egg with salt and pepper, then place the tray in the center of the oven and bake for 10 minutes.

3. Pull the tray out of the oven, and carefully lay the cheddar slices on top of the eggs to completely cover the top surface. You can also sprinkle them with some bread crumbs and a touch of cayenne or paprika. Return the tray to the oven for another 5 to 10 minutes, or until the cheese is bubbly and the eggs are *just* set.

4. Carefully transfer each container to a plate, and serve right away. (Remind your guests that the dishes are hot.)

VARIATIONS   For each variation, follow the main recipe with these adjustments. (Each of these serves 4.)

EGGS FLORENTINE

(Add 15 minutes to the preparation time.)

Have ready and heated:

• Classic Creamed Spinach (page 171)

Lightly spray 4 individual gratin dishes with nonstick spray, and divide the spinach mixture among them, spreading it into place. Proceed with step 2 of the main recipe.

BAKED EGGS ON A BED OF MUSHROOMS

(Add 35 minutes to the preparation time.)

Have ready and heated:

• All-Purpose Breakfast Mushrooms (page 172)

Lightly spray 4 individual gratin dishes with nonstick spray, and divide the mushroom mixture among them, spreading it into place. Proceed with step 2 of the main recipe.

Egg "Muffins"

You (and the children in your life) will love these neat little egg "packages." Eat them on a plate with a fork, or just pick one up and take a bite. They're highly portable.

- Use nonstick pans, generously greased, to be sure these don't stick.
- Whole milk ricotta is best for this, although the lowfat kind will also work.
- You can store these for up to 2 days in a tightly covered container in the refrigerator and reheat them in a microwave.

YIELD: 4 to 8 servings (8 medium-sized "muffins" containing 1 egg apiece)
PREPARATION TIME: 10 minutes, plus 20 minutes to bake

Nonstick spray

4 tablespoons (half a stick) butter

⅓ cup bread crumbs

8 large eggs

1 cup ricotta cheese

½ teaspoon salt (scant measure)

½ cup minced scallion (both white and green parts)

Freshly ground black pepper

2 tablespoons grated parmesan

1. Preheat the oven to 350°F. Generously spray the bottoms and sides of 8 nonstick, standard (2½-inch-diameter) muffin cups with nonstick spray, then place about 1½ teaspoons butter into each cup. Place the pans in the preheating oven for a minute or so to melt the butter, then take them out and divide the bread crumbs among them.

2. Combine the eggs, ricotta, and salt in a blender and whip until smooth. Stir in the scallion and a generous amount of freshly ground black pepper.

3. Pour the egg mixture into the prepared cups, filling them right up to the rim. Bake in the center of the oven for 10 minutes, then reach in and carefully sprinkle the top of each "muffin" with a little parmesan. Bake for another 10 minutes, or until the tops are puffy, golden, and just barely firm to the touch.

4. Remove the pans from the oven and let the "muffins" cool in the pans for about 5 minutes, during which time they will deflate a little. Run a knife around the edges and lift or invert each "muffin" onto a cooling rack or a plate. Serve hot, warm, or at room temperature.

VARIATIONS   AUGMENTED EGG MUFFINS

Follow the main recipe, and add up to ½ cup of any of the following when you stir in the scallion in step 2:

- Halved cherry tomatoes
- Minced red and/or green bell pepper
- Crumbled bacon, "veggie bacon," or soy-based bacon-flavored bits

EGG SALAD FOR BREAKFAST

Strong flavors can turn that old standby, egg salad, into something downright vibrant. We usually think of egg salad as lunch box fare, but it is really good for breakfast as well. Stuff one of these perky salads into a pita—or just pile it on a piece of toast—and top it with a slice or two of cucumber or ripe tomato. It's quite an eye-opener!

If you're anticipating a busy day when you'll need to grab a quick lunch on the run that will hold you all the way until dinner, egg salad might be the perfect choice.

- For information about hard-boiled eggs, see page 117.
- Chipotle chiles (smoked jalapeños) are available canned in a tomato sauce (adobo) in the imported foods section of many grocery stores and specialty shops.
- Egg salad will keep for up to a week in a tightly covered container in the refrigerator.

YIELD: **Each makes 4 servings**
PREPARATION TIME: **5 minutes (once the eggs are already boiled)**

Egg Salad with Capers and Olives

4 hard-boiled eggs

2 tablespoons minced red onion

2 tablespoons mayonnaise

1 teaspoon prepared mustard

2 tablespoons minced red bell pepper

2 tablespoons minced pitted kalamata olives

1 tablespoon minced parsley

1 tablespoon capers

Salt and pepper

1. Finely chop the eggs and transfer them to a medium-sized bowl.

2. Add the remaining ingredients, including salt and pepper to taste, and mix well.

DEVILED EGGS ARE A GREAT MORNING FOOD

You can easily make either of the egg salad recipes into deviled eggs, for a convenient, portable breakfast item. Simply cut the eggs in half lengthwise, and pop the yolks into a small bowl. Mash the yolks with the remaining ingredients, then stuff this filling back into the "yolk compartment" of the egg whites. Chill in a tightly covered container until serving time.

Smoky Egg Salad

4 hard-boiled eggs

2 tablespoons sour cream

½ teaspoon minced chipotle

1 tablespoon minced cilantro

Salt and pepper

1. Finely chop the eggs and transfer them to a medium-sized bowl.

2. Add the remaining ingredients, including salt and pepper to taste, and mix well.

Basic Cheese Soufflé

An ideal soufflé is light and airy but also moist and creamy. The key lies in beating the egg whites to just the right consistency. Everything else will just . . . rise into place. Truly! Be sure your guests are ready when the soufflé emerges from the oven, so its ephemeral puffy splendor can be admired by all.

- Separate the eggs well ahead of time, placing the whites in a large bowl and the yolks in a smaller one. Cover both bowls with plastic wrap, and let them come to room temperature.
- You can substitute other types of flavorful, medium-firm cheese for sharp cheddar. Gruyère works especially well. Experiment with your favorites.

YIELD: 3 to 4 servings
PREPARATION TIME: 15 minutes, plus 40 minutes to bake

Nonstick spray

1¼ cups milk

3 tablespoons unsalted butter

3 tablespoons unbleached all-purpose flour

2 teaspoons dry mustard

6 large eggs, separated and at room temperature

¾ teaspoon salt

Freshly ground black pepper

Cayenne

1½ cups (packed) grated sharp cheddar

1. Preheat the oven to 375°F. Lightly spray a 1½-quart soufflé dish with nonstick spray.

2. Heat the milk, either in a saucepan on the stove or in a glass or ceramic container in the microwave. When it is very hot but not yet boiling, remove it from the heat and set it aside.

3. Melt the butter in a medium-sized saucepan over medium-low heat. Sprinkle in the flour and mustard, whisking constantly. Turn the heat down to low, and continue to cook the resulting paste (roux) for about a minute or two longer, stirring often.

4. Slowly drizzle in the hot milk, whisking steadily. Cook over low heat for 5 minutes, stirring frequently with a whisk and then a wooden spoon as it thickens. Remove from the heat, and transfer to a large bowl.

5. Beat the egg yolks with a fork just until they lose their shape and become runny, then drizzle them into the hot sauce, beating vigorously. Add the salt, some black pepper, and cayenne to taste.

6. Beat the egg whites until they form peaks that don't fall over when the whisk or beaters are lifted, and just a little liquid is left in the bottom of the bowl. (More details about this are on the opposite page.)

7. Fold the beaten whites into the sauce, sprinkling in the grated cheese as you fold, until the egg whites are mostly incorporated. The mixture will not be uniform—there will be little puffs of "cloud" here and there—and that is fine. (It's best not to overfold, as this will deflate the egg whites.) Transfer the mixture to the prepared dish.

8. Bake in the center of the oven for 35 to 40 minutes, or until golden brown all over the puffy top surface. Bring to the table and serve immediately.

For each variation, follow the main recipe with these adjustments. (Use a 2-quart soufflé dish.)

BROCCOLI SOUFFLÉ

Steam until tender:

• 1½ cups chopped broccoli

Sprinkle lightly with salt and pepper, and fold it in with the egg whites and cheese.

ASPARAGUS SOUFFLÉ

Steam until tender:

• 1½ cups asparagus tips

Sprinkle lightly with salt and pepper. Add:

• ½ teaspoon dried tarragon
• 3 tablespoons minced fresh dill

Fold in with the egg whites and cheese. (You might want to use a milder cheddar for this soufflé.)

SPINACH SOUFFLÉ

Omit the milk, butter, flour, and mustard. Use as the sauce:

• Classic Creamed Spinach (page 171)

Skip steps 2, 3, and 4, and proceed with step 5. You may use mild cheddar instead of sharp.

MUSHROOM–GOAT CHEESE SOUFFLÉ

Reduce the milk to ¾ cup. Add:

• All-Purpose Breakfast Mushrooms (page 172)

to the roux when you add the milk in step 4. Replace the cheddar with:

• 1 cup crumbled goat cheese

WITH A SOUFFLÉ, EGG WHITES ARE EVERYTHING

Attention to these details will reward you with a fine soufflé every time:

• Use fresh eggs for soufflés, because the fresher the whites, the more stable they will be after they're beaten—and you will get a sturdier (although still tender) soufflé. Note that fresh egg whites will take longer to beat than older whites, but the result will be worth the slight extra time and trouble.

• Don't salt the whites—it will destabilize them. If you wish, you can add a little acid (cream of tartar or a drop of vinegar) to speed up the process and add stability.

• Beating time is related to temperature—the colder the egg whites, the longer it takes for them to whip.

• If you are using a whisk instead of an electric mixer, beating time is related to the structure of the whisk. "A whisk of many tines" works faster than one with fewer. Use a large balloon whisk for the most efficient action.

• Frozen, defrosted whites work fine. (See page 122.)

• Make sure there is absolutely no yolk in the whites, and be sure you beat them with very clean utensils. The presence of any oil at all will inhibit their ability to puff.

• Don't overbeat the whites. It's easy to do, especially when you're using an electric mixer. When to stop beating? When soft peaks form and just a tiny amount of liquid is left in the bottom of the bowl. Another sign: When you tilt the bowl, the foam should slide just a little.

Sunlight Soufflé

Peaches and creamy cheese are delightful together in this rich-tasting soufflé. If you don't have access to ripe, fresh peaches, make this with the equivalent amount of drained canned peaches (packed in water or juice); it will still be absolutely delicious.

- Separate the eggs well ahead of time, placing the whites in a large bowl and the yolks in a smaller one. Cover both bowls with plastic wrap, and let them come to room temperature.
- Zest the lemons before juicing them.

YIELD: About 4 servings
PREPARATION TIME: 15 minutes, plus 45 minutes to bake

Nonstick spray

2 cups ricotta or cottage cheese

6 large eggs, separated and at room temperature

2 teaspoons vanilla extract

⅛ teaspoon almond extract

6 tablespoons unbleached all-purpose flour

½ teaspoon salt

¼ cup sugar

1 tablespoon grated lemon zest

2 medium-sized ripe peaches, peeled and sliced

2 teaspoons fresh lemon juice

1. Preheat the oven to 375°F. Lightly spray a 1½-quart soufflé dish with non-stick spray.
2. Place the ricotta in a large bowl and add the egg yolks, extracts, flour, salt, sugar, and lemon zest. Whisk together until fluffy and smooth. (If using cottage cheese, do all of this in a food processor fitted with the steel blade, whipping the cottage cheese for a minute or so by itself first to smooth the curds.)
3. Beat the egg whites until they form peaks that don't fall over when the whisk or beaters are lifted and just a little liquid is left in the bottom of the bowl. (More details about this are on the preceding page.)
4. Fold the beaten whites into the cheese mixture until they are mostly incorporated. The mixture will not be uniform—there will be little puffs of "cloud" here and there—and that is fine. (It's best not to overfold, as this will deflate the egg whites.) Transfer the mixture to the prepared dish.
5. Toss together the peach slices and the lemon juice, then arrange the peaches in a design on top of the soufflé.
6. Bake in the center of the oven for 45 minutes, or until the soufflé seems solid when you gently shake the dish. Serve immediately.

 THE IRONY OF THE SOUFFLÉ

Here is a generally unacknowledged culinary paradox: Even though it is standard procedure to bring a soufflé to the table the second it emerges, in all its fleeting glory, from the oven—and all traditional soufflé recipes remind us that the guests had better wait for the soufflé, which in turn, waits for no one—the truth is a soufflé is actually much too hot to eat when it is fresh from the oven. It needs to cool down first, during which time it deflates. Cruel fact of life! (Not to mention that when you break into a soufflé to serve it, it deflates anyway.) I've concluded that the true purpose of rushing a fresh soufflé to the table is to have people *admire and applaud it*—to create a spectacle, as it were. The eating opportunity realistically happens about 10 minutes later, making this a classic "hurry up and wait" situation. But it's worth it!

Giant Cauliflower-Cheese Puff

Keep this recipe in mind when you need a noteworthy brunch dish but you're not in the mood to fuss. All this requires is some cooked cauliflower and onions and an egg mixture that gets whipped up in the blender. Combine everything in a pan, put it in the oven, and 40 minutes later you have an impressive brunch entrée. I love it when that happens.

- Rondelé is a creamy cheese accented strongly with garlic and herbs. If you can't find it, use a garlic- and herb-enhanced goat cheese or something similar. This recipe is quite flexible.
- Leftovers can be stored for up to 5 days in a tightly covered container in the refrigerator and reheated in a 350°F oven or a microwave.

YIELD: 4 to 6 servings
PREPARATION TIME: 20 minutes, plus 40 minutes to bake

Nonstick spray

Butter for the pan

1 tablespoon olive oil

2 cups chopped onion

¾ teaspoon salt

5 cups cauliflower florets

6 large eggs

1 cup milk

1 cup unbleached all-purpose flour

¾ cup Rondelé Garlic and Herb cheese (5 ounces)

1. Preheat the oven to 350°F. Lightly spray a 9- by 13-inch pan with nonstick spray, then add a small chunk (about 3 tablespoons) of butter. Place the pan in the preheating oven for a minute or so to melt the butter, then take it out and carefully tilt it in all directions to let the butter coat the bottom. Set aside.

2. Place a 10-inch skillet over medium heat and wait a few minutes. Add the olive oil, wait about 10 seconds, then swirl to coat the pan. Add the onions, sauté for 5 minutes, then stir in the salt and the cauliflower. Sauté over medium heat for 8 to 10 minutes, or until the cauliflower is just tender. Transfer this mixture to the prepared pan.

3. While the cauliflower is cooking, combine the eggs, milk, flour, and cheese in a blender. Whip into a smooth batter and pour it over the cauliflower mixture in the pan.

4. Bake in the center of the oven for 35 to 40 minutes, or until puffed and golden. Serve hot or warm, cut into squares.

VARIATIONS   For each variation, follow the main recipe, adding any of the following in any combination—as much as will fit.

GIANT BROCCOLI-CHEESE PUFF

Replace the cauliflower with:

- 5 cups chopped broccoli

Replace the Rondelé cheese with:

- 1 cup grated sharp cheddar

GIANT MUSHROOM PUFF

Replace the cauliflower mixture with:

- All-Purpose Breakfast Mushrooms (page 172)

GIANT ASPARAGUS-MUSHROOM PUFF

Lightly steam:

- 1½ cups asparagus tips

and add them to the mushroom variation just described.

MY TWO FAVORITE QUICHES

These quiches are my all-time favorites. Fried green tomatoes and sharp cheddar cheese grace the first one, and the second is brimming with sweet onions, red peppers, and sumptuous gruyère. Try serving the two quiches side by side for a dazzling brunch duet—they go really well together.

- The crust can be made well ahead and refrigerated for several days. It can also be stored in the freezer in a sealed plastic bag. You don't need to defrost it before assembling the quiche.

YIELD: Each makes 4 to 6 servings
PREPARATION TIME: 30 minutes, plus 40 minutes to bake

Gruyère Quiche with golden onion and red pepper

- You can prepare the sautéed vegetables (steps 1 and 2) up to several days ahead.

1 tablespoon olive oil

3 cups sliced onion

½ teaspoon salt

¼ teaspoon dried thyme

¼ teaspoon dried sage

1 teaspoon dry mustard

1 unbaked Quiche Crust (recipe follows)

1 tablespoon balsamic vinegar

1 cup thinly sliced red bell pepper

1 cup (packed) grated gruyère

3 large eggs

1 cup milk

Freshly ground black pepper

1. Place a medium-sized skillet over medium heat and wait about 2 minutes. Add the oil and swirl to coat the pan. Add the onion, sauté for 5 minutes, and then add the salt, herbs, and mustard. Cover the pan, lower the heat, and cook for 15 minutes, stirring occasionally. (During this time, preheat the oven to 375°F, and place the unbaked crust on a baking tray.)

2. Sir the vinegar and bell pepper into the onions, turn the heat up to medium, and cook, uncovered, for another 5 minutes. Remove from heat.

3. Sprinkle the cheese into the crust, then spoon the onion-pepper mixture on top of the cheese.

4. Whisk together the eggs, milk, and black pepper to taste, and slowly pour this over the vegetables and cheese.

5. Bake on the baking tray in the lower third of the oven for 35 to 40 minutes, or until the custard is set. Cool for at least 10 minutes before slicing, and serve at any temperature.

Fried Green Tomato Quiche

• Prepare the tomatoes up to several hours in advance, and leave them on the cooling rack until you need them.

1 unbaked Quiche Crust
(recipe follows)

1 cup (packed) grated cheddar

Fried Green Tomatoes (page 169)

3 large eggs

1 cup milk

¼ teaspoon salt (rounded measure)

Freshly ground black pepper

A few dashes of cayenne

1. Preheat the oven to 375°F. Place the unbaked crust on a baking tray.
2. Sprinkle the grated cheese into the bottom of the crust.
3. Cut the fried tomatoes in half, and arrange them over the cheese. They will overlap, and that's fine.
4. Whisk together the eggs, milk, salt, pepper to taste, and cayenne, and slowly pour this mixture over the tomatoes and cheese.
5. Bake on the baking tray in the lower third of the oven for 35 to 40 minutes, or until the custard is set. Cool for at least 10 minutes before slicing, and serve at any temperature.

Quiche Crust

This generous recipe enables you to make a nice edge on your crust, whether you're building it in a 9-inch pie pan or a 10-inch springform tart pan.

1½ cups unbleached all-purpose
flour

¼ teaspoon salt

½ cup (1 stick) cold unsalted
butter

Up to 3 tablespoons cold water,
milk, or buttermilk

1. Place the flour and salt in the bowl of a food processor fitted with the steel blade. Cut the butter into slices, add to the processor, and buzz several times, until the mixture is uniform and resembles coarse meal. (If you don't have a food processor, use a pastry cutter or 2 forks instead.)
2. Continue to process in quick spurts as you add the water, 1 tablespoon at a time. As soon as the dough adheres to itself when pinched, stop adding water and turn the dough out onto a floured surface. Gather it gently into a ball.
3. Roll the dough into a circle 11 inches or so in diameter (slightly bigger than a 10-inch round). Lift the dough and ease it into a 9-inch pie pan or 10-inch springform tart pan, nudging it gently into the corners. Form a generous, even edge all the way around the sides. If you're not going to use the crust right away, wrap it tightly in plastic wrap and refrigerate or freeze it until use.

6

POTATOES, BEANS, TEMPEH & HASHES

CONTENTS

POTATOES, BEANS, TEMPEH & HASHES

Some people like sweet breakfasts; others prefer savory. Many of us alternate, depending on the weather, the time of day, the day of the week—and whether or not the savory offering includes crisp, hot potatoes! When potatoes are perfectly cooked, not only are they delicious and texturally enthralling, but I'm convinced they also take on psychologically beneficial properties. They manage, magically, to have substance without weight, to make us feel like children being held. And potatoes have broad potential for combining beautifully with other nutritious ingredients, which is so important when one is trying to eat well in a busy life.

Traditional American farm breakfasts have always showcased potatoes, which are larder vegetables that keep well over the winter. In the preindustrial era, rural life demanded more physical labor in one morning—*before* breakfast—than most of us modern urban dwellers expend in a week. Breakfast needed to be hearty, because it had to provide the fuel for plowing the lower forty and then some. These days, we don't really need that kind of hearty breakfast, unless we are professional athletes in training. But we do want a big plateful (or a tastefully medium-sized plateful) of potatoes every once in a while, especially on cold mornings when we know it's going to be a long wait until lunch.

Hashes and potatoes present a good opportunity to incorporate fresh or leftover vegetables into a tasty breakfast dish. Many of the recipes in this chapter have colorful variations that really pack in the greenery, providing an easy head start on the day's vegetable quota.

I've also included a few bean and tempeh dishes. Beans and tempeh are great sources of protein, fiber, and minerals, and like potatoes, they blend well with vegetables. Tempeh especially is a good meat substitute—not just for vegetarians but for anyone who wants a high-protein alternative to eggs.

I know you're not going to get up at dawn on a busy workday to make these savory dishes from scratch. But they all are designed to reheat really well—and fast! So put some of these recipes together in the evening or on a weekend, and store them in tightly covered containers in the refrigerator. You will thank yourself in the morning the minute those savory seasonings hit the hot pan.

Mustard-Roasted Potatoes with dill

Bite-sized pieces of potato acquire dreamy qualities when coated with olive oil and mustard and roasted at a very high temperature until crisp on the outside and creamy within. Light touches of salt, pepper, and minced fresh dill are added when the potatoes come out of the oven, giving new meaning to the phrase "crowning touch."

• This will work with any waxy variety of potato. In the winter, I like to use red or yellow creamers. In the summer and fall, if you have access to a good farmers' market, look for freshly harvested fingerlings.

YIELD: 4 to 6 servings
PREPARATION TIME: 25 minutes (5 minutes of work)

4 tablespoons olive oil

⅓ cup Dijon mustard

2 pounds small potatoes, cut into 1-inch pieces (unless they're already that size)

¼ teaspoon salt (rounded measure)

⅛ teaspoon black pepper

1 to 2 tablespoons minced fresh dill

1. Adjust the oven rack so that it is about one third of the way up from the bottom of the oven, then preheat the oven to 450°F. Line a baking tray with foil, add 1 tablespoon of the olive oil, and brush to distribute it over the foil.

2. Whisk together the remaining 3 tablespoons oil and the mustard in a medium-sized bowl. Add the potatoes and toss to coat.

3. Spread the potatoes in a single layer on the prepared tray, and place the tray in the oven on the rack you adjusted in step 1. Roast until the potatoes can be pierced fairly easily with a fork—about 20 minutes, depending on the size and shape of the pieces.

4. Remove the tray from the oven, and sprinkle the potatoes lightly with the salt and pepper. Transfer to a serving bowl, toss with fresh dill, and serve hot, warm, or at room temperature.

VARIATION **WASABI-ROASTED POTATOES**

Follow the main recipe with this adjustment.

Replace the mustard with the following:

• ⅓ cup wasabi (Japanese green horseradish paste)
• 3 to 4 tablespoons water

Place the wasabi in a small bowl, and add enough water to thin it to the consistency of prepared mustard. Whisk this mixture together with the oil, as described in step 2, and proceed with the recipe, omitting the dill.

For more intense flavor, you can double the wasabi-oil mixture and brush another layer of it onto the potatoes when they come out of the oven.

Home Fries at Home

My fourth-grader wanted to know why they're called home fries when the only place we ever ate them was in restaurants. Good question—why indeed? Deciding that home fries should be true to their name, I developed this recipe to correct the situation. Many cooking adventures later, with a house full of potatoes, I'm happy to report that home fries made at home are not only eminently doable but also fantastic—better than even the best restaurant version. When I serve these for breakfast, my kids brag about me in school. What better motivation could there possibly be?

To get home fries right, you need to perform three simple cooking processes. First you boil the potatoes. Then you fry them in hot oil to get them brown and crisp. The third stage introduces onions, seasonings, and other embellishments, adding the crisped potatoes back in at the very end. It only sounds complicated. Homemade home fries are actually very straightforward and a lot of fun!

You can boil the potatoes up to several days ahead. Prepare all the other ingredients ahead, too, and then assemble the home fries just before serving. You can also store the completed recipe in a tightly covered container in the refrigerator for up to a week. Home fries reheat beautifully, either in a hot, lightly oiled frying pan or spread out on a tray in a 350°F oven.

Any type of potato will work, and you can combine the various kinds. Waxy varieties, like Yukon Gold or Yellow Finn, hold together very well, whereas russets are drier and more crumbly but fry up nicely, even though they fall apart somewhat. It's actually fine for the potatoes used in home fries to fall apart, and it can even lead to a more interesting texture.

My basic recipe for home fries (following page) is quite plain—potatoes with just onions, bell peppers, and a few seasonings. From there we depart into the vast world of variations, from "Kitchen Sink" to the Southwest and beyond. Recipes for Mexican, Indian, and Peruvian-style versions follow. You will never look at a potato in the same way again.

PREPPED POTATOES

Here is the procedure for preparing potatoes for home fries. This amount works for all of the recipes that follow.

- 2 pounds potatoes (any kind)

Scrub the potatoes, and cut them into ½-inch cubes. (You should have about 5 to 6 cups of cubes.) Place them in a large saucepan, add water to cover, and bring to a boil. Cook until just tender, then drain and set aside.

If you are going to make home fries right away, you don't need to cool them first. Just proceed with any of the recipes.

If you are prepping the potatoes in advance, store them in fresh water in a tightly covered container in the refrigerator. Drain and dry completely before using. (You don't need to bring them to room temperature.)

USING LEFTOVER POTATOES

You can use leftover cooked potatoes (any kind—4 to 5 cups) for home fries. In fact, I'm sure that home fries were the invention of some frugal, unknown American cook of yesteryear, intent on finding a creative use for last night's spuds. Even baked potatoes, although crumbly, will work. And it's okay to include the skins—just be sure to cut them up.

Basic Home Fries

My basic home fries are very simple, focusing on the potatoes themselves—most notably their texture. The cooking method requires patience but not a lot of work. You need to sauté the already-cooked ("prepped") potatoes in a hot pan with hot oil and plenty of space to allow maximum contact with direct heat. This gets them truly, divinely crisp. This step is critically important, as crispness is the main point. Flavor is also very important, and I keep it straightforward in the basic recipe, seasoning with just onion, a few dried herbs, bell pepper, and garlic. In the variations that follow, the potatoes are still the main event, but they share the spotlight with various other ingredients. The possibilities abound!

- Please read "Home Fries at Home" (preceding page), and have the Prepped Potatoes on hand.

YIELD: **About 4 servings (slightly more for the variations)**
PREPARATION TIME: **1 hour (once Prepped Potatoes are done)**

---

3 tablespoons olive oil

Prepped Potatoes (page 145)

½ teaspoon salt (possibly more)

1 to 2 teaspoons unsalted butter
(optional)

1½ to 2 cups chopped onion

1 teaspoon dried basil

½ teaspoon dried thyme

1 cup diced bell pepper (any color)

1 to 2 tablespoons coarsely
chopped garlic

Freshly ground black pepper

OPTIONAL TOPPINGS

Sour cream

Minced scallions or chives

Salsa (pages 250 to 255)

Chipotle Cream (page 256)

Tomato Jam (page 262)

1. Place a 10-inch skillet or sauté pan over medium heat. After several minutes, add 1 tablespoon of the olive oil, wait about 10 seconds, then swirl to coat the pan. Turn the heat up to medium-high and add half the cooked potatoes, spreading them into a single layer in the hot oil. Let them cook without stirring for 5 minutes.

2. After 5 minutes, sprinkle in about ⅛ teaspoon of the salt and turn the potatoes over, using a metal spatula. Spread them into a single layer again. Let them cook without stirring for another 5 to 8 minutes, or until golden. Scrape from the bottom to loosen the potatoes, and toss them around in the pan. Cook for another minute or two, then transfer them to a plate or a bowl, scraping out and saving all the tasty brown tidbits from the bottom of the pan. Repeat this procedure with the remaining potatoes, using another tablespoon of the oil and another ⅛ teaspoon salt.

3. After cooking the potatoes, scrape out the pan (saving the scrapings), and wipe it out with a damp paper towel. Return the pan to the heat, and when it is hot, add the remaining tablespoon of oil. (You can also melt in some butter.) Wait 10 seconds, then swirl to coat the pan. Add the onion and sauté over medium heat for 5 to 8 minutes, or until it becomes very soft. Sprinkle in the remaining ¼ teaspoon salt, along with the herbs, bell pepper, and garlic. Continue to cook, stirring often, for another 5 minutes or so.

4. Return the potatoes to the pan and stir them into the onion mixture. Sauté over medium heat for another 10 or 20 minutes, or until everything is done to your liking.

5. Taste to adjust the salt, and grind in some black pepper. Serve hot or warm, topped with sour cream and minced scallions or chives, or any other of the suggested toppings.

For each variation, follow the main recipe with these adjustments.

KITCHEN SINK HOME FRIES

In step 3, after the onion becomes soft, add:

- 4 cups (packed) chopped spinach
- 1 small zucchini or summer squash, diced or sliced
- 1 to 2 cups sliced cherry tomatoes
- 1 cup corn (fresh or frozen/defrosted)

At the end of step 4, stir in:

- A few tablespoons of pesto and/or some grated cheese of your choice (You can broil the cheese on top, for a dramatic effect.)

SOY-ENHANCED HOME FRIES

In step 3, after the onion becomes soft, add either:

- 1 cup sliced pressed tofu (smoked or "savory baked")

or:

- 1 cup Basic Browned Tempeh (page 156)

SMOKY BEAN HOME FRIES

In step 3, after the onion becomes soft, add:

- 1 can (15 ounces) pinto beans, rinsed and drained

Choose one of the following, and add it with the beans:

- Up to 1 teaspoon minced chipotle chiles
- Up to ½ teaspoon liquid smoke
- Up to 1 cup crisped soy bacon

SOUTHWEST HOME FRIES

When you begin cooking the onion, add:

- 1 tablespoon pure ground chile powder

In step 3, after the onion becomes soft, add:

- ¾ cup minced anaheim or poblano chiles
- 2 to 3 tablespoons fresh lime juice

Mexican Home Fries

Home fries travel south, picking up a few surprise additions along the way.

- Please read "Home Fries at Home" (page 145), and have the Prepped Potatoes on hand.
- You can cut the tortillas into any size and shape. Children love to do this with scissors.
- Anaheim and poblano chiles are moderately hot. For a milder flavor, remove and discard the seeds. (Wash your hands after handling these or any other hot peppers.) You can also substitute canned green chiles.

YIELD: **5 to 6 servings**
PREPARATION TIME: **1 hour (once Prepped Potatoes are done)**

3 tablespoons olive oil

Prepped Potatoes (page 145)

3 to 4 corn tortillas

¾ teaspoon salt (possibly more)

1 to 2 teaspoons unsalted butter (optional)

1½ to 2 cups chopped onion

2 teaspoons cumin

1 cup diced bell pepper (any color)

¾ cup minced anaheim and/or poblano chiles

2 teaspoons minced garlic

1 cup cooked pinto beans (optional)

3 tablespoons fresh lime juice

Freshly ground black pepper

Red pepper flakes or cayenne

OPTIONAL TOPPINGS

1 cup (packed) grated jack cheese

Lightly toasted pumpkin seeds

Sour cream

Salsa (pages 250 to 255)

Minced cilantro and/or parsley

1. Place a 10-inch skillet or sauté pan over medium heat. After several minutes, add 1 tablespoon of the olive oil, wait about 10 seconds, then swirl to coat the pan. Turn the heat up to medium-high and add half the cooked potatoes, spreading them into a single layer in the hot oil. Let them cook without stirring for 5 minutes. During this time, cut the tortillas into small pieces (approximately 2-inch strips, but the shape is unimportant), and set aside.

2. After 5 minutes, sprinkle in about ⅛ teaspoon of the salt and turn the potatoes over, using a metal spatula. Spread them into a single layer again. Let them cook without stirring for another 5 to 8 minutes, or until golden. Scrape from the bottom to loosen the potatoes, and toss them around in the pan. Cook for another minute or two, then transfer them to a plate or a bowl, scraping out and saving all the tasty brown tidbits from the bottom of the pan. Repeat this procedure with the remaining potatoes, using another tablespoon of the oil and another ⅛ teaspoon salt.

3. After cooking the potatoes, scrape out the pan (saving the scrapings), and wipe it out with a damp paper towel. Return the pan to the heat, and when it is hot, add the remaining tablespoon of oil. (You can also melt in some butter.) Wait 10 seconds, then swirl to coat the pan. Add the onion and sauté over medium heat for 5 to 8 minutes, or until soft. Stir in the cumin, bell pepper, chiles, and the remaining ½ teaspoon salt, and sauté for about 5 minutes longer. Add the tortilla pieces and the garlic and continue to cook, stirring often, for about 10 minutes more.

4. Return the potatoes to the pan—adding the beans, if desired—and stir them into the onion mixture. Sauté over medium heat for another 10 or 20 minutes, or until everything is done to your liking. Sprinkle in the lime juice, and add black and red pepper—and possibly more salt—to taste.

5. Serve hot or warm, with any combination of the suggested toppings.

Indian Home Fries

Potatoes and Indian spices are a blessed match. This spunky and pretty dish, crowned with bright green peas, will be even more beautiful if you make it with red onions and unpeeled red potatoes.

- Defrost frozen peas by placing them in a strainer under cold or tepid running water for just a minute or two. No cooking is necessary.
- If you are using fresh peas, steam them lightly before using.
- Please read "Home Fries at Home" (page 145), and have the Prepped Potatoes on hand.

YIELD: 4 to 5 servings
PREPARATION TIME: 50 minutes (once Prepped Potatoes are done)

3 tablespoons olive oil

Prepped Potatoes (page 145)

¾ teaspoon salt (possibly more)

1 to 2 teaspoons unsalted butter (optional)

2 cups chopped onion

1 to 2 tablespoons minced fresh ginger

2 teaspoons mustard seed

1 teaspoon cumin seed

1 teaspoon ground cumin

1 teaspoon ground coriander

½ teaspoon ground cardamom

1 to 2 tablespoons minced garlic

3 to 4 tablespoons fresh lemon juice

Cayenne

1½ cups green peas (defrosted if frozen)

Yogurt or Breakfast Raita (page 216; optional)

1. Place a 10-inch skillet or sauté pan over medium heat. After several minutes, add 1 tablespoon of the olive oil, wait about 10 seconds, then swirl to coat the pan. Turn the heat up to medium-high and add half the cooked potatoes, spreading them into a single layer in the hot oil. Let them cook without stirring for 5 minutes.

2. After 5 minutes, sprinkle in about ⅛ teaspoon of the salt and turn the potatoes over, using a metal spatula. Spread them into a single layer again. Let them cook without stirring for another 5 to 8 minutes, or until golden. Scrape from the bottom to loosen the potatoes, and toss them around in the pan. Cook for another minute or two, then transfer them to a plate or a bowl, scraping out and saving all the tasty brown tidbits from the bottom of the pan. Repeat this procedure with the remaining potatoes, using another tablespoon of the oil and another ⅛ teaspoon salt.

3. After cooking the potatoes, scrape out the pan (saving the scrapings), and wipe it out with a damp paper towel. Return the pan to the heat, and when it is hot, add the remaining tablespoon of oil. (You can also melt in some butter.) Wait 10 seconds, then swirl to coat the pan. Add the onion, ginger, mustard seed, and cumin seed, and sauté over medium heat for 8 to 10 minutes, or until the onions are very soft and the seeds begin to pop. Sprinkle in the remaining ½ teaspoon salt, along with the other seasonings and the garlic. Continue to cook, stirring often, for another 5 minutes or so.

4. Return the potatoes to the pan and stir them into the onion mixture. Sauté over medium heat for another 10 or 20 minutes, or until everything is done to your liking. Stir in the lemon juice and cayenne to taste, and adjust the salt, if necessary.

5. Serve hot or warm, topped with the peas and with some yogurt or raita on the side, if desired.

Peruvian Blue Home Fries

Many people think potatoes originated in Ireland—or maybe Idaho—but in fact, they are native to the rugged Andean highlands of South America. This dish features a traditional Peruvian combination of potatoes and peanuts and will be even more authentic if you make it with Peruvian blue potatoes (available in farmers' markets and in some grocery stores). Other types of potato will also work.

- Please read "Home Fries at Home" (page 145), and have the Prepped Potatoes on hand.
- Anaheim and poblano chiles are moderately hot. For a milder flavor, remove and discard the seeds. (Wash your hands after handling these or any other hot peppers.) You can also substitute canned green chiles.

YIELD: **About 4 servings**
PREPARATION TIME: **50 minutes (once Prepped Potatoes are done)**

3 tablespoons olive oil

Prepped Potatoes (page 145)

¾ teaspoon salt (possibly more)

1 to 2 teaspoons unsalted butter (optional)

1½ to 2 cups minced onion

1 cup minced anaheim and/or poblano chiles

1 cup chopped red and yellow bell peppers

1 to 2 tablespoons minced garlic

¾ cup (packed) grated jack or cheddar (optional)

3 tablespoons fresh lemon juice

1 cup lightly toasted peanuts, coarsely chopped

Minced cilantro and/or parsley

Squeezable lemon wedges

1. Place a 10-inch skillet or sauté pan over medium heat. After several minutes, add 1 tablespoon of the olive oil, wait about 10 seconds, then swirl to coat the pan. Turn the heat up to medium-high and add half the cooked potatoes, spreading them into a single layer in the hot oil. Let them cook without stirring for 5 minutes.

2. After 5 minutes, sprinkle in about ⅛ teaspoon of the salt and turn the potatoes over, using a metal spatula. Spread them into a single layer again. Let them cook for another 5 to 8 minutes, or until golden. Scrape from the bottom to loosen the potatoes, and toss them around in the pan. Cook for another minute or two, then transfer them to a plate or a bowl, scraping out and saving all the tasty brown tidbits from the bottom of the pan. Repeat this procedure with the remaining potatoes, using another tablespoon of the oil and another ⅛ teaspoon salt.

3. After cooking the potatoes, scrape out the pan (saving the scrapings), and wipe it out with a damp paper towel. Return the pan to the heat, and when it is hot, add the remaining tablespoon of oil. (You can also melt in some butter.) Wait 10 seconds, then swirl to coat the pan. Add the onion and sauté over medium heat for 5 to 8 minutes, or until it becomes very soft. Add the chiles and bell peppers, along with the remaining ½ teaspoon salt. Continue to cook, stirring often, for another 5 to 8 minutes.

4. Return the potatoes to the pan and stir them into the onion mixture, along with the garlic. Sauté over medium heat for another 10 or 20 minutes, or until everything is done to your liking. Sprinkle in the cheese and lemon juice during the last few minutes of cooking, and, if necessary, adjust the salt.

5. Serve hot or warm, topped with peanuts and minced cilantro or parsley, and with lemon wedges tucked into the side.

Cajun Scalloped Sweet Potatoes

When you combine different-colored sweet potatoes (deep garnet and pale orange), this beautiful dish becomes stunning—an edible sunburst! With its deep, baked-in spicy/aromatic flavors and brilliant color, this is perfect for an autumn brunch. Serve it with scrambled eggs or tofu, a Breakfast Salad (page 167), and, for dessert, Bittersweet Mocha Coffee Cake (page 284) and some fresh fruit.

- Chipotle chiles (smoked jalapeños) are available canned in a tomato sauce (adobo) in the imported foods section of many grocery stores and specialty shops. They are very strong and hot, and they keep forever if stored in a tightly covered container in the refrigerator. Use little bits at a time.
- You can prepare this dish through step 4 up to 2 days ahead and save the last 20 minutes of baking time for the next day. (Leaving the foil in place, cool the dish to room temperature and then refrigerate. Bring it back to room temperature before the final baking.)

YIELD: 6 to 8 servings
PREPARATION TIME: 15 minutes, plus 1 hour to bake

1 tablespoon olive oil

Nonstick spray

2½ pounds sweet potatoes (4 medium)

1 teaspoon salt

1 tablespoon pure ground chile powder

⅛ teaspoon black pepper

1 teaspoon dried thyme

1 to 2 tablespoons minced garlic

1 teaspoon minced chipotle chiles (optional)

2 cups milk (plain soy milk will also work)

1 to 2 teaspoons sugar (optional)

2 tablespoons fresh lemon juice

Squeezable lemon wedges

Tomato Jam (page 262; optional)

1. Preheat the oven to 425°F. Coat the bottom of a 1½- to 2-quart baking pan or gratin dish with the olive oil. Spray a large sheet of aluminum foil on one side with nonstick spray.
2. Peel the sweet potatoes and slice them paper-thin. (If you have a food processor with a thin slicing attachment, you can use it for this.) Spread them in the oiled pan.
3. Combine the salt, seasonings, garlic, and chiles in a 4-cup liquid measure. Pour in the milk, stir until blended, and slowly pour the seasoned milk over the sweet potato slices in the pan.
4. Cover the pan tightly with the prepared piece of foil (sprayed side down), and bake it in the center of the preheated oven for about 40 minutes.
5. Pull out the oven rack, remove the foil, and use a long-handled spoon to carefully "stir" (that is, lift and rearrange) the potatoes a few times to redistribute the seasonings.
6. Return the pan to the oven and bake, uncovered, for 20 minutes more, or until the sweet potatoes look slightly shriveled and golden on top. If you like a sweet touch, you can sprinkle the top with the sugar during the last 10 minutes or so of baking.
7. Remove from the oven, drizzle with the lemon juice, and cool for about 15 minutes before serving. Any extra liquid will get absorbed during this waiting period. Serve warm, with a lemon wedge tucked into the side and a dab of Tomato Jam on top, if desired.

American Potato Cutlets

For an unusual skillet breakfast, serve these mashed potato cakes with Fried Green Tomatoes (page 169). The timing is good, because you can prepare the tomatoes first and then let them cool while you fry the potato cakes. (The tomatoes need time to cool anyway.)

- Why russets? Because they are a dry, mealy variety that mashes well. Other, waxier types can turn gluey when mashed.
- You can use leftover mashed potatoes for this. If they've been salted, adjust the amount of salt accordingly.
- If you're cooking the potatoes just for this recipe, use 1 pound. Peel them, cut them into chunks, and boil until soft. Drain very well, and mash until smooth.
- You can make and coat the patties up to a day in advance, storing them on a plate, tightly covered with plastic wrap, in the refrigerator. Dredge them again in bread crumbs just before frying.

YIELD: **About 4 servings (2 patties each)**
PREPARATION TIME: **30 minutes**

1½ cups cooked, mashed russet potatoes

2 tablespoons Dijon mustard

2 tablespoons minced fresh dill

1 teaspoon minced garlic

½ cup finely minced scallion

1 hard-boiled egg, minced or grated

¾ teaspoon salt, or to taste

⅛ teaspoon black pepper

1 large egg, beaten

⅓ to ½ cup fine bread crumbs

2 to 3 tablespoons olive oil

A little butter (optional)

OPTIONAL TOPPINGS

Sour cream or Chipotle Cream (page 256)

Fire-Roasted Pepper Salsa (page 254)

Smoky Tomato Salsa (page 253)

Caramelized Onion and Lemon Marmalade (page 258)

1. Place the mashed potatoes in a medium-sized bowl. Add the mustard, dill, garlic, scallion, hard-boiled egg, salt, and pepper. Mix until everything is thoroughly blended.
2. Break the egg onto a dinner plate, and beat it with a fork until smooth. Place the bread crumbs on another plate.
3. Use your hands (wet them if you like, for easier handling) to form the mixture into 3-inch patties, using about ¼ cup for each.
4. Carefully dip both sides of each patty in egg and dredge them lightly in the bread crumbs to coat on all sides.
5. Place a 10-inch skillet over medium heat. After a minute or two, add the olive oil, wait for about 10 seconds, then swirl to coat the pan. If you like, you can also melt in some butter.
6. When the pan is hot enough to sizzle a bread crumb, fry the cutlets for about 5 minutes on each side, or until golden and crisp. Remove the cutlets from the pan, and transfer them to a wire rack over a tray to cool. (This retains their crispy texture.)
7. Serve hot or warm, with any of the suggested toppings.

(VARIATION) **BROCCOLI-POTATO CUTLETS**

Follow the main recipe with these adjustments.

Add to the potato mixture:

- 1½ cups finely minced broccoli (florets and peeled stems)

For a touch of color, replace the scallion with:

- ½ cup finely minced red onion

Crispy Southwest Polenta Hash

In this fun breakfast or brunch dish, you sauté Polenta Pieces in a hot skillet with savory southwestern seasonings. Be sure to use a large enough skillet (or two skillets, side by side) so the polenta can have maximum contact with the hot oil. That is what gives this dish its ultra-crisp texture.

- This hash is good with eggs or by itself and it's *really* good with salsa. Use your favorite commercial brand, or make your own (pages 250 to 255).
- You can make the Polenta Pieces several days ahead of time and store them in an airtight container in the refrigerator.
- The jalapeño adds a bit of heat. For a milder flavor, remove and discard the seeds. (Wash your hands after handling this or any other hot pepper.) You can also substitute canned green chiles.

YIELD: **4 to 6 servings (depending on the context)**
PREPARATION TIME: **30 minutes (once the Polenta Pieces are made)**

2 to 3 tablespoons olive oil

1 to 2 teaspoons butter (optional)

Polenta Pieces (page 59),
  not yet fried

Nonstick spray (optional)

1 heaping cup minced onion

2 to 3 tablespoons minced jalapeño
  (a 3-inch chile)

2 teaspoons pure ground chile
  powder

1 teaspoon minced garlic

1 to 2 cups fresh corn kernels
  (optional)

1 to 2 cups cherry tomatoes, halved
  (optional)

1½ cups cooked black beans
  (a 15-ounce can), drained

Salsa (pages 250 to 255; optional)

1. Place a 10-inch sauté pan over medium-high heat for about 2 minutes. Add 1 tablespoon of the oil, wait another 10 seconds or so, then swirl to coat the pan. You can also melt in some butter for a richer flavor.
2. Add the Polenta Pieces (you should hear a nice sizzle on contact), and sauté in a single layer for a good 12 to 15 minutes, loosening and moving them around every 5 minutes with a metal spatula to keep them from sticking. They will crumble somewhat, which is actually desirable, as it makes a crisper result. Don't move the pieces any more often than every 5 minutes; letting them sit over the heat is what gets them crisp. If the polenta appears to be sticking, push it to one side, lightly spray the pan with nonstick spray—or add a little more olive oil—and resume sautéing until all surfaces are golden.
3. When the polenta turns golden, move it over to one side of the pan, and pour in a little additional oil. Add the onions, jalapeño, and chile powder, and sauté for 8 to 10 minutes, or until the onions are very soft. Stir in the garlic, and sauté for another 5 minutes.
4. Push the polenta pieces back into the center, and mix everything together in the pan, still over the heat. Gently stir in the corn, tomatoes, and beans, and cook just until heated through. (Be careful not to break the beans as you stir. The dish looks nicer if they remain whole.)
5. Serve hot or warm, with salsa if desired.

Hash Browns

The secret to heartbreakingly perfect hash browns is to maximize their direct contact with very hot oil while they are cooking. This means you must choose the right oil—one that can safely and effectively be heated to a high temperature. It also means you must use a sufficiently large pan so the grated potatoes can have plenty of room to bathe in the hot oil. It's best to cook just a few portions at a time so you won't crowd the pan. You can have two pans going at the same time, or just make serial batches.

The ideal oil to use for high-temperature frying is high-oleic safflower oil. It cooks very effectively at a high temperature. If you're worried about ingesting too much oil by eating hash browns, here's the key: When you use the right oil, and you get it hot enough before *adding the potatoes, they will absorb very little of it. The proof is in the pan: When you remove the cooked potatoes with a slotted spoon, you'll see that most of the oil remains behind. And you can safely use the same oil over again for the next batch. This is a clean frying process with a very crisp, nongreasy result.*

- Use a food processor with the medium grating attachment to grate the potatoes.
- Don't worry if the grated raw potato discolors as it sits around. It will come back to life when it cooks.
- Both russets and waxier varieties work very well. Russets yield a more feathery result, while waxier potatoes make slightly chewier hash browns. You can also combine the different types.

YIELD: **2 to 3 servings (easily multiplied)**
PREPARATION TIME: **25 minutes**

---

2 cups (packed) grated potato
(¾ pound), peeled or not

High-oleic safflower oil for frying

Salt

1. Place a 10-inch sauté pan over medium heat and wait about 3 minutes. Pour in enough oil to make a pool about ⅛ inch deep. Wait another minute or two for the oil to heat up.
2. When the oil is hot enough to instantly and dramatically sizzle a bread crumb, *slowly*—so as not to cause the hot oil to splash—add the grated potatoes in a single layer. (I find it easiest to do this with a fork.) Two cups of grated potato should just fit into the pan.
3. Once all the potatoes are in, turn the heat up to medium-high and let the potatoes cook undisturbed in the bubbling oil for about 7 or 8 minutes. They will form a large, round cake. Lift a section with a metal spatula to see if it is brown enough underneath. (This is your judgment call.) If they look perfect to you, loosen the potatoes all around with the spatula, and carefully flip them to the other side. If you'd like them darker, leave them there for another 2 minutes or so before turning them over. The second side will brown faster, so check it after 5 minutes.
4. Line a plate with a double layer of paper towels. Use a slotted spoon to lift the potatoes out of the pan—leaving much of the oil behind—and transfer them to the prepared plate. Sprinkle lightly with salt to taste.
5. Serve hot, warm, or at room temperature.

VARIATIONS

Hash browns made from sweet potatoes or spaghetti squash are delicious! Note that because of their high sugar content, sweet potatoes and spaghetti squash have a greater tendency to burn than regular potatoes do. So watch them carefully, and keep the heat at medium. Also, these variations don't stay as crisp as hash browns made with regular potatoes. If necessary, refresh them in a 300°F oven or toaster oven. Spread them out in a single layer on a foil-lined tray, and they will turn crisp in minutes.

HASH-BROWN SWEET POTATOES

Follow the main recipe, replacing the potatoes with:

- 2 cups (packed) peeled, grated sweet potatoes

HASH-BROWN SPAGHETTI SQUASH

Follow the main recipe, replacing the potatoes with:

- 2 cups "prepared" spaghetti squash (instructions are at the bottom of page 191)

FEAR OF FRYING? HIGH-OLEIC SAFFLOWER OIL TO THE RESCUE!

High-oleic safflower oil is not the same as regular safflower oil, which is much less stable and can't withstand strong heat. High-oleic safflower oil is extracted from safflower seeds that have been cultivated expressly for high oleic (omega-9) levels and enhanced monounsaturated content without the use of toxic chemicals or solvents. This increases the oil's stability and shelf life and enables it to fry your food cleanly and efficiently at high temperatures without breaking down—and with very little absorption. Look for high-oleic safflower oil in natural food stores.

Basic Browned Tempeh

Tempeh is a partially cooked product, and it needs to be cooked further before it is edible. After years of experimenting, I have found this browning treatment to be the very best way to go about it. When you brown tempeh in hot oil in an uncrowded pan, it becomes crunchy on the outside and chewy on the inside, with a delightful nutty-toasty flavor. Basic Browned Tempeh is a terrific staple for your cooking repertoire—a launching pad for many variations and a very satisfying protein solution, especially for breakfast.

- This recipe uses two 8-ounce packages of tempeh. Several different types of tempeh are available (some are made with grains, some are straight soy). You can use any kind here.
- You can brown the tempeh up to several days ahead of time. Store it in a tightly covered container in the refrigerator, and reheat it shortly before serving in a hot pan lightly sprayed with nonstick spray or in a microwave.
- Another great use for Basic Browned Tempeh: Throw some into your dinner salad as high-protein, full-flavored "croutons."

YIELD: **4 to 5 servings, depending on the context**
PREPARATION TIME: **About 20 minutes**

---

1 to 2 tablespoons olive oil

1 pound tempeh, cut into ½-inch dice

½ teaspoon salt

Nonstick spray (optional)

2 tablespoons balsamic vinegar

Freshly ground black pepper

OPTIONAL TOPPINGS

Salsa (pages 250 to 255)

Tomato Jam (page 262)

Caramelized Onion and Lemon Marmalade (page 258)

Beet, Lemon, and Ginger Marmalade (page 259)

1. Place a 10-inch sauté pan over medium-high heat for about 2 minutes. Add 1 tablespoon of the oil, wait another 10 seconds or so, then swirl to coat the pan.

2. When the pan is hot enough to sizzle a bread crumb, add the tempeh and spread it into a single layer. Sprinkle in the salt, and cook for a good 10 to 12 minutes, stirring occasionally, until the tempeh turns golden brown on all surfaces. If it appears to be sticking, push it to one side, lightly spray the pan with nonstick spray—or add up to another tablespoon of olive oil—and then resume sautéing until all surfaces are golden.

3. Sprinkle in the vinegar, letting it hit the hot surface of the pan (it makes a great sizzling sound) so it can reduce slightly on contact. Stir and cook over medium heat for another 5 minutes or so.

4. Serve hot, warm, or at room temperature, passing a pepper mill and the topping of your choice. Or go on to make Tempeh Hash (opposite page).

 WHAT EXACTLY IS TEMPEH?

Originally from Indonesia, tempeh is a firm, chewy, fermented "cake" made from partially cooked soybeans (sometimes with grain added) that have been inoculated with spores and then incubated. It is a very versatile, high-protein food that can be used in a wide range of savory dishes. Look for tempeh in the refrigerator or freezer section of natural food stores, shrink-wrapped in 8-ounce packages. If it's frozen, defrost it before using.

Tempeh Hash

You can augment Basic Browned Tempeh with as many vegetables as you feel like adding (and can fit). This is one of the most satisfying breakfast dishes ever—you'll feel quite complete for a long time following.

If you are making this hash right after browning the tempeh, simply transfer the tempeh to a plate, then return the pan to the heat and proceed with step 1 below. There's no need to clean the pan in between.

- You can also add leftover cooked vegetables to this hash. Have them at room temperature first, then add them with the tempeh so they can heat through.
- It's fine to make this up to several days ahead of time. Store it in a tightly covered container in the refrigerator, and reheat shortly before serving in a hot pan lightly sprayed with nonstick spray or in a microwave.

YIELD: **5 to 6 servings**
PREPARATION TIME: **About 20 minutes**

1 tablespoon olive oil

2 cups sliced or chopped onion

1 heaping teaspoon minced garlic

¼ teaspoon salt (possibly more)

Basic Browned Tempeh
   (opposite page)

Freshly ground black pepper

OPTIONAL ADDITIONS

Chopped vegetables (spinach, broccoli, zucchini, peppers, cherry tomatoes)

Cooked whole grains (up to 1 cup)

OPTIONAL TOPPINGS

Chopped walnuts, lightly toasted

Cooked beets, cut into small dice

Salsa (pages 250 to 255)

Apple-Balsamic Syrup (page 246)

1. Place a 10-inch sauté pan over medium-high heat for about 2 minutes. Add the oil, wait another 10 seconds or so, then swirl to coat the pan.
2. Add the onion and garlic and sauté for 5 to 8 minutes, or until just tender (it's okay if they're still a little crunchy), adding the salt as you go. If the pan seems too hot, reduce the heat a little.
3. Stir in the optional vegetables after the onion has been cooking for about 3 minutes, and sauté until they're done to your liking. Stir in the tempeh and the optional cooked grains and cook over medium heat for another 5 minutes or so, stirring occasionally, until everything is heated through. Taste and correct the salt.
4. Serve hot, warm, or at room temperature. Pass a pepper mill and some fresh salsa or other suggested toppings.

(VARIATION) **TEMPEH HASH WITH SHIITAKE MUSHROOMS**

Follow the main recipe with this adjustment.

After the onion has been cooking for about 3 minutes, add:

- **12 to 14 medium-sized shiitake mushrooms (½ to ¾ pound), stemmed and thinly sliced**

Continue to cook over medium-high heat for about 5 minutes longer, or until the mushrooms are soft, then add the tempeh and proceed from the middle of step 3.

Red Flannel Hash

Traditional New England red flannel hash contains bacon in addition to the standard potatoes and beets (which bestow their lovely rosy hue, hence the name). This intensely colorful vegetarian version features sweet potatoes and a bacon presence from soy-based "veggie bacon" or smoked tofu, imparting a similar smoky flavor, a crisp texture—and a significant amount of protein.

- You will notice two kinds of oil in the recipe. The first, high-oleic safflower oil, can be heated safely and effectively to very high temperatures, which gets whatever you're frying *really* crisp. (See page 155.) The second, canola oil, is a good all-around oil for sautéing at medium temperatures. If you can't find high-oleic safflower oil, use olive oil in its place.

YIELD: **4 to 6 servings, depending on the context**
PREPARATION TIME: **25 to 30 minutes**

1 tablespoon high-oleic safflower oil

6 ounces "veggie bacon" or smoked tofu, cut into strips

1 tablespoon canola oil

2 cups minced onion

1 pound sweet potatoes, cooked, peeled, and diced

½ pound beets, cooked, peeled, and diced

1 tablespoon minced garlic

½ teaspoon salt

OPTIONAL TOPPINGS

Hard-boiled eggs, cut into wedges

Apple-Balsamic Syrup (page 246)

1. Heat the high-oleic safflower oil in a medium-sized skillet over medium heat. When the oil is hot enough to sizzle a bread crumb, add the veggie bacon or tofu in a single layer. Fry over medium-high heat for about 5 minutes on each side (until crisp), then remove from the pan with a slotted spoon and drain on a double thickness of paper towels. Set aside.
2. Reheat the skillet over medium heat. (It's okay if some of the safflower oil is still left in it.) When the pan is hot, add the canola oil and the onions, and sauté for 5 to 8 minutes, or until the onion is soft and translucent.
3. Stir in the sweet potatoes, beets, garlic, and salt, and spread the mixture out to allow maximum contact with the hot pan. Let it cook without stirring for about 5 minutes, then stir it around and continue to cook until it is lightly crisped all over.
4. Stir in the bacon or tofu and serve hot, topped with slices of hard-boiled egg and a drizzle of Apple-Balsamic Syrup, if desired.

PEELING SWEET POTATOES AND BEETS

Both beets and sweet potatoes peel more easily if cooked first.

- Cut unpeeled sweet potatoes crosswise into 1-inch circles and boil or steam them until tender. When they're cool enough to handle, strip the skin off by hand.
- Roast or boil whole, unpeeled beets until tender. After they're cooked and cooled, simply peel them with a paring knife. (Information about roasting beets is on page 259.)

Ful Medames

In Egypt, small, purple beans (a variety of fava beans) are a popular street food, frequently eaten in the morning. This is my own version of the traditional Egyptian preparation. It makes a complete breakfast on its own—and an even heartier one when served with scrambled eggs and toast.

Fresh fava beans are ideal for this, but you can also use dried or canned favas or any kind of broad bean or small, plump brown bean (such as pintos or habas), dried or canned. If using dried beans, soak and cook them ahead of time. If using canned, rinse and thoroughly drain them before using.

- Be sure to use a high-quality, flavorful extra virgin olive oil as the seasoning. You can use a less expensive virgin or pure olive oil for sautéing.

YIELD: 2 hearty servings, or 3 to 4 dainty ones
PREPARATION TIME: 20 to 30 minutes

1 tablespoon olive oil

1 cup minced onion

1½ cups cooked fava beans,
   broad beans, or brown beans
   (a 15-ounce can)

2 to 3 teaspoons minced garlic

½ pound plum (Roma) tomatoes
   (about 3 medium-sized tomatoes)

¾ teaspoon salt, or to taste

1 to 2 tablespoons fresh lemon juice

Extra virgin olive oil for the top

1 handful coarsely chopped
   flat-leaf parsley

Freshly ground black pepper

1. Place a medium-sized sauté pan over medium-high heat for about 2 minutes. Add the olive oil, wait another 30 seconds or so, then swirl to coat the pan. Reduce the heat to medium, add the onion, and sauté for 5 to 8 minutes, or until it becomes very soft.

2. Add the beans and the garlic and stir gently, so you don't break the beans. Lower the heat, cover, and cook for about 5 more minutes. Meanwhile, prepare the tomatoes.

3. Cut the tomatoes in half crosswise; squeeze out and discard the seeds. Chop the flesh into ½-inch pieces, and add it to the beans. Stir, cover, and cook for about 5 minutes.

4. Stir in the salt and lemon juice. Cook only a minute or two longer, then dish into bowls. Drizzle each serving with a high-quality extra virgin olive oil, and sprinkle with coarsely chopped flat-leaf parsley. Serve hot, and pass a pepper mill.

FRESH FAVA BEANS

Fresh fava beans in their pods are available in the spring and summer in some specialty produce markets. Preparing them is a project, but it's well worth the trouble. Put a large pot of water on to boil while you shell the beans. (Discard the pods.) Add the beans to the simmering water for about a minute, then scoop them out with a flat, fine-mesh strainer, leaving the water on the stove. Run the beans under very cold tap water until they cool down, then peel them. (You might have to use a fingernail to loosen the skins.) Return the peeled beans to the simmering water to cook for 8 to 10 minutes longer, or until tender. Drain them in a colander, and they're finally ready!

Bean Porridge

Almost like a bean risotto, with beans suspended in their own thickened cooking liquid, this comforting bowlful is brimming with protein, minerals, fiber, and, most important, flavor. You will be surprised by how good this is for breakfast! Have it on its own or topped with a poached egg and/or Roasted Herbes de Provence Tomatoes (page 168) and accompanied by some hot buttered toast.

This porridge is easy to reheat in the morning if you make it the night before while you are busy doing other things. It takes practically no work.

- The best way to reheat this is in a microwave.
- Most kinds of beans will work, but white beans (navy, pea, cannelloni, great northern, and so on) make prettier-looking porridge than darker varieties. Soybeans are not a good choice for this, because they remain too firm to turn into porridge, no matter how long they are cooked.

YIELD: 2 servings (easily doubled)
PREPARATION TIME: 45 minutes (5 minutes of work)

1½ to 2 cups cooked white beans
(a 15-ounce can)

½ cup water (possibly more)

1 medium clove garlic, peeled

¼ teaspoon dried sage or thyme

Coarse salt

Freshly ground black pepper

Extra virgin olive oil

Balsamic vinegar

Chopped flat-leaf parsley

Caramelized Onion and Lemon
Marmalade (page 258; optional)

1. Without rinsing or draining them first, transfer the beans directly from the can or cooking liquid to a small to medium saucepan. Add ½ cup water, bring to a boil, then lower the heat to a simmer and partially cover. Cook for 30 minutes.

2. Add the garlic and the sage or thyme, partially cover again, and let it simmer another 10 minutes. (Check the water level during this time. It should be fine—slightly soupy—but if for some reason the beans are running dry, add more water, a tablespoon or two at a time.)

3. Remove the pot from the heat, and use a potato masher to mash the beans until they turn thick and creamy but still retain some texture. You can be the judge of how far to take this.

4. Season to taste with coarse salt and a generous amount of freshly ground black pepper. Serve hot or very warm, in bowls, topped with a drizzle of extra virgin olive oil, a small splash of balsamic vinegar, and a sprinkling of minced parsley. Pass a small dish of the marmalade, if available.

Silver Dollar Bean Cakes

Crunchy little bean patties (similar to falafel, which are common breakfast street food in the Middle East) make an unusual and satisfying light breakfast or midmorning snack. This easy recipe is a fun way to incorporate more beans into your diet. Any kind will work, but white beans make prettier-looking cakes than darker varieties. Soybeans are also a good option for this.

Serve with grits (page 58) and the toppings of your choice.

- These cakes store well in the refrigerator or freezer if packed in a tightly covered container or wrapped in a sealed plastic bag. If frozen, defrost them thoroughly before reheating. Reheat on the stovetop in a lightly oiled pan or in a microwave or a 300°F oven.
- You can replace the egg with 3 to 4 tablespoons milk or soy milk. The eggless cakes may fall apart a little but will still taste good.

YIELD: About 3 servings (10 small cakes)
PREPARATION TIME: 30 minutes

¾ cup cooked beans (about half a 15-ounce can)

1 large egg, beaten

¼ cup cornmeal or polenta

¼ teaspoon salt

Freshly ground black pepper

1 teaspoon minced garlic

1 scallion, finely minced

2 tablespoons finely minced parsley (optional)

Olive oil or high-oleic safflower oil

OPTIONAL TOPPINGS

Citrus-Papaya Salsa with a Chipotle Haze (page 251)

Smoky Tomato Salsa (page 253)

Chipotle Cream (page 256)

Basic Guacamole (page 257)

Creamy Tahini Sauce (page 256)

1. Rinse and drain the beans, and transfer them to a medium-sized bowl. Mash them roughly with a potato masher or a fork. (It's okay if they retain some texture.)
2. Stir in the beaten egg, along with the cornmeal, salt, pepper to taste, garlic, scallion, and parsley, if desired. Mix well.
3. Place a large skillet (or two smaller ones) over medium heat, and wait a minute or two. Add about 1 tablespoon oil, wait about 10 seconds, then swirl to coat the pan.
4. When the oil is hot enough to sizzle a bread crumb, add tablespoons of batter to the pan, flattening it down into small cakes. (If you're using the safflower oil, which gets hotter than olive oil, be careful not to splatter.) Fry for about 5 minutes on each side, or until golden.
5. Remove the cakes with a slotted metal spatula, and place them on a plate lined with paper towels. Pat to absorb any excess oil. (There won't be much.)
6. Serve hot, warm, or at room temperature, with your chosen toppings.

7

VEGETABLES FOR BREAKFAST

CONTENTS

VEGETABLES FOR BREAKFAST

We don't normally think of breakfast when we're making our vegetable plans—nor of vegetables when we're making our breakfast plans. But including vegetables in your breakfast is a *great* way to get a head start on your daily quota, and it's easier than you think.

Cooking vegetables doesn't have to be a big production, especially if you do a little planning. Cut (and possibly also cook) a few extra vegetables the night before when preparing dinner, and put them aside for breakfast. Then, in the morning, you can throw some into a hot pan for a minute or two before scrambling eggs—or add some to your potatoes or toast. And when you're out shopping for lunch and dinner vegetables, remember to think about breakfast, too.

The best breakfast vegetables—those that go down most easily in the morning—are potatoes, tomatoes, mushrooms, sweet potatoes, onions, scallions, bell peppers, chiles, cucumbers, squash, corn, spinach, asparagus (surprisingly nice), and artichoke hearts. Many other vegetables can also find their place at the morning table, especially if the meal expands into brunch. In addition to the recipes in this chapter, there are many other ideas throughout the book that will inspire you to include vegetables. Suggestions for what I like to call "vegetable delivery systems" appear throughout most of the chapters, even the one on cakes and other sweets!

VEGETABLE JUICE

If you would like to enhance your vegetable intake, but it seems like a chore to actually *eat* more vegetables, consider investing in a juicer and *drinking* your vegetables. Homemade juice will give you all the vitamins and nutrients—minus the bulk and fiber—of the vegetables from which it was extracted, enabling you to consume a greater quantity of vegetable goodness than you possibly could otherwise. And vegetable juice is easy to drink in the morning.

Try a combination of carrot and celery juice—in equal parts—as a basic blend. To this, you can add smaller amounts of juice from other vegetables, like leafy greens (especially spinach or watercress), bell peppers, fennel, parsley, cabbage, cucumbers, and beets. And if you want to sweeten the mix, add some fresh-pressed apple juice as well—it will soften the edges. (Normally, fruit and vegetable juices don't combine successfully, but apple juice is an exception—it seems to go with everything.)

For information about juicers, see page xvii.

VEGETABLE JUMP-STARTS

The National Cancer Institute recommends that we eat at least five servings a day of fruit and vegetables. And that's a minimum—ideally, they suggest we try to get that number up to nine servings! This amount may seem overwhelming, but with a little planning and some creative fun in the kitchen, it definitely can be done. It's really important to include a fruit or vegetable with our earliest meal, and for many of us, fruit is an easier start-of-the-day choice. But here are some ideas for getting in a portion of vegetables right out of the gate—or soon thereafter.

LEFTOVER SALAD IN A TORTILLA OR A PITA

Make a little extra dinner salad (ideally one that is full of spinach), and put it aside, undressed. Refrigerate it overnight in a plastic bag, and in the morning toss it with some dressing while you heat a flour tortilla or a piece of pita bread in the toaster oven. Roll—or stuff—the salad into the tortilla or pita, perhaps with a little cheese, and enjoy it for breakfast.

LEFTOVER VEGETABLES IN A TORTILLA, PITA, CRÊPE, OR OMELET

In a similar spirit, prepare an extra serving of vegetables at dinnertime. In the morning, reheat the leftovers in a microwave or a small, hot pan coated with olive oil, and you'll have an instant filling for a tortilla, pita, crêpe (page 195), or omelet (page 129).

VEGETABLES SCRAMBLED INTO EGGS

This is really quick and easy! Details are on page 121.

RAW VEGETABLES ON A BAGEL

Cucumbers! Scallions or red onion slices! Shredded carrots and beets! Tomatoes! Sprouts! Bell pepper slices! Pile them high on a toasted bagel spread with cream cheese, and eat it over a plate, to catch the pieces that fall off.

VEGETABLES IN COTTAGE CHEESE

Eat this delicious mélange with a spoon, or spread it on toast. Details are on page 218.

FLASH-COOKED VEGETABLES IN A POTATO

Make an extra baked potato for dinner. The next morning, reheat it in the microwave while you flash-cook some vegetables (page 174). Scoop some of the potato out of its skin, and replace it with the vegetables for a perfect hand-held breakfast.

VEGETABLE-ENHANCED QUICHE

Make a Gruyère Quiche with Golden Onion and Red Pepper (page 138), and add some extra vegetables (steamed, chopped broccoli or cauliflower, chopped spinach, sautéed mushrooms—whatever will fit). Bring a slice of it to work with you. It's highly portable and delicious at room temperature.

VEGETABLE-BASED BEVERAGES

These preparations make vegetable consumption easy! Breakfast Gazpacho (page 165), Cucumber-Mint Lassi (page 15), vegetable juices (preceding page).

STEALTH VEGETABLES

Here are some other good ways to consume vegetables without even noticing: Pumpkin–Chocolate Chip Protein Bread (page 88), Pumpkin Muffins (page 80), Pumpkin-Orange Marmalade (page 260), Zucchini-Pecan Protein Bread (page 89), Carrot-Currant Muffins (page 81), Carrot-Almond-Oat Gems (page 276), Spaghetti Squash Pancakes (page 191), and Zucchini-Carrot Pancakes (page 190).

Breakfast Salad

Consider having a little vegetable salad for breakfast! This one is very light yet full of protein—enough to get you through the morning with plenty of energy. Choose a brightly colored bell pepper and it will be especially beautiful.

- Make most of the salad the night before and store it in a tightly covered container in the refrigerator. (This is designed not to wilt overnight.) Cook and add the eggs in the morning.
- Here is a very good opportunity to incorporate flax-seed oil into your diet. It has a deeply nutty taste and is a rich source of omega-3 fatty acids, which are enormously healthful. (For more information about flax-seed oil, see page 274.)

YIELD: 3 to 4 servings
PREPARATION TIME: 15 minutes

1 medium-sized cucumber

3 to 4 large radishes, quartered and thinly sliced

1 medium-sized bell pepper, diced

1 medium-sized ripe tomato, seeded and diced

3 tablespoons extra virgin olive oil

¾ cup (packed) crumbled cheese (feta or ricotta salata)

¼ teaspoon salt (possibly more)

2 large eggs

3 medium-sized scallions, minced

1 tablespoon red wine vinegar

¼ cup sunflower seeds, lightly toasted

Freshly ground black pepper

Flax-seed oil (optional)

1. Peel the cucumber, if necessary, and cut it in half lengthwise. Scrape out and discard the seeds (unless they're tiny and tightly packed), and cut the cucumber into small pieces. Transfer to a medium-sized bowl, and add the radishes, bell pepper, and tomato.
2. Drizzle with the olive oil, and toss gently. Crumble in the cheese, and toss again. Add salt to taste. (At this point, the salad can be covered tightly and refrigerated overnight.)
3. Shortly before serving, boil the eggs to your liking. (For more information about boiling eggs, see page 117.) While the eggs are cooking, add the scallions and vinegar to the salad, and mix thoroughly.
4. When the eggs are done, transfer them to a strainer, and refresh under cold running water until cool enough to handle. Peel the eggs, and cut them directly into the salad while they're still warm. Mix gently, letting the yolks—whether firm, soft, or even runny—become a delicious enrichment to the "dressing."
5. Sprinkle with sunflower seeds, and add black pepper to taste. If desired, you can drizzle each serving with flax-seed oil. Serve in bowls, with thick slices of toast to sop up the juices. You can also stuff the salad into lightly toasted pita bread.

Roasted Herbes de Provence Tomatoes

Serve these with just about anything. They are especially delicious with eggs, beans, potatoes—or scrambled tofu or tempeh. I also love serving them with cheese and toast.

Herbes de Provence is a dried blend that usually includes thyme, fennel seed, oregano or marjoram, summer savory, and, delight of delights, lavender. You should be able to find this heavenly mixture in the spice department of your favorite grocery store or specialty food market. Note: Dried herbs lose their intensity and fade over time, with exposure to heat and light. Solution: Keep them in the freezer.

- Use small tomatoes (1½ to 2 ounces each). They'll absorb more flavor and be easier to eat than larger ones. Allow 2 tomatoes per person. (Some people will probably want more, so consider making extra.)
- Juices from the tomatoes will leak out during roasting and might cause the oven to get smoky. You can lessen this effect by spooning out the juices a few times during the process. (A baster works well for this.) This will also help concentrate the rich tomato flavor.

YIELD: 4 to 5 servings, depending on the context
PREPARATION TIME: 5 minutes, plus 30 to 50 minutes to roast

---

1 to 2 tablespoons extra virgin olive oil

1 pound plum (Roma) tomatoes—about 10 small ones

1 tablespoon herbes de Provence (possibly more)

Coarse salt to taste

Freshly ground black pepper to taste

Lavender flowers for garnish (optional)

1. Preheat the oven to 425°F. Line a baking tray with foil, and brush it with about 1 tablespoon olive oil.

2. Thinly slice off the stem ends of the tomatoes, then hold each tomato over a sink and squeeze out the seeds through the sliced opening. Cut the tomatoes in half lengthwise, and place them cut side up on the foil.

3. Roast the tomatoes in the center of the oven for 20 to 30 minutes, or until they reduce in volume by about a third and the tops look nicely "done." Remove the tray from the oven, and drizzle the tomatoes with a little olive oil while they rest, still hot, on the tray. Sprinkle each with about ⅛ teaspoon herbes de Provence. After they've cooled for about 10 minutes, sprinkle the tomatoes lightly with coarse salt and freshly ground black pepper.

4. You can serve them at this point or deepen their flavor by returning the tray to the just-turned-off oven and leaving it in there for another 30 minutes or so. The tomatoes will become chewier, and their flavor will intensify. (The yield will be slightly lower, because the tomatoes will shrink.)

5. Serve warm or at room temperature, garnished with lavender flowers, if desired.

 LAVENDER

We normally think of lavender as a lovely flash of scented color in the garden. But it is also a transcendent culinary herb, with a flowery, clean, sharp—and pleasantly bitter—taste.

The leaves contain the strongest fragrance; the lovely blossoms are more subtle. You can use them both in cooking. In addition to being the star ingredient in herbes de Provence, lavender also goes well in sweet breads. (See Lemon-Glazed Rosemary/Lavender Raisin Buns, page 105.)

Fried Green Tomatoes

Tart, crunchy, and dripping with juice, fried green tomatoes are rarely considered a breakfast food. But picture a few slices—coated with golden cornmeal—on the plate next to your scrambled eggs or tofu, and I think you'll reconsider. They're also a perfect partner for American Potato Cutlets (page 152) and among my favorite quiche fillings (page 139).

Serve these warm, not hot, as the insides of the tomatoes retain a lot of heat and could burn your mouth.

- The tomatoes don't have to literally be green, as long as they're unripe and really hard. They soften up so much during the cooking process that if they're at all ripe to begin with, you'll have mush when you're done.
- Use a metal spatula for turning the tomatoes, and scrape the surface of the pan when you lift them. This ensures that you won't accidentally separate the cornmeal coating from the tomato.

YIELD: 2 to 3 servings (2 to 3 thick slices per serving)
PREPARATION TIME: 5 minutes, plus 20 minutes to cook

---

2 large unripe tomatoes (about 1 pound)

⅓ cup cornmeal or polenta (rounded measure)

¼ teaspoon salt

Nonstick spray and a little butter for the pan

OPTIONAL TOPPINGS

Coarse salt

Freshly ground black pepper

Chipotle Cream (page 256)

1. Core the tomatoes, and thinly slice off the ends. Cut the tomatoes into half-inch-thick slices (you'll get about 3 or 4 slices per tomato) and set aside.
2. Combine the cornmeal and salt on a dinner plate. Mix until uniformly blended.
3. Dredge the tomato slices in the cornmeal mixture, pressing it into the cut surfaces of the tomatoes to create a thick coating.
4. Place a large skillet or sauté pan over medium heat for several minutes. Spray the hot pan with nonstick spray, and melt in a little butter. After a few seconds, tilt the pan to distribute the butter, then add the coated tomatoes.
5. Fry the tomatoes on each side for 8 to 10 minutes, or until crisp and golden. You might need to add a little more butter at some point to keep them from sticking.
6. Remove the tomatoes from the pan, and transfer them to a wire rack over a tray to cool. (This retains their crispy texture.) Wait at least 5 minutes before serving, as the insides of the tomatoes will have become very hot and will need to cool down a little.
7. Serve warm, and pass some coarse salt, a pepper mill, and if you like, some Chipotle Cream to spoon on top.

VARIATION · **FRIED GREEN TOMATOES WITH MELTED CHEDDAR**

Follow the main recipe with this adjustment.

Preheat the broiler. Place the fried tomatoes in a baking dish and sprinkle with:

- ½ cup (packed) grated sharp cheddar

Broil just long enough to melt the cheese. Serve right away.

Cinnamon-Spiced Fried Tomatoes

You will love this easy, exotic fried tomato departure. And you will also love the incredible aroma that fills your kitchen the minute the tomato slices hit the hot pan! This is another excellent way to use not-quite-ripe tomatoes. Serve them as a side dish with just about anything. I like them for breakfast with eggs and steamed, buttered corn tortillas.

YIELD: 2 servings (easily multiplied)
PREPARATION TIME: About 10 minutes

2 medium-sized firm tomatoes
(¾ pound)

2 teaspoons unbleached
all-purpose flour

1 teaspoon cinnamon

½ teaspoon ground cumin

A big pinch of coarse salt
(plus extra for serving)

About 1 tablespoon olive oil

1. Cut the tomatoes in half and gently squeeze out and discard the seeds. (This step is unnecessary if you're using Roma, or plum, tomatoes.) Cut the tomatoes into thick slices.

2. Combine the flour, cinnamon, cumin, and salt on a dinner plate. Dredge the tomato slices in this mixture, turning to coat both sides of each piece.

3. Place a medium-sized heavy skillet over medium heat for several minutes. When the skillet is hot, add the olive oil, wait for about 10 seconds, then swirl to coat the pan. Fry the coated tomato slices in the hot oil on both sides until crisp. (It goes fast—only a minute or two. Don't let them burn!)

4. Transfer the fried tomatoes to a plate and wait for 3 to 5 minutes before serving, as the juices inside will be very hot. Pass coarse salt at the table, so each person can add an extra pinch, if desired.

Classic Creamed Spinach

Rich and pure, this is a luxurious way to bestow a touch of green onto your breakfast plate. Serve Classic Creamed Spinach over toast or next to eggs (or in an omelet). For an elegant treat, use this as a filling for Folded French Crêpes (page 195).

- For your convenience, this recipe was designed to use frozen chopped spinach. You can also make it with 10 ounces of chopped *fresh* spinach, if you prefer.
- You can use any kind of milk (whole, lowfat, soy, and so on). Heat the milk ahead of time in a saucepan or in a glass measuring cup (easy to pour from!) in the microwave.
- This keeps for up to a week if stored in a tightly covered container in the refrigerator. You can easily reheat individual servings in a microwave.

YIELD: About 4 side-dish servings (or enough to fill 6 omelets or 10 crêpes)
PREPARATION TIME: 15 minutes (once spinach is defrosted)

---

1 package (10 ounces) frozen chopped spinach, defrosted

3 tablespoons unsalted butter

¼ teaspoon dry mustard

⅛ teaspoon nutmeg (possibly more)

¼ cup unbleached all-purpose flour

2 cups hot milk (any kind)

¾ teaspoon salt

White pepper

1. Place the defrosted spinach in a fine-mesh strainer, and press out as much of the liquid as you can. Let it stand over a bowl to drip until needed.
2. Melt the butter in a 10-inch sauté pan over low heat. Add the mustard and nutmeg as it melts.
3. Use a fine-mesh strainer to slowly sift in the flour with one hand while you whisk the butter with the other. Keep whisking for a minute or so after all the flour has been added.
4. Slowly pour in the milk, still whisking. As the milk is incorporated, it will become a medium-thick sauce. Keep whisking to keep it smooth.
5. Add the spinach all at once. Use a fork to spread out the spinach, stirring it in as you go. It will take a minute or so to distribute the spinach evenly throughout the sauce.
6. Cook the sauce for about 2 minutes more over low heat, stirring frequently with a wooden spoon. Remove the pan from the heat, and add white pepper to taste. Serve hot.

All-Purpose Breakfast Mushrooms

Sautéed mushrooms fit perfectly in many contexts, and here is my basic recipe. Use these mushrooms for omelets or as an accompaniment to just about any kind of savory egg dish. Spoon them on top of Zucchini-Carrot Pancakes (page 190), tuck them around the sides of Savory Rosemary-Olive Waffles (page 205), stuff them into Folded French Crêpes (page 195), or transform them into Buckwheat Blini with Mushroom Filling (page 202). And when you mince the mushrooms instead of slicing them, they become a perfect topping for brie or camembert (page 223).

- For deeper flavor use a combination of domestic and wild mushrooms (such as shiitakes, chanterelles, oyster mushrooms, and morels)—if available. The proportions should be about half domestic and half wild mushrooms.
- These mushrooms store and reheat well. They should last for about a week in the refrigerator if kept in a tightly covered container. Reheat in the microwave or over very low heat on the stovetop.

YIELD: About 4 servings, depending on the context (2 cups total)
PREPARATION TIME: About 35 minutes

1 tablespoon olive oil

A little butter (optional)

1 cup minced onion

4 heaping cups mushrooms
 (1 pound), sliced or minced

¾ teaspoon salt (possibly more)

½ teaspoon dried thyme

1 tablespoon fresh lemon juice

Freshly ground black pepper

1. Place a 10-inch skillet over medium heat. After a minute or two, add the olive oil, wait for about 10 seconds, then swirl to coat the pan. If you like, you can also melt in some butter.
2. When the cooking surface is hot enough to sizzle a bread crumb, add the onion and sauté for about 8 minutes, or until soft.
3. Add the mushrooms, salt, and thyme, and turn the heat up to medium-high. Sauté until the mushrooms are cooked through and their juices evaporate. This should take only a few minutes if the pan is hot and large enough.
4. Toss in the lemon juice, and add black pepper (and possibly more salt) to taste.
5. Serve hot, warm, or at room temperature in the context of your choice.

CLEANING MUSHROOMS

Wash them? Peel them? Actually, neither of these is ideal. Mushrooms should be wiped clean with a damp paper towel. If you wash them under running water, they absorb some of it and become diluted. If you peel them, you lose some of the flavor and possibly some volume as well. Exception to the latter: If the mushrooms are borderline (that is, too funky to clean with just the towel but still salvageable), peel them with a very sharp paring knife. And unless the stems are tight and pristine, slice them away.

Quick Individual All-Purpose Mushrooms

Mushrooms are great breakfast food—too good to put on hold until the rare occasion when you're making a fancy meal for others. Why not throw together a single serving of mushrooms for just you—whether it's for a spontaneous omelet or to spoon onto a piece of toast? To save time, heat the pan while you're cutting the mushrooms. This will go very fast!

YIELD: **1 serving (about ⅓ cup cooked)**
PREPARATION TIME: **10 minutes**

1 teaspoon olive oil

1 heaping cup sliced mushrooms
(4 ounces)

⅛ teaspoon salt (possibly more)

2 dashes garlic powder, or ½
teaspoon minced fresh garlic

1 heaping tablespoon minced
scallion

Freshly ground black pepper

1. Place an 8-inch nonstick crêpe or omelet pan—or a plain small frying pan—over medium heat. After a minute or two, add the olive oil, wait for about 10 seconds, then swirl to coat the pan. Continue to heat the olive oil over medium heat for a minute or so.
2. When the cooking surface is hot enough to sizzle a bread crumb, add the mushrooms, spreading them out for maximum contact with the heat. Sprinkle in the salt (and the garlic powder, if you're using it) and turn the heat up to medium-high. Cook for about 5 minutes, tossing or stirring frequently.
3. Add the fresh garlic, if you're using it, and the scallion, and cook for about 1 minute longer. Transfer to a plate and add black pepper (and possibly more salt) to taste.
4. Serve hot, warm, or room temperature. (If you're continuing on to make an omelet, transfer the mushrooms to a plate and proceed. See page 129.)

 STORING MUSHROOMS

Mushrooms need to be kept dry, so it's important not to store them in plastic bags, which retain moisture and hasten deterioration. Store mushrooms in a paper bag instead. This enables them to "breathe" and keeps them viable for a longer time. If mushrooms get a little old looking while waiting around in your refrigerator, that's okay, as long as they aren't wet. Dry mushrooms will come back to life and taste fine once they are cooked. Wet ones, on the other hand, are pretty much unsalvageable and should be tossed.

Flash-Cooked Vegetables

Flash-cooking vegetables in a very hot pan is really as quick as it sounds, especially if you are making only one or two servings at a time. With a large enough, hot enough pan—and a few swift chopping strokes to prepare the produce—you are ready to toss together a quick "side of vegetables" for your morning eggs (or scrambled tofu, or whatever else you have on the menu). Strong heat is essential! In fact, my favorite aspect of this recipe (next to eating this, of course) is the audible sizzle when the vegetables hit the pan. It's as though the "snooze" button of the alarm clock followed you into the kitchen.

- You can save time by chopping a vegetable or two while the pan is heating.
- To multiply this recipe, use a second (or larger) pan so the vegetables won't be crowded. (Crowding slows down the cooking process and compromises the texture.)
- You can season this with a combination of savory herbs or with cumin. Your choice!

YIELD: 2 to 3 servings (about 2 cups cooked vegetables); easily multiplied
PREPARATION TIME: 12 minutes

1 tablespoon olive oil

1½ cups sliced onion

6 mushrooms, thinly sliced

1 cup thinly sliced bell pepper

2 cups thinly sliced zucchini

½ teaspoon salt

1 to 2 teaspoons cumin or dried thyme, marjoram, or basil

1 teaspoon minced garlic

2 to 3 handfuls fresh spinach leaves, clean and dry

Freshly ground black pepper

Crushed red pepper flakes (optional)

OPTIONAL ADDITIONS

Cherry tomatoes (halved, unless they're tiny)

Minced scallion

Sliced vegetarian sausage, sautéed until crisp

Basic Browned Tempeh (page 156)

1. Place a large (10-inch) sauté pan over medium-high heat for about 2 minutes. Add the olive oil, wait another 30 seconds or so, then swirl to coat the pan. Wait another minute or so for the oil to get really hot.
2. When the cooking surface is hot enough to sizzle a bread crumb, add the onion and mushrooms, turn the heat up to high, and toss or stir for about 2 minutes.
3. Add the bell pepper and zucchini, and continue to cook over high heat, keeping the vegetables moving, for another minute.
4. Sprinkle in the salt, cumin or herbs, and garlic, and toss to distribute. Add a few handfuls of fresh spinach, and cook just a minute or so longer, or until the spinach wilts but is still bright green. (You may want to mix it with tongs once you've added the spinach.) Stir in as many of the optional additions as you desire, keeping the pan on the heat just long enough to mix these in and heat them through.
5. Remove the pan from the heat, and add black pepper to taste, as well as crushed red pepper flakes to taste, if desired. Serve hot, warm, or at room temperature.

Calabacitas

A vegetable mélange influenced by Pueblo cuisine, this simple dish makes a stunning little breakfast when served with Cinnamon-Spiced Fried Tomatoes (page 170) and Basic Corn Muffins (page 76) or warm tortillas (flour or corn).

- You can make this up to several days ahead. Store it in a tightly covered container in the refrigerator, and reheat in a microwave or in a covered dish in a 300°F oven.
- Anaheim and poblano chiles are moderately hot. For a milder flavor, remove and discard the seeds. (Wash your hands after handling these or any other hot peppers.) You can also substitute canned green chiles.
- Fresh corn, shaved right off the cob, is ideal. But defrosted frozen corn is fine, too.

YIELD: 3 to 4 servings, depending on the context
PREPARATION TIME: 30 minutes

1 tablespoon olive oil

1 cup minced onion

1 cup minced anaheim and/or poblano chiles

½ teaspoon salt (possibly more)

1 to 2 teaspoons pure ground chile powder (optional)

2 cups diced zucchini (about 10 ounces, or two 6-inch zucchini)

2 cups corn kernels (cut from 2 ears, or defrosted frozen corn)

2 teaspoons minced garlic

¾ cup cooked pinto beans (half a 15-ounce can; optional)

Grated jack or cheddar cheese (optional)

Freshly ground black pepper

Squeezable wedges of lime

1. Place a medium-sized skillet over medium heat for a minute or two. Add the olive oil, wait about 30 seconds, then swirl to coat the pan.

2. When the cooking surface is hot enough to sizzle a bread crumb, add the onion, chiles, salt, and optional chile powder, and cook, stirring frequently, for 8 to 10 minutes, or until the vegetables become quite soft.

3. Add the zucchini, corn, garlic, and optional beans, and continue to cook, stirring gently to avoid breaking the beans, for about 5 minutes longer, or until the zucchini is *just* tender. (Don't overcook the zucchini.) Remove the pan from the heat.

4. Sprinkle in grated cheese to taste, if desired, and stir to distribute it as it melts. Add black pepper (and possibly more salt) to taste. Serve hot, warm, or at room temperature, with squeezable wedges of lime tucked into the side of each serving.

Portobello Pizzas

Portobello mushrooms are perfect little containers for vegetables and cheese.

The "Mushroom Treatment" (step 1) greatly firms up the portobellos and condenses their flavor. Mushrooms prepared in this manner can be used in many ways beyond these pizzas. Keep "treated" mushrooms in your refrigerator for up to a week. They're a great convenience item that can perform double duty as both something to eat and something to "hold" other food, like scrambled eggs or tofu, cooked grains, potatoes, beans, or any kind of leftovers. This can greatly expand your repertoire!

- If you're eating breakfast on the run, keep in mind that these fit perfectly onto toasted English muffins and can thus be portable.
- The fully cooked pizzas reheat beautifully. Store in a tightly covered container in the refrigerator, and bring to room temperature before reheating in a 300°F oven or a microwave.

YIELD: About 2 servings (2 small pizzas apiece)
PREPARATION TIME: 40 minutes

4 medium (4-inch) firm portobello
mushrooms, caps intact

1 tablespoon olive oil

1 medium tomato (8 ounces),
not too ripe

Half a medium bell pepper

About 1 handful fresh spinach
leaves, clean and dry

Dried thyme

Salt

Freshly ground black pepper

About 6 ounces mozzarella cheese,
grated

Crushed red pepper flakes (optional)

1. The Mushroom Treatment: Remove and discard the mushroom stems, and wipe the caps clean with a damp paper towel. Place a large, heavy skillet over medium heat for about 2 minutes. Add the olive oil, wait about 30 seconds, then swirl to coat the pan. Place the mushrooms cap side down in the hot oil, and let them cook undisturbed for about 10 minutes. Turn them over and cook on the other side for 10 minutes, then flip them over one more time and cook for 5 to 10 minutes more on their cap side once again. Leave them in the pan and set aside.

2. Core the tomato and gently squeeze out the seeds through the opening. Cut the tomato and the bell pepper into very thin slices.

3. Preheat the broiler. While it is heating, place the mushrooms cap side down in a Pyrex or ceramic baking dish. Top each mushroom with a few spinach leaves, some slices of tomato and bell pepper, and pinches of dried thyme, salt, and pepper. Take your time covering the top with grated cheese, tucking it into every crevice and cavity and trying to cover everything (including the edges of the mushrooms, so they won't burn under the broiler).

4. Broil until the cheese melts and is turning golden. Watch carefully, as this will take only about 5 minutes or less. Serve hot, warm, or at room temperature, sprinkled lightly with red pepper flakes, if desired.

Nut-Crusted Mushroom Fritters

Thin strips of meaty portobello mushrooms hold a crunchy nut coating very well. When you sauté them in olive oil, they become a wonderfully satisfying light breakfast entrée or side dish (great next to eggs!)—or a midmorning snack, eaten at room temperature. The coating is full of protein, so these fritters will definitely take the edge off your appetite.

- Milk or soy milk can replace some of the beaten egg.
- You can prepare the coated mushroom slices in the evening and store them overnight in a tightly covered container in the refrigerator. Frying them in the morning will then take less than 15 minutes.
- Alternative cooking method: Instead of sautéing them, spread the coated mushroom slices on a foil-lined baking tray brushed or sprayed lightly with olive oil, and bake in a preheated 425°F oven for 12 to 15 minutes. Turn the mushrooms over halfway through the process.

YIELD: 4 to 6 servings (4 to 6 slices per serving)
PREPARATION TIME: 30 minutes

4 medium (4-inch) portobello mushrooms

1 cup almonds or hazelnuts

¼ cup grated parmesan

¼ teaspoon salt

⅛ teaspoon black pepper

⅛ teaspoon garlic powder (possibly more)

3 large eggs

2 to 3 tablespoons olive oil

Fire-Roasted Pepper Salsa (page 254; optional)

1. Remove and discard the mushroom stems and wipe the caps clean with a damp paper towel. Cut them into long slices about ½ inch thick, and set aside.

2. Place the nuts and cheese in a blender or food processor, and turn the machine on and off a few times until the nuts are ground to the consistency of cornmeal. (You can also use a small electric spice grinder and grind the nuts in batches.) Transfer this mixture to a plate, and stir in the salt, pepper, and garlic powder. Mix until uniformly blended.

3. Break the eggs into a pie pan, and beat until smooth.

4. Dip both sides of each mushroom slice in the beaten egg, then press the wet surfaces firmly into the nut mixture. (*Really* push it in there, so a *lot* of coating can stick to the mushrooms. Thick is good in this case!) Transfer the coated mushrooms to another plate.

5. Place a skillet or sauté pan over medium heat and wait several minutes. Add a tablespoon of the olive oil, wait about 30 seconds, then swirl to coat the pan. When the cooking surface is hot enough to sizzle a bread crumb, arrange the coated mushroom slices in the pan. They can be touching but should not overlap. Sauté them for about 5 minutes on each side, adding more oil if necessary. (Note: If some of the coating falls off, save and include it. It's delicious!) When the mushrooms are golden all over, transfer them to a wire rack over a tray to cool. This retains their crispy texture.

6. Serve hot, warm, or at room temperature, with Fire-Roasted Pepper Salsa on the side, if desired.

GRIDDLE FOODS: PANCAKES, WAFFLES, BLINTZES, CRÊPES & FRENCH TOAST

CONTENTS

GRIDDLE FOODS:
PANCAKES, WAFFLES, BLINTZES, CRÊPES & FRENCH TOAST

In Asian cuisines, pancakes are savory accompaniments to lunch or dinner. In Europe, pancakes—and sometimes waffles—are dessert. Only in the United States are these foods served for breakfast, dating back to an era when homes on the prairie (and cowherders in transit) lacked ovens, and breakfast breads needed to be "baked" on a griddle. So necessity was the mother of pancakes (at least on these shores)—luckily for us!

This chapter contains recipes for many different kinds of pancakes and waffles, including:

- Many variations of "regular" cakelike pancakes and waffles (studded with berries and other kinds of fruit, dressed up in gingerbread spices, enhanced with protein, wheat-free, cornmeal and buttermilk-based, whole grain, and more)
- Crispy vegetable and potato pancakes with savory seasonings
- Crêpes, blintzes, and blini, which are various forms of thin pancakes, folded or rolled around delicious fillings

French toast and matzoh brei (fried matzoh), also stars of the griddle, make an honorary appearance at the end of this chapter.

ABOUT PANCAKES

There are certain challenges to creating a good pancake, and they are quite easily addressed. Just remember these pointers:

- Be careful not to undercook pancakes or they will be unpleasantly damp and raw tasting.
- Don't overhandle cakelike pancakes or they will become tough. Minimally mix the batter, and turn them only once. Be absolutely sure they are done on the underside before turning them over. (Vegetable-based pancakes, on the other hand, can be mixed—and turned over—to your heart's content.)
- Cakelike pancakes should be served immediately and not kept warm or left to stand after being cooked. (Vegetable-based pancakes and crêpes, blintzes, and blini can be kept warm in the oven.)
- For all kinds of pancakes, always preheat the griddle, and keep the heat at medium-high throughout the cooking process.
- Pancakes come out best when cooked in a combination of nonstick spray and a little butter. Although the butter is optional in these recipes, I recommend you use it.

ABOUT WAFFLES

What are the most important traits for a really good waffle? For me, they would be an elusive combination of lightness and creaminess encased in a crisp exterior that, after the initial delicate crunch, proceeds to dissolve in your mouth. How's that for some wordy prose? You'll talk this way, too, once you try the waffle recipes in this chapter. Here's why they work so well:

• The batters are thin. (A thin batter is key to good waffle texture.)
• The batters contain a significant amount of melted butter or canola oil. (Fat is necessary for crispness.)
• The sugar content is low. (Too much sugar causes the waffles to become too brown—or worse, to burn—before they become crisp.)
• The batters are not overmixed. (Overmixing causes the waffles to become tough.)

Not all waffle irons are alike. Get a good waffle iron—one that can become very hot. Look for old-fashioned metal waffle irons in antique appliance shops or at garage sales, or buy a high-quality new one that has a thermostat. Get to know your waffle iron, and hone your powers of observation. Peek during the cooking process to see how things are progressing. Many cookbooks advise following the "manufacturer's instructions." But who keeps the manufacturer's instructions? Just preheat the iron and pay careful attention. Those are *my* instructions.

Whether or not your waffle iron has a nonstick coating, oil and/or butter it anyway. A combination of non-stick spray and butter works best. Reapply both *before cooking each waffle!*

Pancake and waffle batters are not interchangeable. (Pancakes have less liquid and fat than waffles.) Belgian waffles use the same batter as standard ones. The main difference is that they use approximately twice the amount of batter and take longer to cook. They also require a special waffle iron.

All of the waffles in this chapter freeze well in heavy zip-style plastic bags and reheat beautifully in a toaster oven without being defrosted first. If you are intending to freeze waffles, underbake them slightly. Toasting will finish the job perfectly.

KEEPING THE BATTER

Most of us tend to think of a pancake or waffle breakfast as a weekend event, but it is actually quite easy to have these treats during the week as well. All the batters in this chapter keep very well for several days or longer in a tightly covered container in the refrigerator. This means you can put together a batter in the evening and enjoy freshly made pancakes or waffles the next morning. Several days later, you can enjoy an encore performance from the same batter.

During storage, the top surface of the batter may turn a harmless dark color from oxidation. Just stir it back in and it will disappear. Also, refrigeration will often cause the batter to thicken, which is fine. Just spread each pancake with the back of a spoon when it hits the griddle. You can also thin pancake or waffle batter to its original consistency by adding a little water or milk.

TOPPINGS

We usually expect some combination of softened butter, maple syrup, fresh fruit, and powdered sugar as the standard toppings for most pancakes and waffles. (Make that a dab of sour cream for savory variations.) But there are many other delicious accoutrements that can add color and excitement to your griddled breakfast foods. Look through the "Condiments, Sauces, Toppings & Spreads" chapter to get more ideas. And don't forget that waffles are great "catchers" of raspberries, blueberries, peas, corn, pomegranate seeds, or chocolate chips. Garnishing waffles with tidbits-that-fit can be a whole lot of fun!

Mollie's Basic Pancake and Waffle Mix

Even though it's very easy to throw together the dry ingredients for any batter, many people have a psychological block in this department. It seems we're fine with adding whatever wet ingredients are required, but there's something intimidating about the dry stuff—hence the wild success of commercial mixes. Without trying to analyze this syndrome, let me just provide you with a lovely recipe for making your own pancake and waffle mix. With homemade mix, you know exactly what's in it and you can choose your ingredients carefully (organic stone-ground flour, for example). There's also the added benefit of being able to feel ambitious and accomplished one day (when you're energetic enough to spend the 5 minutes it takes to put this mix together) and somewhat lazy the next (when you pull out the mix and throw breakfast together while still half asleep).

This mix works for both pancakes and waffles. The only difference is the amount of liquid and fat you'll add when you prepare the batter. (Waffles need more of both.)

- This mix just fills a quart jar and will keep for a long time in the refrigerator and forever in the freezer.
- To make this mix into pancakes, see the following page. For waffle instructions, see page 204.

YIELD: **Enough for 3 batches of pancakes or waffles**
PREPARATION TIME: **5 minutes**

2¼ cups unbleached
 all-purpose flour

¾ cup soy protein powder

¾ cup unprocessed wheat bran

¾ teaspoon salt (rounded measure)

4½ teaspoons baking powder
 (1 tablespoon plus 1½ teaspoons)

½ teaspoon baking soda

3 tablespoons sugar (optional)

1. Combine everything in a large bowl and stir until uniformly blended.

2. Transfer to a clean, dry jar with a tight-fitting lid and store in the refrigerator or freezer.

Mollie's Basic Buttermilk Pancakes

My kids were amazed and impressed with themselves for loving these "healthy" pancakes. The truth is, when you use protein powder and bran in the right proportions, and you don't overwork the batter, "healthy" pancakes can be light and fluffy enough to earn a thumbs-up from the under-20 crowd but still have sufficient nutritional complexity to slow down the carbohydrate load so you won't crash in midmorning. Everyone wins!

• Canola oil can be substituted for some or all of the butter.

YIELD: 3 to 4 servings (ten 4-inch pancakes)
PREPARATION TIME: 15 minutes

1⅓ cups Mollie's Basic Pancake and Waffle Mix (preceding page), or use the Pancake Mix Substitute below

1⅓ cups buttermilk

2 large eggs

½ teaspoon vanilla extract

1½ tablespoons unsalted butter, melted

Nonstick spray

Butter for the pan (optional)

PANCAKE MIX SUBSTITUTE

¾ cup unbleached all-purpose flour

¼ cup soy protein powder

¼ cup unprocessed wheat bran

¼ teaspoon salt

1½ teaspoons baking powder

⅛ teaspoon baking soda

1 tablespoon sugar (optional)

1. Place the pancake mix in a medium-sized bowl.
2. Measure the 1⅓ cups buttermilk into a 2-cup liquid measure. Add the eggs and beat gently with a fork or a small whisk until smooth. Stir in the vanilla.
3. Pour the buttermilk mixture, along with the melted butter, into the dry ingredients. Using a spoon or a rubber spatula, stir from the bottom of the bowl until the dry ingredients are all moistened. Don't overmix; a few small lumps are okay.
4. Place a griddle or skillet over medium heat. After a minute or two, spray it lightly with nonstick spray, and if you like, melt in a little butter. Using a ¼-cup measure with a handle, scoop up batter and pour it onto the hot griddle.
5. Cook the pancakes for 3 to 4 minutes on the first side, or until golden on the bottom. (Don't turn them too soon. The trick is to flip them only once, which keeps them light and tender.) The second side will go a little faster; 2 to 3 minutes will usually do it, depending on the heat.
6. Serve right away with your chosen toppings.

For each variation, follow the main recipe with these adjustments.

LIGHT WHOLE-GRAIN PANCAKES

Right after you've poured the batter onto the hot griddle, sprinkle onto each pancake:

- Up to 2 tablespoons cooked grains—any kind (page 46)

Use a dinner knife to gently spread the batter over the grains, and proceed with step 5.

TOASTED OAT-COATED PANCAKES

For each pancake, you'll need:

- 2 tablespoons rolled oats

After you add the butter to the griddle in step 4, sprinkle pancake-sized circles of oats—1 tablespoon apiece—onto the hot griddle. Pour the batter directly over the oat circles, then sprinkle another tablespoon of rolled oats on top of each pancake so they'll be on the bottom when you flip them over. Proceed with step 5.

GINGERBREAD PANCAKES

Add to the dry ingredients:

- 1 teaspoon cinnamon
- ½ teaspoon ground ginger
- ½ teaspoon allspice
- ⅔ cup minced crystallized ginger

Proceed with step 2.

APPLE OR BANANA PANCAKES

Right after you've poured the batter onto the hot griddle, add to each pancake:

- 4 to 5 *thin* slices peeled apple or banana

Use a dinner knife to gently spread the batter over the fruit so it won't be too "tall," and proceed with step 5.

BLUEBERRY, RASPBERRY, OR STRAWBERRY PANCAKES

Use the smallest berries you can find. (Strawberries should be sliced.) If you're using frozen berries, defrost them first. Right after you've poured the batter onto the hot griddle, add to each pancake:

- 1 to 2 tablespoons berries (fresh or frozen)

Use a dinner knife to gently spread the batter over the berries so they won't be too "tall," and proceed with step 5.

Wheat-Free Pancakes

We don't often get to experience the subtle flavors of flour made from grains other than wheat. This is because wheat flour, with its uniquely high gluten content, is necessary to the actual structure of most baked goods. Pancakes and waffles are an exception, though, and can be made successfully with no wheat flour at all. You can use any combination of "alternative" flours for this. My own favorite mix is oat flour and barley flour. Look for non-wheat flours at natural food stores. (I buy Arrowhead Mills brand—which comes packed in 2-pound bags—and I keep it in the freezer for maximum freshness.)

- Canola oil can be substituted for some or all of the butter.
- The variations for Mollie's Basic Buttermilk Pancakes (preceding page) will also work with this batter.

YIELD: 4 servings (about a dozen 4-inch pancakes)
PREPARATION TIME: 15 minutes

1½ cups rice flour, oat flour, barley flour, and/or millet flour

¼ cup arrowroot or cornstarch

½ teaspoon salt

½ teaspoon baking powder

1 tablespoon sugar (optional)

1¼ cups milk

1 large egg

1 tablespoon unsalted butter, melted

Nonstick spray

Butter for the pan (optional)

1. Combine the dry ingredients in a medium-sized bowl.
2. Measure the 1¼ cups milk into a 2-cup liquid measure. Add the egg, and beat gently with a fork or a small whisk until thoroughly combined.
3. Pour the milk-egg mixture, along with the melted butter, into the dry ingredients. Using a spoon or a rubber spatula, stir from the bottom of the bowl until the dry ingredients are all moistened. Don't overmix; a few small lumps are okay.
4. Place a griddle or skillet over medium heat. After a minute or two, spray it lightly with nonstick spray, and if you like, melt in a little butter. Using a ⅓-cup measure with a handle, scoop up batter and pour it onto the hot griddle.
5. Cook the pancakes for 3 to 4 minutes on the first side, or until golden on the bottom. (Don't turn them too soon. The trick is to flip them only once, which keeps them light and tender.) The second side will go a little faster; 2 to 3 minutes will usually do it, depending on the heat.
6. Serve right away with your chosen toppings.

VARIATION   **WHEAT-FREE WAFFLES**

Make the batter in the main recipe, using:

- 2 large eggs
- 3 tablespoons unsalted butter, melted

Preheat a waffle iron, spray it with nonstick spray, and brush with a little melted butter. Add about ⅓ cup batter for each standard waffle (⅔ cup batter for each Belgian waffle), and bake until crisp. Serve right away, or reheat in a toaster later on. This will make about 4 servings (8 to 9 standard waffles, or 4 Belgian waffles).

Enriched High-Protein Pancakes

If you love pancakes but avoid them out of fear that your energy will crash an hour later from the pure carbohydrate load, this is the recipe for you. The high-protein ingredients are very unobtrusive, yet they do their job well. You should be able to run all morning on the "fuel" of these eggy, chewy-light pancakes, especially if you serve them with yogurt and some high-fiber fresh fruit on the side.

- Powdered egg whites are sold in a can and can usually be found with the baking ingredients in the supermarket. Once you've opened the can, store it in the refrigerator or freezer, and use as desired.
- For information about soy protein powder, see page xv.
- Canola oil can be substituted for some or all of the butter.
- Add less baking powder if you want the pancakes to be less puffy.

YIELD: 3 to 4 servings (ten to twelve 4½-inch pancakes)
PREPARATION TIME: 15 minutes

¾ cup soy protein powder

¼ cup soy flour

¼ cup unbleached all-purpose flour

2 tablespoons powdered egg whites (optional)

½ cup dry milk powder

¼ teaspoon salt

½ to 2 teaspoons baking powder

1 tablespoon sugar

1¼ cups milk

2 large eggs

1 tablespoon unsalted butter, melted

Nonstick spray

Butter for the pan (optional)

1. Combine the dry ingredients in a medium-sized bowl.
2. Measure the 1¼ cups milk into a 2-cup liquid measure. Add the eggs, and beat gently with a fork or a small whisk until smooth.
3. Pour the milk and egg mixture, along with the melted butter, into the dry ingredients. Using a spoon or a rubber spatula, stir from the bottom of the bowl until the dry ingredients are all moistened. Don't overmix; a few small lumps are okay.
4. Place a griddle or skillet over medium heat. After a minute or two, spray it lightly with nonstick spray, and if you like, melt in a little butter. Using a ¼-cup measure with a handle, scoop up batter and pour it onto the hot griddle.
5. Cook the pancakes for 3 to 4 minutes on the first side, or until golden on the bottom. (Don't turn them too soon. The trick is to flip them only once, which keeps them light and tender.) The second side will go a little faster; 2 to 3 minutes will usually do it, depending on the heat.
6. Serve right away with your chosen toppings.

> **VARIATION**   **ENRICHED HIGH-PROTEIN PANCAKES WITH BLUEBERRIES**
>
> Follow the the main recipe with this adjustment.
>
> Right after you've poured the batter onto the hot griddle, add to each pancake:
>
> - 1 tablespoon small blueberries (or about 6 larger ones)
>
> Poke the berries in with your fingers and/or spread batter over them with a dinner knife so they'll be level with the pancake surface. Proceed with step 5.

Buttermilk Corn Cakes

Sweet accents of vanilla and sugar play against the slightly bitter cornmeal and tart buttermilk in these fluffy pan-cakes, creating a wonderful balance of flavor. Not surprisingly, these corn cakes taste great with just the simple touch of butter and maple syrup. They are also quite versatile and are very compatible with a wide variety of toppings. So try the ones I suggest below, and thumb through the "Condiments, Sauces, Toppings & Spreads" chapter to get some wild ideas. You'll be amazed at what you can get away with!

- Use a fine grade of cornmeal (not the coarser polenta) for best results.

YIELD: 3 servings (about ten 4½-inch pancakes)
PREPARATION TIME: 15 minutes

½ cup cornmeal

½ cup unbleached all-purpose flour

½ teaspoon salt

1 teaspoon baking powder

½ teaspoon baking soda

1 tablespoon sugar

1 cup buttermilk

2 large eggs

1 teaspoon vanilla extract

1 tablespoon unsalted butter, melted

Nonstick spray

Butter for the pan (optional)

OPTIONAL TOPPINGS

Avocado-Grapefruit-Mango Salsa (page 252)

Passionfruit or guava syrup (page 246)

Pumpkin-Orange Marmalade (page 260)

Citrus-Papaya Salsa with a Chipotle Haze (page 251)

1. Combine the dry ingredients in a medium-sized bowl.
2. Measure the 1 cup buttermilk into a 2-cup liquid measure. Add the eggs, and beat gently with a fork or a small whisk until thoroughly combined. Beat in the vanilla.
3. Pour the buttermilk mixture, along with the melted butter, into the dry ingredients. Using a spoon or a rubber spatula, stir from the bottom of the bowl until the dry ingredients are all moistened. Don't overmix; a few small lumps are okay.
4. Place a griddle or skillet over medium heat. After a minute or two, spray it lightly with nonstick spray, and if you like, melt in a little butter. Using a ¼-cup measure with a handle, scoop up batter and pour it onto the hot griddle.
5. Cook the pancakes for 3 to 4 minutes on the first side, or until *really* golden on the bottom. (Don't turn them too soon. The trick is to flip them only once, which keeps them light and tender.) The second side will go a little faster; 2 to 3 minutes will usually do it, depending on the heat.
6. Serve right away with your chosen toppings.

VARIATION **BLACKBERRY CORN CAKES**

Follow the main recipe with this adjustment.

If you're using frozen berries, defrost them first. Right after you've poured the batter onto the hot griddle, add to each pancake:

- 1 to 2 tablespoons blackberries, sliced in half

Use a dinner knife to gently spread batter over the berries so they won't be too "tall," and proceed with step 5.

Savory Buttermilk Corn Cakes

When you add a few vegetables and some savory accents to Buttermilk Corn Cakes, they not only make a perfect brunch dish but can even be served for supper as a first course or light entrée.

- Use finely ground cornmeal (not the coarser polenta) for best results.
- For a milder flavor, remove and discard the jalapeño seeds. (Wash your hands after handling these or any other hot peppers.) You can also substitute canned green chiles.
- To keep the pancakes warm, transfer them to a rack on a baking tray, and place the tray in a 200°F oven until serving time. (The rack keeps them crisp.)

YIELD: 4 servings (about twelve 4½-inch corn cakes)
PREPARATION TIME: 20 minutes

---

1 tablespoon olive oil

¼ cup finely minced red bell pepper

Up to ¼ cup minced jalapeño (optional)

2 cups corn kernels (defrosted if frozen)

¼ cup minced scallion

½ cup cornmeal

½ cup unbleached all-purpose flour

½ teaspoon salt

1 teaspoon baking powder

½ teaspoon baking soda

1 cup buttermilk

2 large eggs

Nonstick spray

Butter for the pan (optional)

OPTIONAL TOPPINGS

Chipotle Cream (page 256)

Apple-Jalapeño Syrup (page 246)

Cilantro leaves

Smoky Tomato Salsa (page 253)

Basic Guacamole (page 257)

1. Heat the olive oil in a small skillet. Add the bell pepper, jalapeño, and corn, and sauté over medium heat for about 10 minutes. Remove from the heat, stir in the scallion, and set aside.
2. Combine the dry ingredients in a medium-sized bowl.
3. Measure the 1 cup buttermilk into a 2-cup liquid measure. Add the eggs, and beat gently with a fork or a small whisk until smooth.
4. Pour the buttermilk mixture and the sautéed vegetables (scraping the pan to include all the butter or oil) into the dry ingredients. Using a spoon or a rubber spatula, stir from the bottom of the bowl until the dry ingredients are all moistened. Don't overmix; a few small lumps are okay.
5. Place a griddle or skillet over medium heat. After a few minutes, spray lightly with nonstick spray, and if you like, melt in a little butter. When the griddle is hot enough to sizzle a bread crumb, use a ¼-cup measure with a handle to scoop up batter and pour it onto the hot griddle. Cook for 2 to 3 minutes on each side, or until golden.
6. Serve hot or warm, topped with a drizzle of Chipotle Cream or Apple-Jalapeño Syrup and a few torn cilantro leaves. If desired, pass any of the other suggested toppings at the table.

Zucchini-Carrot Pancakes

Cheerful flecks of orange and green make these light pancakes otherworldly and beautiful. This recipe is a good way to get children (or anyone, for that matter) to eat vegetables.

- Use a food processor with the medium grating attachment to grate both the zucchini and the carrot. There's no need to clean it in between. You can grate the vegetables up to several days ahead and store them in a tightly covered container in the refrigerator.
- The batter keeps well for up to 5 days if stored in a tightly covered container in the refrigerator.
- To keep the pancakes warm, transfer them to a rack on a baking tray, and place the tray in a 200°F oven until serving time. (The rack keeps them crisp.) They are also good at room temperature.

YIELD: 4 to 5 servings (sixteen 3½-inch pancakes)
PREPARATION TIME: 30 minutes

4 large eggs

¾ teaspoon salt

⅛ teaspoon black pepper

2 cups (packed) grated zucchini

2 cups (packed) grated carrot

½ cup finely minced scallion

½ teaspoon dried thyme

½ teaspoon dried sage

1 teaspoon dried basil

⅓ cup unbleached all-purpose flour or rice flour

Nonstick spray

Butter for the pan (optional)

OPTIONAL TOPPINGS

Sour cream or yogurt

Minced fresh mint leaves

All-Purpose Breakfast Mushrooms (page 172)

Mango Ketchup (page 261)

Tomato Jam (page 262)

1. Combine the eggs, salt, and pepper in a medium-sized bowl and beat with a whisk until frothy.
2. Gradually beat in the zucchini, carrot, scallion, and herbs. Keep beating as you sprinkle in the flour.
3. Place a griddle or skillet over medium heat. After a few minutes, spray it lightly with nonstick spray, and if you like, melt in a little butter. When the griddle is hot enough to sizzle a bread crumb, use a ¼-cup measure with a handle to scoop up batter and pour it onto the hot griddle. Cook for 4 to 6 minutes on each side, or until golden and crisp.
4. Serve hot—plain or topped with a dab of sour cream or yogurt and some minced fresh mint leaves. For a special touch, serve with a side of All-Purpose Breakfast Mushrooms, and pass a small dish of Mango Ketchup or Tomato Jam.

Spaghetti Squash Pancakes

Tender, eggy, delicate, soft, and slightly chewy, these pancakes have such a mysterious quality that people will have difficulty guessing what they're made from. In addition to being great for breakfast, they also work well as a side dish or a light entrée for lunch or dinner.

- Prepare the squash well ahead of time. Instructions follow the recipe.
- The batter keeps well for up to 5 days if stored in a tightly covered container in the refrigerator.
- To keep the pancakes warm, transfer them to a rack on a baking tray, and place the tray in a 200°F oven until serving time. (The rack keeps them crisp.)

YIELD: 4 servings (about 8 pancakes)
PREPARATION TIME: 15 minutes (once the squash is baked)

2 cups (packed) prepared spaghetti squash (see the box below)

1 cup minced onion

¼ cup unbleached all-purpose flour or rice flour

½ teaspoon salt (scant measure)

4 large eggs

Nonstick spray

Butter for the pan (optional)

OPTIONAL TOPPINGS

Sour cream or yogurt

Tomato Jam (page 262)

1. Place the squash in a medium-sized bowl and separate the strands a little with a fork. Continue to use the fork to mix in the onion, flour, and salt, and then beat in the eggs.
2. Place a griddle or skillet over medium heat. After a minute or two, spray it lightly with nonstick spray, and if you like, melt in a little butter. When the griddle is hot enough to sizzle a bread crumb, use a ¼-cup measure with a handle to scoop up batter and pour it onto the hot griddle.
3. Cook the pancakes for a good 8 to 10 minutes on each side—until truly golden. Unlike cakier pancakes, which toughen when turned repeatedly from side to side, these can be turned more than once, if necessary, without compromising their texture. Get them really well done on the outside, and you will have an exquisite chewy-crisp result.
4. Serve hot or warm—plain or with any of the suggested toppings.

"PREPARED" SPAGHETTI SQUASH

Spaghetti squash is a plain, large, yellowish-green oval-shaped vegetable with a hard, woody stem. Once cooked, the flesh forms strands that resemble spaghetti (hence the name) with a light and crunchy texture, a subtle, slightly sweet taste, and an ethereal golden color. Spaghetti squash is a good source of fiber and vitamin A.

To prepare spaghetti squash for this recipe, you'll need:

1 spaghetti squash (3 pounds)

Preheat the oven to 350°F. Cut the squash in half lengthwise, and scrape out the seeds. Bake the halves cut sides down on a lightly oiled baking tray for about 30 minutes, or until the skin can just barely be pierced with a fork. (It should be tender but not too soft.) Remove the squash from the oven and let it cool to room temperature. Scoop out the flesh, place it in a strainer over a bowl, and squeeze out enough of the juices to reduce its final volume to 2 packed cups.

Wild Rice Pancakes with mushrooms and goat cheese

Savory, earthy, and pungent, these incredibly satisfying pancakes are almost like individual omelets. They reheat well in a microwave or a toaster oven and also taste good at room temperature, so try packing a few for a late-morning breakfast break or for lunch.

- The batter keeps well for several days in a tightly covered container in the refrigerator.
- Cook the wild rice ahead of time. (Guidelines are on page 46.)
- To keep the pancakes warm, transfer them to a rack on a baking tray, and place the tray in a 200°F oven until serving time. (The rack keeps them crisp.) They are also good at room temperature.

YIELD: 4 to 5 servings (twelve 4-inch pancakes)
PREPARATION TIME: About 35 minutes

1 tablespoon olive oil

12 medium-sized mushrooms
   (1½ inches in diameter), sliced

1 teaspoon salt

1 teaspoon minced garlic

2 teaspoons fresh lemon juice

4 large eggs

⅓ cup unbleached all-purpose flour
   or rice flour

4 scallions, minced

1 cup cooked wild rice

1 cup (about 5 ounces) crumbled
   goat cheese

⅛ teaspoon black pepper

Nonstick spray

Butter for the pan (optional)

OPTIONAL TOPPINGS

Sour cream or yogurt

Flat-leaf parsley (torn leaves)

Minced chives

Fire-Roasted Pepper Salsa
   (page 255)

Chive blossoms

1. Place a medium-sized skillet over medium heat for about 1 minute. Add the olive oil and the mushrooms, and sauté over medium heat for 5 minutes. Stir in ½ teaspoon of the salt and sauté 5 minutes longer. Stir in the garlic and lemon juice and remove the pan from the heat without cooking the mixture any further.

2. Beat the eggs in a medium-sized bowl. Whisk in the flour and the remaining ½ teaspoon salt. When this mixture is uniform, stir in the cooked mushrooms, including all their juices. Add the scallions, wild rice, goat cheese, and black pepper, and stir until well combined.

3. Wipe out the skillet used to cook the mushrooms, and return it to medium heat. After a minute or two, spray it lightly with nonstick spray, and if you like, melt in a little butter. When the pan is hot enough to sizzle a bread crumb, use a ¼-cup measure with a handle to scoop up batter and pour it into the hot pan. Cook for 2 to 3 minutes on each side, or until golden.

4. Serve hot, warm, or at room temperature with one or more of the suggested toppings. Decorate with purple chive blossoms, if you're lucky enough to have some.

Potato Pancakes

The very same potato pancakes, or latkes, that are traditional supper fare for Chanukah make an exciting breakfast treat as well.

I went through a phase of trying to politely sauté latkes instead of frying them, in an attempt to make them lower in fat. They always turned out disappointing, if not depressing, because you can't get potato pancakes really crisp if they're not really fried. And crispness is the whole point! Then I discovered high-oleic safflower oil—an ingredient that makes it possible to fry efficiently at a very high temperature—and my potato pancakes just took off. Crisp doesn't begin to describe them—they practically shatter when you take a bite!

- For information about high-oleic safflower oil, see page 155.
- Rice flour can be substituted for the all-purpose flour.
- For a delicious variation, replace up to half the potato with grated sweet potato.
- The batter lasts for several days if kept in a tightly covered container in the refrigerator, so you can keep it around and fry up a few latkes on this morning or that, when the opportunity arises. Allow 12 to 15 minutes' frying time once the frying pan and the oil are hot.
- Leftover potato pancakes can be reheated in an ungreased, preheated skillet over medium heat.

YIELD: **About 4 servings (12 to 14 medium-sized pancakes)**
PREPARATION TIME: **30 minutes**

1½ pounds potatoes (any kind)

1 medium onion (about 6 ounces)

¼ cup unbleached all-purpose flour

½ teaspoon salt (rounded measure)

2 large eggs, beaten

High-oleic safflower oil for frying

OPTIONAL TOPPINGS

Sour cream

Applesauce

Mixed Fruit Compote (page 32)

1. Use a hand grater—or the fine grating attachment of a food processor—to grate the potato and onion together. (Peeling the potatoes is optional.)
2. Transfer the grated vegetables to a medium-sized bowl, and sprinkle in the flour and salt. Add the beaten eggs, and stir until thoroughly combined.
3. Place a large, deep skillet over medium heat for about 3 minutes. Add enough oil to make a ⅛-inch-deep pool in the pan. Wait another minute or two to heat the oil. When the oil is hot enough to instantly and dramatically sizzle a bread crumb, use a ¼-cup measure with a handle or a large spoon to scoop up batter and pour it into the pan. (Go slow, so you don't splash hot oil.) Spread each pancake out so it is very thin.
4. Fry the pancakes on each side for 7 or 8 minutes, or until deep golden and crisp all over.
5. Line a platter with a triple thickness of paper towels. Remove the pancakes from the pan, using a slotted metal spatula, and hold each over the pan for a moment or two to drain off any excess oil. Place the pancakes in a single layer on the prepared platter for a few minutes before serving. There should be plenty of oil left in the pan to fry the remaining batter.
6. Serve hot or warm, with any of the suggested toppings.

Matzoh Meal Pancakes

Jewish food (especially the kind I grew up with, courtesy of my grandmother and great-aunt) is not particularly known for being ethereal. These pancakes are my favorite exception to the "heavy food lets you know you've really eaten" rule. They are so light and fluffy, you'll think you're eating clouds, but you'll know you've eaten.

- Separate the eggs well ahead of time so they can come to room temperature. Place the whites in a large bowl and the yolks in a small one, and cover the bowls with plastic wrap.
- Serve these pancakes right away! They will toughen if kept in a warm oven or reheated.

YIELD: **2 SERVINGS (5 or 6 pancakes); very easily multiplied**
PREPARATION TIME: **15 minutes**

3 large eggs, separated

1 teaspoon sugar

½ cup matzoh meal

¼ teaspoon salt

Nonstick spray

Butter for the pan

OPTIONAL TOPPINGS

Fresh fruit

Preserves

Honey

Cinnamon sugar

1. Place the egg whites in a large bowl, add the sugar, and beat with a hand-held electric mixer until they form stiff peaks.
2. In a small bowl, lightly beat the egg yolks with a fork, then drizzle them on top of the beaten whites. Sprinkle the matzoh meal and salt over the whites as well.
3. Use a rubber spatula to fold everything together until uniform but still inflated. This will happen pretty easily with just a few strokes. Be sure to scrape from the bottom of the bowl.
4. Place a griddle or skillet over medium heat. After a minute or two, spray it lightly with nonstick spray, and melt in a little butter. Using a ½-cup measure with a handle, scoop up batter and pour it onto the hot griddle.
5. Cook on both sides until golden brown, and serve hot with any of the suggested toppings.

Folded French Crêpes

Similar to blintzes but sturdier, Folded French Crêpes can be wrapped around a great variety of spreads and fillings. My favorite filling for these is Classic Creamed Spinach (page 171), but you can try just about anything that comes to mind and it will probably work. Think of them as a kind of French tortilla, and I'll bet the ideas will start pouring in.

• The unfilled crêpes will keep in the refrigerator for up to a week, stacked on a plate and tightly covered with plastic wrap.
• Crêpes reheat well in a hot, lightly buttered pan or a microwave, so you can just warm up a few at a time as needed. I like to reheat unfilled crêpes and then add a hot, warm, or room-temperature filling and serve right away.

YIELD: **4 to 5 servings (about 10 crêpes)**
PREPARATION TIME: **20 minutes**

1 large egg

1¼ cups milk

¼ teaspoon salt

1 cup unbleached all-purpose flour

Nonstick spray

Butter for the pan

1. Place the egg, milk, salt, and flour in a blender, and process until smooth. Let the batter rest for 10 to 15 minutes.
2. Place an 8-inch nonstick crêpe or omelet pan over medium heat. After a minute or two, spray it lightly with nonstick spray, and melt in a little butter. Pour a scant ¼ cup batter into the hot pan, wait a few seconds, then slowly tilt the pan in all directions until the batter climbs a little way up the sides.
3. Cook over medium heat until the top surface is dry, then loosen the edges with the tip of a knife and turn, using a small spatula. Cook on the second side for about 30 seconds, then turn the cooked crêpe out onto a plate.
4. Immediately return the pan to the heat and repeat the procedure until you've run out of batter. (If you keep the pan hot, you won't need additional nonstick spray or butter.) Stack the cooked crêpes on the plate.
5. Fill the crêpes shortly before serving. To fill, place a small amount of filling (whatever *looks* as though it will fit—this is inexact) in the center of each crêpe, then fold over the sides, one at a time. Serve hot, warm, or at room temperature.

 WHAT TO PUT IN A CRÊPE?

Almost anything!

• Last night's leftovers
• Classic Creamed Spinach (page 171)
• Scrambled eggs
• Any kind of cheese—grated or crumbled
• Fresh or cooked fruit (See the "Fruit" chapter)

• Steamed fresh whole asparagus, green beans, or broccoli spears, with a drizzle of Homemade Crème Fraîche (page 263) or Hollandaise Sauce (page 265)
• All-Purpose Breakfast Mushrooms (page 172)
• Nutella (very French!)
• Cinnamon sugar

Classic Cheese or Fruit Blintzes

My mother makes blintzes only one precious time a year—in June, for the Jewish festival of Shavuot. To me, they symbolize the summer solstice, and I just can't eat them any other time of year. However, you can—and I hope you will!

- The pancakes can be made up to several days in advance. Stack them on a plate, cover tightly with plastic wrap, and refrigerate until ready to use.
- Blintzes can be filled the night before and refrigerated.
- Freeze filled, unfried blintzes in a tightly covered container. You can fry them without defrosting if you cover the pan. Turn them twice during the frying, so they can heat through *and* turn crisp.

YIELD: 6 to 8 servings (about 16 blintzes)
PREPARATION TIME: 1¼ hours (including time to prepare the filling)

3 large eggs

1⅓ cups milk

2 tablespoons unsalted butter, melted

¼ teaspoon salt

¾ cup unbleached all-purpose flour

Nonstick spray

Butter for the pan

Cheese or Fruit Filling (recipes follow)

OPTIONAL TOPPINGS

Sour cream or yogurt

Fresh fruit

Powdered sugar

1. Place the eggs, milk, melted butter, salt, and flour in a blender, and process until smooth. Let the batter rest for 10 to 15 minutes.
2. Place an 8-inch nonstick crêpe or omelet pan over medium heat. After a minute or two, spray it lightly with nonstick spray, and melt in a little butter. Pour a scant ¼ cup batter into the hot pan, wait a few seconds, then slowly tilt the pan in all directions until the batter climbs a little way up the sides.
3. Cook over medium heat until the top surface is dry and the edges release easily with the tip of a knife. This will happen quickly. Don't let the pancake brown or turn crisp.
4. Turn the cooked pancake out onto a plate, then immediately return the pan to the heat. Repeat the procedure until you've run out of batter. (If you keep the pan hot, you won't need additional nonstick spray or butter.) Stack the cooked pancakes on the plate.
5. To fill, place about 1 heaping tablespoon of either filling in the center of each blintz, then fold the top and bottom of the pancake—followed by the sides—over the filling. Store the filled blintzes seam side down on a plate or in a flat container. Cover and refrigerate until shortly before serving time.
6. Place a skillet over medium heat for several minutes, then spray it with nonstick spray. Melt in a little butter, and fry the filled blintzes for 6 to 8 minutes on each side, or until golden and crisp. Serve hot with the suggested toppings.

Cheese Filling for Blintzes

1½ pounds fresh cheese (cottage, ricotta, farmer's, or pot cheese)

1 large egg, beaten

1 teaspoon vanilla extract

2 to 3 tablespoons sugar (possibly more)

¼ teaspoon salt

3 tablespoons unbleached all-purpose flour

1. If you're using cottage cheese, press it through a sieve into a medium-sized bowl. Place any of the other cheeses directly in the bowl.
2. Add the remaining ingredients and mix well. Taste and add more sugar, if needed.

Fruit Filling for Blintzes

• This filling needs 20 minutes to cook, plus time to cool.

4 cups blueberries or sliced stone fruit (pitted cherries, apricots, plums, or peaches)

2 tablespoons fresh lemon juice

3 tablespoons unbleached all-purpose flour

⅛ teaspoon salt

1 tablespoon sugar (possibly more)

1 teaspoon grated lemon zest

1. Place the fruit in a medium-sized saucepan over medium heat and partially cover. Cook for about 5 minutes with no added liquid. (It's okay if it reaches a boil.)
2. Turn the heat down to medium-low, stir in the lemon juice, and use a fine-mesh sieve to sift in the flour as you continue to stir. Add the salt and sugar to taste and cook, uncovered, for another 5 minutes, stirring frequently.
3. Remove from the heat, stir in the lemon zest, and set aside to cool for at least 15 minutes before filling the blintzes.

Ricotta Crêpes

My husband invented these delightful crêpes, which have become our family's new Sunday morning tradition. After several weeks of following him around, writing down what he was doing (he didn't measure), I finally got it. Now it can be your Sunday morning tradition, too.

- These taste best made with whole-milk ricotta but will work with the lowfat variety as well.
- Cook as many crêpes as you need, then store the remaining batter in an airtight container in the refrigerator for another day. Stir from the bottom before using. It should keep for 3 to 4 days.
- If using frozen berries, defrost and drain them first. Save the beautiful, delicious "defrosting juices" to spoon onto the serving plate.

YIELD: 4 to 5 servings (8 to 10 crêpes)
PREPARATION TIME: 40 minutes (including time for the batter to rest)

---

4 large eggs

⅓ cup ricotta cheese

1 cup milk

1 teaspoon vanilla extract

⅛ teaspoon almond extract

2 tablespoons sugar (optional)

⅔ cup unbleached all-purpose flour

¼ teaspoon salt (rounded measure)

Nonstick spray

Butter for the pan

1 to 1¼ cups berries (optional)

OPTIONAL TOPPINGS

Powdered sugar

Pure maple syrup or fruit syrup (page 246)

Yogurt

1. Place the eggs, ricotta, milk, vanilla and almond extracts, sugar (if desired), flour, and salt in a blender, and process until smooth. Let the batter rest for at least 15 minutes (and up to an hour or longer). If your kitchen is warm and you plan to let it rest for longer than an hour, store the batter in a tightly covered container in the refrigerator.

2. Place an 8-inch nonstick crêpe or omelet pan over medium heat. After a minute or two, spray it lightly with nonstick spray, and melt in a little butter. When the pan is hot enough to sizzle a bread crumb, use a ⅓-cup measure with a handle to scoop up batter and pour it into the hot pan. Wait a few seconds, then slowly tilt the pan in all directions until the bottom is coated and the batter climbs a little way up the sides. (In other words, swirl the batter around the edges until it stops.) If there appears to be too much batter in the pan, pour some off (back into the mother batter).

3. Cook over medium heat until the top surface is dry and the edges release easily with the tip of a knife. This will happen quickly. If you're using the berries, place a tablespoon or two directly in the center of each crêpe while still in the pan. Without flipping the crêpe, fold it into quarters (top to bottom and side to side) in the pan. Serve hot with any of the optional toppings.

4. Cook the rest of the batter in this manner, or save some to cook another time, stirring from the bottom of the bowl each time you scoop some out. (It settles fast!) If you keep the heat constant, you probably won't need to add any more nonstick spray or butter to the pan. Serve each crêpe fresh from the pan, or keep them warm for up to 15 minutes in a 200°F oven.

Corn Crêpes

Plain, simple, and wheat-free, these crêpes are one of the best places to put sliced fresh strawberries! You can also take them in a savory direction by serving them with any of the suggested savory toppings.

Although they get rubbery as they cool, these bright yellow crêpes soften up like magic when reheated in a hot, buttered pan, becoming perfectly tender and slightly crisp. Delicious!

- Make the crêpes ahead of time and pile them on a plate. Reheat and fill just before serving.
- Unfilled crêpes, wrapped airtight and refrigerated, will keep for a week.
- For extra crunch you can substitute about 2 tablespoons polenta for the same amount of cornmeal.

YIELD: **7 servings (14 crêpes)**
PREPARATION TIME: **50 minutes (including time for the batter to rest)**

2 large eggs

1 cup milk

1 to 2 tablespoons unsalted butter, melted

½ teaspoon salt (rounded measure)

1 cup cornmeal

½ cup arrowroot or cornstarch

1 tablespoon sugar (optional)

Nonstick spray

Butter for the pan (optional)

OPTIONAL SWEET TOPPINGS

Sliced strawberries

Powdered sugar

OPTIONAL SAVORY TOPPINGS

Sour cream or Homemade Crème Fraîche (page 263)

Smoked salmon

Minced red onion and/or chives

Capers

1. Place the eggs, milk, melted butter, salt, cornmeal, arrowroot or cornstarch, and optional sugar in a blender, and process until smooth. Let the batter rest for at least 15 minutes (and up to an hour or longer). If your kitchen is warm and you plan to let the batter rest for longer than an hour, store it in a tightly covered container in the refrigerator.

2. Place an 8-inch nonstick crêpe or omelet pan over medium heat. After a minute or two, spray it lightly with nonstick spray and, if you like, melt in a little butter. When the pan is hot enough to sizzle a bread crumb, use a ¼-cup measure with a handle to scoop up batter and pour it into the hot pan. Wait a few seconds, then slowly tilt the pan in all directions until the bottom is coated and the batter climbs a little way up the sides. If there appears to be too much batter in the pan, pour some off (back into the mother batter).

3. Cook over medium heat until the top surface is dry and the edges release easily with the tip of a knife. This will happen quickly. For a softer crêpe, turn it out onto a dinner plate after cooking it on only one side. For a crisper one, cook it a little longer and on both sides.

4. Continue with the rest of the batter, stirring from the bottom of the bowl each time you go to scoop it. (It settles fast!) If you keep the heat constant, you probably won't need to add any more nonstick spray or butter.

5. Serve hot, folded around strawberries and topped with powdered sugar, or with some combination of the suggested savory toppings. If you won't be serving the crêpes right away, reheat them just before serving. To reheat, lightly spray a preheated skillet with nonstick spray and melt in a little butter. Place the crêpes in the pan one at a time, and heat on both sides until golden but still supple.

Vietnamese Coconut–Rice Flour Crêpes
with hot-sweet-sour dipping sauce

Bright yellow from the turmeric—and crispy if you cook them long enough—these lovely, thin pancakes are studded throughout with vegetables and tofu, creating fantastic contrasts of texture and color.

Cook the vegetables separately first, as you would for an omelet. (You can do this well ahead.) Then, when it's time to serve, make four separate vegetable-studded crêpes, one at a time. Each one takes only a couple of minutes, so don't begin the process until just before you intend to eat them. You can keep the finished crêpes warm in a 200°F oven, but they are best eaten right after they're cooked.

- Make the dipping sauce ahead of time. It takes only 5 minutes to prepare.
- Rice flour is available in natural food stores. You can also use unbleached all-purpose flour.
- The vegetables can be cooked—and the crêpe batter made—a day ahead. Store everything in the refrigerator, and bring to room temperature before the final cooking.
- Keep the clean, dry lettuce refrigerated until just before you serve so it can provide a sublimely crisp and cold contrast.
- Freeze the unused coconut milk in an ice cube tray (page 11), and store the cubes in a sealed plastic bag to defrost for future use in smoothies, curries, or soups—or for more of these crêpes.

YIELD: **4 servings (4 crêpes)**
PREPARATION TIME: **About 50 minutes**

½ pound very firm tofu

About 2 tablespoons canola oil

1 medium onion, thinly sliced

4 medium shiitake mushrooms, stemmed and thinly sliced

2 tablespoons minced fresh ginger

1 small bell pepper, thinly sliced

4 scallions, minced

¾ teaspoon salt

4 ounces mung bean sprouts

4 large eggs

½ cup coconut milk (lowfat okay)

½ teaspoon ground turmeric

¼ cup rice flour

1 small head green leaf lettuce, separated into leaves

Sprigs of fresh mint

Hot-Sweet-Sour Dipping Sauce

1. Cut the tofu into thin slices (about ⅛ inch thick and ¾ inch square) and set aside.

2. Place a medium to large sauté pan (preferably nonstick) over medium heat for a few minutes. When the pan is hot, add 1 tablespoon of the oil, wait 30 seconds, then swirl to coat the pan. Add the onion, mushrooms, and ginger, and sauté over medium-high heat for about 5 minutes, or until the mushrooms wilt and begin to shrink.

3. Stir in the tofu, bell peppers, and scallions, along with ½ teaspoon of the salt, and sauté for about 3 minutes more. Add the bean sprouts, and toss everything over the heat for about 2 minutes more. Remove the pan from the heat, and set aside.

4. Break the eggs into a medium-sized bowl. Add the coconut milk and beat with a whisk until smooth. Keep whisking as you sprinkle in the turmeric, rice flour, and remaining ¼ teaspoon salt. Pour the mixture into a 2-cup liquid measure, and set aside.

5. Place an 8-inch nonstick crêpe pan over medium heat. After a minute or two, add a scant teaspoon of canola oil, wait 30 seconds, then swirl to coat the pan. When the pan is hot enough to sizzle a bread crumb, add approximately one fourth of the cooked vegetable-tofu mixture, spreading it into a flat layer.

6. Slowly pour about one fourth of the egg mixture over the vegetables. Then lift the pan and slowly tilt it in all directions so the batter can flow to the edges. Return it to the heat, and let it sit for 2 to 3 minutes, or until the batter is set.

7. Loosen the edges with a dinner knife, then gently insert a large spatula underneath and flip the crêpe over. Cook on the second side until golden and crisp, about 3 minutes more. (If it breaks a little during this process, don't worry. Just flip over the pieces and continue.)

8. Transfer the finished crêpe to a plate, and serve right away, or keep it warm in a 200°F oven until you have made the other 3 crêpes. (Wipe out the pan with a paper towel in between crêpes, and add another scant teaspoon of canola oil each time.)

9. To serve, pass a plate of crisp lettuce leaves and mint sprigs, and have ready a bowl of Hot-Sweet-Sour Dipping Sauce with a small spoon. Use the lettuce as a wrapper, placing large pieces of crêpe, drizzled with the dipping sauce and a sprig or two of mint inside the crisp leaves. Roll up and eat from your hand, remembering to pass the napkins.

Hot-Sweet-Sour Dipping Sauce

YIELD: ½ cup
PREPARATION TIME: 5 minutes

2 small (1½-inch) red or green serrano chiles

¼ cup light-colored honey

½ cup cider vinegar

⅓ cup minced peanuts (optional)

1. Slice the chiles into very thin rounds. (For a milder flavor, scrape out and discard the seeds from inside the chiles. Wash your hands after handling these or any other hot peppers.)

2. Measure the honey into a small glass or ceramic bowl. Add the vinegar, and stir until the honey dissolves.

3. Stir in the chiles. Let stand at room temperature until serving time. Sprinkle in the peanuts just before serving.

Buckwheat Blini with mushroom filling

In this recipe, the traditional Russian buckwheat pancake is fortified with cooked whole buckwheat groats (kasha) and a rich mushroom–cottage cheese filling. Serve these for a winter brunch, and you and your guests will stay warm for hours.

- Buckwheat flour is available in natural food stores. (I buy Arrowhead Mills brand, which comes packed in 2-pound bags, and keep it in the freezer for maximum freshness.)
- Cook the buckwheat groats (kasha) well ahead of time. (Guidelines are on page 46.)
- The pancakes can be made up to several days in advance. Stack them on a plate, cover tightly with plastic wrap, and refrigerate until ready to use.
- The filling can be made up to a day ahead and stored in a tightly covered container in the refrigerator. Let it come to room temperature before filling the blini.
- To keep the filled blini warm, transfer them to a baking tray or an ovenproof plate, and place in a 200˚F oven until serving time.
- Blini are delicious sprinkled with caviar, if you are so inclined.

YIELD: About 6 servings (about 12 blini)
PREPARATION TIME: 45 minutes (once All-Purpose Breakfast Mushrooms are made)

---

1 large egg

1¼ cups milk

1 cup buckwheat flour

½ teaspoon salt

½ cup cooked buckwheat groats (page 46)

Nonstick spray

Butter for the pan

Mushroom Filling, at room temperature (recipe follows)

OPTIONAL TOPPINGS

Extra Mushroom Filling

Sour cream or Homemade Crème Fraîche (page 263)

Minced chives or scallions

Paprika

Slices of smoked salmon

Caviar

1. Place the egg, milk, flour, and salt in a blender, and process until smooth. Transfer the batter to a medium-sized bowl, and crumble in the buckwheat groats with your fingers, breaking up any clumps.
2. Place an 8-inch nonstick crêpe or omelet pan over medium heat. After a minute or two, spray it lightly with nonstick spray, and melt in a little butter. Swirl to coat the pan, making sure to get butter into the corners. When the pan is hot enough to sizzle a bread crumb, use a ¼-cup measure with a handle to scoop up batter and pour it into the hot pan, tilting and turning the pan in a continuous direction until the bottom is coated and the batter climbs a little bit up the sides. (The groats make this a tad cumbersome, but if you tilt and turn the pan patiently, it will work.)
3. After a minute or so, the batter will become dry on top, and you will have a fully cooked, flexible pancake. Loosen the edges with a dinner knife, flip the pancake over, and cook it on the other side for about 30 seconds. Turn it out onto a plate. Repeat this process until you've used up all the batter. Stack the cooked pancakes on the plate and set aside until shortly before serving time. (Cover with plastic wrap and refrigerate if you are making these in advance.)
4. Shortly before serving time, place a skillet over medium heat, and wait a minute or two. Spray it lightly with nonstick spray, and melt in a little butter. Add a pancake and wait a minute or so for it to heat up a little. Add 3 to 4 tablespoons room-temperature Mushroom Filling, spreading it almost to the edges.

RIGHTEOUS BUCKWHEAT

Buckwheat—or "kasha," as buckwheat groats are called when they've been roasted—is actually not a wheat, nor is it a true cereal grain. It's a relative of rhubarb, of all things! Who would have guessed? With its strong, toasty aroma, easy cooking procedure, and friendly, soft texture—not to mention its reasonable price—buckwheat is a pleasure to prepare and eat. It is also a nutritional force, containing all eight essential amino acids, calcium, vitamin E, and almost the entire spectrum of B-complex vitamins.

5. Top with a second pancake, like a sandwich. Cook until crisp on the bottom, then flip it over, and cook until crisp on the second side. Transfer the filled blin (that's the singular of blini) to a cutting board, and cut it into 4 wedges, like a quesadilla. Repeat with the remaining pancakes and filling.

6. Serve hot, topped with a small spoonful of extra Mushroom Filling, a dollop of sour cream or Homemade Crème Fraîche, and a light sprinkling of chives and paprika. Pass small dishes of smoked salmon or caviar, if desired.

Mushroom Filling

All-Purpose Breakfast Mushrooms
   (page 172)

½ cup cottage cheese

1 tablespoon sour cream or
   Homemade Crème Fraîche
      (page 263)

2 teaspoons minced fresh dill

⅛ teaspoon black pepper

Place everything in a medium-sized bowl and stir until thoroughly combined. Taste and adjust the seasonings.

Mollie's Basic Buttermilk Waffles

There are several criteria for a good waffle. It must be light and crisp but also moist and almost creamy in the center. It needs to rise just enough, but not so much that the batter fails to cook through. Ideally, it should also be substantial enough to keep you from feeling light-headed two hours later. This recipe covers all the bases.

- To keep the waffles warm, transfer them to a rack on a baking tray, and place the tray in a 200°F oven until serving time. (The rack keeps them crisp.)
- Canola oil can be substituted for some or all of the butter.

YIELD: 3 to 4 servings (6 or 7 standard waffles, or 3 Belgian waffles)
PREPARATION TIME: 20 minutes

1⅓ cups Mollie's Basic Pancake and Waffle Mix (page 183), or use the Pancake Mix Substitute below

1 cup buttermilk

3 tablespoons water

3 large eggs

½ teaspoon vanilla extract

6 tablespoons unsalted butter, melted

Nonstick spray

Butter for the waffle iron

PANCAKE MIX SUBSTITUTE

¾ cup unbleached all-purpose flour

¼ cup soy protein powder

¼ cup unprocessed wheat bran

¼ teaspoon salt

1½ teaspoons baking powder

⅛ teaspoon baking soda

1 tablespoon sugar (optional)

1. Preheat the waffle iron.
2. Place the pancake mix in a medium-sized bowl.
3. Measure the buttermilk and then the water into a 4-cup liquid measure. Add the eggs and beat gently with a fork or a small whisk until smooth. Stir in the vanilla. Pour this mixture, along with the melted butter, into the dry ingredients. Stir until thoroughly blended, scraping from the bottom and sides of the bowl, but don't overmix. A few lumps are okay.
4. Lightly spray the hot waffle iron on both the top and bottom surfaces with nonstick spray, then rub on a little butter. (This is most easily accomplished by generously buttering a chunk of bread and using it as a nifty, edible utensil to butter the waffle iron.) Add enough batter to just cover the cooking surface—approximately ½ cup for a standard waffle (1 cup for a Belgian waffle).
5. Cook for 2 to 3 minutes, depending on your waffle iron. Don't overbake—you want it crisp and brown but not too dark. It's perfectly okay to peek.
6. Serve hot with your chosen toppings.

THE FALLACY OF LOWFAT WAFFLES

If you want crisp waffles, there is no way around using a generous amount of butter or oil. It's just one of those cruel facts of life. The crispness of the waffle is proportionate to the thinness of the batter, the fat content, and the temperature of the iron. Lowfat waffles simply won't stand up to a fork.

Each of these variations gets topped with a special ingredient that falls perfectly into the crevices of the waffles. Follow the main recipe with these adjustments.

LEMON WAFFLES WITH BLUEBERRIES

Add to the basic mix:

- 2 to 3 tablespoons sugar
- 1 tablespoon grated lemon zest

Replace the water with:

- 3 tablespoons fresh lemon juice

Increase the vanilla extract to 1 teaspoon.

Top the finished waffles with:

- 1½ cups fresh blueberries or frozen, defrosted blueberries

CHOCOLATE WAFFLES

Add to the basic mix:

- 3 to 5 tablespoons sugar
- 3 tablespoons unsweetened cocoa

Replace the buttermilk and water with:

- 1¼ cups milk

Increase the vanilla extract to 2 teaspoons.

Top the finished waffles with:

- 1½ cups semisweet chocolate chips

The chocolate chips will melt slightly into the top surface of each hot waffle. Serve with powdered sugar and fresh raspberries, if available.

ORANGE WAFFLES WITH POMEGRANATE

Add to the basic mix:

- 2 tablespoons sugar
- 1 tablespoon grated orange zest

Replace the water with:

- 3 tablespoons orange juice

After the waffles are cooked, sprinkle with:

- 1 cup pomegranate seeds

Serve drizzled with pomegranate molasses (available in specialty markets and Middle Eastern groceries).

HERBED SWEET CORN WAFFLES

If you're making this in mid- to late summer—or in early fall—shave fresh sweet corn directly from the cob. (If corn is not in season, use frozen corn. To defrost, place it in a strainer and run it under room-temperature tap water. Drain and dry it thoroughly before adding to the batter.)

Omit the vanilla extract.

Soak in the melted butter for a few minutes:

- 2 cups fresh corn kernels (from about 3 cobs)
- ¼ teaspoon dried sage
- ½ teaspoon dried thyme
- ½ teaspoon dried basil

Add 1½ cups of the corn-butter-herb mixture to the batter, reserving the rest for sprinkling on top of the cooked waffles. Serve with Apple-Jalapeño Syrup (page 246).

SAVORY ROSEMARY-OLIVE WAFFLES WITH PEAS

You can steam fresh peas or use frozen ones. (To de-frost, place them in a strainer and run them under room-temperature tap water. No cooking necessary. Drain and dry them thoroughly before using.)

Omit the sugar and vanilla extract.

Replace half the melted butter with olive oil.

Add to the batter:

- ½ teaspoon crumbled dried rosemary
- 1 cup minced pitted Greek (kalamata) olives

Top the finished waffles with:

- 1½ cups green peas

Serve with Roasted Garlic Aïoli (page 264).

Oatmeal Waffles

Regular rolled oats work beautifully in this recipe, but if you can find the thicker kind (usually labeled "thick rolled oats" in the bulk bins in natural food stores), these waffles will have more substance and body, yet they'll still be light.

- If the batter gets too thick as it sits, you can thin it with some plain milk. It should be the consistency of a thick cream that pours easily.
- To keep the waffles warm, transfer them to a rack on a baking tray, and place the tray in a 200°F oven until serving time. (The rack keeps them crisp.)
- For an even chewier texture—and for additional nutrition and whole-grain goodness—stir in up to a cup of cooked oat groats (page 46).
- Canola oil can be substituted for some or all of the butter.

YIELD: 3 to 4 servings (6 or 7 standard waffles, or 3 Belgian waffles)
PREPARATION TIME: 20 minutes

1 cup rolled oats

1 cup unbleached all-purpose flour

½ cup oat bran

¾ teaspoon salt

1 teaspoon baking powder

¼ teaspoon baking soda

2 tablespoons sugar

1½ cups buttermilk

½ cup water or milk

2 large eggs

3 tablespoons unsalted butter, melted

Nonstick spray

Butter for the waffle iron

1. Preheat the waffle iron.
2. Combine the dry ingredients in a medium-sized bowl.
3. Measure the buttermilk and then the water into a 4-cup liquid measure. Add the eggs, and beat gently with a fork or a small whisk until smooth. Pour this mixture, along with the melted butter, into the dry ingredients. Stir until thoroughly blended, scraping from the bottom and sides of the bowl, but don't overmix. A few lumps are okay.
4. Lightly spray the hot waffle iron on both the top and bottom surfaces with nonstick spray, and rub on a little butter. (This is most easily accomplished by generously buttering a chunk of bread and using it as an edible utensil to butter the waffle iron.) Add just enough batter to cover the cooking surface—approximately ½ cup for a standard waffle (1 cup for a Belgian waffle).
5. Cook for 2 to 3 minutes, depending on your waffle iron. Don't overbake— you want it crisp and brown but not too dark. It's okay to peek.
6. Serve hot with your chosen toppings.

Polenta Waffles with berries

An extra benefit from making these delicious waffles is that the berries emit an amazing aroma when they hit the hot waffle iron. It will fill your kitchen with the best of breakfast smells! I use polenta instead of regular cornmeal for these waffles because its coarse grind gives them a slightly crunchy texture.

You can use any kind of berry—and frozen ones work beautifully—so you can have these any time of year. I like to use a mixture of different types. You can buy an unsweetened frozen berry mix in most supermarkets. Don't defrost them before adding them to the batter, but do cut larger berries into smaller pieces. (You can do this while they are still frozen.)

- To keep the waffles warm, transfer them to a rack on a baking tray, and place the tray in a 200°F oven until serving time. (The rack keeps them crisp.)
- Canola oil can be substituted for some or all of the butter.

YIELD: **4 servings (8 standard waffles, or 4 Belgian waffles)**
PREPARATION TIME: **20 minutes**

1¾ cups unbleached all-purpose flour

¼ cup polenta

¼ teaspoon salt (rounded measure)

2½ teaspoons baking powder

1 tablespoon sugar

3 large eggs

1½ cups milk

4 tablespoons (half a stick) unsalted butter, melted

2 cups berries (any kind)

Nonstick spray

Butter for the waffle iron

1. Preheat the waffle iron.

2. Combine the dry ingredients in a medium-sized bowl.

3. Break the eggs into a second medium-sized bowl and beat with a whisk until frothy. Drizzle in the milk.

4. Add the egg-milk mixture to the dry ingredients, along with the melted butter and the berries. Mix with decisive strokes from the bottom of the bowl until all the dry ingredients have been moistened. Try not to over-mix, and also try to avoid breaking the berries. You'll break some anyway, but just do your best.

5. Lightly spray the hot waffle iron on both the top and bottom surfaces with nonstick spray, and rub on a little butter. (This is most easily accomplished by generously buttering a chunk of bread and using it as an edible utensil to butter the waffle iron.) Add just enough batter to cover the cooking surface—approximately ½ cup for a standard waffle (1 cup for a Belgian waffle).

6. Cook for 2 to 3 minutes, depending on your waffle iron. Don't overbake—you want it crisp and brown but not too dark. It's okay to peek.

7. Serve hot with your chosen toppings.

Amazing Overnight Waffles

Leavened with yeast, these ever-so-slightly sourdough waffles are the lightest and crispiest I've ever tasted. You begin the batter the night before and finish it in the morning—just 5 minutes here and 5 minutes there, and you're ready for the waffle iron. Don't be scared off by the yeast! Just mix it into the flour: no proofing, no kneading, no dough. This is truly easy batter!

- To keep the waffles warm, transfer them to a rack on a baking tray, and place the tray in a 200°F oven until serving time. (The rack keeps them crisp.)
- Canola oil can be substituted for some or all of the butter.

YIELD: 3 to 4 servings (6 to 8 standard-size waffles, or 3 or 4 Belgian waffles)
PREPARATION TIME: 5 minutes in the evening, 20 minutes in the morning

2 cups unbleached all-purpose flour

1 teaspoon yeast

1 tablespoon sugar

½ teaspoon salt

2 cups milk

6 tablespoons unsalted butter, melted

1 large egg

Nonstick spray

Butter for the waffle iron

1. Combine the flour, yeast, sugar, and salt in a medium-sized bowl. Add the milk, and whisk until blended. Cover the bowl tightly with plastic wrap, and let it stand overnight at room temperature. (If the room is warmer than 70°F, put it in the refrigerator.)

2. In the morning, preheat the waffle iron and melt the butter. Beat the egg in a small, separate bowl, then beat it into the batter along with the melted butter. The batter will be quite thin.

3. Lightly spray the hot waffle iron on both the top and bottom surfaces with nonstick spray, and rub on a little butter. (This is most easily accomplished by generously buttering a chunk of bread and using it as an edible utensil to butter the waffle iron.) Add just enough batter to cover the cooking surface—approximately ⅔ cup for each waffle (1⅓ cups for a Belgian waffle).

4. Cook for 2 to 3 minutes, depending on your waffle iron. Don't overbake—you want it crisp and brown but not too dark. It's okay to peek.

5. Serve hot with your chosen toppings.

VARIATIONS You can take the basic recipe for Amazing Overnight Waffles in a number of directions. For each variation, follow the main recipe with the following adjustments.

QUINOA WAFFLES

Stir into the batter:

- 1½ cups cooked quinoa (page 46)
- Up to 2 teaspoons additional sugar

The added sugar offsets the naturally bitter flavor of the quinoa. These waffles taste great served with Blackberry Maple Syrup (page 246) and yogurt.

CRUNCHY MILLET WAFFLES

Stir into the batter:

- ⅔ cup uncooked millet
- A pinch of cinnamon (optional)

Top with orange marmalade.

WILD RICE WAFFLES

Stir into the batter:

- Up to 1½ cups cooked wild rice (page 46)
- Up to 2 teaspoons additional sugar

These waffles go beautifully with sliced fresh peaches.

PROTEIN POWDER WAFFLES

For information about protein powder, see page xv.

Replace 1 cup of the flour with:

- 1 cup soy protein powder

Increase the milk to 2½ cups.

You will get a slightly higher yield with this variation. Serve with Passionfruit Syrup (page 246).

PECAN WAFFLES

Add to the batter:

- ¾ cup finely chopped pecans, lightly toasted

Top with Lemon-Thyme Honey Syrup (page 247).

Crunchy Coated French Toast

French toast tastes best when the bread has been soaked all the way through so it stays moist and creamy on the inside even after it's been cooked. I also want my French toast to be so crisp you can hear me take a bite from two rooms away. Is that a tall order? Not with this recipe! An extra coating of almonds, oats, or crunchy millet ensures that the texture will be just right and adds a wonderful layer of flavor.

- For best results, use either challah or a country-style bread with a crisp crust and an airy, chewy interior (what's known in bread-speak as a "high crust to crumb ratio"). These breads are often called sweet *bâtarde, ciabatta,* or *pugliese.* If you can't find any of these, use stale French or Italian bread. Fresh bread will also work, but it tends to fall apart.
- Any kind of milk (including soy milk or half-and-half) will work.

YIELD: **2 servings (easily multiplied)**
PREPARATION TIME: **15 minutes**

3 large eggs

A pinch of salt

½ teaspoon vanilla extract

½ cup milk (possibly more)

A pinch of cinnamon (optional)

3 or 4 slices bread

⅔ cup sliced almonds, rolled oats, or uncooked millet

Butter for the pan

1. Begin heating a griddle or skillet over medium heat.
2. Break the eggs into a pie pan, add the salt, and beat with a fork until smooth. Beat in the vanilla.
3. Continue to stir the mixture as you drizzle in the milk and sprinkle in the cinnamon, if desired. When it is well blended, place the slices of bread into the mixture, pressing them down with the back of the fork.
4. Let the bread sit in the egg mixture for about 2 minutes, then turn it over and let it sit for another 2 minutes. It should be soaked all the way through.
5. Spread the almonds, oats, or millet out on one or two plates. Lay the soaked bread on top and press gently until coated on the bottom. Turn the bread over and coat the other side.
6. Melt some butter on the hot griddle, then add the coated bread. Fry over medium heat for 8 to 10 minutes on each side, or until the coating is golden. (If it begins to brown too much or too fast, turn the heat down. It's important that the French toast be cooked all the way through.)
7. Serve hot with the toppings of your choice.

Matzoh Brei

Matzoh brei is similar in concept to French toast, but instead of soaking bread in eggs and milk, you soften matzoh in a little water and then drain it off, mix it with beaten egg, and fry it in butter. It's actually very easy!

- If you have any matzoh brei left over, it reheats well in an oven or toaster oven. Line the tray with foil and spread out the leftover matzoh brei in a thin layer. Reheat for about 10 minutes at 200°F.

YIELD: **1 large or 2 smaller servings (easily multiplied)**
PREPARATION TIME: **15 to 20 minutes**

2 matzohs

2 large eggs

Salt

About 1 tablespoon butter

OPTIONAL TOPPINGS

Fresh fruit

Preserves

Honey

Cinnamon sugar

1. Break the matzoh into 3-inch pieces (approximate, of course!) and place them in a bowl. Add tap water (any temperature) to cover, and let it stand for 3 to 5 minutes.
2. Drain off the water. You don't need to press it out—just get rid of any that is standing in the bowl.
3. Break the eggs into a second, smaller bowl, and beat with a fork until smooth.
4. Pour the eggs over the matzoh, add a few dashes of salt, and mix until the matzoh is completely coated. It's okay if the matzoh breaks further into smaller pieces.
5. Place a 10-inch skillet over medium heat and wait for a few minutes. When it is hot, add the butter, wait a few seconds longer, and then swirl so it coats the pan as it melts.
6. Add the matzoh-egg mixture to the hot pan, distributing it evenly to the edges of the pan so that it forms a large, round unit.
7. Let it cook undisturbed over medium heat for a good 5 to 8 minutes (possibly a little longer), or until golden on the bottom.
8. Lift the matzoh brei gently with a spatula, add a little extra butter to the pan, and wait a few seconds for it to melt. Flip the matzoh brei over to cook on the second side until golden all over. (If it breaks during the flipping process, don't worry about it. You need to break it up to eat it anyway.) Serve hot or warm with your chosen toppings.

 ## ACCORDING TO MY GRANDMA . . .

It was impossible to extract a precise recipe for matzoh brei from my grandmother, because she never measured anything. She owned no cookbooks (not even recipes on scraps of paper) and had never heard of measuring cups or spoons. Both cooking and baking were done by "feel" or by sight—judging things in relationship to the size of her hand, for example. That said, this is a close approximation of our family "recipe" for matzoh brei. It might not be *your* family's recipe, but that's okay. If you are Jewish and you remember your grandmother making it differently (for instance, going a savory route with sautéed onions and leaving off the sweet toppings), please, by all means improvise in that direction. There is neither a right nor a wrong way to make it!

9

YOGURT & CHEESE

CONTENTS

YOGURT & CHEESE

Cheese and yogurt originated as nature's way of transforming, and thus preserving, milk. Over the centuries, even as many variations and means of production for cheese and yogurt have been perfected, these noble dairy products remain pretty much unchanged. They're the cornerstone of many cuisines and a traditional morning food in many cultures.

Consider a light breakfast of bread and cheese, perhaps with a few slices of apple, some grapes, or a fresh fig. It's also fun to expand this idea—grouping several cheeses together, European style—for a leisurely weekend morning. Treat yourself to a trip to the cheese shop, and pick up a small variety of great-tasting cheeses that complement one another, not only in flavor but also in color, texture, and shape. Arrange them on a wooden or marble board, and serve it with chunks of fresh bread, fresh fruit (ideally apples, pears, figs, grapes, and melon), small bowls of nuts and dried fruit, and maybe a few savory touches (scallions, celery, cucumber, bell pepper, tomatoes, and olives). Then you can sit around tasting and relaxing, reading the paper or talking, and sipping your favorite hot beverage—it's a great way to spend a morning!

Or picture a small bowl of yogurt waiting for you first thing in the morning, crowned with a few colorful berries and a swirl of honey—or topped with raisins and toasted almonds. A modest serving of high-quality yogurt can be a wonderful solution for those of us who don't have a huge appetite in the morning but would like just a few easy mouthfuls of something wholesome and gratifying. And don't forget that yogurt can be a perfect topping for your breakfast cereal—a thick, tart, and refreshing alternative to plain milk.

In this chapter you'll find a range of ideas for incorporating yogurt and cheese into your morning menu, adding a touch of luxury and some good nutrition in the process. If I had to define dairy products in a single sentence, I think I would put it like this: They are the world's most sensuous delivery system for calcium and protein. Just think about it.

Breakfast Raita

Add a little Indian seasoning and a scattering of fresh vegetables to a bowlful of yogurt and you have raita—a general term for yogurt sauces served as a cooling contrast to hot curries. When you serve raita by itself, it becomes a refreshing light breakfast dish. Scoop it up with some freshly baked flatbread (page 96), and wash it down with a cup of Backward Chai (page 17).

- Raita tastes best—and is most satisfying—when made with whole-milk yogurt.
- I haven't given exact measures for the optional additions. You can decide how much to add per your taste and judgment. Raita is very flexible.
- Make this a maximum of 1 day ahead of time. It doesn't keep well for much longer than that.

YIELD: **3 to 4 servings** (possibly more, depending on how many extras you add)
PREPARATION TIME: **5 minutes**

---

1 teaspoon cumin seed

2 cups yogurt

¼ teaspoon salt

⅛ teaspoon cayenne

Up to 1 cup minced cucumber
(peeled and seeded)

OPTIONAL ADDITIONS

Minced fresh fennel

Minced bell pepper

Minced red onion

Grated carrot

Diced ripe tomato

Minced or torn cilantro leaves

1. Lightly toast the cumin seed in a toaster oven or a small skillet over medium heat. Watch it carefully so it doesn't burn. When the cumin gives off a strong, toasty aroma, remove it from the heat.
2. Place the yogurt in a medium-sized bowl, and add the cumin, salt, cayenne, and cucumber—and whatever optional additional vegetables you prefer. (Don't add the diced tomato and cilantro until shortly before serving.) Mix until thoroughly blended, cover, and refrigerate.
3. Serve cold, topped with a scattering of diced tomato and minced or torn cilantro leaves, if desired.

 IN PRAISE OF YOGURT

Many of us think of yogurt as something sweet, eaten straight out of small, decorative containers from the convenience store. But there is also some very good *real* yogurt available in supermarkets these days. You can find unflavored whole-milk yogurt—made with live cultures—that is fresh tasting and pure. In fact, high-quality yogurt can be so delicious, all it needs is perhaps a drizzle of pure maple syrup or honey or a sprinkling of coarse salt, freshly ground black pepper, and an aromatic spice mixture (page 260). You'll find that you can happily get lost in a bowl of it.

Homemade Ricotta

Homemade ricotta cheese is not only more soulful than anything you can buy, it's also more economical, producing approximately 1 pound of cheese for the price of a half-gallon of milk, which is usually a pretty good deal. I love this cheese, and I love what it contributes to the spirit of my kitchen.

You can control the thickness of the cheese simply by keeping watch over the project and wrapping it up (literally) when the cheese achieves your preferred texture. The longer it drains, the firmer it becomes.

- The whey (liquid) that drains off during the process is full of flavor and nutrients and can be used in place of water when you make yeasted dough.
- Use a yogurt that is made with live, active cultures (such as *Streptococcus thermophilus, Lactobacillus bulgaricus,* or *L. acidophilus*). This will be indicated on the label.

YIELD: 2 cups
PREPARATION TIME: A few minutes of work, plus time to heat and 4 to 5 hours to stand

½ gallon whole milk

1 cup yogurt

½ cup fresh lemon juice

½ teaspoon salt, or to taste

1. Pour the milk and yogurt into a large saucepan or a kettle, and whisk until smooth. Place the pan over medium heat, and warm the mixture until small bubbles form along the sides and the top surface bulges slightly.

2. Remove the pan from the stove, and pour in the lemon juice without mixing. Let the mixture stand at room temperature for an hour to curdle.

3. Prepare a 4-layer cheesecloth net about 16 inches long and 8 to 10 inches wide. Spread this into a medium-sized fine-mesh strainer or colander balanced over a bowl. Long pieces of cheesecloth will drape over the sides. Pour the curdled mixture into the net so the liquid (whey) drips into the bowl and the solids (curds) remain in the cheesecloth. Don't press it or try to hurry the process along in any way, or you'll lose some of the cheese. The whey needs to drip at its own natural pace.

4. After about an hour, lift the side flaps of cheesecloth and, without actually knotting them, tie them neatly around the cheese. (The cheesecloth wrap should be snug enough to press but not squeeze the cheese.) Let it stand, slowly dripping, for another hour or two—or even longer, if you like a firmer, drier cheese.

5. Salt the cheese to taste, transfer it to a tightly covered container, and refrigerate. It will keep for about 5 days.

 YOGURT CHEESE—SIMPLEST OF ALL

With equipment no more complicated than a plain coffee filter—and with no cooking or heating—you can make a great, tangy alternative to cream cheese out of any kind of yogurt—flavored or plain, whole milk or lowfat.

Place a large, paper-lined coffee filter over a container (I use a 1-cup liquid measure), and spoon in some high-quality yogurt—any amount that will fit. Let it stand for about 6 hours at room temperature or in the refrigerator. The whey will drain, and the yogurt will firm up and become a soft cheese. As with homemade ricotta, the longer it drains, the thicker it gets. You will end up with about half the original volume.

Vegetable-Flecked Cottage Cheese

Plain, fresh cottage cheese on a piece of toast is a quick and delicious breakfast. You can also augment cottage cheese by adding diced fruit or vegetables and a few choice accoutrements, thus making it more colorful and varied. Enjoy this mixture heaped on toast, or just eat it with a spoon.

- This keeps for a day or two in a tightly covered container in the refrigerator.
- Grind the flax seed shortly before you need it, using an electric spice grinder.

YIELD: 4 to 6 servings
PREPARATION TIME: 10 minutes

2 cups (1 pound) cottage cheese

½ cup grated carrot

½ cup minced celery

½ cup minced bell pepper

½ cup minced cucumber

1 small scallion, minced

¼ cup toasted sunflower seeds

2 to 3 tablespoons ground flax seed (optional)

Salt

Freshly ground black pepper

OPTIONAL TOPPINGS

Cherry tomatoes, halved unless they're tiny

Chopped hard-boiled egg

1. In a medium-sized bowl, combine everything except the toppings, adding salt and pepper to taste. Gently stir until thoroughly combined. Cover and chill until serving time.
2. Serve cold, topped with cherry tomatoes and chopped egg, if desired.

VARIATION   COTTAGE CHEESE WITH FRUIT

You can use any fruit that is fresh and in season. Try peaches, cantaloupe, honeydew, apple, oranges, or pineapple. This mixture doesn't keep well, so try to eat it soon after you make it.

Begin with 2 cups cottage cheese, as in the main recipe. Replace the other ingredients with:

- ½ cup seedless grapes, halved if large
- 2 cups (1 pound) cottage cheese
- 2 cups diced fresh fruit in season
- 2 teaspoons poppy seeds
- ¼ cup raisins or currants
- ½ cup chopped toasted nuts
- Honey and lemon juice to taste

Gently mix until thoroughly blended, and serve cold. This will serve 4 to 6.

Breaded Sautéed Goat Cheese Patties

Crisp on the outside and creamy on the inside, these patties are a luxurious treat. Eat them plain or accompanied by little toasts and some vegetables and olives. They also fit perfectly on an English muffin or tucked inside a cooked portobello mushroom. (See page 176 for the "Mushroom Treatment.")

- You can make these ahead of time and store them in an airtight wrapper or container in the refrigerator for up to a week. They reheat very quickly (about 20 seconds on High) in a microwave. You can also keep the patties warm in a 300°F oven just after cooking them.

YIELD: **About 4 servings (2 patties each); easily multiplied**
PREPARATION TIME: **15 minutes**

1 cup soft goat cheese

¼ cup fine bread crumbs

Freshly ground black pepper

1 to 2 tablespoons olive oil

OPTIONAL ACCOMPANIMENTS

English muffins or little toasts

Olives

Thinly sliced radishes

Thinly sliced cucumber

Tiny cherry tomatoes

1. Place about 2 tablespoons of the cheese on a piece of plastic wrap. Cover with another piece of plastic wrap, and gently pat and "massage" the cheese into a patty 2 inches in diameter and ¾ inch thick. (You can also skip the plastic wrap, and just use your hands. Dampen them first, so the cheese won't stick.) Repeat with the rest of the cheese. You should have 8 patties.

2. Place the bread crumbs on a plate, grind in some fresh black pepper, and stir to mix. Press the cheese patties into the crumbs until coated on both sides and around the edges.

3. Place a heavy, nonstick skillet over medium heat for about 2 minutes. Add 1 tablespoon of olive oil, wait about 30 seconds, then swirl to coat the pan. When the skillet is very hot, add the coated cheese patties and sauté for 2 to 3 minutes on each side, or until golden brown, adding more oil if necessary. When they are done to your liking, transfer the sautéed patties to a plate lined with a double thickness of paper towels.

4. Serve hot or very warm, sprinkled with more freshly ground black pepper, along with your choice of accompaniments.

Scrambled Cheese

Did you know that you can scramble ricotta just as you would eggs or tofu? Scrambled cheese can provide a terrific hit of protein for breakfast, especially when you need a break from eggs (sorry).

I'm always surprised by how interesting the flavor of plain ricotta cheese can be, all on its own. For some reason, its flavor is more detectable (and delectable) when the cheese has been heated or cooked than when experienced straight from the container. Give this a try.

• You can eat scrambled cheese by itself—delicious with just salt and pepper—or expand it by adding vegetables. (See the variations.)

YIELD: 1 serving (easily multiplied)
PREPARATION TIME: About 12 minutes

1 teaspoon olive oil

¾ cup ricotta cheese (whole milk or lowfat)

Salt

Freshly ground black pepper

1. Place an 8-inch crêpe or omelet pan over medium heat for 2 minutes. Add the olive oil, wait about 10 seconds, and swirl to coat the pan. Then wait about 30 seconds longer to let the oiled pan get really hot.

2. Spoon the cheese into the hot pan, distributing it as evenly as possible. (Be careful not to get splattered, especially when using lowfat cheese.) Let it cook without stirring for about 5 minutes.

3. Move the cheese around in the pan a little, turning the cheese over and rearranging it to maximize contact with the heat. Sprinkle in a little salt, then let the cheese cook for about 5 minutes longer.

4. Rearrange the cheese again. This time it will suddenly come together in a soft mass. Transfer it to a plate, and serve right away. Pass a pepper mill.

VARIATIONS   For each variation, follow the main recipe with these adjustments. (Each of these takes about 20 minutes and serves 4.)

SCRAMBLED CHEESE WITH VEGETABLES

Make a double batch of Scrambled Cheese, and add:

• Flash-Cooked Vegetables (page 174)

Mix everything together—or place side by side—and serve right away.

SCRAMBLED CHEESE WITH MUSHROOMS

Make a double batch of Scrambled Cheese, and add:

• Quick Individual All-Purpose Mushrooms (page 173)

Mix everything together—or place side by side—and serve right away.

Baked Ricotta

Ricotta is generally considered an ingredient and not an "eating" cheese. Usually made into something else, it rarely, if ever, gets to shine on its own. That's a shame, because ricotta can be incredibly soothing, and its natural flavor, while subtle, is quite lovely. Yet we're hardly ever given a chance to notice it!

Here is that chance. When you bake ricotta, the texture firms up and the flavor deepens. It becomes more of an eating cheese, similar in many ways to an Italian cheesecake. Serve baked ricotta slightly warm or at room temperature, cut into wedges or slices. It's perfect for breakfast or for a midmorning snack.

- Store baked ricotta in an airtight container in the refrigerator for up to a week. Bring it to room temperature before serving.
- You can make this with whole-milk ricotta or with the lowfat variety. It will come out fine either way. If you use lowfat ricotta, it will give off some liquid (whey) as it bakes, but then reabsorb it as it cools.

YIELD: 3 to 4 servings
PREPARATION TIME: 5 minutes, plus 40 minutes to bake

Nonstick spray

1 pound ricotta cheese

1. Preheat the oven to 350°F. Lightly spray a 9-inch pie pan with nonstick spray.
2. Place the ricotta in the pan, and spread it to make a circle about 6 inches in diameter and ½ inch thick.
3. Bake in the center of the oven for 35 to 40 minutes, or until the edges turn light golden and the top is firm to the touch and just beginning to turn pale brown. (The cheese might spread and/or "weep" a little during baking. This is fine.)
4. Remove from the oven and allow to cool in the pan for at least 15 minutes before slicing.

VARIATIONS For each variation, follow the main recipe with these adjustments.

FRUIT-FLAVORED BAKED RICOTTA

Mix and mash into the ricotta:

- 2 tablespoons of your favorite jam or preserves

Proceed as described in the main recipe.

RUM-RAISIN BAKED RICOTTA

Combine in a glass or ceramic bowl:

- ⅓ cup raisins
- ¼ cup rum

Microwave on High for 30 to 40 seconds. Stir into the ricotta, and proceed as described in the main recipe.

DATE-NUT BAKED RICOTTA

Stir into the ricotta:

- ½ cup chopped dates
- ½ cup chopped toasted walnuts
- 1 teaspoon grated lemon zest (optional)

Proceed as described in the main recipe.

Filo Packets

With very little effort, plain soft cheese can be wrapped in filo pastry and transformed into neat and crispy little packets. Convenient and elegant, these quick breakfast bites are easy and fun to make. They also travel well, so consider bringing a stash with you to work.

- Plain nonstick spray works fine, but olive oil-based cooking spray will give extra flavor.
- This recipe uses approximately half of a 1-pound package of filo pastry. You can wrap the unused filo in a zip-style plastic bag and refrigerate for future use.
- Filo packets store well in an airtight container or zip-type plastic bag in the refrigerator for a week or longer. Freshen them up for 5 to 10 minutes in a preheated 350°F toaster oven before serving.

YIELD: 4 to 6 servings (12 packets); easily multiplied
PREPARATION TIME: 10 minutes, plus 20 minutes to bake

Nonstick spray (plain or olive oil)

12 sheets filo pastry

1 cup soft cheese (goat cheese, ricotta, or farmer's cheese)

¾ cup lightly toasted pistachio nuts or pine nuts (optional)

3 tablespoons unsalted butter, melted

1. Preheat the oven to 350°F. Lightly spray a baking tray with nonstick spray.
2. Unfold the filo, and leave it in a stack. Spray the top sheet with nonstick spray, then fold it into thirds lengthwise—first one flap, then the other. You should have one long, 3-layer strip. Spray the top surface with nonstick spray.
3. Place a heaping tablespoon of cheese about 2 inches from one end of the folded pastry. If you like, you can also add a tablespoon of nuts. Fold the 2-inch end of the filo up and over the cheese, then fold in the narrow margins. Wrap the cheese up in the pastry, beginning at the cheese end and flopping it over and over until you have a little square or rectangular package. Transfer to the prepared baking tray, and repeat until you have 12 packages.
4. Lightly brush the tops of the packets with melted butter, and bake in the center of the oven for 20 minutes, or until golden brown. Transfer to a rack to cool for at least 10 minutes before serving. These can be eaten hot, warm, or at room temperature.

CHEESE-BASED TOAST TOPPINGS

Cheese can transform a piece of plain toast into a meal that will keep you satisfied for hours. Here are some ideas for topping a piece of freshly toasted bread:

- Thin slices of aged cheddar, topped with slices of date and tart apple and sprinkled with fresh lemon juice.

- Brie or camembert topped with a spoonful of All-Purpose Breakfast Mushrooms (page 172).

- Cream cheese topped with watercress and thin slices of radish and cucumber.

- Lemon juice–soaked raisins topped with grated gruyère and broiled.

- Homemade ricotta or yogurt cheese (page 217) drizzled with Lemon-Thyme Honey Syrup (page 247) or with plain honey that has been warmed slightly.

- Muenster or emmenthaler, thinly sliced, with a dab of mustard and a sprinkling of celery seed. Top with thinly sliced cucumbers and radishes.

- Sharp cheddar topped with walnuts and then broiled. Drizzle on some fruit syrup (page 246).

- Tartine Mistral: Spread a toasted half-baguette with a thick layer of goat cheese and a generous topping of sliced roasted peppers (bottom of page 255), and sprinkle with salt and pepper. For a luxurious touch, finish it off with a touch of Homemade Crème Fraîche (page 263).

SOME PRACTICAL CHEESE POINTERS

- Shop for cheese frequently, and buy it in small amounts to ensure freshness.

- To keep hard cheese moist, rub it all over with oil before wrapping it.

- The ideal way to keep hard or medium-firm cheese is to wrap it in a paper towel that you've dampened with vinegar. Then put the whole thing inside a plastic bag and close loosely, but don't seal it—it needs some air. Store it in the refrigerator, checking the paper towel daily, and reapplying vinegar, if necessary. This method keeps cheese longer and inhibits the formation of mold.

- Medium-firm cheeses (cheddar, swiss, jack) grate more easily when very cold. Hard cheeses (pecorino, parmesan) grate more easily at room temperature.

- If you're going to use the grating attachment of a food processor to grate cheese, spray it with nonstick spray beforehand. This will make cleanup easier.

- For a time-saver, grate extra cheese and freeze it. Spread out the freshly grated cheese on a tray that has been coated with nonstick spray, and freeze for about 30 minutes. (This keeps the cheese from clumping when frozen.) Then transfer the semifrozen cheese to a heavy zip-style plastic bag, seal it, and store it in the freezer. Use as needed.

- Ricotta and cottage cheese stay fresh longer if stored upside down.

FOUR IRRESISTIBLE CHEESE SPREADS

Sometimes the flavor of cheese is complex, and sometimes it is fresh and simple. Each of the following recipes builds on the essence of a particular cheese, adding various sweet, savory, tart, and pungent touches, some of them quite unusual. The first two spreads are savory and go perfectly on toast and/or vegetables. The second two, both blue cheese–based, are also good on toast and taste downright sublime with figs (fresh or dried) or spread onto slices of fresh pear.

- Serve cheese spreads at room temperature or cold.
- Each spread keeps for a week or longer if stored in a tightly covered container in the refrigerator.

YIELD: Each makes 4 to 6 servings
PREPARATION TIME: 10 minutes or less

Creamy Feta with Ground Walnuts

Try this on sourdough or pumpernickel toast with tomatoes or minced red bell pepper. It's also good on herb bread, topped with dates or golden raisins. Or use it to fill a hollowed-out cucumber for a delicious commuter breakfast.

1 cup walnuts, lightly toasted

A handful of parsley

1 cup crumbled feta

½ teaspoon minced garlic (optional)

½ cup milk, cream, or Homemade
  Crème Fraîche (page 263)

1 teaspoon mild paprika

Cayenne

1. Combine the walnuts and parsley in a food processor or blender. Buzz until the nuts are finely ground and the parsley is finely minced.
2. Add the cheese, garlic, milk, and paprika, and purée until smooth. Transfer to a bowl and add cayenne to taste.
3. Serve at room temperature or cold.

Ricotta with Artichoke Hearts and Parmesan

Spread this tangy mixture on toast. You can also take it a few steps further by topping it with a slice of ripe tomato and a sprinkling of additional parmesan—and broiling it until the cheese browns.

4 jars (6 ounces each) marinated artichoke hearts

1 cup ricotta cheese

6 tablespoons grated parmesan

Freshly ground black pepper

1. Drain the artichoke hearts, and transfer them to a food processor.
2. Add the ricotta and parmesan, and purée until smooth.
3. Season to taste with black pepper. Transfer to a tightly covered container, and refrigerate until use. Serve cold.

Stilton with Dates and Lemon

Sweet, pungent, and tart flavors are in perfect balance in this intense spread.

• Zest the lemons before juicing them. Use a vegetable peeler to remove the zest, then chop it coarsely with a knife.

½ cup mashed pitted soft dates

¼ cup fresh lemon juice

1 cup crumbled stilton

3 tablespoons chopped lemon zest

1. Combine the dates and lemon juice in a medium-sized bowl, and slowly mash them together until blended.
2. Add the cheese and lemon zest, and stir until uniformly combined.
3. Serve at room temperature or cold.

Mascarpone and Gorgonzola with Pine Nuts

Mascarpone is a sublimely smooth, somewhat sweet Italian cream cheese that acquires a slightly provocative edge when laced with gorgonzola. If you can't find mascarpone, substitute a high-quality cream cheese.

• Note: This tastes best at room temperature.

⅓ cup mascarpone

3 tablespoons crumbled gorgonzola

1 teaspoon fresh lemon juice

A dash of salt (optional)

¼ cup pine nuts, lightly toasted

Light honey

Lavender flowers and/or leaves for garnish (optional)

1. Place the mascarpone in a small bowl and stir to soften. (Be patient—it's a bit sticky.) Slowly stir in the crumbled gorgonzola and the lemon juice, and mix until well blended. Add a dash of salt, if desired. Stir in 3 tablespoons of the pine nuts.
2. To serve, spread a small amount on a slice of fruit or piece of toast. Drizzle the top of each serving with a little honey and sprinkle on a few extra pine nuts. A scattering of fresh lavender blossoms and/or leaves is the perfect finishing touch.

10

PUDDINGS & CUSTARDS

CONTENTS

PUDDINGS & CUSTARDS

Who says comfort foods are only for the end of the day or for weekend afternoons in winter? There is definitely such a thing as Morning Comfort Food, which I define as a dish you can happily face on mornings when you might not be able to face anything else. It's as simple as that.

We all have days when we just want to crawl out of bed and spoon-feed ourselves a gentle something that barely requires chewing. The recipes in this chapter are for those days. They're also a great choice for non-breakfast eaters in general who want to cultivate a new habit of eating something early in the day.

Some of the puddings, flans, and custards in this chapter are basically desserts that cross over nicely to breakfast, taking care of our sweet tooth and our protein needs at the same time. Others are cozy savory dishes that provide several levels of nourishment, both physical and psychological. Savory puddings can also double as supper.

Many of the recipes are made in individual portions, so consider investing in a set of 6-ounce ceramic ramekins or ovenproof glass custard cups. You'll use them a lot once you get into the pudding habit! The cups are portable, so you can bring one or two to work with you for a snack or a late, light breakfast.

The bread puddings, spinach-feta pudding, and cornmeal-cheddar pudding—which are baked in larger pans—can also travel with you to work. Pack them in individual containers and reheat in a microwave for a terrific—and inconspicuous—desk-side meal. They are also good cold or at room temperature, so if you don't have a microwave at work, take some with you anyway.

ABOUT THE MILK

You can use just about any kind of milk—or a combination of different types—for these recipes. If you like a rich taste, include some cream. My favorite combination for most of these dishes is whole milk and half-and-half (in about a 3-to-1 ratio). You can also get luxurious, lower-fat results by combining lowfat milk with lowfat or skim evaporated milk. Plain soy milk can be used for all of these recipes as well.

Honey or Maple Breakfast Flan

Dreamy and light—and just sweet enough—this is an easy way to slip down a nutritious breakfast on mornings when you can't face something weightier.

Traditionally, flan has a caramel topping that is made separately and poured into the bottom of the baking cup. The custard is baked on top of the caramel, and the flan is inverted when served. This user-friendly version avoids that extra step, incorporating a built-in topping that "makes itself" right in the bottom of the cup. It's very shiny and impressive when the flan is inverted for serving. You can prepare a batch of flan in the evening while you're home puttering around and then enjoy it for breakfast the next morning (or for several mornings). If you vary the toppings, using the ideas that follow this recipe, you can get an assortment of flavors from a single effort.

- This flan keeps very well in the refrigerator for up to a week. Cover each cup with plastic wrap, and unmold just before serving.
- Some flans are very rich. This one can go in either direction—rich or light—depending on the type of milk you use.
- Options for the milk are discussed on the preceding page.

YIELD: 5 or 6 small servings
PREPARATION TIME: 10 minutes, plus 35 to 40 minutes to bake

Nonstick spray

4 large eggs

⅛ teaspoon salt

2 cups milk

1½ teaspoons vanilla extract

11 tablespoons light honey or pure maple syrup

1. Half-fill a 9- by 13-inch pan with water and place it on a rack in the center of the oven, then preheat the oven to 350°F. Lightly spray five 6-ounce ramekins—and a tablespoon—with nonstick spray.

2. Break the eggs into a medium-sized bowl, add the salt, and beat lightly with a fork or whisk until the yolks are broken. Continue to beat lightly as you slowly pour in the milk and vanilla. Use the sprayed tablespoon from step 1 to measure out 6 tablespoons of the honey or syrup, and keep whisking as you drizzle it in. Mix slowly until everything is uniformly blended.

3. Use the sprayed tablespoon again to measure 1 tablespoon honey or maple syrup into each of the prepared ramekins. Pour the custard over the honey, dividing it equally among the 5 cups. If you have enough custard to fill another cup, go ahead and prepare a sixth. If you have only a little custard left over, just make the 5 cups very full.

4. Gently place the ramekins in the panful of hot water in the oven. Bake for 35 to 40 minutes, or until a knife inserted all the way into the flan—about halfway between the edge and the center of each ramekin—comes out clean. (The center might still be soft, but it will continue to cook after it comes out of the oven.) Carefully remove the pan from the oven, then take out the ramekins one by one and place them on a rack to cool. (Tongs are very useful for this sometimes-awkward process.)

5. Cool to room temperature or chill before serving. To serve, run a knife around the sides, then invert onto a small plate. Be sure to scrape out all the honey or syrup. Flan tastes best at room temperature or cold.

For each variation, follow the main recipe with these adjustments.

OTHER TOPPINGS FOR FLAN

In step 3, replace the honey or maple syrup with any of the following (1 tablespoon per ramekin). Try making an assortment!

BROWN SUGAR CARAMEL FLAN

• Light or dark brown sugar

BITTERSWEET CHOCOLATE FLAN

• Semisweet chocolate chips

BLACKBERRY OR RASPBERRY FLAN

• Blackberry or raspberry preserves

ORANGE MARMALADE FLAN

• Orange marmalade

CINNAMON-SUGAR CARAMEL FLAN

Combine:

• 1 tablespoon cinnamon
• 5 tablespoons sugar

MILK CHOCOLATE FLAN

Replace the milk with:

• 2 cups chocolate milk (any kind)

In step 2, replace the honey or maple syrup in the custard with:

• 2 tablespoons sugar

In step 3, replace the honey or maple syrup in the ramekins with:

• 6 tablespoons chocolate syrup

RICE OR NOODLE PUDDING CUPS

You can make flan into rice pudding or noodle pudding. Add to each cup before pouring in the custard:

• About 3 tablespoons cooked rice or broken vermicelli

The baking time will be about the same. This is a great way to use up leftover cooked rice or noodles. The yield will increase slightly.

Orange-Vanilla Custard

Imagine having an orange Creamsicle for breakfast! That's the closest I can come to describing this lovely, smooth custard. And it tastes fantastic *(and becomes a more complete light breakfast) when served with fresh fruit—ideally, a combination of pink grapefruit sections, sliced strawberries, and sliced kiwi.*

- You can take this in a tart or sweet direction, depending on your deft touch with the orange zest.
- This custard keeps very well in the refrigerator for up to a week, if you cover each cup tightly with plastic wrap.
- Options for the milk are discussed on page 229.

YIELD: 5 or 6 servings
PREPARATION TIME: 20 minutes, plus 35 to 40 minutes to bake

Nonstick spray

4 large eggs

½ teaspoon salt (scant measure)

2 cups orange juice

½ cup evaporated milk or half-and-half

¼ cup sugar

1 teaspoon orange extract (optional)

2 teaspoons vanilla extract

2 tablespoons unbleached all-purpose flour

Up to 1 tablespoon grated orange zest (optional)

1. Half-fill a 9- by 13-inch pan with water and place it on a rack in the center of the oven. Then preheat the oven to 350°F. Lightly spray five 6-ounce ramekins with nonstick spray.
2. Break the eggs into a medium-sized bowl, sprinkle in the salt, and beat lightly with a fork or whisk until the yolks are broken. Continue to beat lightly as you slowly pour in the orange juice, milk, sugar, and extracts. Place the flour in a fine-mesh sieve, and sift it into the mixture, mixing constantly. Add the zest, if desired, and stir slowly until everything is uniformly blended. (Slow mixing avoids incorporating air and thus produces a dense, creamy custard.)
3. Pour the custard into the ramekins, distributing it equally among the 5 cups. If you have enough custard to fill another cup, go ahead and prepare a sixth. If you have only a little custard left over, just make the 5 cups very full.
4. Gently place the ramekins in the panful of hot water in the oven. Bake for 35 to 40 minutes, or until a knife inserted all the way into the custard—about halfway between the edge and the center of each ramekin—comes out clean. (The center might still be soft, but it will continue to cook after it comes out of the oven.) Carefully remove the pan from the oven, then take out the ramekins one by one and place them on a rack to cool. (Tongs are very useful for this sometimes-awkward process.)
5. Cool to room temperature or chill before serving. The custard tastes best at room temperature or cold.

Sweet Potato Pudding

How indulgent is this pudding? Golden, sweet, and slightly spicy, it's like having a cupful of sweet potato pie filling for breakfast. Top it with blackberries and the color combination will be as exciting as the taste! Vitamins and protein are all generously present. If you're aspiring to the proverbial five servings a day of fruits and vegetables, this delightful pudding sneaks in vegetable serving number one before you're even out the door.

- Cooked, mashed pumpkin or squash can be substituted for the sweet potato.
- This pudding keeps very well in the refrigerator for up to a week, if you cover each cup tightly with plastic wrap.
- Options for the milk are discussed on page 229.

YIELD: 6 servings
PREPARATION TIME: 10 minutes (once the sweet potato is cooked), plus 35 to 40 minutes to bake

---

Nonstick spray

1½ cups cooked, mashed sweet potato (about ½ pound)

½ teaspoon salt (scant measure)

¼ cup (packed) light brown sugar

⅛ teaspoon cinnamon

⅛ teaspoon nutmeg

⅛ teaspoon ground cloves

⅛ teaspoon powdered ginger

4 large eggs, lightly beaten

1½ cups milk

1 teaspoon vanilla extract

OPTIONAL ACCOMPANIMENTS

Squeezable lime wedges

Blackberries (fresh or frozen, defrosted if frozen)

1. Half-fill a 9- by 13-inch pan with water and place it on a rack in the center of the oven. Then preheat the oven to 350°F. Lightly spray six 6-ounce ramekins with nonstick spray.
2. Place the mashed sweet potato in a medium-sized bowl, sprinkle in the salt, sugar, and spices, and continue to mash until very smooth. Slowly pour in the beaten eggs and mix until they are completely blended in. Pour in the milk and vanilla extract and mix until everything is uniformly combined.
3. Spoon the pudding into the prepared ramekins, distributing it equally among the 6 cups. Gently place the ramekins in the panful of hot water in the oven.
4. Bake for 35 to 40 minutes, or until a knife inserted all the way into the pudding—about halfway between the edge and the center of each ramekin—comes out clean. (The center might still be soft, but it will continue to cook after it comes out of the oven.) Carefully remove the pan from the oven, then take out the ramekins one by one and place them on a rack to cool. (Tongs are very useful for this sometimes-awkward process.)
5. Cool to room temperature or chill before serving. This pudding tastes best at room temperature or cold, with some fresh lime juice squeezed onto each serving and a few choice blackberries on top.

VARIATION　　**SWEET POTATO–COCONUT PUDDING**

Follow the main recipe with these adjustments:

- Replace the milk with coconut milk (lowfat okay).
- Use granulated sugar instead of brown sugar.
- Increase the vanilla extract to 1½ teaspoons.

Before baking, sprinkle each ramekin with:

- 2 tablespoons unsweetened shredded coconut
- 1½ teaspoons sugar

233

Coconut-Honey-Masala Flan

Small touches of intense spice go a long way when suspended in a gentle, coconut-laced custard. The result is subtle and smooth.

- This flan keeps very well in the refrigerator for up to a week. Cover each cup with plastic wrap, and unmold just before serving.
- Some flans are very rich. This one can go in either direction, rich or light, depending on the type of milk used. Options for the milk are discussed on page 229.
- Leftover coconut milk can be made into ice cubes and used for smoothies (see page 11).

YIELD: 5 or 6 servings
PREPARATION TIME: 10 minutes, plus 35 to 40 minutes to bake

Nonstick spray

4 large eggs

½ teaspoon salt (scant measure)

¼ teaspoon cinnamon

¼ teaspoon ground cardamom

¼ teaspoon ground cloves

¼ teaspoon ground coriander

1 cup evaporated milk (lowfat okay)

1 cup coconut milk (lowfat okay)

2¼ teaspoons vanilla extract

11 tablespoons light honey

1. Half-fill a 9- by 13-inch pan with water and place it on a rack in the center of the oven, then preheat the oven to 350°F. Lightly spray five 6-ounce ramekins—and a tablespoon—with nonstick spray.

2. Break the eggs into a medium-sized bowl, sprinkle in the salt and spices, and beat lightly with a fork or whisk until the yolks are broken. Continue to beat lightly as you slowly pour in the milk, coconut milk, and vanilla. Use the sprayed tablespoon from step 1 to measure out 6 tablespoons of the honey, and keep whisking as you drizzle it in. Mix slowly until everything is uniformly blended. (Slow mixing avoids incorporating air and thus produces a dense, creamy custard.)

3. Use the sprayed tablespoon again to measure 1 tablespoon honey into each of the prepared ramekins. Pour the custard over the honey, dividing it equally among the 5 cups. If you have enough custard to fill another cup, go ahead and prepare a sixth. If you have only a little custard left over, just make the five cups very full.

4. Gently place the ramekins in the panful of hot water in the oven. Bake for 35 to 40 minutes, or until a knife inserted all the way into the flan—about halfway between the edge and the center of each ramekin—comes out clean. (The center might still be soft, but it will continue to cook after it comes out of the oven.) Carefully remove the pan from the oven, then take out the ramekins one by one and place them on a rack to cool. (Tongs are very useful for this sometimes-awkward process.)

5. Cool to room temperature or chill before serving. To serve, run a knife around the sides, then invert onto a small plate. Be sure to scrape out all the honey. Flan tastes best at room temperature or cold.

Tiramisù in a Cup

"Tiramisù for breakfast? Am I dreaming?" Traditionally, tiramisù is made with mascarpone (a very rich Italian cream cheese) and eggs. This lighter variation is made with ricotta, which is much leaner and higher in protein than mascarpone, so you can feel entitled to eat it for breakfast—a guilty pleasure without the guilt!

You can prepare this recipe with absolutely no dessert-making experience whatsoever and still feel most *accomplished. Just assemble individual servings the night before, let them soak, covered, in the refrigerator overnight, and you're all set in the morning. It's portable, too, so you can take a cup to work with you for a significant midmorning mood booster.*

- I recommend using lowfat ricotta for this, because it is lighter than whole-milk ricotta and yields a fluffier result.
- Have available two 6-ounce ramekins. You can also use custard cups of the same size.
- If you don't have ladyfingers, you can substitute cake (sponge, pound, or angel food), cut into slices approximately the size of ladyfingers or into thin rounds that will fit inside the ramekins.

YIELD: 2 servings (easily multiplied)
PREPARATION TIME: 10 minutes, plus at least 4 hours in the refrigerator

¼ cup semisweet chocolate chips

¾ cup lowfat ricotta cheese

1 tablespoon sugar, or to taste

12 ladyfingers

About ½ cup espresso (or brewed strong, black coffee), at room temperature

1. Place the chocolate chips in an electric spice grinder or a blender and—in a few short spurts—grind them to a coarse meal. (You can also chop the chocolate by hand.)
2. Place the ricotta in a medium-sized bowl. Add the sugar and mix it in with a fork or a small whisk.
3. Spoon about 2 tablespoons of the sweetened ricotta into each of two 6-ounce ramekins. Sprinkle about 1 tablespoon of the ground chocolate over the ricotta.
4. Lay 3 ladyfingers on top of the chocolate. (It's okay if they overlap.) Sprinkle the ladyfingers with 1 to 2 tablespoons of the espresso.
5. Repeat the layers: cheese, chocolate, ladyfingers, espresso.
6. Add a final dab of cheese, and sprinkle the top with a little more chocolate for a finished look. Wrap each ramekin tightly in plastic wrap, and refrigerate for a minimum of 4 hours (preferably overnight) to let the layers meld. Serve cold.

Cherry-Peach Bread Pudding

Delicious on its own, this beautiful dish, studded with cherries and peaches, doesn't really need a cream topping. But plain yogurt goes very well and makes it into a more complete breakfast. Sour cream or Crème Fraîche are equally good. I like to serve this pudding warm, with cold toppings, accompanied by big mugs of hot chocolate.

About the bread: For best results, use a country-style bread with a crisp crust and an airy, chewy interior (what's known in bread-speak as a "high crust to crumb ratio"). These breads are often called sweet bâtarde, ciabatta, *or* pugliese. *If you can't find any of these, use stale French or Italian bread.*

- You can use fresh or frozen fruit. If using frozen fruit, defrosting is not necessary.
- Options for the milk are discussed on page 229.

YIELD: 6 to 8 servings
PREPARATION TIME: 15 minutes, plus 35 to 40 minutes to bake

Nonstick spray

3 cups bread cubes (½-inch pieces)

2½ cups pitted cherries, or 8 ounces frozen cherries

2½ cups sliced peaches, or 8 ounces frozen peaches

4 large eggs

2 cups milk

¼ teaspoon salt

2 teaspoons vanilla extract

⅛ teaspoon almond extract

½ cup sugar

½ teaspoon grated lemon zest

¾ cup chopped almonds (optional)

Sour cream, yogurt, or Homemade Crème Fraîche (page 263; optional)

1. Preheat the oven to 350°F (325°F for a glass pan). Lightly spray a 9- by 13-inch baking pan with nonstick spray.

2. Spread the bread cubes in the pan. Cut the cherries in half, and cut the peaches into bite-sized pieces. (If using frozen fruit, cut it without defrosting it first. It's not difficult.) Place the cherries and peaches among the pieces of bread, tucking the fruit into any crevices. Shake the pan to distribute everything somewhat evenly.

3. Combine the eggs, milk, salt, extracts, sugar, and lemon zest in a blender or a food processor and process until smooth. Pour this mixture over the bread, and let it sit for about 5 minutes. Use your finger or a spoon to poke the bread into the liquid until all the pieces are soaked. Sprinkle chopped almonds over the top, if desired.

4. Bake in the center of the oven for 35 to 40 minutes, or until the custard is *almost* set. (It's okay if it is still slightly wet on top, as it will continue to cook from its own heat for a few minutes after it comes out of the oven.)

5. Cool for at least 15 minutes before serving. Serve warm or at room temperature—plain or with a little yogurt, sour cream, or crème fraîche on the side.

Banana Bread Pudding

Usually, overripe bananas are preferable for baking. But in this case, you will have the best results if you simply use bananas that are eating-ripe, whatever that means to you. (To me, it means past green but still firm, with no dark spots.)

This recipe calls for the pudding to be served with a squeezable wedge of lime. Take that wedge seriously! Fresh lime juice squeezed onto each serving gives this dish a sparkle that truly sets it apart.

- Options for the milk are discussed on page 229.
- For the best bread to use, see the note at the top of the opposite page.

YIELD: 6 to 8 servings
PREPARATION TIME: 15 minutes, plus 35 to 40 minutes to bake

Nonstick spray

3 cups bread cubes (½-inch pieces)

3 medium-sized ripe bananas

4 large eggs

2 cups milk

¼ teaspoon salt

½ cup (packed) brown sugar

1½ teaspoons vanilla extract

⅛ teaspoon almond extract

A pinch of nutmeg

1 to 2 tablespoons cold butter, thinly sliced (optional)

Squeezable lime wedges

Sour cream, yogurt, or Homemade Crème Fraîche (page 263; optional)

1. Preheat the oven to 350°F (325°F for a glass pan). Lightly spray a 9- by 13-inch baking pan with nonstick spray.

2. Spread the bread cubes in the pan. Peel the bananas, cut them into slices, and gently tuck them among the pieces of bread. Shake the pan to distribute everything somewhat evenly.

3. Combine the eggs, milk, salt, sugar, extracts, and nutmeg in a blender or a food processor and process until smooth. Pour this mixture over the bread, and let it sit for about 5 minutes. Use your finger or a spoon to poke the bread into the liquid until all the pieces are soaked. Top with slices of butter, if desired.

4. Bake in the center of the oven for 35 to 40 minutes, or until the custard is *almost* set. (It's okay if it is still slightly wet on top, as it will continue to cook from its own heat for a few minutes after it comes out of the oven.)

5. Cool for at least 15 minutes before serving. Serve warm or at room temperature, with a squeezable wedge of lime on the side and a dab of yogurt, sour cream, or crème fraîche on top of each serving.

 BANANA HISTORY

Although they were abundant for centuries in the West Indies, bananas were virtually unknown in the United States before the mid-19th century. A few bunches made their way north beginning around the time of the Civil War, arriving via boat in New Orleans, with each fruit wrapped individually in foil like a precious object. At that time, a single banana was worth a dollar—a huge amount of money in those days! Because of the intense perishability of the fruit, it took a while for people to figure out how to create a viable banana trade, which developed over time with improved packing and transportation methods. Now, of course, bananas are so common and plentiful that we take them for granted.

Chocolate Bread Pudding

Good at any temperature (even cold), Chocolate Bread Pudding is downright transcendent when served warm or hot, and it reheats well in a microwave. So take some to work with you to heat up for a midmorning break, or dazzle your coworkers by bringing some to share.

- Do step 1 well ahead, so the mixture has time to cool to room temperature.
- Options for the milk are discussed on page 229.
- For the best bread to use, see the note at the top of page 236.

YIELD: 6 to 8 servings
PREPARATION TIME: 25 minutes, plus 35 to 40 minutes to bake

1¾ cups milk

1¼ cups semisweet chocolate chips

Nonstick spray

3 cups bread cubes (½-inch pieces)

14 pitted dried plums (prunes), cut into small pieces

4 large eggs

¼ teaspoon cinnamon

¼ teaspoon salt

2 teaspoons vanilla extract

¼ cup sugar

Up to 1 tablespoon minced orange zest (optional)

OPTIONAL TOPPINGS

Lightly sweetened whipped cream or Homemade Crème Fraîche (page 263)

Raspberry Sauce (page 249)

Powdered sugar

Fresh fruit (raspberries, chopped mango, orange sections, sliced banana)

1. Pour the milk into a medium-sized saucepan, and add ¾ cup of the chocolate chips. Place over very low heat until the chocolate melts. Don't boil or otherwise cook the milk. As soon as the chocolate is melted, remove the pan from heat, and let the mixture cool to room temperature.

2. Preheat the oven to 350°F (325°F for a glass pan). Lightly spray a 9- by 13-inch baking pan with nonstick spray.

3. Spread the bread cubes in the pan. Sprinkle in the dried plums and the remaining ½ cup chocolate chips, and shake the pan to distribute everything somewhat evenly.

4. Break the eggs into the jar of a large blender or the work bowl of a food processor, and process until they are well beaten. Add the cinnamon, salt, vanilla, and sugar, and process again until smooth. Keep the machine running while you drizzle in the chocolate milk, being sure to scrape in all the chocolate, some of which may cling to the bottom of the saucepan. Blend until smooth, adding the grated orange zest, if desired.

5. Pour the chocolate mixture over the bread mixture, and let it sit for about 5 minutes. Use your finger or a spoon to poke the bread into the liquid until all the pieces are soaked.

6. Bake in the center of the oven for 35 to 40 minutes, or until the custard is *almost* set. (It's okay if it is still slightly wet on top, as it will continue to cook from its own heat for a few minutes after it comes out of the oven.)

7. Cool for at least 15 minutes before serving. Serve warm or at room temperature (or even cold)—plain or with a little whipped cream or crème fraîche and/or Raspberry Sauce on the side. You can also sprinkle some powdered sugar on top and garnish with fresh berries or other fruit.

Mushroom Bread Pudding

Try this savory, aromatic dish for brunch or supper, as well as for breakfast. It's definitely one of those morning foods that becomes an evening food when served with a green salad. Mushroom Bread Pudding tastes best served hot or warm and reheats perfectly well in a microwave. In fact, sometimes it tastes even better reheated, which should encourage you to make this dish at any time.

- If you can't find fresh shiitakes, it's fine to use all domestic mushrooms.
- Options for the milk are discussed on page 229.
- For the best bread to use, see the note at the top of page 236.

YIELD: 6 to 8 servings
PREPARATION TIME: 40 minutes, plus 35 to 40 minutes to bake

Nonstick spray

1 to 2 tablespoons olive oil

1½ cups chopped onion

½ teaspoon dried thyme

1¼ teaspoons salt

6 to 8 cups sliced mushrooms
 (1½ pounds)

5 ounces fresh shiitake mushrooms,
 chopped

2 tablespoons minced garlic

¼ cup dry sherry

2 tablespoons fresh lemon juice

Freshly ground black pepper

3 cups bread cubes (½-inch pieces)

5 large eggs

2 cups milk

Sour cream, yogurt, or
 Homemade Crème Fraîche
 (page 263; optional)

1. Preheat the oven to 350°F (325°F for a glass pan). Lightly spray a 9- by 13-inch baking pan with nonstick spray.
2. Place a large skillet or sauté pan over medium heat, and add the oil. When the oil is hot, add the onion, thyme, and ½ teaspoon of the salt. Sauté over medium heat for about 8 minutes, or until the onion is soft.
3. Add the mushrooms and the remaining ¾ teaspoon salt. Sauté for about 5 minutes, then cover and cook for 10 minutes longer over medium heat.
4. Stir in the garlic, sherry, and lemon juice. Cook, stirring, for just a few minutes longer, then remove from the heat. Grind in black pepper to taste.
5. Distribute the bread cubes evenly in the prepared pan. Spread the mushroom mixture on top of the bread, being sure to include all the liquid.
6. Combine the eggs and milk in a blender or a food processor, and process until smooth. Pour this mixture over the bread and mushrooms, and let it sit for about 5 minutes. Use your finger or a spoon to poke the bread into the liquid until all the pieces are soaked.
7. Bake in the center of the oven for 35 to 40 minutes, or until the custard is *almost* set. (It's okay if it is still slightly wet on top, as it will continue to cook from its own heat for a few minutes after it comes out of the oven.)
8. Cool for at least 15 minutes before serving. Serve warm or at room temperature, with a dab of sour cream, yogurt, or Crème Fraîche on top of each serving.

TO GET A DEEPER MUSHROOM FLAVOR

You can give this pudding an even deeper flavor by adding up to ½ ounce of dried shiitake, oyster, or porcini mushrooms to the sautéed mixture in step 4. Soak the dried mushrooms in hot water for about 30 minutes, then drain, stem, and chop them, and they're ready to use. Save the flavorful soaking liquid for use in a soup or sauce, if desired.

Baked Cornmeal-Cheddar Pudding

In this simple, smooth-textured dish, the classic combination of cornmeal and cheese is spiked with a surprise hit of mustard, which both blends in and stands out at the same time, waking up not only your taste buds but hopefully your brain and spirit as well.

- Use a fine grade of cornmeal (not the coarser polenta) for best results.
- Options for the milk are discussed on page 229.
- Once baked, this recipe freezes and reheats well. To freeze individual squares, wrap each one tightly in plastic wrap and then seal them in a heavy zip-style plastic bag. Defrosting and reheating are easy in a microwave.

YIELD: 6 servings
PREPARATION TIME: 15 minutes, plus 30 minutes to bake

Nonstick spray

3 cups milk

1 cup cornmeal

½ teaspoon salt

1 tablespoon Dijon mustard

4 large eggs, beaten

1 cup (packed) grated extra-sharp cheddar

OPTIONAL TOPPINGS

Chipotle Cream (page 256)

Sour cream with chives

Basic Guacamole (page 257)

Salsa of your choice
(pages 250 to 255)

1. Preheat the oven to 350°F (325°F for a glass pan). Lightly spray an 8- by 8-inch pan with nonstick spray.
2. Heat the milk in a medium-sized saucepan until it *almost* boils. Turn the heat down, and whisk steadily as you sprinkle in the cornmeal. Cook for 5 minutes over medium heat, stirring constantly.
3. Remove from the heat and stir in the salt, mustard, beaten eggs, and half of the cheese. When it is thoroughly combined, transfer the mixture to the prepared pan.
4. Bake for 20 minutes, then sprinkle the top with the remaining cheese and bake for 10 minutes longer—or until the pudding is firm in the center.
5. Cut into squares and serve hot or warm, with the topping of your choice.

> **VARIATION**   **TAWNY CORN AND VEGETABLE PUDDING**
>
> You will get a slightly larger yield from this textured, seasoned version of the above recipe—and it will take about 15 minutes longer to prepare.
>
> Heat in a medium-sized skillet over medium heat:
>
> - 1 tablespoon olive oil or butter
>
> Add:
>
> - 1 cup minced fresh chiles (poblano or anaheim) or canned green chiles
> - ¾ teaspoon salt
>
> Sauté for 5 to 8 minutes, or until soft. Add:
>
> - 2 cups corn kernels (fresh or frozen, defrosted if frozen)
> - 1 tablespoon pure ground chile powder
> - ¼ cup minced scallion
>
> Sauté for another 3 minutes or so. Remove the pan from the heat.
>
> Begin preparing the main recipe, using a 9- by 13-inch pan instead of the 8- by 8-inch pan. When you get to step 3, add the sautéed chile mixture in place of the mustard and the salt. Continue with the remaining steps.

Baked Spinach-Feta Pudding

Put this on your A-list of portable savory breakfasts that you can grab while running out the door. It stores, travels, and reheats incredibly well. You can warm up a square in the microwave and then eat it as a handheld meal, wrapped in a napkin, during your commute.

- If using frozen spinach, be sure it is thoroughly defrosted and well drained, with all the liquid firmly squeezed out.
- Once baked, this recipe freezes and reheats well. To freeze individual squares, wrap each one tightly in plastic wrap and then seal them in a heavy zip-style plastic bag. Defrosting and reheating are easy in a microwave.

YIELD: About 6 servings
PREPARATION TIME: 40 minutes, plus 45 minutes to bake

Nonstick spray

1½ tablespoons butter and/or olive oil

2 cups minced onion

10 ounces fresh spinach, chopped, or 10 ounces frozen chopped spinach, defrosted and drained

½ teaspoon salt

½ teaspoon dried oregano or basil

2 teaspoons minced garlic

2 tablespoons unbleached all-purpose flour

1 cup crumbled feta

¼ cup minced fresh mint leaves

2 cups (1 pound) cottage cheese

4 large eggs

Freshly ground black pepper

Cayenne

Paprika

½ cup sunflower seeds or chopped pistachios (optional)

1. Preheat the oven to 350°F (325°F for a glass pan). Lightly spray an 8- by 8-inch pan with nonstick spray.
2. Melt the butter and/or heat the oil in a deep skillet over medium heat. Add the onion and sauté for 8 to 10 minutes, or until soft.
3. Using tongs, stir in the spinach, salt, and oregano, and continue to cook over medium heat, stirring occasionally, for about 5 minutes, or until the spinach is wilted (if fresh) or heated through (if frozen). Add the garlic and cook for another minute or so, then sprinkle in the flour. Cook for about a minute longer, stirring once or twice. Remove from the heat, and sprinkle in the feta and mint. Mix well.
4. Combine the cottage cheese and eggs in a blender or food processor, and process until smooth. Pour this into the spinach mixture, and use a wooden spoon to stir until thoroughly combined. Season to taste with black pepper and cayenne.
5. Spread the mixture into the prepared pan, dust the top with paprika, and, if desired, sprinkle with sunflower seeds or chopped pistachios. Bake in the center of the oven for 45 minutes, or until solid in the center when you shake the pan. Serve hot or warm, cut into squares.

11

CONDIMENTS, SAUCES, TOPPINGS & SPREADS

CONTENTS

CONDIMENTS, SAUCES, TOPPINGS & SPREADS

Sometimes, even if the alarm clock has succeeded in getting us vertical, we still find ourselves sleep-walking through the morning. On these days, we might need a touch of unexpected, assertive flavor in our breakfast to *truly* wake us up. This fun chapter presents a range of toppings that you can drizzle over, puddle under, sprinkle around, spoon next to, or spread upon many of the various sweet and savory dishes found throughout this book (and beyond). Some of these recipes will wake you up gently; others, while not exactly hitting you over the head, will give you a good kick.

Condiments are a big "category" in the commercial food world, and that category is rapidly expanding. Many excellent salsas, jams, and marmalades are available, not only in grocery stores and gourmet shops, but also from the artisans themselves, at farmers' markets or via mail order and the Internet. Definitely look into these products! Some of them are quite wonderful (even organic), and it's good to support these small, creative ventures.

But perhaps you find these items too expensive to purchase often. Or perhaps you are in the mood to put something together in your own kitchen with your own hands, and you want to experience that extra level of connection with your food (and your creative spirit). You want to fill shakers with spice mixtures to shower onto freshly baked flatbreads—or with vanilla- or lavender-scented powdered sugar to "snow" onto your crêpes. Or you long to pour brightly colored guava or blackberry syrup onto buttermilk pancakes or spoon a smoky tomato salsa next to your eggs. Most of all, you want these to be *your own concoctions*. These recipes will give you the map.

Read through the chapter, and picture the many ways you can transform plain toast, cereal, eggs, or cheese into an event—something you might even be motivated enough to get up early to enjoy! Although varied, these recipes have in common a clean-tasting brightness that will shine upon even the foggiest morning.

A SPECTRUM OF SYRUPS

A pitcher of warm maple syrup is an American breakfast table emblem. Although maple syrup is delicious on its own, it also tastes wonderful when augmented with other ingredients. Below I share my two favorite ways of enhancing maple syrup.

These are followed by a great formula for making homemade fruit syrups from fruit juice concentrate. These syrups are incredibly easy—you simply reduce the concentrate by slowly boiling it. The flavors and colors intensify, and the result is unusual and exciting.

I've given formulas rather than recipes for the fruit syrups. You can make any amount of syrup—just figure that you will end up with slightly less than half the volume with which you started.

• Store all syrups in a tightly capped bottle or jar in the refrigerator, and serve at any temperature. They will keep indefinitely.

BLACKBERRY MAPLE SYRUP

This is my favorite remedy for underripe blackberries. It manages to mutually infuse the berries and the syrup so that each enhances the other, and you get a syrup with brilliant blackberry flavor and a deep, dark purple hue that looks gorgeous on your pancakes.

Simply combine equal amounts of blackberries and syrup in a glass or ceramic dish, and microwave on High for 2 minutes. (You can also use the stovetop: Combine the berries and syrup in a saucepan, bring to a boil, and simmer for 2 minutes.) Straining is unnecessary.

PECAN OR WALNUT MAPLE SYRUP

In a glass or ceramic dish, combine one part minced, toasted pecans or walnuts with two parts pure maple syrup, Place it in the microwave and heat on High for 1 minute. (You can also use the stovetop: Combine the nuts and syrup in a saucepan, bring to a boil, and simmer for 1 minute.)

APPLE SYRUP
GUAVA SYRUP
PASSIONFRUIT SYRUP

Defrost a can of frozen juice concentrate, and transfer the contents to a shallow saucepan. Bring it to a boil, turn the heat down, and simmer, uncovered, for 20 to 30 minutes (possibly longer), until it is reduced by slightly more than half. Remove from heat, and let it cool to room temperature. Serve in small glass pitchers for a beautiful sunlight meal!

APPLE-JALAPEÑO SYRUP

For every 12-ounce can of defrosted apple juice concentrate, add a 2-inch jalapeño chile, sliced in half lengthwise. Follow the procedure above for making fruit syrup; remove and discard the chile after the syrup has cooled.

APPLE-BASIL SYRUP

Add a handful (about ¼ cup packed) fresh basil leaves to 12 ounces defrosted apple juice concentrate. Follow the procedure above for making fruit syrup; remove and discard the basil after the syrup has cooled.

APPLE-BALSAMIC SYRUP

Combine equal amounts of defrosted apple juice concentrate and balsamic vinegar in a shallow saucepan. Follow the procedure above for making fruit syrup. Open the windows during the cooking—there will be fumes!

Lemon-Thyme Honey Syrup

Honey and thyme have a natural affinity for each other, and hence this happy marriage. Lemon juice gives it a slight edge that keeps it from being too sweet.

YIELD: ⅓ cup (easily multiplied)
PREPARATION TIME: 5 minutes, plus 1 minute to cook

⅓ cup light honey

½ teaspoon minced fresh thyme leaves

1 tablespoon fresh lemon juice

1. Combine the honey and thyme in a glass or ceramic dish and microwave on High for 1 minute. (You can also use the stovetop: Put the honey and thyme in a saucepan, bring to a boil, and simmer for 2 minutes.) Remove from the heat, and let it cool to room temperature, leaving in the thyme.

2. Stir in the lemon juice, and serve at any temperature. This syrup keeps for months in a tightly covered container in the refrigerator.

LAVENDER-SCENTED POWDERED SUGAR

Add 2 tablespoons coarsely chopped fresh lavender leaves to 1 cup powdered sugar. Transfer to a clean, dry, tightly capped jar. Let it stand for at least 24 hours to infuse the sugar with the lavender, and then transfer to a shaker and use as desired.

VANILLA-SCENTED POWDERED SUGAR

Split a 3-inch piece of vanilla bean in half lengthwise. Add this to 1 cup powdered sugar, and transfer to a clean, dry, tightly capped jar. Let it stand for at least 24 hours to infuse the sugar with the vanilla, then transfer the sugar to a shaker, and use as desired. (It's okay to leave the vanilla bean in the sugar.)

CHEATING AT HOMEMADE JAM

Formal jam making can be quite a process, requiring sterilized jars, hot-packing procedures, and so on. Caramelized Fruit (page 27), Roasted Fruit (page 36), or Mixed or Dried Fruit Compote (pages 32 and 34) are all easy recipes that can double as fruit jam for pancakes—or as a topping for toast. No one will ever know you didn't go through the old-fashioned, laborious home-preserving ritual to make these delicious toppings!

BERRY SAUCES

A deeply colored berry sauce can have many applications and will always add sparkle to your breakfast. You can soak the oats for Muesli (page 52) in Strawberry Sauce, drizzle Raspberry Sauce over just about any of the flans (pages 230 to 231), or spoon some Blueberry Sauce around your pancakes. These are just a few suggestions, as I'm sure you'll have many other brilliant ideas for using these sauces.

- These sauces take only about 2 minutes to prepare once the fruit is defrosted.
- Each of these recipes will keep for about 5 days in a tightly covered container in the refrigerator.

Blueberry Sauce

You might find it interesting to note that this recipe—and the Strawberry or Raspberry Sauce on the opposite page—use frozen, unsweetened fruit. That is because frozen berries give off a generous amount of delicious juices as they defrost, making an almost instant sauce. (And my feeling is, if you're lucky enough to have good fresh *berries, for heaven's sake just eat them!)*

YIELD: **About 1½ cups**
PREPARATION TIME: **About 2 minutes, once the berries are defrosted**

---

10 ounces frozen blueberries

3 tablespoons light honey

3 tablespoons fresh lemon juice

1. Defrost the berries in the bowl you will be using to make the sauce.
2. When the berries are defrosted, spoon some of the juices into a second, smaller bowl, and stir in the honey and lemon juice. Pour this liquid back into the berries, stirring gently so they don't break.
3. If you want a thicker sauce, purée a few spoonfuls of the blueberries (including some of the liquid) in a blender. Don't purée too much of it, though, as puréed blueberries are somewhat grainy.

 BLUEBERRIES ARE POWERFUL!

They might be diminutive, but blueberries are a nutritional giant, containing iron, vitamins A and C, fiber, carotenoids, antioxidants, and anthocyanosides. It's possible that regular consumption of blueberries (½ cup a day) can reduce various signs of aging. Blueberries are good for the eyes; they have been shown to improve night vision and may also protect against cataracts and glaucoma. In addition to all this, folk medicine has it that blueberries are good for treating stomach ailments. So eat these little overachievers for breakfast as often as you can—they're well worth the price!

Strawberry or Raspberry Sauce

Strawberries and raspberries are interchangeable in this deep red sauce. You can even combine them if you like.

YIELD: About 1 cup
PREPARATION TIME: About 2 minutes, once the berries are defrosted

10 ounces frozen strawberries
or raspberries

½ teaspoon fresh lemon juice

1 tablespoon or more sweetening
(sugar, apple juice concentrate,
light honey)

1. Defrost the berries in the bowl you will be using to make the sauce.
2. When the berries are defrosted, add the lemon juice, and purée all or part of the mixture in a blender. Transfer back to the bowl, and sweeten to taste.

NOTE: Straining out the seeds is optional. I prefer to leave them in, for the texture, especially since this is a breakfast sauce and can be more informal and "down home" than if it were intended for a fancy dessert.

Cranberry-Ginger Sauce

Cranberry-Ginger Sauce has a complex tart flavor with a touch of heat. Mix it into a bowl of plain yogurt or use it to adorn a steaming bowl of Soft Breakfast Polenta (page 59). You can also just eat this plain, with a muffin or a piece of toast.

- Cranberries can be stored indefinitely in the freezer, so you can make this recipe any time of year.
- This sauce will keep for up to 2 weeks in a tightly covered container in the refrigerator.

YIELD: About 2 cups
PREPARATION TIME: 2 minutes of work, plus 20 minutes to cook and time to chill

1 cup fresh cranberries

1 can (12 ounces) frozen cranberry
juice concentrate, defrosted

3 tablespoons corn syrup, or
to taste

A few slices fresh ginger

1. Combine everything in a small to medium saucepan, bring to a boil, and cook over medium heat for about 20 minutes, or until the berries pop and the liquid is reduced by about one third.
2. You can leave the sauce as is or purée some or all of it in a blender for a thicker sauce. (Fish out the ginger slices first.)
3. Cool to room temperature, then adjust the corn syrup to taste and chill until cold.

Pineapple-Coconut-Ginger Salsa

Here's a salsa so good you might just want to eat it plain, with a spoon. It also is a refreshing accompaniment to just about any savory dish.

- For a milder flavor, scrape out and discard the seeds from the chiles. (Wash your hands after handling these or any other hot peppers.)

YIELD: 4 cups
PREPARATION TIME: 15 minutes, plus time to chill

½ cup minced red onion

3 cups boiling water

3 cups minced ripe pineapple

3 tablespoons fresh lemon or lime juice

½ cup minced crystallized ginger

½ cup shredded sweetened coconut

1 tablespoon minced serrano chiles

Mint leaves (optional)

1. Place the onion in a strainer over a bowl in the sink. Pour the boiling water over the onion, remove the strainer from the bowl, and let it drain for at least 5 minutes.
2. Combine the pineapple, lemon or lime juice, ginger, coconut, and chiles in a medium-sized bowl. Add the drained onion, and mix well. Chill.
3. Serve cold, garnished with mint leaves, if desired. Store in a tightly covered container in the refrigerator for up to 2 weeks.

 GINGER TIDBITS

When using fresh ginger, seek out the very freshest you can find, for the best flavor and the easiest handling. Choose young, smooth, light-colored "knobs" with skin so tight and thin that you can scratch it off with your fingernail. (Older roots tend to be tough and fibrous and can have a strong, harsh flavor.)

Crystallized ginger is made by boiling slices of ginger in a sugar syrup, which causes the texture to become chewy and the flavor to both intensifiy and mellow at the same time. You can buy crystallized ginger in chunks or in flat slices. I prefer the latter, as it is easier to cut into the tiny pieces required in most recipes where it is used.

Here's one of my favorite obscure culinary facts: Botanically, ginger is a distant relative of the *banana*. (Keep this in mind, just in case you're ever quizzed on the subject.)

Citrus-Papaya Salsa with a chipotle haze

Mysterious and intense, this salsa has a gradual impact that sneaks up on you. The flavors intensify the longer it sits around. Serve it with any savory dish, or with toast and cheese.

- Blood oranges are especially nice-looking for this, but any kind will work.
- For information about chipotle chiles, see page 133.

YIELD: A generous 2 cups
PREPARATION TIME: 15 minutes, plus time to chill

½ cup minced red onion

3 cups boiling water

3 or 4 medium oranges

1 ripe papaya (1 pound)

¼ teaspoon salt

1 teaspoon minced chipotle chiles

1 tablespoon fresh lemon or
   lime juice

1 tablespoon cider vinegar

1½ teaspoons sugar

1 to 2 tablespoons light honey

1. Place the onion in a strainer over a bowl in the sink. Pour the boiling water over the onion, remove the strainer from the bowl, and let it drain for at least 5 minutes.
2. Peel the oranges, then section them over a medium-sized bowl, to save all the juices.
3. Cut the papaya in half lengthwise, and scoop out the seeds. (You can reserve the seeds for use as a garnish.) Dice the pulp, and add it to the oranges *au jus.*
4. Add the remaining ingredients (including the onions from step 1), and mix until thoroughly combined. Chill.
5. Serve cold, topped with the reserved papaya seeds, if desired. Store in a tightly covered container in the refrigerator for up to 2 weeks.

 THE WHOLE PAPAYA

Papayas, with their lush, pink-to-orange flesh, are the archetype of voluptuousness. In addition to being sexy, they are actually quite practical—you can use the entire fruit! The crunchy, peppery-hot seeds are edible and taste a little like pellets of mustard. And after you scoop out *most* of the flesh from the papaya—leaving some of the fruit behind to keep the shell sturdy—it's fun to use the skin as a serving container for whatever dish you've created, giving the meal a Caribbean ambience.

Avocado-Grapefruit-Mango Salsa

Bright green bits of avocado shine through in stunning contrast to the red onion, pink grapefruit, and sunny mango. The mango pulp thickens the grapefruit juices, giving this wonderful recipe a texture so luxurious that I was tempted to put it in the "Fruit" chapter as a tropical fruit salad. (It landed in this section only because of the onion.) This salsa tastes wonderful on its own (it's a great brunch appetizer!) and also goes well with any savory dish, especially those that are cornmeal-based.

- Try to find a perfectly ripe avocado that is still firm (see page 257).
- Before you add the avocado, this will keep for up to 2 weeks in a tightly covered container in the refrigerator. After the avocado is mixed in, it will keep for only a day or so before the avocado begins turning mushy.

YIELD: 2½ cups
PREPARATION TIME: 15 minutes, plus time to chill

⅓ cup minced red onion

2 cups boiling water

2 pink grapefruit

1 ripe mango

⅛ teaspoon salt, or to taste

1 teaspoon sugar

1 ripe avocado

Cayenne

Torn cilantro leaves (optional)

1. Place the onion in a strainer over a bowl in the sink. Pour the boiling water over the onion, remove the strainer from the bowl, and let it drain for at least 5 minutes.
2. Peel the grapefruit, then section them over a medium-sized bowl, to save all the juices.
3. Cut the mango away from its pit, then peel it and cut the flesh into small pieces on a cutting board. Add the mango to the grapefruit, scraping in as much of the messy, delicious mango pulp as you can retrieve from the cutting board.
4. Stir in the onion from step 1, along with the salt and sugar. Cover and refrigerate until shortly before serving.
5. Pit, peel, and dice the avocado just before serving, and gently stir it into the mixture. Add cayenne to taste, and garnish with a few torn cilantro leaves, if desired. Serve cold.

Smoky Tomato Salsa

Chipotle chiles (smoked jalapeños—very hot!) are the perfect partner for sweet, ripe tomatoes in this spunky salsa.

• For information about chipotle chiles, see page 133.

YIELD: About 2 cups
PREPARATION TIME: 10 minutes, plus time to chill

2 large, ripe tomatoes (1 pound)

1 teaspoon minced garlic

1 teaspoon minced chipotle chiles

½ teaspoon salt

1 tablespoon cider vinegar

1 tablespoon olive oil

1 tablespoon fresh lime juice

2 medium-sized scallions, minced

3 tablespoons minced parsley and/or cilantro

1. Cut the tomatoes into ½-inch dice and place in a medium-sized bowl.

2. Add the garlic, chipotle, salt, vinegar, olive oil, and lime juice, and mix well. Cover and refrigerate until shortly before serving.

3. Stir in the scallions and parsley just before serving. Serve cold.

TOMATOES ARE POTENT

Tomatoes are rich in antioxidants that are believed to have cancer-fighting properties. It's interesting to note that both fresh *and* processed tomatoes—including tomato-based products like tomato juice, canned tomatoes, tomato paste, and even ketchup—have been found to contain significant levels of antioxidants. So you don't have to wait until tomato season to reap the rewards.

Tomato-Tomatillo Salsa

Use only the ripest, sweetest tomatoes in season to complement the refreshingly sour flavor of the tomatillos in this very simple salsa.

YIELD: About 2 cups
PREPARATION TIME: 10 minutes, plus 30 to 40 minutes to chill

5 medium-sized tomatillos
(6 ounces)

1 large, ripe tomato (½ pound)

¼ teaspoon plus a pinch of salt

A handful of minced parsley

Cayenne

1. Remove the husks from the tomatillos. Dice the tomato and tomatillos, and combine them in a small to medium bowl with a big pinch of salt. Chill the mixture for at least 30 to 40 minutes to bring out the flavor and the juices.
2. Shortly before serving, stir in ¼ teaspoon salt and the parsley. Add cayenne to taste, and serve cold.

 TOMATILLOS

Dating back to the Aztecs and Mayans, tomatillos are grown today in Mexico and Guatemala. Although they resemble miniature green tomatoes wrapped in paper, they are actually a separate species in the nightshade family. Look for tomatillos in good produce markets or in the imported food section of your grocery store. If you can't find fresh tomatillos, it's okay to use canned ones. If the canned variety eludes you as well, substitute green tomatoes, which are similarly tart.

Fire-Roasted Pepper Salsa

Bell peppers acquire a subtle, smoky flavor when broiled. You can also get a similar effect by charring them directly on a gas burner or on a charcoal grill, cooked close to the coals. This salsa looks especially beautiful if you make it with an assortment of colored peppers. Serve it with any savory dish.

- This salsa keeps for up to a month in a tightly capped jar in the refrigerator. It actually tastes best after it's had a chance to sit around for a while. The flavors develop over time.

YIELD: About 2 cups
PREPARATION TIME: 1 hour (10 minutes of work)

Olive oil

2 pounds red, yellow, or orange bell peppers

1½ teaspoons minced garlic

½ teaspoon salt, or to taste

2 teaspoons cider vinegar

1 tablespoon fresh lemon or lime juice

Cayenne

OPTIONAL ADDITIONS

½ teaspoon sugar

½ teaspoon ground cumin

1. Preheat the broiler and lightly brush a baking tray with olive oil. Place the whole peppers on the tray.
2. Broil the peppers—or char them directly on the burner of a gas stove over medium heat—turning them every 5 minutes, until they are blackened all over, about 15 minutes total.
3. Transfer the peppers to a bowl, and cover the bowl with a plate. Let the peppers cool for at least 45 minutes, during which time they will give off a good amount of delicious juice. (Save all the juices! They will become part of the sauce.)
4. Peel the peppers, and remove and discard the seeds and stems. Mince the flesh, and return the minced peppers to the bowl. Stir in the remaining ingredients, and adjust the salt and cayenne to taste.
5. Serve cold or at room temperature.

VARIATION **FIRE-ROASTED PEPPER SALSA WITH CUCUMBER AND AVOCADO**

Prepare the salsa as in the main recipe. Just before serving, add:

- Finely minced cucumber (peeled and seeded)
- Ripe avocado, cut into tiny dice

Adjust the salt to taste. Serve within a few hours for the best quality.
Note: This will have a slightly higher yield.

 ROASTED PEPPERS AS A KITCHEN STAPLE

Fire-Roasted Pepper Salsa is a wonderful condiment, but if you don't have the time or inclination to make the whole recipe, just roast and peel the peppers and store them, coated in olive oil, in a tightly covered container in the refrigerator. They will keep for a week or longer and can be used in many ways. (Don't forget to save the juices—they make the world's most brilliant soup stock!)

Creamy Tahini Sauce

Serve this classic Middle Eastern sauce with freshly baked flatbread and some cucumbers and tomatoes, or with Silver Dollar Bean Cakes (page 161).

- For more details about sesame tahini, see page 275.
- This sauce keeps for weeks if stored in a tightly covered container in the refrigerator.

YIELD: About 1½ cups
PREPARATION TIME: 10 minutes

¾ cup sesame tahini

5 tablespoons fresh lemon juice

½ teaspoon minced garlic,
   or to taste

3 or 4 sprigs parsley

½ teaspoon salt, or to taste

About 1 cup water

Cayenne

1. Combine the tahini, lemon juice, garlic, parsley, and salt in a food processor or a blender, and process until uniform.
2. Keep the machine running as you slowly drizzle in the water. When all the water is incorporated, check the consistency. If you'd like it thinner, drizzle in a little extra water.
3. Transfer the sauce to a bowl or container. Add cayenne to taste, and possibly add more salt or garlic. Serve at room temperature or cold.

Chipotle Cream

Sour cream and/or yogurt provide a soothing vehicle for the hot, smoky flavor of chipotle chiles. Serve this with any south-of-the-border-style savory dish.

- For information about chipotle chiles, see page 133.

YIELD: 1 cup
PREPARATION TIME: 5 minutes

1 cup sour cream or yogurt
   (or a combination)

½ to 1 teaspoon minced
   chipotle chiles

1. Place the sour cream in a small bowl, add ½ teaspoon minced chipotles, and whisk until smooth.
2. Let the mixture sit for about 10 minutes, to allow the flavor to develop. Taste, and add more chipotle if you prefer it stronger.
3. Serve cold or at room temperature. Store in a tightly covered container in the refrigerator, where it will keep for up to 2 weeks.

Basic Guacamole

Authentic guacamole is a very simple preparation—basically just pure, ripe avocado with touches of seasoning. Although best known as a dip for chips, guacamole is tremendously versatile, providing a substantial, colorful accompaniment to many savory dishes, especially those featuring eggs, beans, tomatoes, or cornmeal.

• This keeps for only a day or so, tightly covered and refrigerated, and is best eaten right after it's made.

YIELD: **4 servings**
PREPARATION TIME: **5 minutes**

2 tablespoons fresh lemon or lime juice

2 firm, ripe avocados

½ teaspoon salt

2 tablespoons minced red onion

Cayenne

1. Place the lemon or lime juice in a small to medium bowl. Cut the avocados in half, remove the pits, and scoop the flesh into the bowl.

2. Use a fork to slowly mash the avocado into the juice, adding the salt as you go. When the avocado reaches your desired consistency (and that could well include a few lumps), stir in the onion and add cayenne to taste.

3. Serve at room temperature or cold.

 AVOCADO NOTES

Avocados are a rich source of vitamin E, potassium, and good monounsaturated oil. When shopping, select avocados that are heavy for their size and free of blemishes. Buy them unripe (meaning hard), unless you plan to use them right away, and let them ripen at room temperature, watching over them carefully, so they won't overripen. (They are ripe when they yield ever so slightly to gentle finger pressure.) Plan to use avocados as soon as they are ripe, as they don't like to be refrigerated. (Chilling will cause discoloration and dilute the flavor.)

Caramelized Onion and Lemon Marmalade

Serve this delicious sweet-sour marmalade with any savory dish or with toast and cheese. It also goes well with scrambled eggs or tofu.

- Remove the lemon zest before juicing the lemon. It's easiest to strip the zest with a vegetable peeler and then chop it on a cutting board with a sharp knife.

YIELD: 1 cup
PREPARATION TIME: 10 minutes, plus 35 minutes to cook

1 tablespoon canola oil

4 cups minced onion

½ teaspoon salt

1 tablespoon balsamic vinegar

3 tablespoons fresh lemon juice

1 tablespoon sugar

1 tablespoon chopped lemon zest

1. Place a medium to large skillet over medium heat and wait about 2 minutes. Add the oil and swirl to coat the pan. Add the onion, sauté for 5 minutes, then cover the pan and lower the heat.
2. Cook, covered, for 15 minutes, stirring once or twice during this time. Stir in the salt and vinegar. Cover and cook for another 5 minutes. Stir in the lemon juice and sugar and cook, uncovered, for about 5 more minutes.
3. Remove from the heat, and stir in the lemon zest. Cool to room temperature, then pack into a tightly capped jar. Cover and refrigerate for up to 3 weeks. Serve cold or at room temperature.

 ONIONS WITHOUT TEARS

Folklore abounds about how to prevent the painful eye irritation caused by sulfurous onion fumes. Some people say it helps to hold the non-striking end of a kitchen match in your teeth, while others believe the trick is to wet your forearms with water. I've also heard recommendations to burn a candle to "distract" the sulfur or to leave the root end of the onion intact while cutting the rest of the bulb. These exotic techniques may be effective in some cases, but I've got one that I guarantee will work. Just put the peeled onion in the freezer about an hour before you intend to cut it, then cut it in its semifrozen state, using a very sharp knife.

Beet, Lemon, and Ginger Marmalade

A real color-flavor zinger, this marmalade is bound to enhance your relationship with beets forever, even if it was good to begin with. Serve it with any savory dish, especially Tempeh Hash (page 157).

- To cook the beets, boil them in their skins until fork-tender. Drain and cool them, and they will then peel easily under cold running water. You can also roast the beets (see below).
- See the note about lemon zest in the preceding recipe.

YIELD: A generous 2 cups
PREPARATION TIME: 10 minutes (once the beets are cooked)

1 pound cooked beets

½ teaspoon salt

5 tablespoons fresh lemon juice

2 tablespoons light honey

2 to 3 tablespoons chopped lemon zest

⅓ cup minced crystallized ginger

1. Peel and coarsely grate—or mince—the beets, and transfer to a medium-sized bowl.
2. Add the remaining ingredients and mix thoroughly. Transfer to a tightly capped jar. Cover and refrigerate for up to 3 weeks. Serve cold.

ROASTING BEETS

Consider *roasting* the beets for this recipe instead of boiling them. It doesn't take much longer, requires very little work, and is well worth the slight effort. The dry, high heat of the roasting process causes the beets to cook from their own inner moisture, intensifying their flavor and enhancing their natural, rich sweetness. Here's how to do it:

Preheat the oven to 400°F. Use small or medium-sized beets, 1 to 2 inches in diameter. Trim the greens but leave on the stems. Place the beets in a small pan (I use a pie pan) with a splash of water, and cover loosely with foil. Roast for 35 to 45 minutes—or possibly longer. The beets are done when a fork slides in easily. Cool to room temperature, and then rub off the skins.

Pumpkin-Orange Marmalade

Use this golden blend wherever you would plain orange marmalade. It's similar, but earthier and less sweet. You can increase the proportion of pumpkin if you would like the marmalade to be deeper and more nutritious.

YIELD: 1 cup
PREPARATION TIME: 5 minutes

½ cup canned pumpkin

½ cup orange marmalade

¼ teaspoon salt, or to taste

1. Combine everything in a bowl, and mix until well blended. Taste to adjust the salt.
2. Store in a tightly capped jar in the refrigerator for up to 2 weeks. Serve cold.

A SHOWER OF SPICE

Here's a wonderful touch for your kitchen: Make an aromatic spice mixture, and keep it in a shaker on the table. Sprinkle it onto freshly baked flatbreads, scrambled eggs, salads, yogurt, cheese—anything you can think of! My two favorite mixtures are both of Middle Eastern origin. Each of these yields about ⅓ cup.

BAHARAT

Combine:

- 2 tablespoons each cinnamon, coriander, cumin, and paprika
- 1½ teaspoons each nutmeg and cloves
- ½ teaspoon black pepper

ZA'ATAR

Grind to a powder in an electric spice grinder:

- 3 tablespoons toasted sesame seed

Mix with:

- 2 tablespoons dried thyme
- 1 tablespoon dried marjoram
- 1 teaspoon salt

Mango Ketchup

Mangoes have a terrific capacity to harmonize with both sweet and savory foods. This ketchup is a good example. Serve it with just about anything—pancakes, omelets, potatoes, tempeh—and it will always be a delicious fit.

YIELD: **1 cup**
PREPARATION TIME: **25 minutes, plus time to chill**

1 medium-sized ripe mango
  (1 pound)

⅛ teaspoon salt

2 tablespoons (packed) brown sugar

2 tablespoons cider vinegar

1. Use a sharp paring knife to carve the mango flesh from the pit, then remove and discard the peel. (The process will be a bit messy.) Transfer the mango to a small saucepan, and mash it with a fork or a masher until pulpy—it doesn't have to be completely smooth.
2. Place the pan over medium heat until the mango pulp begins to boil. Turn the heat to low and simmer, uncovered, for 10 minutes, stirring occasionally. Stir in the salt, sugar, and vinegar.
3. Continue to let the mixture simmer, uncovered, for another 10 minutes, stirring once or twice during this time. Remove the pan from the heat, and let it cool for about 10 minutes.
4. Transfer to a tightly covered container and refrigerate. It will keep for at least 3 weeks. Serve cold.

 ### MUSINGS ON MANGOES

Mangoes are members of the sumac family and are related to cashews. In the tropical zones where they grow, mango groves are a real sight: The trees, with their thick umbrella of shiny leaves, form a true oasis—and the fruit grows like giant upside-down lollipops on long stems, hanging down.

  Fragrant and delicious though they are, mangoes can be a real source of frustration when you are trying to cut one. The pit always seems to be too large for the amount of fruit, and it is impossible to simply slice a mango in half without knocking up against that clunky centerpiece. Also, a lot of the pulp clings to the seed and thus is not accessible to your project. So we just have to resign ourselves to cutting mangoes about one third of the way in, salvaging as much of the flesh as we can to use in our recipe, and relegating that large, messy-but-delicious central unit to snack status. It might be nature's way of telling us to slow down and take a healthy break.

Tomato Jam

You can make this jam with tomatoes of any color or degree of ripeness. Ripe tomatoes will give you a sweeter jam; hard ones will produce a delightfully tart result. I like it both ways.

Tomato Jam fits well in any context where you might serve tomato ketchup—it's more complex, yet basically similar. I like it with potatoes, on top of Tempeh Hash (page 157), and with just about any cornmeal- or polenta-based dish.

- To peel and seed a tomato, plunge it into simmering water for a slow count of 10 (for a ripe tomato) or 20 (if the tomato is only medium-ripe). Remove the tomato from the water, and pull off the skin. Then cut the tomato in half, and squeeze out and discard the seeds. Note: You only need to do this with ripe or medium-ripe tomatoes. Unripe tomatoes do not need to be peeled.
- The two different vinegars add layers of flavor.

YIELD: About 1⅓ cups
PREPARATION TIME: 5 minutes, plus 45 minutes to cook

---

2 pounds tomatoes, peeled and seeded if ripe or medium-ripe

¼ teaspoon salt

3 to 4 tablespoons sugar or light-colored honey

2 tablespoons balsamic vinegar

2 teaspoons cider vinegar

1 or 2 sprigs fresh basil (optional)

1. Cut the tomatoes into small cubes, and place them in a medium-sized saucepan. Cover the pot, and place it over medium heat.

2. When the tomatoes begin to boil, reduce the heat to medium, uncover the pot, and let them cook for 10 minutes.

3. Stir in the salt, sugar, vinegars, and optional basil sprigs, and continue to cook, uncovered, over medium heat for another 35 minutes, or until the mixture is reduced in volume by about two thirds. (In other words, it should be approximately one third of its original volume. This is inexact— you can eyeball it.)

4. Remove the pot from the heat, and fish out and discard the basil. Let the mixture cool to room temperature, then transfer to a clean, tightly capped jar, and store for up to several weeks in the refrigerator. Serve cold.

Homemade Crème Fraîche

Rich but light, this silky, subtle, fresh-tasting cultured cream—with just a highlight of tartness—is a luxurious topping for both sweet and savory dishes. It has mystery and soul. And it's really easy to make!

• Use a yogurt that is made with live, active cultures (such as *Streptococcus thermophilus*, *Lactobacillus bulgaricus*, or *L. acidophilus*). This will be indicated on the label.

YIELD: 2 cups
PREPARATION TIME: 2 minutes, plus time to stand and to chill

1½ cups heavy cream

½ cup cultured buttermilk

2 tablespoons plain yogurt

1. Combine the cream and buttermilk in a glass or ceramic bowl or container, and whisk in the yogurt.
2. Cover the container, and let it stand overnight at a warm room temperature (about 75°F is optimal). In the morning, put it in the refrigerator to stop the fermentation and to chill it. When it's cold, it's ready to serve. It will stay fresh for at least a month, and thickens a bit as it ages.

 A HIGH-CLASS, LOW-TECH DAIRY PRODUCT

In some areas of France, crème fraîche is still made the traditional way, which is to say largely by accident. Unpasteurized cream pretty much self-cultures through its own naturally occurring lactic bacteria—and from the agitation and lack of refrigeration during the journey on its way to the market. When it arrives at its destination, voilà! "Instant" crème fraîche!

Roasted Garlic Aïoli

Aïoli is a garlic mayonnaise that is traditional in—and quite central to—the esteemed cuisine of Provence, France. This tawny-colored version uses roasted garlic, which has a handsomely bitter flavor that is both deeper and milder than that of fresh garlic. Serve this creamy, dreamy sauce on or next to any savory dish, or alone as a dip for vegetables.

- Unlike most homemade mayonnaise recipes, which use raw egg yolks, this version cooks the yolks to remove the risk of salmonella.
- You can use the egg whites to make Scrambled Egg Whites (page 122).
- You can roast the garlic up to several days ahead of time. Store it, drizzled lightly with olive oil, in a tightly capped container in the refrigerator.
- The aïoli will keep for up to 3 weeks in a tightly covered container in the refrigerator.
- Roast extra garlic (steps 1 and 2), and keep it around to use as a seasoning for eggs, vegetables, sauces, and anything else you can think of. It is a terrific kitchen staple!

YIELD: 1 scant cup

PREPARATION TIME: 10 minutes, preceded by 1 hour to roast and cool the garlic

1 whole bulb garlic

A little olive oil for roasting
   the garlic

2 egg yolks

2 tablespoons balsamic vinegar

2 tablespoons water

¼ teaspoon salt (rounded measure)

¼ teaspoon dry mustard

10 tablespoons (½ cup plus
   2 tablespoons) extra virgin
   olive oil

1. Preheat the oven to 375°F. Brush a small baking tray with olive oil.
2. Stand the garlic bulb root side down on the prepared tray, and roast for 35 to 40 minutes, or until it feels soft when gently squeezed. Remove the tray from the oven, and let the bulb cool until you can handle it comfortably. Separate the cloves, and squeeze each one over a small bowl, releasing the pulp. Mash the pulp with a fork until smooth, and set aside.
3. Fill a medium-sized bowl with water and set aside.
4. Combine the egg yolks, vinegar, and water in a small saucepan and whisk until smooth (it will be frothy). Place the pan over very low heat, and begin heating it slowly, whisking constantly. (Open a window—the vinegar will produce fumes!)
5. After 3 or 4 minutes, the mixture will begin to thicken and cling to the bottom of the pan. At this point, remove the pan from the heat, and immediately dip the bottom of the pan in the cold water, holding it there for about 2 minutes, to cool it off a little.
6. Transfer the mixture to a blender. Add 1 tablespoon of the roasted garlic paste, along with the salt and mustard, and blend until smooth.
7. Keep the machine running as you gradually drizzle the olive oil, in a thin, steady stream, through the feed tube of the blender. As the oil is incorporated, the mixture will thicken. (You might need to stop the motor once or twice during this process to scrape the sides of the blender.)
8. Transfer the aïoli to a serving dish or storage container, and serve right away at room temperature or chill and serve cold.

Hollandaise Sauce

The queen of classic sauces, hollandaise provides a luxurious, lemony blanket for eggs (Eggs Benedict, page 118, in particular), crêpes, or vegetables, bestowing a perfect richness without becoming heavy. Hollandaise has an undeserved reputation as being difficult to prepare—and even trickier to keep after it's made. Don't pay attention to those warnings! If you just follow the recipe, you'll find this sauce very straightforward and forgiving.

- You can use the egg whites to make Scrambled Egg Whites (page 122).
- Hollandaise can be stored in the refrigerator in an airtight container for up to several days. Reheat it in the top of a double boiler, whisking it until smooth.

YIELD: **1 scant cup**
PREPARATION TIME: **10 minutes**

½ cup (1 stick) unsalted butter

3 egg yolks

2 tablespoons fresh lemon juice

¼ teaspoon salt

1. Melt the butter in a small saucepan over medium heat. While it is melting, place about 2 inches of water in the bottom of a double boiler or in a medium-sized saucepan and heat it to simmering. (Note: After the butter melts, keep it hot over very low heat.)
2. Combine the egg yolks and lemon juice in the top of the double boiler or in a bowl that fits snugly over the saucepan. Whisk the mixture until smooth, then place the container over the gently simmering water.
3. Cook the yolk mixture, whisking constantly, for 3 or 4 minutes, or until it begins to thicken and clings to the bottom of the pan. Slowly drizzle in the hot, melted butter a few drops at a time, whisking after each addition, until the butter is absorbed. The sauce will thicken as the butter is incorporated.
4. As soon as you've added all the butter, remove the bowl or the top of the double boiler from the heat, and stir in the salt.
5. Serve hot, warm, or at room temperature. You can keep the sauce hot for up to 1 hour by simply setting the top of the double boiler—or the bowl—back over the simmering water with the heat turned off.

VARIATION   **ORANGE HOLLANDAISE WITH DILL AND CHIVES**

Follow the main recipe with these adjustments.

Replace the lemon juice with:

- 2 tablespoons orange juice

In step 4, stir in:

- 1 tablespoon minced fresh dill
- 2 tablespoons minced fresh chives
- 1 teaspoon grated orange zest

⑫

BREAKFAST BARS, COFFEE CAKES & SWEET SOMETHINGS

CONTENTS

BREAKFAST BARS, COFFEE CAKES & SWEET SOMETHINGS

People always perk up when something sweet is on the menu. The presence of even the simplest coffee cake can infuse an ordinary morning with excitement and optimism. You probably won't be baking fresh cake for breakfast on a regular basis. But you can feel secure in the knowledge that when a special occasion arises—or when you need to *create* a special occasion just to make everyone around you feel good—you have an excellent collection of delicious coffee cake recipes from which to choose.

In addition to addressing the grand coffee cake theme, this chapter also offers a selection of smaller goodies that you actually can (and hopefully will) embrace as part of your general breakfast repertoire. These include Homemade Protein Bars, Breakfast Biscotti, and Polenta–Pine Nut Cookies, as well as a series of delicious, nutritionally potent little nuggets and gems (some of them unbaked) that you can grab and carry for your commute or for a midmorning pick-me-up. I call these "sweet somethings," as they have the multiple talent required to sedate your sweet tooth, even out your blood sugar, boost your energy and concentration, perk up your palate, *and* take the edge off your mood—all at the same time! I know this sounds grandiose, especially for such small items, but I speak from experience: I eat these regularly.

Speaking of nutrition, some of the cakes in this chapter are filled with ingredients of real substance (such as cottage cheese, fresh fruit, nuts, soy protein powder, and bran), and many can be further enhanced nutritionally. Enriched or not, they all share the ability to provide a very elusive substance that is neither a macronutrient nor a micronutrient, but rather a *soul* nutrient. It's called *satisfaction,* and I hope that these recipes will bring more of it into your life (or at least into your mornings).

Note: The coffee cakes in this chapter are batter cakes. Those made from yeasted dough (babkas and various sweet rolls) can be found in the "Muffins, Biscuits, Breads & Buns" chapter.

Homemade Protein Bars

Making your own granola bars is much easier than you may think, and it's really fun. These homemade bars are very economical, and you get to select all the ingredients according to your own standards, needs, and taste. Try adding some or all of the protein boosters that follow the recipe. You may never make these the same way twice.

- For nondairy bars, replace the yogurt with unsweetened applesauce, canned pumpkin, or mashed banana. (Or try the silken tofu option in the Protein Boosters box.) Add an extra pinch of salt if using pumpkin or silken tofu.
- The range of sugar allows you to make these bars sweeter or not, according to your taste.
- For information about protein powder, see page xv.

YIELD: About 20 medium-sized bars
PREPARATION TIME: 10 minutes, plus at least 30 minutes to bake

Nonstick spray

1 cup soy protein powder

½ cup unbleached all-purpose flour

2 cups rolled oats

½ cup oat bran

½ teaspoon cinnamon

¾ teaspoon salt

½ to ⅔ cup (packed) brown sugar

1 cup semisweet chocolate chips

1½ cups plain or vanilla yogurt

¼ cup canola oil

2 teaspoons vanilla extract

1. Preheat the oven to 350°F (325°F for a glass pan). Lightly spray a 9- by 13-inch baking pan and a baking tray with nonstick spray.

2. Mix together the protein powder, flour, oats, oat bran, cinnamon, and salt in a large bowl. Crumble in the brown sugar, rubbing it with your fingers to break up any clumps. Stir in the chocolate chips.

3. Measure the yogurt, oil, and vanilla into a second bowl, stirring until well combined. Add the wet mixture to the dry, and mix patiently until thoroughly blended. (You may have to use your hands—it will be a thick batter, verging on a dough.)

4. Transfer the mixture to the prepared pan, patting it evenly into place with your hands. Bake in the center of the oven for 15 minutes, then remove from the oven and cut into bars of any size or shape. Place the bars on the prepared baking tray and bake for another 15 minutes, or until golden around the edges. (For extra-crunchy bars, turn off the oven and leave them in there for up to 45 minutes longer.) Remove the bars from the oven, and place them on a rack to cool.

5. Eat the bars within a few hours, or seal them in a heavy zip-style plastic bag and store in the freezer. For maximum crispness, "refresh" them in a toaster oven after defrosting.

VARIATIONS PROTEIN BOOSTERS

You can make the main recipe with any combination of the following adjustments:

- Replace the canola oil with ½ cup peanut butter or almond butter (softened in a microwave).

- Replace the flour with quinoa, ground to a powder in a blender or an electric spice grinder.

- Replace the yogurt with mashed silken tofu (soft or firm). Add an extra pinch of salt.

- Add 2 to 3 tablespoons powdered egg whites (see page 187).

- Add up to 1 cup chopped nuts and/or sunflower seeds.

Chewy Fruit and Nut Bars

I always carry a small plastic bag of these with me on early-morning plane trips and can thus happily decline the less-than-inspiring airline breakfast, knowing I've got something much better. These bars are very simple, but they add up to far more than the sum of their humble ingredients. You must try them!

- My favorite fruit combination for this recipe is dried plums (prunes), apricots, figs, and cherries. But any kind of dried fruit will work, as long as it is neither crystallized nor parched and leathery.
- Nonstick spray prevents the honey from sticking to the measuring cup.
- Rice flour can be substituted for the all-purpose flour.

YIELD: 12 small to medium bars
PREPARATION TIME: 10 minutes, plus 30 minutes to bake

Nonstick spray

4 cups mixed dried fruit

1½ cups finely chopped walnuts and/or pecans

¼ cup all-purpose unbleached flour

¼ teaspoon salt

¼ cup light honey

¾ cup mashed silken tofu, soft or firm

1. Preheat the oven to 350°F (325°F for a glass pan). Lightly spray an 8-inch square baking pan with nonstick spray.
2. Use scissors or a knife to cut the larger pieces of dried fruit into slices approximately the size of a dried cherry. Combine the dried fruit with the nuts in a medium-sized bowl.
3. Sprinkle in the flour and salt, and toss until all the fruit is evenly coated.
4. Spray a ¼-cup measure with nonstick spray. Measure in the honey, then pour it into the fruit mixture. Add the mashed tofu, and mix with a spoon—or your hands—until everything is thoroughly combined.
5. Spread the mixture into the prepared pan, and bake in the center of the oven for 30 to 40 minutes, or until it turns brown around the edges and the top surface is dry to the touch. You can take the pan out of the oven at this point or, for an even chewier result, turn off the oven and leave the pan in there for up to 40 minutes longer.
6. Remove the pan from the oven, cool for about 20 minutes, then cut the mixture into about a dozen small bars. Transfer them to a rack, and let them sit for about an hour. (They'll become chewy while "airing out" on the rack.) Keep the bars in a cookie tin at room temperature—or, if you'll be keeping them for more than a few days, seal them in a heavy zip-style plastic bag and store in the refrigerator or freezer. Eat at any temperature. (They're even good frozen!)

VARIATION **TO USE EGGS INSTEAD OF TOFU**

Follow the main recipe with these adjustments. In step 3, crumble in:

- ½ cup (packed) brown sugar

In step 4, omit the honey and tofu. In a separate bowl, beat:

- 4 to 6 large eggs

and add to the fruit mixture. (You can use just the egg whites, if you prefer.)

271

Breakfast Biscotti

It seems that most people in this country now include "biscotti" in their vocabulary, if not their cookie jars—a very positive trend indeed! Taking this good development even further, I've created for your dunking and gnawing pleasure a comprehensive breakfast version of the now-famous Italian treat, kind of like a cross between the real thing and a granola bar.

- Use a fine grade of cornmeal (not the coarser polenta) for best results.
- For information about protein powder, see page xv.
- These keep very well in a cookie tin at room temperature or in the freezer.

YIELD: 30 biscotti
PREPARATION TIME: 15 minutes, plus about 40 minutes to bake

Nonstick spray

3 large eggs

⅓ cup (packed) brown sugar

¼ cup granulated sugar

⅓ cup canola oil

1 teaspoon grated orange zest

1 teaspoon vanilla extract

⅛ teaspoon almond extract

1½ cups unbleached all-purpose flour

¾ cup rolled oats

½ cup soy protein powder

¼ cup cornmeal

½ teaspoon salt

¾ cup minced almonds

6 dates, pitted and minced (optional)

1. Preheat the oven to 375°F. Lightly spray a baking tray with nonstick spray.
2. Break the eggs into a large bowl. Add the sugars, oil, orange zest, and extracts, and beat together until smooth.
3. In a second, medium-sized bowl, combine the remaining ingredients, and mix until completely blended.
4. Add the dry ingredients to the wet ones and mix thoroughly, using a spoon at first and then mixing with your hands as it thickens. (It will be a stiff batter—almost a dough.)
5. Divide the batter in half, and form it into 2 equal logs, each about 2 inches in diameter. Place them side by side on the prepared baking tray. (They can be close together but should not touch.)
6. Bake for 20 minutes, then remove the tray from the oven. Transfer the logs to a cutting board, and cut them into ½-inch-thick slices. (Use a serrated knife and a sawing motion, to prevent crumbling.)
7. Return the pieces to the tray, laying them flat on their sides, and bake for 8 minutes longer. Turn them over, and bake for another 8 minutes on the other side. For extra-crunchy biscotti, turn off the oven, and leave the tray in there for an additional 15 minutes or so.
8. Remove the tray from the oven, transfer the biscotti to a rack, and allow them to cool for at least 10 minutes before consuming.

 LINGUISTIC RELATIVES

Derived from the Latin roots *bi* (twice) and *coquere* (cook, cuisine, concoct, kitchen), "biscotti" means "twice-baked." And as you can see from the recipe on this page, that is a literal description of how the cookies are made. Any similarity to the word "biscuit" is no coincidence. The original early American biscuit was designed to be kept for a long time in the larder and then baked a second time to freshen it up just before it was served.

Polenta-Pine Nut Cookies

Keep a tin of these sunny little treats on your desk. They come in handy on days when you might not have had time to eat a good breakfast—just dunk them in your midmorning latte, hot chocolate, or chai, and your energy (and mood) will be restored.

Sometimes it's nice to chop lemon zest instead of grating it. Chopped zest is more of a presence—an ingredient—in a cookie, whereas grated zest is more of a seasoning. To chop the zest, shave off the outermost peel of the lemon with a vegetable peeler, and then chop the shavings into smaller pieces with a sharp knife.

- For best results, use organic stoneground polenta (coarse cornmeal), which you can usually find in the bulk bins at natural food stores.
- You can store these in a sealed zip-style plastic bag in the freezer. They defrost quickly and are even good frozen!

YIELD: 2 dozen small cookies
PREPARATION TIME: 15 minutes, plus 15 minutes to bake

Nonstick spray

2 large eggs

½ teaspoon salt

¼ cup pure maple syrup

2 tablespoons canola oil

½ teaspoon vanilla extract (optional)

1⅓ cups unbleached all-purpose flour

⅔ cup polenta

¾ cup pine nuts

1 tablespoon chopped lemon zest

½ cup minced crystallized ginger (optional)

Sugar for the tops

1. Preheat the oven to 350°F. Line a baking tray with foil, and spray it generously with nonstick spray.
2. Break the eggs into a medium-sized bowl, and beat until smooth. Stir in the salt, maple syrup, oil, and optional vanilla.
3. Sprinkle in the flour, polenta, pine nuts, lemon zest, and optional ginger. Mix with a wooden spoon until completely blended.
4. Wet your hands, and pick up a small piece of dough, about 2 teaspoons' worth. Roll it into a ball about 1 inch in diameter, then flatten it into a small circle. Place on the prepared baking tray, patting it down to about ⅛ inch thick. (The thinness will allow the edges to brown and turn crisp.) Repeat with the remaining dough. Sprinkle each unbaked cookie with a pinch or two of sugar.
5. Bake in the center of the oven for 15 minutes, or until the cookies turn golden brown around the edges and on the bottoms. (You can peek.) If you like the cookies sweeter, sprinkle them with a little additional sugar as soon as they come out of the oven. It will melt into the tops of the cookies and form a subtle, sweet crust.
6. Cool on a rack for at least 15 minutes before eating.

Date–Peanut–Flax Seed Nuggets

Pondering a good vehicle for flax seed (which can't really be effectively consumed alone) and absentmindedly munching out of the jars of wholesome goodies I keep in my kitchen, I discovered the great flavor combination of dates and peanuts by what I call an "absentminded snacking accident." This "no-bake" recipe then quickly fell into place.

- Use a high-quality, unprocessed *salted* peanut butter for best results.
- These will keep for weeks or even months, if you don't eat them sooner.

YIELD: **About 2 dozen nuggets**
PREPARATION TIME: **15 minutes**

1⅓ cups pitted dates
(about ½ pound)

½ cup flax seed

½ cup peanuts

½ cup dried cranberries (optional)

½ to ¾ cup peanut butter

1 to 2 tablespoons flax-seed oil
(optional)

½ cup shredded unsweetened
coconut (optional)

1. Place the dates in a medium-sized bowl. Mash them with a spoon if they are soft and sticky. If you're using dates that are drier or are in rolled form, just break them into smaller pieces with your fingers or scissors, put them in the bowl, and push them together with the spoon.
2. Grind the flax seed—and then the peanuts—to a fine meal in an electric spice grinder or a blender. (Process with a few short bursts rather than long pulses, to be sure they don't get too oily and turn into a paste.) Add them to the dates, using a fork or your fingers to rub everything together. Mix in the dried cranberries, if desired, as you go.
3. Add the peanut butter, mixing and mashing it in with a spoon (or your hands). You can also add the optional flax-seed oil at this point, to help hold everything together (and for an extra nutrition component).
4. Use your hands, or two spoons, to scoop up heaping teaspoons of the mixture, and shape each piece into a tight little ball about 1 inch in diameter. Roll each one in coconut, if desired, place in a shallow plastic container with a tight-fitting lid, and refrigerate or freeze as soon as you're done. Eat the nuggets at room temperature or cold—or even frozen, if you like.

 ABOUT FLAX SEED

Tiny, flat, brown flax seeds are the richest source of omega-3 oil in the plant world. Omega-3 oil is ultra-nutritious, promoting and supporting healthy brain function, hormones, blood, nerves, arteries, skin, and hair—and transporting fat-soluble vitamins throughout our system. Purchase inexpensive flax seed in bulk at natural food stores, and store it in a cool, dark place. Flax-seed oil is concentrated (and thus more expensive) and should be stored in the freezer. Note that flax seed needs to be ground and left *uncooked* to be nutritionally useful. (Whole flax seeds are indigestible, and exposure to heat damages the oil.)

Pistachio-Currant Halvah Nuggets

Welcome to my new favorite snack! These unbaked nuggets are so satisfying and good for you that I predict you will soon incorporate them into your busy lifestyle as a grabbed breakfast-on-the-run or as an afternoon pick-me-up snack. I keep them at my desk and munch on them whenever I feel my blood sugar level dropping. Low in carbohydrates and high in protein and good fat, they spruce me right up again. It never fails!

- These will keep for weeks or even months, if you don't eat them sooner.

YIELD: **2 dozen nuggets**
PREPARATION TIME: **10 minutes**

1 cup sesame tahini

2 tablespoons light honey

½ teaspoon salt (scant measure)

⅔ cup currants

⅔ cup minced or ground pistachio nuts, lightly toasted

⅓ cup sesame seeds

1. Combine the tahini, honey, and salt in a medium-sized bowl, and use a fork or the back of a spoon to mix and/or mash them together until reasonably well blended.
2. Add the currants and pistachio nuts, mashing them in as best you can. The mixture will be a little stiff.
3. Place the sesame seeds on a plate. Use your hands (wetting them if necessary) to form the mixture into 1-inch balls, then roll each ball in the sesame seeds until thoroughly coated.
4. Place the coated nuggets in a shallow plastic container with a tight-fitting lid, and store in the refrigerator or freezer. Eat them at room temperature or cold—or even frozen, if you like.

 A BRIEF SESAME LESSON

Sesame is an ancient plant (documented as far back as 1800 B.C.) and was one of the earliest to be used for both the seeds and the oil within the seeds. Sesame seeds are high in protein, vitamin E, calcium, and other minerals. They also contain a good-for-you type of monounsaturated fat. The oil is stable and highly resistant to oxidation (rancidity), due to the presence of a lignan called sesamin. Lignans are natural preservatives, stabilizers, and antioxidants. Although sesame seeds are very nutritious, it is difficult to eat enough of them to get the health benefits. And even if you could eat a sufficient quantity, they are not easily digested. It is much more nutritionally efficient to consume sesame seeds in the form of a paste (such as sesame butter or tahini).

Carrot-Almond-Oat Gems

Soft and chewy, and brimming with grated carrot and almonds, these dense bar cookies can also be made into a torte with the simple addition of beaten eggs. Either way, this recipe is deeply satisfying and makes a great portable snack—full of fiber and vitamins—that will fill you up just the right amount and also take care of your sweet tooth.

- This recipe is truly quick and easy if you use a food processor for grinding the almonds and grating the carrots. If you don't have a food processor, you can do step 2 in a blender and grate the carrots by hand.
- Light honey or pure maple syrup can replace the sugar. If you're using either of these, add it with the grated carrot in step 3.

YIELD: About 12 small bars
PREPARATION TIME: 10 minutes, plus 30 minutes to bake

Nonstick spray

2 cups whole almonds

¼ cup rolled oats

3 to 4 tablespoons sugar

½ teaspoon salt (scant measure)

1½ cups (packed) finely shredded carrot (about ½ pound)

1 to 2 teaspoons grated lemon zest

1 teaspoon vanilla extract

⅛ teaspoon almond extract

1. Preheat the oven to 350°F. Lightly spray an 8-inch round cake pan with nonstick spray.
2. Place 1½ cups of the almonds in a food processor fitted with the steel blade. Add the oats, sugar, and salt, and process in a few long pulses until they combine and become a powder. Transfer to a medium-sized bowl. Finely chop the remaining ½ cup almonds, and stir these in.
3. Add the carrots to the almond mixture, along with the lemon zest and extracts, and mix with a fork until thoroughly combined.
4. Transfer the batter to the center of the prepared pan, and shape it into a disk about an inch high and 6½ inches in diameter. Bake in the center of the oven for 30 minutes, or until dry on top.
5. Remove from the oven, and cut into pieces while still hot, leaving the pieces in the pan. (You get to choose the size and shape of the pieces. I like to cut it into about a dozen wedges.) Cool in the pan for about 20 minutes, then transfer to a rack to cool for at least 15 minutes longer. Store in a tightly covered container in the refrigerator, and serve cold or at room temperature.

(VARIATION) **CARROT-ALMOND-OAT TORTE**

For a moist cake that will serve 6 to 8, follow the main recipe with these adjustments:

Increase the salt to ½ teaspoon (*level* measure, not scant). Beat and add to the almond mixture in step 3:

- 3 or 4 large eggs

Bake for 35 minutes. Cool for at least 15 minutes before slicing.

Light Breakfast Gingerbread with cranberries, bran, and walnuts

A combination of fresh and crystallized ginger, with touches of orange and spice, creates complex layers of flavor that will wake you up gently but thoroughly—and happily.

• Unwrap the butter ahead of time and place it directly in the mixing bowl to soften.

YIELD: About 8 servings (one 8-inch square cake)
PREPARATION TIME: 15 minutes, plus 35 to 40 minutes to bake

Nonstick spray

6 tablespoons unsalted butter, softened

¼ cup grated fresh ginger

½ cup (packed) brown sugar

2 tablespoons molasses

1 large egg

1 teaspoon vanilla extract

1½ cups unbleached all-purpose flour

1 teaspoon baking powder

¼ teaspoon baking soda

½ teaspoon salt

1 teaspoon cinnamon

½ teaspoon allspice

½ cup unprocessed wheat bran

2 teaspoons grated orange zest

⅓ cup minced crystallized ginger

½ cup dried cranberries

½ cup chopped walnuts

1¼ cups buttermilk

Yogurt or Homemade Crème Fraîche (page 263; optional)

1. Preheat the oven to 350°F (325°F for a glass pan). Lightly spray an 8-inch square pan with nonstick spray.

2. In a medium to large bowl, beat the butter for several minutes with an electric mixer at high speed. Add the fresh ginger, brown sugar, and molasses and beat for several minutes longer. Add the egg and vanilla, and continue beating for 2 to 3 more minutes.

3. In a second bowl, combine the flour, baking powder, baking soda, salt, spices, bran, and orange zest, slowly mixing them together with a whisk.

4. Add the crystallized ginger, rubbing it in with your fingers to separate the pieces. (You can also cut the ginger pieces smaller with scissors. It's easier to do this when they are coated with the flour.) Stir in the cranberries and walnuts.

5. Add the dry ingredients to the butter mixture in 3 installments, alternating with the buttermilk (dry-wet-dry-wet-dry). After each addition, use a spoon or rubber spatula to stir from the bottom of the bowl just enough to blend. Don't overmix.

6. Transfer the batter to the prepared pan, spreading it into place. Bake in the middle of the oven for 35 to 40 minutes, or until a toothpick inserted all the way into the center comes out clean. Cool for at least 15 minutes before slicing.

7. Serve at any temperature, plain or with yogurt or Homemade Crème Fraîche.

Divine Apple-Pear Crostada with cornmeal crust

Inspired by one of the many beautiful desserts sold at The Phoenix Pastificio's bakery counter in Berkeley, this rustic galette-style fruit tart, with a rich cornmeal crust and lattice top, is a perfect breakfast pastry. I like it best in the winter, made with a combination of tart apples and sweet pears. You can also try making it in the summer with peaches and blackberries or blueberries. The crust is sturdy and reliable—a good inaugural for those of you who are venturing into tart making for the first time.

- If you don't have a food processor, you can use the paddle attachment of an electric mixer—or a pastry cutter or two forks—to cut the cold butter into the cornmeal-flour mixture.
- Use a fine grade of cornmeal (not the coarser polenta) for best results.
- The pastry can be made ahead and refrigerated, sealed in a zip-style plastic bag, for up to a week. Let it warm up a bit before rolling it out.
- The recipe calls for 1½ pounds mixed apples and pears, and you can use any combination. My own favorite formula is 3 Granny Smith apples and 2 very ripe Anjou pears.

YIELD: About 8 servings (one 10-inch tart)
PREPARATION TIME: 30 minutes, plus about 40 minutes to bake

PASTRY

1½ cups cornmeal

1½ cups unbleached all-purpose flour

¼ cup sugar

½ teaspoon salt

½ cup (1 stick) cold unsalted butter

1 large egg

About ⅓ cup cream or half-and-half

1. To make the pastry, combine the cornmeal, flour, sugar, and salt in a food processor fitted with the steel blade.
2. Use a dinner knife to cut the butter into thin slices (working quickly to keep it cold), then lay the pieces on top of the dry ingredients in the food processor. Process in a few long pulses until the butter is evenly distributed and the mixture resembles a coarse meal.
3. Add the egg and pulse once or twice—just until it is incorporated—then pulse in enough cream to bring the dough together. Remove the dough from the food processor, and push it together into one mass.
4. Break the dough into 2 uneven pieces, approximately two thirds and one third. Form each piece into a ball, and flatten each ball into a thick disk. Place each disk between 2 sheets of plastic wrap, and roll until about ⅛ inch thick. Ease the larger circle into a 10-inch tart pan with removable bottom, and trim the edges. Cut the smaller circle into strips about ½-inch wide. Meanwhile, preheat the oven to 375°F.

BAKING WITH PEARS

The mother of a friend of mine was locally famous for her apple pies. In public, she would never reveal her recipe. But in private, she confessed the secret of her success: She made her apple pies with a combination of apples and *pears*. And indeed, I have found over the years that when I add pears to apples in baked goods, the flavor is indescribably—if subtly—enhanced.

Pears are almost always harvested green, as they ripen best off the tree. So when you find pears in the market, they are in various stages of ripeness, and you have to examine them carefully. Pears are at their best when they emit an aroma and yield to gentle pressure. And because they ripen from the inside out, a pear that is really soft on the outside is probably already overripe (and possibly rotten) within. When you bake with pears, be sure they are not too ripe, or they will "melt" into oblivion during the baking process, and you will lose texture and volume.

For baking, use any type of pear except Asian pears and Bosc pears, which are terminally crunchy and can become gritty when exposed to heat.

FILLING

2½ pounds mixed apples and pears

2 tablespoons fresh lemon or lime juice

2 tablespoons unbleached all-purpose flour

3 tablespoons sugar

¼ teaspoon salt

Homemade Crème Fraîche (page 263; optional)

5. To make the filling, peel the fruit and cut it into thin slices. Transfer to a medium-sized bowl, and drizzle with the lemon or lime juice. Combine the flour, sugar, and salt in a small bowl, then sprinkle it into the fruit and toss to coat.

6. Spread the fruit in the crust. Arrange the strips of dough on top in a criss-cross pattern, then push the ends of the strips into the sides of the crust to hold them in place. (You might need to wet them a little to make them stick.) Place the filled tart on a baking tray, and bake in the lower half of the oven for about 40 minutes, or until light golden on the top and around the edges.

7. Cool for at least 15 minutes before removing the rim of the pan and slicing the tart. Serve warm or at room temperature. This tastes especially good with a dollop of Homemade Crème Fraîche on the side.

Classic Buttermilk Coffee Cake

When I was growing up, sour cream coffee cake was a specialty of our next-door neighbor, Mrs. Buerschaper, who magically appeared at our kitchen door early on the morning of my 15th birthday with a freshly baked panful. She did it just that one time, but boy, did it make an impression! This act of delicious thoughtfulness has remained one of my most inspiring memories and has moved me to create my own version, which I make with buttermilk.

- Unwrap the butter ahead of time and place it directly in the mixing bowl to soften.
- You can substitute soy protein powder for up to ½ cup of the flour. The batter will be stiff—just be patient when spreading it in the pan. (For information about soy protein powder, see page xv.)
- The range of sugar allows you to make these sweeter or not, according to your taste.

YIELD: 6 or 7 servings (one 8-inch round or square cake)
PREPARATION TIME: 15 minutes, plus 20 to 25 minutes to bake

Nonstick spray

½ cup (1 stick) unsalted butter, softened

⅓ to ½ cup granulated sugar

2 large eggs

1 teaspoon vanilla extract

1½ cups unbleached all-purpose flour

½ teaspoon salt

1 teaspoon baking powder

⅛ teaspoon baking soda

½ cup buttermilk

TOPPING

2 tablespoons (packed) brown sugar

½ teaspoon cinnamon

½ cup chopped walnuts or pecans (optional)

1. Preheat the oven to 350°F (325°F for a glass pan). Lightly spray an 8-inch round or square pan with nonstick spray.
2. In a large bowl, beat the butter for several minutes with an electric mixer at high speed. Add the sugar and beat for several minutes longer. Add the eggs, one at a time, beating well after each, then beat in the vanilla.
3. In a second bowl, combine the flour, salt, baking powder, and baking soda, slowly mixing them together with a whisk.
4. Add the dry ingredients in 3 installments to the butter mixture, alternating with the buttermilk, beginning and ending with the dry (dry-wet-dry-wet-dry). After each addition, use a spoon or rubber spatula to stir from the bottom of the bowl just enough to blend. Don't overmix.
5. Transfer the batter to the prepared pan, spreading it evenly into place. Mix together the brown sugar and cinnamon and the optional nuts, and sprinkle this on top before baking.
6. Bake in the middle of the oven for 20 to 25 minutes, or until a toothpick or sharp knife inserted all the way into the center comes out clean. Cool for at least 15 minutes before cutting and serving.

For each variation, follow the main recipe with these adjustments.

CARAMEL NUT-CRUSTED COFFEE CAKE

In step 1, melt into the sprayed pan:

- 2 tablespoons unsalted butter

(You can do this in the preheating oven.) Sprinkle into the melted butter:

- 3 tablespoons (packed) brown sugar
- ⅔ cup chopped pecans

Invert the cake onto a plate after it's cooled. Scrape onto it any topping remaining in the pan.

BUTTERMILK-RHUBARB COFFEE CAKE

Before making the batter, toss the following together in a small bowl:

- 2 cups chopped rhubarb (¼-inch pieces)
- 2 tablespoons granulated sugar
- 1 tablespoon unbleached all-purpose flour

Let the mixture stand while you prepare the batter. Increase the sugar in the batter to ⅔ cup, and fold the rhubarb mixture in with the last installment of dry ingredients in step 4. Bake the cake for 30 to 40 minutes.

BURIED TREASURE COFFEE CAKE

For a bigger cake that you can fill with extra goodies, double the recipe and use a standard-sized Bundt or tube pan. Instead of sprinkling the topping on the top, put it in the center of the cake. To do this, spoon half the batter into the prepared pan, sprinkle the topping (now a filling) over it, and then spoon on the rest of the batter. You can also add to the filling up to ½ cup of any or all of the following:

- Semisweet chocolate chips
- Additional chopped nuts
- Sliced dried fruit
- Shredded unsweetened coconut
- Jam or marmalade (spooned in, blob by blob)

Bake this larger cake at 350°F for 45 to 50 minutes. Cool it in the pan for 30 minutes, then rap the pan sharply, and invert the cake onto a plate (if you used a Bundt pan) or pull out the tube and gently lift the cake off and onto a plate (if it's in a tube pan). Cool for another 10 to 15 minutes before slicing. This cake makes 12 to 16 servings.

Plum-Studded Morning Cake

Baked in a tart pan, this little cake is downright elegant, with an impressive fluted edge. The buttery, tender crumb and fresh flavor are so evocative, you'll feel as though you went to bed at home and woke up in the south of France! To render the experience plus français, *serve the cake with* chocolat chaud *(hot chocolate) or* café au lait.

• Unwrap the butter ahead of time and place it directly in the mixing bowl to soften.

YIELD: 6 to 8 servings (one 10-inch cake)
PREPARATION TIME: 15 minutes, plus 35 to 40 minutes to bake

Nonstick spray

½ cup (1 stick) unsalted butter, softened

⅔ cup plus 1 tablespoon sugar

2 large eggs

1 teaspoon vanilla extract

1 cup plus 1 tablespoon unbleached all-purpose flour

½ teaspoon salt

1 teaspoon baking powder

½ cup milk

4 or 5 firm, ripe plums

1 tablespoon fresh lemon juice

OPTIONAL TOPPINGS

Vanilla yogurt

Homemade Crème Fraîche (page 263)

1. Preheat the oven to 350°F. Lightly spray the bottom of a 10-inch tart pan with removable bottom with nonstick spray.
2. In a medium to large bowl, beat the butter for several minutes with an electric mixer at high speed. Add ⅔ cup of the sugar and beat for several minutes longer. Add the eggs, one at a time, beating well after each, and then beat in the vanilla.
3. In a second bowl, combine 1 cup of the flour with the salt and baking powder, slowly mixing them together with a whisk.
4. Add the dry ingredients to the butter mixture in 2 installments, alternating with the milk (dry-wet-dry). After each addition, use a spoon or rubber spatula to stir from the bottom of the bowl just enough to blend. Don't overmix.
5. Transfer the batter to the prepared pan, spreading it evenly into place. Let it rest while you prepare the topping.
6. Halve the plums and remove the pits. You can leave the halves intact or slice them again, lengthwise, into quarters. Place the plums in a small bowl, add the lemon juice and the remaining 1 tablespoon sugar, and toss to distribute. Then sprinkle in the remaining 1 tablespoon flour and toss again until the plum pieces are fairly evenly coated. Arrange them on top of the batter in the pattern of your choice.
7. Put the pan on a baking tray, and place it in the middle of the oven for 35 to 40 minutes, or until the cake is golden and springy to the touch. Cool for at least 20 minutes before removing the rim of the pan. Without removing it from the bottom of the pan, place the cake on a serving plate and cool for another 10 minutes or so before slicing.
8. Serve warm or at room temperature, with vanilla yogurt or Homemade Crème Fraîche. (It's also good plain.)

For each variation, follow the main recipe with these adjustments.

MANGO SUNBURST CAKE

In this beautiful variation, the mango looks as though it's bursting through the top of the cake! I can't imagine anyone having a bad day after being served this for breakfast.

Cut lengthwise into 2 pieces:

- 1 ripe mango (about 1 pound)

Peel it, and cut the fruit off the pit. Measure ½ cup of the mango flesh, and place it in a blender with:

- 1 tablespoon fresh lemon juice

Purée until smooth. Cut the remaining mango into small slices or pieces the size of dice.

Follow the main recipe, reducing the sugar to ½ cup and adding to the flour mixture in step 3:

- 1 tablespoon grated lemon zest

Replace the milk with the mango purée, and replace the plums with the mango pieces.

FIG-STUDDED MORNING CAKE

This is probably the most subtle of all these variations. Note: You can use imperfect figs and it will still be good.

Follow the main recipe, replacing the plums with:

- 4 or 5 firm figs, cut lengthwise into halves or quarters

STONE FRUIT–STUDDED MORNING CAKE

Celebrate the summer with a cake that you've bedecked with as much fruit as can fit! Follow the main recipe, replacing the plums with:

- A combination of sliced peaches, plums, apricots, and pitted cherries

Bittersweet Mocha Coffee Cake

I created this cake for a fund-raiser brunch at my daughter's school. Everyone wanted seconds and thirds, and then, of course, they all had to have a chunk to take home, and there simply wasn't enough to go around. Over the next week or so, I baked a few more cakes to share. By then my husband and kids got wind of the situation and expressed feelings of neglect, so I had to bake yet another cake for the home front. No one seems to be able to get enough of this deep, dark, yummy thing!

- You can adjust the proportion of coffee and milk to get a stronger or milder coffee flavor. Just make sure the total liquid adds up to 1 cup.
- Unwrap the butter ahead of time and place it directly in the mixing bowl to soften.
- You can replace up to half the flour with soy protein powder (see page xv).

YIELD: 12 or more servings (1 tube cake)
PREPARATION TIME: 15 minutes, plus 45 to 50 minutes to bake

Nonstick spray

1 cup (2 sticks) unsalted butter, softened

1¼ cups sugar

4 large eggs

1 tablespoon vanilla extract

2 cups unbleached all-purpose flour

⅓ cup unsweetened cocoa

½ teaspoon salt

1½ teaspoons baking powder

¾ cup strong brewed coffee

¼ cup milk

1 cup semisweet chocolate chips

1. Preheat the oven to 350°F. Lightly spray the bottom and center of a standard-sized tube pan or Bundt pan with nonstick spray.

2. In a large bowl, beat the butter for several minutes with an electric mixer at high speed. Add the sugar and beat for several minutes longer. Add the eggs, one at a time, beating well after each, and then beat in the vanilla.

3. In a second bowl, combine the flour, cocoa, salt, and baking powder, slowly mixing them together with a whisk. Combine the coffee and milk in a measuring cup with a spout.

4. Add the dry ingredients to the butter mixture in 3 installments, alternating with the coffee mixture, beginning and ending with the dry (dry-wet-dry-wet-dry). After each addition, use a spoon or rubber spatula to stir from the bottom of the bowl just enough to blend. Fold in the chocolate chips with the last addition of flour. Don't overmix.

5. Transfer the batter to the prepared pan, spreading it evenly into place. Bake in the middle of the oven for 45 to 50 minutes, or until a sharp knife inserted all the way into the center comes out clean. Cool for at least 30 minutes before removing the cake from the pan. Then invert it onto a plate (if you used a Bundt pan) or pull out the tube and gently lift the cake off and onto a plate (if it's in a tube pan). Cool for another 10 to 15 minutes before slicing.

Cottage Cheese Cake

Have you been searching for a bona fide, scrumptious cheesecake that is nutritionally friendly? Look no further. While you're busy enjoying every mouthful—and feeling like you're getting away with something—you'll actually be eating real food, *full of protein and not overloaded with sugar. (If you make the raspberry variation, you'll also be getting good fiber and vitamins.)*

- Remember to grate the lemon zest before squeezing the juice.
- This cake keeps very well for up to a week if stored in a tightly covered container in the refrigerator. Remove it from the metal bottom of the springform pan if storing it for more than a day.
- If the cottage cheese tastes salty, decrease the salt accordingly.

YIELD: About 10 servings (one 9-inch cake)
PREPARATION TIME: 10 minutes, plus 45 minutes to bake and several hours to chill

---

Nonstick spray

4 cups (2 pounds) cottage cheese

3 eggs

⅓ cup sugar

⅓ cup unbleached all-purpose flour

½ teaspoon salt (scant measure)

1 tablespoon vanilla extract

1 to 2 tablespoons fresh lemon juice

Up to 2 teaspoons grated lemon zest (optional)

1. Preheat the oven to 350°F. Lightly spray the bottom of a 9-inch springform cake pan with nonstick spray.
2. Place the cottage cheese in a food processor, and process until very smooth. (Stop a few times to scrape the sides of the work bowl with a rubber spatula, then continue.) Add the eggs, and continue to process until they are completely incorporated.
3. Add the remaining ingredients, and continue to process until smooth, scraping the sides of the work bowl as needed.
4. Transfer the batter to the prepared pan. Put the pan on a baking tray, and bake it in the middle of the oven for 45 minutes, or until the cake is springy to the touch. Cool to room temperature, then cover the pan very tightly with plastic wrap and refrigerate until cold.
5. Remove the rim of the pan shortly before serving, and serve the cake cold, cut into wedges.

VARIATION **RASPBERRY COTTAGE CHEESE CAKE**

Follow the main recipe with this adjustment.

Increase the sugar to ½ cup. Add at the end of step 3:

- 2 cups raspberries (fresh or frozen, undefrosted)

(If using frozen berries and they are clumped together, break them up with your fingers or chop them into manageable pieces with a knife.) Pulse the motor on and off to distribute the berries throughout the batter, but don't actually purée them. Bake the cake for 50 minutes.

Cornmeal-Millet Toasting Cake

If your idea of a perfect breakfast is a toasty slice of something sweet dunked in your coffee or cocoa, this cake is for you. It has a wonderful texture—full of cornmeal and fluffy cooked millet—and it's just sweet enough to appease your sugar craving without overdoing it. Although designed to be sliced, toasted, and buttered, this cake can also be eaten straight.

- Unwrap the butter ahead of time and place it directly in the mixing bowl to soften.
- Use a fine grade of cornmeal (not the coarser polenta) for best results.
- For information about protein powder, see page xv.
- Freeze the cake in slices, sealed in a heavy zip-style plastic bag. If they're not too thick, the frozen slices can go directly into a toaster oven without being defrosted.

YIELD: **12 or more servings (1 tube cake)**
PREPARATION TIME: **15 minutes, plus 1 hour to bake**

Nonstick spray

½ cup (1 stick) unsalted butter, softened

¼ to ⅓ cup granulated sugar

2 large eggs

2 teaspoons vanilla extract

3 cups unbleached all-purpose flour

1 cup cornmeal

1 cup soy protein powder

¾ teaspoon salt

2 teaspoons baking powder

¼ teaspoon baking soda

1 cup (packed) light brown sugar

1½ cups cooked millet (page 46)

2 cups plain yogurt (lowfat okay)

1. Preheat the oven to 350°F. Lightly spray a standard-sized tube pan or Bundt pan with nonstick spray.
2. In a large bowl, beat the butter for several minutes with an electric mixer at high speed. Add the sugar and beat for several minutes longer. Add the eggs, one at a time, beating well after each. Beat in the vanilla.
3. In a second bowl, combine the flour, cornmeal, protein powder, salt, baking powder, and baking soda, slowly mixing them together with a whisk. Add the brown sugar and millet, rubbing them in with your fingers until the mixture is uniformly blended.
4. Add the dry ingredients to the butter mixture in 3 installments, alternating with the yogurt (dry-wet-dry-wet-dry). After each addition, use a spoon or rubber spatula to stir from the bottom of the bowl just enough to blend. Don't overmix. The batter will be stiff.
5. Transfer the batter to the prepared pan, spooning it in clump by clump. When it is all in the pan, take your time spreading it evenly in place with a rubber spatula.
6. Bake in the middle of the oven for 1 hour, or until a toothpick or sharp knife inserted all the way into the center comes out clean. Cool for at least 45 minutes before removing the cake from the pan. (To remove the cake from a tube pan, pull out the tube with the cake still on it, and set it down. Gently lift the cake off and onto a plate. To remove the cake from a Bundt pan, rap the pan sharply a few times, then invert the cake onto a plate.) Let the cake cool on the plate for at least 15 minutes before slicing.

Black Cherry Clafoutis

A traditional dessert from the farm culture of southern France, a clafoutis *is a puffy cake—much like a jumbo fruit pancake or a filled popover—made from a thick, crêpelike batter studded with black cherries. (The name, pronounced "cla-FOO-tee," derives from a verb meaning "to fill" in a regional French dialect.)*

- It's fun to bring the whole pan to the table straight from the oven, so your guests can admire this beautiful, dramatic-looking dish.
- The pitted cherries are my own adaptation. A traditional French cook would use unpitted fruit, because the pit is believed by some to impart a hint of almond flavor. Also, unpitted cherries are less likely to bleed into the batter. So if you want to make this in the authentic French *mode*, leave the pits in.
- You can use frozen pitted cherries without defrosting them first.

YIELD: 4 or 5 servings
PREPARATION TIME: 15 minutes, plus 30 to 35 minutes to bake

Nonstick spray

About 2 tablespoons butter

1½ cups pitted black cherries

1⅓ cups plus 1 tablespoon unbleached all-purpose flour

1½ cups milk

2 tablespoons sugar

4 large eggs

1 teaspoon vanilla extract

¼ teaspoon salt

Powdered sugar for dusting the top

1. Preheat the oven to 375°F. Lightly spray a 9- by 13-inch pan with nonstick spray, then add the butter in a chunk. Place the pan in the preheating oven for a minute or so to melt the butter, then take it out and carefully tilt it in all directions to let the butter coat the bottom surface. Set the pan aside.

2. In a small bowl, toss together the cherries and 1 tablespoon of the flour, and let them stand for a few minutes.

3. Pour the milk into a blender or food processor fitted with the steel blade. Add the sugar, eggs, vanilla, and salt, and process for a few seconds. Add the remaining 1⅓ cups flour and process until the mixture is uniform. (You may need to stop and scrape the sides with a rubber spatula to get all the flour mixed in.)

4. Pour the batter into the prepared pan, spoon in the fruit, and bake in the center of the oven for 30 to 35 minutes, or until puffed and lightly browned.

5. Serve hot or warm, cut into large squares and dusted with powdered sugar.

STONE FRUIT, BERRIES, AND OTHER OPTIONS

Even though a *clafoutis* is traditionally made with black cherries, you can also use other fruit, or a combination. Try offsetting the sweet, dark cherries with some tart raspberries or blackberries, or substitute other types of stone fruit—peaches, apricots, and/or plums—pitted and sliced. In some parts of France this dish is made with grapes or red currants, which are also delicious. In the winter, use frozen, unsweetened fruit, adding it to the batter without defrosting it first. You can also use canned fruit if you drain it very well ahead of time.

One more option: *Clafoutis* can also be made with dried fruit that has been soaked for an hour or so in fruit juice or a fruity liqueur. If you're using larger pieces of dried fruit, slice them first.

MOLLIE KATZEN'S
SUNLIGHT CAFÉ

"Brunch" is one of those terms that has many connotations beyond the literal translation (late break-fast/early lunch). Above all, brunch is about leisure—about literally taking and extending time, inserting a slice of the extraordinary into our lives whenever possible, regardless of the hour or the day of the week. It's a wonderful way to be with people and to express our creativity—and I hope these ideas will inspire you to carve out time for brunch whenever you can.

I designed the following menus according to my own taste. Of course, you can adjust them in any way you choose, or create your own altogether. Please note that in most of these menus I did not include beverages, assuming that you would fill in this blank with your own selections. (The few exceptions are cases where I felt that a certain drink would just be too perfect not to recommend.)

BRUNCH MENUS

- Avocado-Grapefruit-Mango Salsa (page 252) *(served as an appetizer)*
  Giant Cauliflower-Cheese Puff (page 137)
  Amazing Amaranth Wafers (page 61)
  Divine Apple-Pear Crostada with Cornmeal Crust (page 278)

- Nut-Crusted Mushroom Fritters (page 177)
  Sunlight Soufflé (page 136)
  Raspberry Sauce (page 249)
  Bittersweet Mocha Coffee Cake (page 284)

- Raspberry-Drenched Rhubarb (page 33)
  Frittata of your choice (pages 126 to 127)
  Mustard-Roasted Potatoes with Dill (page 144)
  Pumpkin Muffins (page 80)

- Fried eggs (page 119)
  Roasted Herbes de Provence Tomatoes (page 168)
  Basic Home Fries (page 146)
  Breakfast "meat" (real or soy-based)
  Ginger-Oat Scones (page 92)

BRUNCH MENUS

- Savory Buttermilk Corn Cakes (page 189)
  Red Flannel Hash (page 158)
  Chipotle Cream (page 256)
  Citrus-Papaya Salsa with a Chipotle Haze (page 251)
  Cinnamon-Sugar Caramel Flan (page 231)

- *Fresh blackberries, plain or prepared with the*
  Balsamic Vinegar Treatment (page 26)
  American Potato Cutlets (page 152)
  Fried Green Tomatoes (page 169)
  Simplest Buttermilk Biscuits (page 91)
  Cottage Cheese Cake (page 285)

- *Sliced fresh fruit in season*
  Cajun Scalloped Sweet Potatoes (page 151)
  Breaded Sautéed Goat Cheese Patties (page 219)
  Buttermilk Blueberry Muffins (page 79)

- *Citrus sections*
  Ful Medames (page 159)
  Basic Yeasted Flatbread (page 96)
  Minced fresh vegetables (scallions, radishes,
  bell peppers, cucumbers)
  Creamy Tahini Sauce (page 256)
  Sweet Potato Pudding (page 233)

- Piña Colada Smoothie (page 12)
  Silver Dollar Bean Cakes (page 161)
  Peruvian Blue Home Fries (page 150)
  Smoky Tomato Salsa (page 253)
  Cornmeal-Millet Toasting Cake (page 286)
  Strawberry Sauce (page 249)

BRUNCH MENUS

- Green Apples and Red Grapes with Maple Yogurt (page 31)
  Tempeh Hash (page 157)
  Tomato Jam (page 262)
  Orange-Pecan Skillet Millet (page 53)
  Carrot-Almond-Oat Gems (page 276)

- Winter Fruit Salad with Pomegranate (page 29)
  Scrambled Tofu (page 123)
  Crispy Southwest Polenta Hash (page 153)
  Light Breakfast Gingerbread with Cranberries, Bran,
      and Walnuts (page 277)

- Breakfast Salad (page 167)
  Masfouf (page 56)
  Yogurt
  Black Cherry Clafoutis (page 287)

- Breakfast Gazpacho (page 15)
  Soft Breakfast Polenta (page 59) *topped with
      gorgonzola cheese*
  Poached Eggs (page 118)
  Chewy Fruit and Nut Bars (page 271)

- Faux Fool (page 30)
  Vietnamese Coconut–Rice Flour Crêpes with
      Hot-Sweet-Sour Dipping Sauce (page 200)
  Banana Bread Pudding (page 237)

- Mint-Infused Fruit Salad (page 28)
  Wild Rice Pancakes with Mushrooms and
      Goat Cheese (page 192)
  Fire-Roasted Pepper Salsa (page 254)
  Plum-Studded Morning Cake (page 282)

- Berries in Buttermilk (page 30)
  Folded French Crêpes (page 195) filled with
    Classic Creamed Spinach (page 171)
  Polenta–Pine Nut Cookies (page 273)
  My Family's Favorite Hot Chocolate (page 18)

- *Half grapefruit*
  Egg "Muffins" (page 132)
  Oatmeal Waffles (page 206)
  Passionfruit Syrup (page 246)

- *Sliced mango and kiwi drizzled with lime juice*
  Indian Home Fries (page 149)
  Breakfast Raita (page 216)
  Spiced Basmati-Almond Muffins (page 71)
  Backward Chai (page 17)

- Caramelized Fruit (page 27)
  Portobello Pizzas (page 176)
  Toasted English muffins
  Breakfast "meat" (real or soy-based)
  Tiramisù in a Cup (page 235)

- Roasted Fruit (page 36)
  Baked Spinach-Feta Pudding (page 241)
  Sliced ripe tomatoes
  Chocolate Bread Pudding (page 238)

- Baked Cornmeal-Cheddar Pudding (page 240)
  Flash-Cooked Vegetables (page 174)
  Cinnamon-Spiced Fried Tomatoes (page 170)
  Fruit Crisp (page 38)

INDEX